THE NEW CAMBRID

HERMAN

MU00781766

The New Cambridge Companion to He...... .... provides timely, critical
essays on Melville's classic works. The essays have been specially commissioned
for this volume and present a complete overview of Melville's career. Melville's
major novels are discussed, along with a range of his short fiction and poetry,
including neglected works ripe for rediscovery. The volume includes essays on
such new topics as Melville and oceanic studies, Melville and animal studies,
and Melville and the planetary, along with a number of essays that focus on
form and aesthetics. Written at a level both challenging and accessible, this
New Companion brings together a team of leading scholars to offer students
of American literature the most comprehensive introduction available to
Melville's art.

ROBERT S. LEVINE is Professor of English and Distinguished University
Professor at the University of Maryland, College Park. He is the author of
Conspiracy and Romance (1989); *Martin Delany, Frederick Douglass, and the
Politics of Representative Identity* (1997); and *Dislocating Race and Nation*
(2008) and the editor of a number of volumes, including *The Cambridge
Companion to Herman Melville* (1998). He has received fellowships from the
National Endowment for the Humanities and the Guggenheim Foundation.

A complete list of books in the series is at the back of this book.

THE NEW CAMBRIDGE
COMPANION TO
HERMAN MELVILLE

THE NEW CAMBRIDGE
COMPANION TO
HERMAN MELVILLE

EDITED BY
ROBERT S. LEVINE
University of Maryland, College Park

CAMBRIDGE
UNIVERSITY PRESS

32 Avenue of the Americas, New York, NY 10013-2473, USA

Cambridge University Press is part of the University of Cambridge.

It furthers the University's mission by disseminating knowledge in the pursuit of
education, learning, and research at the highest international levels of excellence.

www.cambridge.org
Information on this title: www.cambridge.org/9781107687912

© Cambridge University Press 2014

First published 2014

A catalog record for this publication is available from the British Library.

Library of Congress Cataloging in Publication data
The New Cambridge Companion to Herman Melville / [edited by] Robert S. Levine,
University of Maryland, College Park.
pages   cm. – (Cambridge Companions to Literature)
Includes bibliographical references and index.
ISBN 978-1-107-02313-0 (hardback) – ISBN 978-1-107-68791-2 (pbk.)
1. Melville, Herman, 1819–1891 – Criticism and interpretation.
I. Levine, Robert S. (Robert Steven), 1953– editor of compilation.
PS2387.N45   2013
813'.31–dc23   2013023409

ISBN 978-1-107-02313-0 Hardback
ISBN 978-1-107-68791-2 Paperback

CONTENTS

CONTENTS

NOTES ON CONTRIBUTORS

HESTER BLUM is Associate Professor of English at the Pennsylvania State University. Her first book, *The View from the Mast-Head: Maritime Imagination and Antebellum American Sea Narratives* (2008), received the John Gardner Maritime Research Award; she has also published a critical edition of William Ray's Barbary captivity narrative, *Horrors of Slavery* (2008). A founder of C19: The Society of Nineteenth-Century Americanists, she is at work on a book about oceanic studies and the print culture of Arctic and Antarctic exploration.

JOHN BRYANT, Professor of English at Hofstra University, is the author of *Melville and Repose: The Rhetoric of Humor in the American Renaissance* (1993); *The Fluid Text: A Theory of Revision and Editing for Book and Screen* (2002); and *Melville Unfolding: Sexuality, Politics, and the Versions of* Typee (2008). In addition to *A Companion to Melville Studies* (1983), he has edited *Typee* (1996, 2005); *Melville's Tales, Poems, and Other Writings* (2001); and (with Haskell Springer) the Longman Critical Edition of *Moby-Dick* (2006). He created and edits *Leviathan: A Journal of Melville Studies* and the electronic edition of *Herman Melville's Typee*. He is currently Director of the Melville Electronic Library.

CHRISTOPHER CASTIGLIA is Liberal Arts Research Professor of English at the Pennsylvania State University. He is the author of *Bound and Determined: Captivity, Culture-Crossing, and White Womanhood from Mary Rowlandson to Patty Hearst* (1996); *Interior States: Institutional Consciousness and the Inner Life of Democracy* (2008); and, with Christopher Reed, *If Memory Serves: Gay Men, AIDS, and the Promise of the Queer Past* (2011). With Dana Nelson, he is coeditor of *J19: the Journal for Nineteenth-Century Americanists*.

GREGG CRANE is Professor of English at the University of Michigan. He is the author of *Race, Citizenship, and Law in American Literature* (2002) and *The Cambridge Introduction to the Nineteenth-Century American Novel* (2007). He is currently working on a book about the figure and theme of intuition in American literature, philosophy, and culture.

JEANNINE MARIE DELOMBARD teaches American literature at the University of Toronto, where she is affiliated faculty with the Centre for the Study of the United States and the Collaborative Program in Book History and Print Culture. She is the author of *Slavery on Trial: Law, Print and Abolitionism* (2007) and *In the Shadow of the Gallows: Race, Crime, and American Civic Identity* (2012).

JENNIFER GREIMAN is Associate Professor of English at the University at Albany, SUNY. She is the author of *Democracy's Spectacle: Sovereignty and Public Life in Antebellum American Writing* (2010) and coeditor with Paul Stasi of *The Last Western:* Deadwood *and the End of American Empire* (2013). Her current project is a study of Herman Melville's political imagination.

WYN KELLEY teaches in the Literature Section at the Massachusetts Institute of Technology. She is the author of *Melville's City: Literary and Urban Form in Nineteenth-Century New York* (1996) and *Herman Melville: An Introduction* (2008), and the editor of the Blackwell *Companion to Herman Melville* (2006). A founding member of the Melville Society Cultural Project, she is also Associate Director of the Melville Electronic Library.

MAURICE S. LEE is Associate Professor of English at Boston University. He is the author of *Slavery, Philosophy, and American Literature, 1830–1860* (2005) and *Uncertain Chances: Science, Skepticism, and Belief in Nineteenth-Century American Literature* (2012). He also edited *The Cambridge Companion to Frederick Douglass* (2009). His current project examines the relationship between aesthetics and quantification in nineteenth-century Anglo-American literature.

ROBERT S. LEVINE is Professor of English and Distinguished University Professor at the University of Maryland, College Park. He is the author of *Conspiracy and Romance* (1989); *Martin Delany, Frederick Douglass, and the Politics of Representative Identity* (1997); and *Dislocating Race and Nation* (2008). Among his edited volumes are *The Cambridge Companion to Herman Melville* (1998), Melville's *Israel Potter* (2008), and (with Samuel Otter) *Frederick Douglass and Herman Melville: Essays in Relation* (2008). He is the general editor of *The Norton Anthology of American Literature.*

TIMOTHY MARR is Bowman and Gordon Gray Distinguished Term Associate Professor in the Department of American Studies at the University of North Carolina. He is the author of *The Cultural Roots of American Islamicism* (2006) and a coeditor (with John Bryant and Mary K. Bercaw Edwards) of *Ungraspable Phantom: Essays on* Moby-Dick (2006). He serves as an executive member of the Melville Society Cultural Project and a project coeditor of the Melville Electronic Library.

SAMUEL OTTER is Professor of English at the University of California, Berkeley. He is the author of *Melville's Anatomies* (1999) and *Philadelphia Stories: America's*

Literature of Race and Freedom (2010) and coeditor (with Robert S. Levine) of *Frederick Douglass and Herman Melville: Essays in Relation* (2008) and (with Geoffrey Sanborn) *Melville and Aesthetics* (2011). He is currently writing a book about what Melville, and we, might mean by literary form.

ELIZABETH RENKER is Professor of English at The Ohio State University. She is the author of *Strike through the Mask: Herman Melville and the Scene of Writing* (1996) and *The Origins of American Literature Studies: An Institutional History* (2007); she also wrote the introduction to the Signet classic edition of *Moby-Dick* (1998). Her book in progress, "The Lost Era in American Poetry, 1866–1912," presents a revisionary account of postbellum poetics, challenging long-standing dismissals of the era as a "twilight interval."

GEOFFREY SANBORN is Professor of English at Amherst College. He is the author of *The Sign of the Cannibal: Melville and the Making of a Postcolonial Reader* (1998) and *Whipscars and Tattoos:* The Last of the Mohicans, Moby-Dick, *and the Maori* (2011) and the coeditor (with Samuel Otter) of *Melville and Aesthetics* (2011). He is currently working on a book titled "Pleasureville: Fun, Money, and Other People's Language in the Work of William Wells Brown."

MICHAEL D. SNEDIKER is Associate Professor of English at the University of Houston. He is the author of *Queer Optimism: Lyric Personhood and Other Felicitous Persuasions* (2009), and he is working on a book titled "Contingent Figure: Aesthetic Duress from Nathaniel Hawthorne to Eve Kosofsky Sedgwick." He has published several volumes of poetry, most recently *The Apartment of Tragic Appliances* (2013).

ELISA TAMARKIN is Associate Professor of English at the University of California, Berkeley, and the author of *Anglophilia: Deference, Devotion, and Antebellum America* (2008). She is completing a book on ideas of relevant and irrelevant knowledge since 1830.

GRAHAM THOMPSON is Associate Professor of American Studies at the University of Nottingham, UK. He is the author of *Male Sexuality under Surveillance* (2003), *The Business of America* (2004), and *American Culture in the 1980s* (2007). He is currently writing a book on Melville's magazine fiction.

ACKNOWLEDGMENTS

Editing this *New Companion* has been a delight and an honor. I am grateful to Ray Ryan, senior editor at Cambridge University Press, for his encouragement and wisdom at every stage of the editorial process. For their expert assistance, I am also pleased to thank editor Louis Gulino, production manager Bindu Vinod, and indexer Diana Witt.

My warm thanks to the contributors, who performed their parts with intelligence, good humor, and grace. They even met deadlines! I learned from them every day I was working on this project. For their help along the way, I am particularly indebted to John Bryant, Ivy Goodman, Sam Otter, Elizabeth Renker, and Robert Wallace. Finally, I would like to thank my colleagues and students at the University of Maryland, who have helped to make Maryland a great place to read and think about Melville.

1819   Born New York City, August 1, third child of Allan Melvill, merchant and importer, and Maria Gansevoort Melvill, daughter of American Revolutionary hero General Peter Gansevoort. Brothers and sisters: Gansevoort (1815–46), Helen Maria (1817–88), Augusta (1821–76), Allan (1823–72), Catherine (1825–1905), Frances Priscilla (1827–85), Thomas (1830–84).

1825   With Gansevoort, enters New-York Male High School.

1829   Enters the grammar school of Columbia College, joining Gansevoort.

1830   After Allan Melvill liquidates his failing business, the Melvills move to Albany. With Gansevoort, Herman enrolls at the Albany Academy. Lemuel Shaw, Allan's friend and Herman's future father-in-law, named chief justice of the Supreme Judicial Court of Massachusetts.

1831–32   For financial reasons, Herman is withdrawn from the Albany Academy in October 1831. Allan journeys to New York in late November 1831 to take care of business matters. On his return to Albany, on December 10, he's forced to cross the frozen Hudson River on foot. Feverish, delirious, and in debt, he dies on January 28, 1832. Herman begins clerking at the New York State Bank. Sometime between 1832 and 1834, perhaps to disassociate the family from the father's failures, Maria adds the "e" to "Melvill."

1833–37   Continues with his bank job until spring 1834, when he begins working at Gansevoort's cap and fur store. Attends the Albany Classical School in 1835 and then the Albany Academy (1836–37). Works for his brother until the business fails in 1837. In the fall of that year he teaches at the Sikes District school near Pittsfield.

1838   Publishes satirical remarks on the area's young men's debating clubs in the March 24 issue of the *Albany Microscope*. In November, after the family's diminished finances force a relocation to Albany, Melville enrolls at Lansingburgh Academy, where he studies surveying and engineering.

1839   Under the pseudonym "L.A.V.," publishes two sketches, "Fragments from a Writing Desk," in the May *Democratic Press, and Lansingburgh Advertiser*. On June 4 he signs on as a "boy" on the merchant ship

St. Lawrence. Sails from New York to Liverpool and back from June 5 to October 1. Shortly after his return, he begins teaching at the Greenbush and Schodack Academy in Greenbush, New York.

1840   Leaves his position at Greenbush because of the school's inability to pay him. Teaches in the spring in Brunswick, New York, and then, accompanied by his friend Eli James Murdock Fly, visits his uncle Thomas Melvill in Galena, Illinois, to explore vocational possibilities in the west. Returning east, he signs on with the whaling ship *Acushnet* in New Bedford after failing to find a job in New York.

21 ז٠٦ .١٨

1841–44   Departs for the South Seas on the *Acushnet* on January 3, 1841. On July 9, 1842, he jumps ship with Richard Tobias Greene at Nukahiva Bay in the Marquesas Islands, remaining among the islanders of Taipi Valley for four weeks before signing on with the Australian whaler *Lucy Ann.* At Tahiti, he is sent ashore and nominally imprisoned as a mutineer, only to escape in October with John B. Troy. He then signs on with the Nantucket whaling ship *Charles and Henry* in November 1842. (At around the same time, his first cousin Guert Gansevoort is involved in putting down the "mutiny" on the U.S. brig *Somers.*) Discharged in May 1843 in the Hawaiian Islands, Melville works at various jobs – pin setter in a bowling alley, clerk in a store – until enlisting in the United States Navy in Honolulu and sailing as an ordinary seaman aboard the frigate *United States* on August 20, 1843. He returns to Boston on October 3, 1844, and soon after his discharge rejoins his family in Lansingburgh.

1845–46   Writes a narrative of his adventures among the Typee islanders, which is rejected by New York's Harper & Brothers in May or June 1845. Gansevoort, after stumping for Polk in 1844, is rewarded in spring 1845 with the position of secretary of the American Legation in London. Once there, he helps to place his brother's *Typee* manuscript with John Murray, who publishes it in his prestigious "Colonial and Home Library" in late February 1846, under the title *Narrative of a Four Months' Residence among the Natives of a Valley of the Marquesas Islands.* On March 17, the book, now titled *Typee,* is published by New York's Wiley & Putnam. After meeting Toby Greene in Rochester, who "authenticates" the facts of *Typee,* Melville prepares a "Revised Edition," with an appended "The Story of Toby," which is published later that year. Gansevoort dies in London on May 12, 1846.

1847   Attempts to find a government job in Washington, DC. *Omoo* published by Murray in London (March) and by Harper & Brothers in New York (May). On August 4, Melville marries Elizabeth Shaw, daughter of Chief Justice Lemuel Shaw. After honeymooning in New Hampshire and Canada, they move into a large row house in Manhattan purchased with the help of Lemuel Shaw. Living with Herman and Elizabeth are Allan Melville and his wife, the four unmarried Melville sisters, mother Maria Melville, and (on occasion) brother Tom Melville. Writes for the *Literary*

World, edited by Evert A. Duyckinck, and for *Yankee Doodle*, edited by Cornelius Mathews.

1849   Rejected by Murray, *Mardi* is published by Richard Bentley in London (March) and by Harper in New York (April). *Redburn* is published by Bentley (October) and Harper (November). Birth of son, Malcolm, February 16. In October, Melville departs for a trip to London and the Continent, returning January 31, 1850.

1850   *White-Jacket* published by Bentley in London (January) and by Harper in New York (March). On August 5, Melville, while vacationing in Pittsfield, meets Hawthorne and they quickly become friends; later that month he publishes "Hawthorne and His Mosses" in the *Literary World*. In September, with money borrowed from his father-in-law, Melville purchases a 160-acre farm in Pittsfield, which he names "Arrowhead," and moves there with his family.

1851   Dedicated to the "Genius" of Nathaniel Hawthorne, *The Whale* published by Bentley in London (October) and, with the title changed to *Moby-Dick*, by Harper in New York (November). Birth of second son, Stanwix, on October 22. In a famous test of the Fugitive Slave Law, Chief Justice Shaw, in April, orders Thomas Sims returned to his Southern owner (in 1854, in another famous case, he orders fugitive slave Anthony Burns returned to his owner).

32 yrs old

1852   Rejected by Bentley, *Pierre* published by Harper in New York (August) and by Sampson Low in London (November).

1853   Between 1853 and 1856, Melville publishes fourteen tales and sketches in *Putnam's Monthly Magazine* and *Harper's New Monthly Magazine*. Birth of daughter, Elizabeth, on May 22. Melville's family makes an unsuccessful effort to secure him a consulship. Evidence suggests he completes a book manuscript, *The Isle of the Cross*, which the Harpers choose not to publish.

1855   Serialized in *Putnam's*, *Israel Potter* published by Putnam in New York (March) and by George Routledge in London (May). Birth of second daughter, Frances, on March 2.

1856   *The Piazza Tales*, which collects five of the pieces in *Putnam's*, including "Bartleby, the Scrivener" (1853) and "Benito Cereno" (1855), published by Dix & Edwards in New York (1856) and distributed in England by Sampson Low. Concerned about his son-in-law's health, Shaw finances Melville's travels to Europe and the Holy Land (October 11, 1856–May 20, 1857). Melville visits Hawthorne in Liverpool in November 1856.

1857–60   *The Confidence-Man* published by Dix & Edwards in New York (April 1857) and by Longman in London (April 1857). Between late 1857 and 1860 Melville undertakes three lecture tours, speaking first on "Statues in Rome" (1857–58), next on "The South Seas" (1858–59), and finally on "Traveling" (1859–60). In 1860, he fails in his efforts to publish a poetry manuscript. With his brother Thomas at the helm, he embarks for

California on May 30, 1860, aboard the clipper ship *Meteor*. Shaken by their perilous journey around Cape Horn, Melville returns via Panama to New York without his brother in November.

1861 Journeys to Washington, DC, in another failed quest to obtain a consulship. Shakes hands with Abraham Lincoln. Lemuel Shaw dies in Boston on March 30.

1863 Purchases his brother Allan's home at 104 East Twenty-Sixth Street and moves to New York. Allan purchases Arrowhead.

1864 Visits Civil War battlefields on the Virginia front with Allan. Hawthorne dies May 19.

1866 Publishes four Civil War poems in *Harper's*. *Battle-Pieces and Aspects of the War*, a collection of Melville's war poetry, published by Harper in New York (August). On December 5, he assumes the duties of district inspector of the United States Customs Service at the port of New York.

1867 Unhappy in her marriage, and evidently fearful of her husband, Elizabeth Melville discusses with her minister, Henry Bellows, the possibility of a legal separation. In May, Bellows proposes a kind of kidnapping scheme to help Elizabeth obtain sanctuary with her Boston relatives, a scheme she and her family eventually reject. On September 11, the Melvilles' son Malcolm dies from a self-inflicted gunshot to the head.

1872 Maria Gansevoort Melville dies April 1 at the age of eighty-two.

1876 *Clarel* published in New York by Putnam (June). Melville's uncle Peter Gansevoort pays for the publishing expenses.

1885 Resigns from his position as district inspector of customs (December 31).

1886 The Melvilles' son Stanwix dies in San Francisco on February 23.

1888 Privately publishes *John Marr and Other Sailors* in an edition of twenty-five copies after receiving a bequest of $3,000 from his sister Frances Priscilla.

1891 Privately publishes *Timoleon* in an edition of twenty-five copies. Dies September 28. An unpublished volume of poems, titled "Weeds and Wildings Chiefly," the sketch "Daniel Orme," and *Billy Budd* are left in manuscript. The first published version of *Billy Budd* appears in 1924.

TEXTS AND ABBREVIATIONS

Most references to Melville's work in this *Companion* are to *The Writings of Herman Melville*, eds. Harrison Hayford, Hershel Parker, and G. Thomas Tanselle, in fourteen volumes (Evanston and Chicago, IL: Northwestern University Press and The Newberry Library, 1968–). See the Selected Bibliography for complete bibliographical information on this edition. Still standard is Harrison Hayford and Merton M. Sealts, Jr., eds., *Billy Budd, Sailor* (Chicago, IL: University of Chicago Press, 1962). Abbreviations for Melville's texts are as follows:

T	*Typee*
O	*Omoo*
M	*Mardi*
R	*Redburn*
WJ	*White-Jacket*
MD	*Moby-Dick*
P	*Pierre*
PT	*The Piazza Tales and Uncollected Prose*
IP	*Israel Potter*
CM	*The Confidence-Man*
L	*Correspondence*
J	*Journals*
PP	*Published Poems*
C	*Clarel*
BB	*Billy Budd*

ROBERT S. LEVINE

Introduction

This volume inaugurates the *New Cambridge Companion* series at a time
when Melville is more vital than ever in American literary studies. Since the
publication of *The Cambridge Companion to Herman Melville* (1998), there
have been new biographies by Hershel Parker and Andrew Delbanco, dis-
coveries about Melville's process of composition and revision, an increasing
interest in Melville the poet, and an abundance of new books on literary and
cultural matters ranging from Melville's literary friendship with Nathaniel
Hawthorne to his less obvious connections with Frederick Douglass.[1]
Melville as a writer and cultural figure remains crucial to conversations in
American literary studies on sexuality, race, travel, religion, literary traditions, and transatlanticism; and over the past fifteen years Melville's writings
have become central to discussions of transnationalism, ecocriticism, posthumanism, imperialism, political theory, and aesthetics. Melville is more vital
than ever outside of the academy as well. In the wake of 9/11, *Moby-Dick*
was invoked by numerous cultural commentators for its prescient insights
into imperialism, globalization, and America's role in Afghanistan (Ishmael's
inclusion of "BLOODY BATTLE IN AFGHANISTAN" in the "grand pro-
gramme of Providence that was drawn up a long time ago"[*MD* 7] could
not help but haunt).[2] In the wake of the financial crisis of 2007–2008 and
the Great Recession of 2009 to the present, the Occupy movement adopted
"Bartleby, the Scrivener" as its sacred text for the tale's seemingly prophetic
account of passive resistance to Wall Street. And, as ever, Melville attracts
new generations of readers with his artistry. His presence can be felt in popular culture, and not only at the coffee shops named after the *Pequod*'s first
mate. Community readings of *Moby-Dick* have become increasingly common; a New York trade house recently published an internationally popular
book on why we should all read *Moby-Dick*; film and TV adaptations of
Moby-Dick are in the offing; and the forty-fourth president of the United
States lists *Moby-Dick* on his Facebook page as one of his two favorite
novels.[3] Novelists and visual artists at their most ambitious regularly find

I

inspiration in *Moby-Dick* and other of Melville's works, and a brilliant oper-
atic version of *Moby-Dick* has taken the music world by storm.[4] Though it
is probably true, as John Bryant writes in his essay in this volume, that
Melville tends to be equated with *Moby-Dick*, and that the many who make
that equation have not actually read the novel (but have instead encountered it via film, popular culture references, and comic books), this is not to
diminish the impact Melville's writings continue to have on our literary and
cultural moment.

It is time for a *New Cambridge Companion to Herman Melville*, a book
for the twenty-first century that situates Melville in relation to current critical conversations and develops new perspectives on reading and interpreting
the full range of his writings. Though you will encounter endnotes in this
volume, it has been conceived for the widest possible audience. It is my hope
that in addition to contributing to interpretive discussions among those who
write about and teach Melville, this *Companion* will also speak to the many
who (rightly) regard Melville as having a vibrant connection to the world
outside of the classroom. This volume has essays on topics ranging from
democracy to art history, and on such fundamental matters as the challenges
of reading *Moby-Dick* and the relatively neglected great poetry. As a group,
all of the contributors pay close attention to Melville's art, taking Melville's
work as their most important guide, even as they assume the function of
guides themselves.

Because this is my second tour of duty as an editor of a Melville *Companion*,
it might be useful to offer a quick consideration of the two complementary
collections. The 1998 *Companion*, like any such work, was of its time, and
at the time (the mid-1990s, when contributors were writing their essays) the
New Historicism and other historicist approaches were in the ascendency.
That collection includes essays on Melville and race, Melville and social
class, Melville and gender, Melville and slavery, Melville and sexuality, along
with essays that consider Melville in relation to Victorian culture and religion. New Historicists tend to implicate authors in the power structures of
their culture, but in that volume, as in this, Melville is accorded considerable
privilege as a writer who could understand and critique his culture as well
as any historicist critic.

In this 2013 *New Cambridge Companion to Herman Melville*, essays
are also organized around key topics, but a glance at the table of contents
will reveal that this collection is a bit quirkier and the topics more varied.
In the spirit of Timothy Marr's essay on "Melville's Planetary Compass,"
this volume offers a much wider compass, addressing the oceans, the nonhuman, art history, biography, digital humanities, philosophical skepticism,
legal judgment, political theory, the problematics of reading, print culture

and book history, along with sexuality (now addressed from the perspective of queer studies) and slavery (now addressed from a legal perspective). In significant ways, this new *Companion* responds to two large impulses in recent American literary studies: an increased questioning of nation-based models of literary study and a renewed interest in the aesthetic. The last fifteen years have seen a turn in American literary studies from national-ist to more expansive hemispheric, transnational, and global approaches. Likewise in Melville studies, we increasingly have a Melville who is some-thing more than an "American" author.[5] I credit this critical turn to devel-opments both inside and outside the academy. Within the academy, there has been much interest in interdisciplinarity, which has had the inevitable impact of challenging the insularity of national study. Outside the acad-emy, the events of 9/11, the global financial crisis, and the impact of the Internet on all aspects of life, including research, have revealed with stark clarity that nations simply do not and cannot exist in isolation. Perhaps in response to several decades of historicist study, canon busting, and now globalization (which can sometimes make the literary a subordinate player in the flow of peoples, capital, and ideas), a number of critics have begun to pay renewed attention to matters of form, language, and reading. The impact of the aesthetic turn within American literary studies can best been seen in this volume in Samuel Otter's essay on *Moby-Dick*, which addresses the broad and sometimes neglected interconnections between form and content in Melville's art.[6] But aesthetic issues are central to all of the essays in this collection, for the good reason that it is nearly impossible to write about Melville without coming under the sway of his language. In some respects, the return to the "old" – form, language, and aesthetics – is some-thing "new" in this *New Companion*.

The fifteen chapters of *The New Cambridge Companion to Herman Melville* survey a wide range of material and explore Melville's writings from a variety of perspectives. The volume begins with three chapters that provide a foundation for what follows, focusing on major concerns of Melville's fiction: nature (specifically animal and plant life), oceans, and democracy. These chapters are followed by seven chapters that consider Melville's writings chronologically from his early sea fiction (with a focus on *White-Jacket*), to the celebrated works of the 1850s (*Moby-Dick, Pierre, The Confidence-Man*, and the magazine fiction), to the poetry (*Battle-Pieces* through *Timoleon*), and finally to the posthumously published *Billy Budd*. The volume concludes with three interpretive chapters on key aspects of Melville's overall career, from *Typee* to *Billy Budd*, followed by two chap-ters – on biography and criticism, respectively – that look to the future of Melville studies.

The opening essay, Geoffrey Sanborn's "Melville and the Nonhuman World," depicts a Melville who is interested in communicating with trees, horses, cows, and other forms of nonhuman life through what Sanborn terms a "mutual summoning." Drawing on recent work in animal studies, sustainability studies, and other ecologically centered critical movements, and adducing examples from numerous texts by Melville, Sanborn portrays an author whose writings are exclamatory, responsive, and charged with a vital sense of life. Sanborn's focus text is Melville's sketch "Cock-A-Doodle-Doo!" (1853), which has at its center the narrator's responsiveness to a crowing cock. Loud as it may be, the cock bears close connections to other forms of nonhuman life in Melville's writing, including quieter whales. Hester Blum's "Melville and Oceanic Studies" takes the reader to the locale of whales and the seamen who pursue them, and of course to the setting of much of Melville's fiction. Attending to the emerging field of oceanic studies, Blum discusses how the oceans' watery worlds can dissolve national identifications while stimulating new ways of thinking about citizenship, economics, and identity. As Blum shows through her readings of *Moby-Dick*, "Benito Cereno," and (surprisingly) the land-bound *Pierre*, the fluid world of the ocean provides opportunities for political and ontological reorientations, as well as formal experimentation. In her essay on "Democracy and Melville's Aesthetics," Jennifer Greiman considers Melville's representations of democracy on land and at sea – and on rivers, too. The subject of democracy is hardly new to Melville studies, and in Greiman's essay there's a refreshing turn to the "old": an effort to read Melville's political philosophy of democracy through the lens of Alexis de Tocqueville's *Democracy in America* (1840). But the essay is also informed by Greiman's engagement with recent debates in political theory. Like all of the writers in this volume, she is interested in aesthetics, and in her account of Melville's astonishingly wide and varied approaches to democracy, she discerns a poetics of democracy in Melville's fiction that makes use of three recurring rhetorical figures: circles, colors, and rivers.

With Jeannine Marie DeLombard's essay on *White-Jacket*, we turn to a series of essays that for the most part examine single works and follow the course of Melville's unfolding career. In "*White-Jacket*: Telling Who Is – and Aint – a Slave," DeLombard makes the bold claim that the relatively neglected *White-Jacket*, more than the canonical "Benito Cereno," constitutes Melville's most profound statement on slavery. Picking up on Ishmael's famous declaration in *Moby-Dick* – "Who aint a slave? Tell me that" (*MD* 6) – DeLombard examines *White-Jacket* in the context of the sometimes competing and sometimes overlapping antislavery and sailors' rights movements, both of which called attention to the horrors of flogging. Like Gregg

Crane in his essay on *Billy Budd* later in the volume, she works with a law and literature approach, showing how *White-Jacket* absorbs and responds to legal rhetoric about seamen and slaves. The law, as both DeLombard and Crane make clear, is about the problem of interpretation, or reading, and reading is given center stage in Samuel Otter's "Reading *Moby-Dick*." After several decades of criticism that has analyzed *Moby-Dick* in various discursive contexts, Otter urges us to reengage such essential matters as form, language, and genre. Working against the grain of the New Historicism, Otter shows how *Moby-Dick* "flouts the choice between form and history" and is "distinguished by an elaborate reflexivity ... that ties its meanings to its materiality." In a short essay that cannot hope to take in all of *Moby-Dick*, Otter concentrates on what can appear to be the paradoxical claim that the novel gives form to formlessness, finding in the novel's depiction of the squid a key locus for Melville's thinking about textuality and reading.

Wyn Kelley takes up the question of how to read the enigmatic Pierre (the character) in her "*Pierre*, Life History, and the Obscure." She addresses an issue that Maurice S. Lee and Michael D. Snediker discuss in their essays as well: that Melville's characters often seem unreal and not even "characters" in the nineteenth-century realist understanding of what characters are supposed to be. Surprisingly, Kelley argues, Melville drew on popular biographies of the time for his portrayal of the eponymous hero of *Pierre*, crafting a character who seems all the more unknowable and unreal when thought of in relation to the (auto)biographical writings of Mason Locke Weems, Ben Franklin, Ralph Waldo Emerson, and Frederick Douglass. *Pierre* suggests that one can perhaps best begin to know a life by *not* knowing it, at least in the conventional ways of biography. One year after publishing *Pierre*, Melville created perhaps his most unknowable character in the figure of Bartleby. In "'Bartleby' and the Magazine Fiction," Graham Thompson presents the magazine world of Melville's time not only as an important context for understanding "Bartleby," but also as that which can help us to *read* "Bartleby." Returning us to the November 1853 print context of the story, which first appeared in *Putnam's Monthly Magazine*, Thompson challenges those who view "Bartleby" as transcending the contingencies of magazine writing and publishing. For Thompson, the nature of the magazines Melville was writing for during the mid-1850s, and the tropes circulating in those magazines (such as figures of lawyers and clerks), are crucial to the meaning of the story. Even so, the character of Bartleby remains as enigmatic as ever, and thus relatively easy to appropriate as a sort of spokesperson for whatever one might prefer not to do.

The Confidence-Man is one of Melville's most enigmatic works, but as Maurice S. Lee explains in "Skepticism and *The Confidence-Man*," enigma and difficulty are integral to the novel's philosophical ambitions to address questions of identity, perception, and the bases of moral judgment. The novel, Lee suggests, is Melville's purest expression of his interest in skepticism, particularly as mediated through his reading of Descartes. Like a number of the contributors, Lee regards Melville as an experimental writer who in *The Confidence-Man* explores fictions of personhood. The novel's difficulties and inconsistencies, he concludes, speak to the challenge of trying to keep faith in a world that can seem beyond one's grasp. Or perhaps the novel speaks to Melville's loss of faith in fiction, for after publishing the novel Melville turned almost exclusively to writing poetry. His approximately thirty-five-year career as a poet far outweighs his approximately ten-year-career as a fiction writer, and yet, as Elizabeth Renker notes in her essay on "Melville the Poet in the Postbellum World," most readers of Melville know little about his poetry. Renker laments the relative neglect of the poetry, which she, along with a number of recent critics, regards as among Melville's greatest literary achievements. As Renker shows in her wide-ranging essay, Melville was fully engaged with the poetry world of the nineteenth century and was writing at a time when poetry was central to the lives of many Americans. Rather than viewing Melville in the late 1850s as "retreating" from fiction to poetry, she sees him as choosing to work in a genre that placed him in an even closer relation to his culture; and though she allows that Melville was committed to a poetics of difficulty, she nonetheless demonstrates through close reading that the poetry is both accessible and moving. Melville the poet continues to await the many readers he deserves.

Billy Budd had no readers in Melville's lifetime because the novella was still in manuscript at his death in 1891. A work that combines his interest in prose and poetry (the novella was inspired by the poem that Melville placed at the end of the manuscript), *Billy Budd* first appeared in 1924, at the time of the Melville revival (when Melville at long last was being discovered by modernist critics), and quickly became canonical. Like the poetry and much of Melville's fiction, *Billy Budd* is richly allusive, difficult, and resistant to interpretation. In "Judgment in *Billy Budd*," Gregg Crane responds to the novella's interpretive difficulties by reading it in a law and literature context, asking us to think about the novella in relation to contemporaneous juridical and philosophical writings on intuition. Putting the novella in conversation with the writings of William James and Oliver Wendell Holmes, Crane makes a case for moving beyond the binary of acceptance and resistance that has dominated discussions of Vere's decision to execute Billy Budd. Consistent with Otter's essay on *Moby-Dick*, Crane underscores the crucial role of reading in the act of judgment.

Turning from discussions of specific works and the poetry, the next three essays in the volume address Melville's broader corpus from varied critical perspectives. In "Melville and Queerness without Character," Michael D. Snediker views Melville's writings through the optics of queer theory, which he differentiates from gay studies. Queerness can be about, or not about, sexual desire; the emphasis is more on departures from normativity, which Snediker discerns in Melville's unreal (queer) characterizations. Because Melville's characters often don't seem "real," then it might be odd to think about them as somehow possessing corporeal desire. Then again, given *Moby-Dick*'s "A Squeeze of the Hand" chapter and the account of Ishmael and Queequeg sleeping together as "a cosy, loving pair" (*MD* 52), to name just two of the many homoerotic-seeming moments in Melville's writings, it's difficult to ignore homoerotic sexuality. But after taking such moments into account, Snediker reads Melville's characters as "irresolvable aesthetic problems" rather than mimetic representations of people. Melville, Snediker observes, anticipated some of the major insights of queer studies by locating pleasure apart from particular sexual acts, and even regarding pleasure (in language) as an aesthetic category of its own. Aesthetic issues are also essential to Elisa Tamarkin's discussion of Melville as a theorist of vision. Though her essay, "Melville with Pictures," considers some of Melville's fiction, her focus is on the writings that followed his 1857 travels to Italy, Turkey, Greece, Palestine, and Egypt, where he developed his great passion for art. Thus, like Elizabeth Renker, she mainly discusses the poetry of Melville's last three decades. Melville's greatest love was for the paintings of Claude Lorrain, which he viewed in Rome's Sciarra Gallery in 1857. As Tamarkin elaborates, Melville was attracted to Claude and other artists whose dreamlike atmospheric effects produced meditative states. Tamarkin's essay offers new readings of ekphrastic descriptions in Melville's poems, a number of which were inspired by Claude's sense of looking at nature as if through a darkened mirror.

In "Melville's Planetary Compass," Timothy Marr emphasizes the Melville who looked directly at nature, asserting that his engagement with the planet informed his literary expression. Taking account of the full sweep of Melville's writings in poetry and prose, Marr identifies three large strains in those writings that emerged from his planetary thinking: a desire for pantheistic merging with a paradisal nature; a fear of perilous encounters with a heartless materialism (or sharkishness) in a world that can seem a type of hell; and a willingness to take consolation in nature's regenerative processes. Marr discusses Melville's awareness of the new geological sciences, which had undercut ideas of fixity, and suggests that such knowledge had an impact on Melville's development as an experimental writer. Ultimately, though, Marr offers a new way of thinking about Melville and religion, depicting a Melville who is less interested in the Bible and other sacred texts than in the planet itself.

The volume concludes with two essays that help us to think about the future of Melville studies. In "Wound, Beast, Revision: Versions of the Melville Meme," John Bryant takes the figure of the meme – a circulating unit for carrying cultural ideas, symbols, and images, particularly on the Internet – and applies the term to Melville himself. Investigating Melville as meme in relation to the traumas he discerns in Melville's life and writings, Bryant raises provocative questions about who or what "Melville" is, making clear that the Melville we think we know may be just one of many revisions and adaptations. Looking to the future, Bryant describes how the *Melville Electronic Library* (MEL), the digital project he created and directs, promises to develop new ways of editing, reading, visualizing, and circulating Melville texts; in other words, MEL will help to create new Melville memes. Moving from digital studies to a book about Melville published in 1949 might seem counterintuitive when considering the future of Melville studies, but as Christopher Castiglia elaborates in "Cold War Allegories and the Politics of Criticism," Richard Chase's *Herman Melville: A Critical Study* (1949), a key text in the modern revival of Melville, though now relatively neglected, can help us to reorient our own thinking about Melville. Chase saw Melville as a visionary allegorist whose imaginative works posed a challenge to conformity, nurtured social ideals, and opened new worlds to readers. We could use more Richard Chases in our own time, Castiglia argues, critics who are willing to think beyond Cold War– and New Historicist–inflected formulations of authorial blindness and complicity to develop new ways of reading for literary and cultural possibility.

A writer as rich, complex, and prolific as Melville cannot be contained by critics or a critical volume, I am happy to say. Even with fifteen essays in this *New Companion*, I am aware of the gaps, and I also know that this volume, like the 1998 *Companion*, must be of its time. Still, it is my hope that the *New Companion* will play a significant role in guiding this and the next generation of Melville readers to a number of the most compelling aspects of Melville's writings. Some of the contributors discuss Melville's work in the context of current critical conversations while others seek to initiate new conversations, but what links all of the essays are the contributors' recognitions of Melville's importance to our lives as readers. In the concluding paragraph of his essay, Christopher Castiglia writes, "Revisiting one of the greatest allegorists of the antebellum period might be an occasion to discover a Melville for our time, and to investigate new approaches for enlivening that Melville, one of which might be to affirm, as Melville

and Chase did, the imaginative idealism possible in and through literature."
These invigorating words about the imaginative genius of Melville and the
regenerative power of literature seem a perfect way of concluding *The New
Cambridge Companion to Herman Melville*.

NOTES

1 See the selected bibliography at the end of this volume for complete bibliographical information on the biographies by Parker and Delbanco and the books on
  Hawthorne and Melville (edited by Argersinger and Person) and Douglass and
  Melville (edited by Levine and Otter). The bibliography displays the wide range
  of work in Melville studies of the last fifteen years.

2 See, for example, the influential article by Edward Said, "Islam and the West Are
  Inadequate Banners," *The Observer*, September 15, 2001, Web (accessed April
  29, 2012), which compared the hunt for Osama bin Laden to Ahab's hunt for the
  white whale.

3 See https://www.facebook.com/barackobama/info (accessed December 11, 2012);
  Obama lists Toni Morrison's *Song of Solomon* as his other favorite novel. On
  the upsurge of community readings of *Moby-Dick*, see David Dowling, *Chasing
  the White Whale: The* Moby-Dick *Marathon; or, What Melville Means Today*
  (Iowa City: University of Iowa Press, 2010). Nathaniel Philbrick's *Why Read*
  Moby-Dick? (New York: Viking Press, 2011) no doubt brought many new read-
  ers to Melville. On the *Moby-Dick* movie and TV show in the offing, see George
  Cotkin, "'Moby-Dick' in the Mainstream," *The Chronicle of Higher Education*,
  November 13, 2012, Web (accessed November 14, 2012).

4 On Jake Heggie and Gene Scheer's new opera, *Moby-Dick*, see Robert K. Wallace,
  Heggie and Scheer's Moby-Dick: *A Grand Opera for the Twenty-First Century*
  (Denton: University of North Texas Press, 2013). For a striking recent example of
  a visual artist's response to *Moby-Dick*, see Matt Kish's Moby-Dick *in Pictures:
  One Drawing for Every Page* (Portland, OR: Tin House, 2011). (The cover image
  on the paperback edition of this *New Companion* is from Kish's volume; see also
  recent Melville-inspired art by Robert Del Tredici, George Klauba, and Kathleen
  Piercefield.) Chad Harbach's *The Art of Fielding* (New York: Little, Brown and
  Company, 2011) is one of a number of novels of the past decade that have found
  inspiration in Melville.

5 See, for example, Wai Chee Dimock and Lawrence Buell, eds., *Shades of the Planet:
  American Literature as World Literature* (Princeton, NJ: Princeton University
  Press, 2007); and Caroline F. Levander and Robert S. Levine, eds., *Hemispheric
  American Studies* (New Brunswick, NJ: Rutgers University Press, 2008).

6 On the aesthetic turn in American literary studies, see Cindy Weinstein and
  Christopher Looby, eds., *American Literature's Aesthetic Dimensions* (New York:
  Columbia University Press, 2012); and Samuel Otter and Geoffrey Sanborn, eds.,
  Melville and Aesthetics (New York: Palgrave Macmillan, 2011).

I

GEOFFREY SANBORN

Melville and the Nonhuman World

> Do you want to know how I pass my time? – I rise at eight – thereabouts –
> & go to my barn – say good-morning to the horse, & give him his
> breakfast. (It goes to my heart to give him a cold one, but it can't be
> helped.) Then, pay a visit to my cow – cut up a pumpkin or two for
> her, & stand by to see her eat it – for it's a pleasant sight to see a cow
> move her jaws – she does it so mildly & with such a sanctity. – My own
> breakfast over, I go to my work-room & light my fire – then spread
> my M.S.S on the table – take one business squint at it, & fall to with
> a will.
>
> Herman Melville to Evert Duyckinck, December 13, 1850 (*L* 174)

Sometime in the early 1850s, the writer Maunsell B. Field and the illustra-
tor Felix O. C. Darley visited Herman Melville at his home in Pittsfield,
Massachusetts. In a collection of reminiscences published two decades later,
Field writes that he and Darley "found Melville, whom I had always known
as the most silent man of my acquaintance, sitting on the porch in front
of his door. He took us to a particular spot on his place to show us some
superb trees. He told me that he spent much time there *patting them upon
the back*." All three men then went to see Melville's neighbor, the poet/physi-
cian Oliver Wendell Holmes. At first, "the talk, in which all tried to participate, dragged," but when "the conversation drifted to East India religions
and mythologies … there arose a discussion between Holmes and Melville,
which was conducted with the most amazing skill and brilliancy on both
sides. It lasted for hours, and Darley and I had nothing to do but to listen. I
never chanced to hear better talking in my life."[1]
   Tree patting and sparkling talk, like cow feeding and novel writing, might
seem to have little in common. But there is, in each case, something subtly
linking these apparently unrelated activities. What Field is most struck by in
Melville's remark about his trees is that he speaks of "*patting them upon the
back*" – that he not only perceives the trees as beings like himself, with nobly
vertical spines, but is moved to socialize with them. Although the nature of
that socialization is, in Field's anecdote, unclear, the evidence of Melville's
work suggests (as I will show) that it involves both receiving inspiration
from the trees and conveying friendly, admiring feelings to them. Something

similar seems to occur in Melville's visits to his barn animals, as described in the letter to Evert Duyckinck; he seems to draw from the animals and transmit to them an energizing feeling of fellowship. The conversational interaction with Holmes and the interaction with the implied reader in the composition of *Moby-Dick* (1851) – the novel he was working on when he wrote to Duyckinck – are, in addition to whatever else might be said about them, similarly oriented toward the prospect of a reciprocal, companionable vitalization. As in his relationships with the trees, the horse, and the cow, moreover, the value of the interaction is dependent on a mutual summoning, of the kind that occurs when, in the first sentence of the first chapter of *Moby-Dick*, our narrator-to-be says, "Call me Ishmael." If the trees, the horse, and the cow do not summon Melville just as much as Melville summons them, they cannot be said to be much more than idealizations, the products of wishful anthropomorphic thinking. If the conversation does not ignite, if the book is dutifully, mechanically read, neither the friend nor the reader can be said to be much more than that either.

Not only in incidents like these, but throughout Melville's nonfiction, fiction, and poetry – in, for example, the stories about a rooster, a chimney, and a beetle; the poems about a shark, a lilac tree, a sea hawk, a kitten, an iceberg, and a piece of kelp; the book of poetry that is chiefly about plants; and, of course, the novel about a whale – the difference between humans and nonhumans is less significant than the difference between isolation and response.[2] "If to affirm, be to expand one's isolated self; and if to deny, be to contract one's isolated self," Melville writes in *Pierre* (1852), "then to respond is a suspension of all isolation" (293). To respond, to move toward the perception of things that the things themselves solicit, is to give oneself over to what Maurice Merleau-Ponty describes as "another self which has already sided with the world, which is already open to certain of its aspects and synchronized with them." That other self, that "prepersonal cleaving to the general form of the world," has, like the things it perceives, a "momentum of existence"; it actively seeks, just as things actively offer, "certain kinds of symbiosis." "The surface which I am about to recognize as the surface of the table," Merleau-Ponty writes, "when vaguely looked at, already summons me to focus upon it, and demands those movements of convergence which will endow it with its 'true' aspect." By the same token, he goes on to say, "I am able to touch effectively only if the phenomenon finds an echo within me, if it accords with a certain nature of my consciousness, and if the organ which goes out to meet it is synchronized with it." We do not need to "open an intercourse with the world," as Hawthorne puts it, in order to experience such convergences; we need only to intensify the momentum of our already existing intercourse with a world that never stops summoning us.[3]

Akin to the idea that earth is porous

The name Melville gives to that momentum is "life," a word that signifies, in his lexicon, the opposite of stasis. Life, in Melville's work, is "a fine rushing" (R 115), an "incessant operation of subtle processes" (M 505), and we encounter its "joyous, jubilant, overflowing, upbubbling" (P 302) presence – and thereby, however glancingly, the "joyous, heartless, ever-juvenile eternities" (MD 444) – at every turn. "In kings, mollusca, and toad-stools, life is one thing and the same" (538), declares Babbalanja in Mardi (1849). "Trust me," he says elsewhere in that novel, "there are more things alive than those that crawl, or fly, or swim. Think you ... there is no sensation in being a tree? feeling the sap in one's boughs, the breeze in one's foliage? think you it is nothing to be a world? one of a herd, bison-like, wending its way across boundless meadows of ether?" (458). That "ruthless democracy" (L 190), that location of an identical life force in all of the elements of creation, extends ultimately to the Creator. After seeing a moose swimming between two islands at dawn, Babbalanja says, "[w]ith Oro" – the Mardian word for God – "the sun is co-eternal; and the same life that moves that moose, animates alike the sun and Oro" (616). Life, not God, is the ultimate reality, a primal motion carrying moose, sun, and God along with it. On a large scale, that reality can be terrifying, as Pip, for one, discovers. On a small scale, however, when comparable instances of life turn toward one another, it can be an animating source of pleasure. In "The Apple-Tree Table" (1856), after a night-long vigil alongside his inexplicably ticking table – a table that is, unbeknownst to him, inhabited by beetles – the narrator sees "a short nibbled sort of crack, from which (like a butterfly escaping its chrysalis), the sparkling object, whatever it might be, was struggling. Its motion was the motion of life. I stood becharmed" (PT 389).

The recent explosion of analytic approaches to the subject of the nonhuman world – animal studies, ecophenomenology, zoosemiotics, sustainability studies, and the new materialism, to name only the most immediately relevant – makes this an ideal moment to return to Melville's peculiar and frequently misunderstood relationship to "nature."[4] Although some of Melville's earliest twentieth-century critics were drawn to the uncanny communications with the nonhuman world that are threaded through his work – with "sheer physical vibrational sensitiveness," D. H. Lawrence writes, "like a marvelous wireless-station, [Melville] registers the effects of the outer world" – most of his more recent critics have tended to reduce his account of the nonhuman world either to exposures of voracity or to evocations of a void.[5] In The Salt-Sea Mastodon, for instance, Robert Zoellner alternately declares, with respect to Moby-Dick, that "sharkishness, the ineluctably rapacious life-dynamism of the self-sustaining individual, [is] the bedrock of animate creation," and that there is "an ontological vacancy beneath appearances." In recent years, some critics have begun to move beyond the standard bottom lines of violence and meaninglessness in their treatment of this topic, suggesting, for instance, that "[a]nimal agency – individual and collective – is not just a counter to human enterprise but a product of it," and that "Melville treats persons as if they were not governed by a set of constraints that differentiate them from other phenomena, as if ... a person were not different from a stone or a manifestation of light." Instead of pitting Man against Nature, as most of the earlier Melvilleans did, these critics start from the assumption of "an intrinsic and irresistible interdependency," in Elizabeth Schultz's words, and spray out in a variety of directions from there.[6]

In what follows, I want to contribute to the development of the latter approach, first by offering a few propositions that draw on Melville's entire body of work, and then by exploring a rarely explored work, "Cock-A-Doodle-Doo!" (1853), in detail. The emphasis, throughout, will be on Melville's tendency to lateralize just about everything that is capable of being hierarchically arranged. "As soon as you say *Me*, a *God*, a *Nature*," he writes to Hawthorne in 1851, "so soon you jump off from your stool and hang from the beam.... Take God out of the dictionary, and you would have Him in the street" (*L* 186). Everywhere in his work, Melville keeps faith with what Merleau-Ponty calls the "antepredicative unity of the world and of our life," the "living relationships of experience" out of which concepts like "Me," "God," and "Nature" are formed. Moved by a desire to represent "life, plain life," Melville repeatedly drops from conceptual oppositions to experiential adjacencies, at first in an impulsive, intuitive way, but ultimately out of a conviction that "[a]ll's picturesque beneath the sun; / I mean, all's picture; death and life / Pictures and pendants, nor at strife – / No, never to hearts that muse thereon."[7] Instead of arraying Life and Death against one another, dialectically, he arranges them alongside one another, compositionally, because that is how he finds them in his experience. Linked, aesthetically, by associative movements of perception, the elements of experience glide into one another in unpredictably generative ways. "Life folded Death; Death trellised Life," says Ishmael of the "green, life-restless," skeleton-adorning bower in the Arsacides, and out of that primal, ceaseless intertwining comes a blossoming of "curly-headed glories" (*MD* 450).

Proposition One: Melville's work is intensely exclamatory. The first sentence of the first chapter of his first book, *Typee* (1846), is an exclamation – "Six months at sea!" – that gives rise to another exclamation: "Yes, reader, as I live, six months out of sight of land; cruising after the sperm-whale beneath the scorching sun of the Line, and tossed on the billows of the wide-rolling

Pacific – the sky above, the sea around, and nothing else!" (3). Thirteen more exclamations tumble out in the first seven paragraphs, marking distress ("Those glorious bunches of bananas which once decorated our stern and quarter-deck have, alas, disappeared! and the delicious oranges which hung suspended from our tops and stays – they, too, are gone!"), desire ("Oh! for a refreshing glimpse of one blade of grass – for a snuff at the fragrance of a handful of the loamy earth!" [3]), dread-tinged delight ("The Marquesas!"), compassion ("Poor old ship!"), and a resilience of spirit ("Hurra, my lads!" [5]). In each of these instances, and in a slew of similar ones in the works that follow – "Moby Dick bodily burst into view!" (557), say, or "Ah, Bartleby!" (*PT* 45), or "God bless Captain Vere!" (*BB* 123) – Melville inflects an otherwise stable utterance with the unstable tonality of a brief cry. We are meant to hear in each of these utterances a special intensity of expression, a sudden heightening of force, and we are meant to experience, as a result, a corresponding surge of life. Communicating that experience, sending words on "errands of life," is in a very real sense the point of Melville's work. When the tingling of a writer is "infused into a song" that he or she is writing, says the poet Yoomy in *Mardi*, "it evermore causes [the song] so to sparkle, vivify, and irradiate, that no son of man can repeat it without tingling himself." This, Babbalanja agrees, is "the test" (559) of a work's value.

Proposition Two: Melville's exclamatoriness is responsive. At times, it is a response to stagnation or stolidity, as when, in the midst of describing the palm-and-cane floor of a Mardian home, Taji cries, "Hypochondriac! Essay the elastic flooring. It shall so pleasantly and gently jolt thee, as to shake up, and pack off the stagnant humors mantling thy pool-like soul" (*M* 189), or when Ishmael's postapocalyptic Whale, "rearing upon the topmost crest of the equatorial flood, spout[s] his frothed defiance to the skies" (*MD* 462). At other times, it is a response to exclamations or their equivalent in the surrounding world. In the song Yoomy sings after presenting his tingle-based theory of literary value, the sun's rays "[f]lash each a sword, – / Sun-music in the air!," and in response, Yillah "rises and flashes! / Rays shooting from out her long lashes, – / Sun-music in the air!" (*M* 560). Similarly, in *Pierre*, when nature "[blows] her wind-clarion from the blue hills," Pierre "neigh[s] out lyrical thoughts, as at the trumpet-blast, a war-horse paws himself into a lyric of foam" (14), and in *Redburn* (1849), when the ship gives "a sort of bound like a horse," Redburn experiences a "wild bubbling and bursting … at [his] heart, as if a hidden spring had just gushed out there" (66). There are, of course, other kinds of responsive interchanges that occur between Melville's characters and their surroundings: attracted to the "calm intelligence and sagacity" of the truck horses in Liverpool, Redburn tries "to get into conversation with them" (197), and upon hearing "the soft, prophetic sighing of the pine, stirred by the first breath of the morning," Israel Potter trembles "[l]ike the leaflets of that evergreen" (*IP* 8). Far more often, however, the content of the transmission is a feeling of buoyancy. When Ahab, upon witnessing the "leaping spout" of Moby Dick, feels "the eternal sap [run] up in [his] bones again" (552), he models the experience of the nonhuman world that Melville values most.

Proposition Three: Melville is acutely aware of the transitoriness of all such states of being. Immediately after Redburn's ecstatic response to the rising of the wind, by means of which he becomes conscious of "a wonderful thing in [him], that responded to all the wild commotion of the outer world, and went reeling on and on with the planets in their orbits, and was lost in one delirious throb at the center of the All," he is set to work cleaning the chicken coops, at which point his mood inverts, and he curses the "[m]iserable dog's life" (*R* 66) of a sailor. There is, Melville writes to Hawthorne in 1851, "some truth" to the "'all' feeling" – the suddenly acute awareness of the "tinglings of life that are felt in the flowers and the woods, that are felt in the planets Saturn and Venus, and the Fixed Stars" – but "what plays the mischief with the truth is that men will insist upon the universal application of a temporary feeling or opinion" (*L* 194). The only final truth, for Melville, is the truth of nonfinality, which means, as he realizes by the time of *Moby-Dick*, that nothing in this slippery world, not even one's awareness of the world's slipperiness, can hold. After advancing in experience and knowledge and finally arriving at "the pondering repose of If," Ahab says, "we trace the round again; and are infants, boys, and men, and Ifs eternally" (492). There is "no faith, and no stoicism, and no philosophy, that a mortal man can possibly evoke," writes the narrator of *Pierre*, "which will stand the final test of a real impassioned onset of Life and Passion upon him.... Amidst his gray philosophizings, Life breaks upon a man like a morning." Even the most phenomenologically correct thought about the intertwining of all things will, like a ghost "raised from the mist, slide away and disappear ... at cock-crow" (289).

Which brings us to "Cock-a-Doodle-Doo! Or, The Crowing of the Noble Cock Beneventano," a story that undoubtedly requires a brief synopsis. Early one morning, our narrator wanders into a pasture because he cannot sleep. The 1848 revolutions have failed; train wrecks have killed hundreds of people, including one of his close friends; he is being crushed by debt; he is dyspeptic. Then he hears a clear, musical, prolonged, triumphant, plucky, fiery, gleeful, exultant, jubilant crow. A burst of admiration, addressed, companionably, to some nearby cows, escapes him. The crowing continues. He finds himself jumping on a log, flapping his elbows, and crowing himself.

He goes home to drink ale, eat steak, and read *Tristram Shandy*. He attacks his bill collector. The next day, he begins searching for the rooster in neighboring farms, starting with the wealthiest farmers, because he assumes it is an expensive imported Shanghai. As it turns out, however, the rooster belongs to a very poor farmer named Merrymusk who lives with his very sick wife and very sick children in a distant shanty. The narrator goes to see Merrymusk's rooster, or, in his terminology, cock. (One of the most prominent signs of the narrator's rooster-induced spiritedness is a penchant for phallic punning.) After a vigorous crowing session in the yard, the narrator, Merrymusk, and the cock enter the shanty, where Mrs. Merrymusk and the four children all ask it to crow some more. Each time it does, the roof jars. The narrator begins to have misgivings; it doesn't seem appropriate to have this kind of crowing in a sick chamber. Merrymusk insists the cock is "better than a 'pothecary" (*PT* 285). The narrator goes away, "not wholly at rest concerning the soundness of Merrymusk's views of things, though full of admiration for him" (286). Some weeks later he returns. Now Merrymusk is sick, too, but insists he is well, and calls on the cock to crow. The roof jars. Merrymusk dies. An "awful fear" seizes the narrator. The roof jars again. The wife dies. The cock marches up to the children and "raise[s] one long, musical, triumphant, and final sort of crow, with throat heaved far back" (287). The children die. The cock strides outside, flies to the apex of the house, crows one more time, and drops dead. The narrator buries the Merrymusks, their children, and the cock in one grave and puts up a stone decorated with an image of a crowing cock and inscribed with the words "Oh! death, where is thy sting? Oh! grave, where is thy victory?" Then, after declaring that he no longer feels "the doleful dumps, but under all circumstances crow[s] late and early with a continual crow," he gives us a sample – "COCK-A-DOODLE-DOO! – OO! – OO! – OO!" (288) – and the story ends.

Nowhere in Melville's work is there a more striking example of the kind of responsive, transitory exclamatoriness that I have just described. Part of what makes "Cock-A-Doodle-Doo!" so striking is that its topic, as announced in its title, is an interjectional "Crowing," a sound that originally proceeds from "the Noble Cock Beneventano" (*PT* 283) but subsequently reverberates between the mountains to such a degree that it seems to proceed from "the East" (275) in general. If "[a]n exclamation point is entire Mardi's autobiography" (*M* 580–81) as Babbalanja puts it, it is because the Life that is expressed in each individual life-expression, the Life that rises again and again from the metaphorical East, is itself exclamatory, a quick shattering of silence. What crows when one crows, what cries when one cries, what sings when one sings is, Melville suggests, a Crowing, a Crying, a Singing, a style of vocalization that did not begin with and will not end with the individual crower, crier, or singer. When "the air is vocal with [the] hymns" of birds, Melville writes in *Israel Potter* (1855), "your own soul joys in the general joy. Like a stranger in an orchestra, you cannot help singing yourself when all around you raise such hosannas" (5–6). "If at times I would relapse into my doleful dumps," says the narrator of "Cock-A-Doodle-Doo!," "straightaway at the sound of the exultant and defiant crow, my soul, too, would turn chanticleer, and clap her wings, and throw back her throat, and breathe forth a cheerful challenge to all the world of woes" (*PT* 278). At such moments, one is not oneself alone; one is an instance of existence, a life among others, simultaneously individuating oneself and slipping into a vast stream of individuations.

In the chorus to which one contributes – a chorus of generalized anti-predatorial displays, charged with libidinal energy but detached from sexual pursuits – there are no species-based distinctions. When the narrator cries, after his first visit to Merrymusk's shanty, "Oh, noble cock! oh, noble man!" (*PT* 286), he is not ascending, rhetorically, from animality to humanity; he is paralleling nonhuman and human "challenge[s] to all the world of woes." What makes those challenges "noble" is that they are (to take a few key adjectives from the story) dauntless, game, defiant, invincible, unappalled, hearty, and stout – that they are bursting with spiritedness, like the "warm verdure" that, touched by "Spring," anti-monotonously "burst[s] all round" (284). "To the Greeks," Melville writes in "Statues in Rome" (1857), "nature had no brute. Everything was a being with a soul" (*PT* 406). To have a soul, for Melville, is to have the capacity to crest, like a billow, to erupt above a dead level, like a mountain, to raise one's voice above a circumambient hum, like the cock – the capacity to say "'NO!' in [the midst of] thunder" (*L* 186). Just as one can deduce from ancient Greek sculptures of "riderless and rearing" (*PT* 405) horses the "enlarged humanity of that elder day, when man gave himself none of those upstart airs of superiority over the brute creation which he now assumes" (406), so can one deduce from the vast array of souls in Melville's work – from what Warner Berthoff describes as his "excruciating animism" – a similarly enlarged understanding of what we share with other forms of existence.[8]

Trees are a useful case in point. Because the noble cock is ambulatory and vocal, and because he decisively acts on the world – at one point, we see him "walk[ing] in front of the shanty, like a peer of the realm, his crest lifted, his chest heaved out, his embroidered trappings flashing in the light," and then "paus[ing], lift[ing] his head still higher," and uttering his "gladdening sound" (*PT* 283) – it is easier to feel akin to him than to a fixed, nonvocal, seemingly passive organism. And yet on a great many occasions, spanning his entire career, Melville represents trees in a way that makes it possible to imagine that they too have nobly resistant spirits, opening responsively and expressively onto the world. A wide variety of trees receive attention in his work – including the breadfruit tree in *Typee*, the cocoa palm in *Omoo* (1847), the palm of Mar Saba in *Clarel* (1876), the maple in "Time's Betrayal" (ca. 1891), and the lilac in "Rip Van Winkle's Lilac" (ca. 1891) – but Melville is especially drawn to pines and oaks, which embody, for him, an inspiringly majestic unyieldingness. The "three pines" of the *Pequod* stand "stiffly up like the spines of the three old kings of Cologne" (*MD* 69), the "gaunt pines" in "The Town-Ho's Story" stand "like serried lines of kings in Gothic genealogies" (*MD* 244), and Ethan Allan, in *Israel Potter*, is said to share "that inevitable egotism relatively pertaining to pine trees, spires, and giants" (149). In *Pierre*, the narrator observes that "ever-shifting Nature hath not so unbounded a sway" over the oak, whose "limbs ... for a long term of years, defy that annual decree" (9), and in *Israel Potter*, the protagonist is compared, toward the end of his life, to "those tough old oaks of the cliffs, which, though hacked at by hail-stones of tempests, and even wantonly maimed by the passing woodman, still, however cramped by rival trees and fettered by rocks, succeed, against all odds, in keeping the vital nerve of the tap-root alive" (169). Most tellingly, in "The Paradise of Bachelors and the Tartarus of Maids" (1855), the very cold narrator, on his way to a paper mill in the middle of the winter, says that the pines, oaks, and other species of trees "here and there skirting the route, feeling the same all-stiffening influence ... strangely groaned – not in the swaying branches merely, but likewise in the vertical trunk – as the fitful gusts remorselessly swept through them" (*PT* 325). Subject to "the same all-stiffening influence" that we are, groaning in their trunks in response to it, but nevertheless rising, spreading, and holding their ground, and doing so on a larger scale and for a longer time than just about any other organism on the planet, trees are, like whales, godlike in the best sense: superior enough to awe and yet comparable enough to give joy. "The thought of heaven's great King afar / But humbles us," Melville writes in *Battle-Pieces* (1866). Only in the more companionable greatness of a fellow creature – a tree, a bird, a horse, a human being, or even a nonliving index of upsurging forces, like a mountain – is there something "cheering," something capable of "lift[ing] the heart" (*PP* 77).

All such manifestations of life belong to what the psychoanalytic theorist Leo Bersani calls a "transversal cut of being," a slice of existence whose elements associatively hang together. Although there are of course many other cuts of being – such as the ones evoked by the mosquitoes of *Omoo*, the iceberg of "The Berg" (1888), and the frisky kitten of "Montaigne and

His Kitten" (ca. 1891) – none matters more to Melville than the cut that contains the noble cock, the white whale, and his "loyal neighbors, the Maples and the Beeches" (P vii). "Life is not equally expressed in all its varied forms," writes the feminist philosopher Elizabeth Grosz, but is most expressed in a life that seeks, in response to its own "joyous excess or super-fluousness of inner force," a "*maximization* of its being." Even though life "always functions in excess of need, survival, stability, and pleasure," it is only in certain exceptional cases that the "desire of each thing, entity, atom, or energy to expand and intensify itself" – to "enjoy life" rather than "avoid death" – is fully perceptible. It is crucial, in this context, that the cock in "Cock-A-Doodle-Doo!" crows solely "on his own account" (PT 275), and that he does so not out of a "sophomorean" ignorance of "what might be to come," but out of a "philosophic" resolution to crow even if "the earth should heave and the heavens should fall." This is what makes it "a crow of all crows" (274), a Crowing with a capital C; it aims only at its own expansion and intensification. Far from evoking in the narrator an Ahabian "rage and hate" (MD 184), it evokes in him a strangely genial feeling of invincibility, a feeling that, by "set[ting] [him] up" (PT 273), places him side by side with everything else in the world. "I felt," he writes, "as though I could meet Death, and invite him to dinner, and toast the Catacombs with him, in pure overflow of self-reliance and a sense of universal security" (279). By infusing the narrator with a "calm, good-natured rapture of defiance," the crowing brings the Life in him to the apex of its expression, to a "pure overflow" (274), a state in which even Death is no longer an antagonist.[9]

In the margins of his Shakespeare volume, Melville scored the passage in As You Like It in which Jaques says of the Duke, "He is too disputable for my company. I think of as many matters as he; but I give heaven thanks, and make no boast of them. Come, warble, come." Alongside the passage, Melville wrote, "There are 75 folio volumes in that." Immediately after Jaques's speech, Amiens and company sing the following verse:

> Who doth ambition shun,
> And loves to live i' th' sun,
> Seeking the food he eats,
> And pleas'd with what he gets,
> Come hither, come hither, come hither.
> Here shall he see
> No enemy
> But winter and rough weather.

Such lines may seem to leave us, critically speaking, with nowhere to go. "What, minstrel," cries the philosophy-fuddled Babbalanja when Yoomy's sun-music song comes to a sudden halt, "must nothing ultimate come of all that melody? no final and inexhaustible meaning? ... Then, Yoomy, is thy song nothing worth" (*M* 561). Songs, human or otherwise, will never get us any closer to what Melville derisively calls in *Pierre* "the Ultimate of Human Speculative Knowledge" (167). They may, however, incite a rejoining of "company," an involuntary inward response to their invitation to "come hither," a response that flows both toward and from a world "alive to its axis" (*M* 458). In that motion, as in the motion of a cow chewing a pumpkin, or a human writing a novel – or, for that matter, of wounded and blood-maddened sharks "viciously snapp[ing], not only at each other's disembowelments, but ... [at] their own" (*MD* 302) – life non-teleologically moves. Whatever knowledge emerges from that motion, from the way in which each creature "'sing[s]' the world," cannot be separated from its means of emergence, and the value of that knowledge depends less on its "disputable" formulation than on its diversion and intensification of the circulation of life. "[N]ature is made better by no mean, / But nature makes that mean," says Polixenes in *The Winter's Tale*. Next to the passage, Melville drew two lines and wrote, "a world here."[10]

NOTES

1 Maunsell Field, *Memories of Many Men and Some Women* (New York: Harpers, 1874), 202; emphasis in original. The dating of the episode is derived from Hershel Parker, *Herman Melville: A Biography, Volume Two* (Baltimore, MD: Johns Hopkins University Press, 2005), 230–31.
2 The references are to "Cock-A-Doodle-Doo!" (1853), "I and My Chimney" (1856), "The Apple-Tree Table" (1856), "The Maldive Shark" (1888), "Rip Van Winkle's Lilac" (ca. 1891), "The Man-of-War Hawk" (1888), "Montaigne and His Kitten" (ca. 1891), "The Berg" (1888), "The Tuft of Kelp" (1888), *Weeds and Wildings* (ca. 1891), and *Moby-Dick* (1851).
3 Maurice Merleau-Ponty, *Phenomenology of Perception*, trans. Colin Smith (London: Routledge, 1962), 251, 97, 370, 369; Hawthorne, "Preface to *Twice-Told Tales*," in *Tales and Sketches* (New York: Library of America, 1982), 1152.
4 For examples of these approaches, see, respectively, Rosi Braidotti, "Animals, Anomalies, and Inorganic Others," *PMLA* 124 (2009): 526–32; Ted Toadvine, *Merleau-Ponty's Philosophy of Nature* (Evanston, IL: Northwestern University Press, 2009); Christopher White, "The Modern Magnetic Animal: *As I Lay Dying* and the Uncanny Zoology of Modernism," *Journal of Modern Literature* 31 (2008): 81–101; Stacy Alaimo, "Sustainable This, Sustainable That: New Materialisms, Posthumanism, and Unknown Futures," *PMLA* 127 (2012): 558–64; and Jane Bennett, *Vibrant Matter: A Political Ecology of Things* (Durham, NC: Duke University Press, 2010).
5 D. H. Lawrence, *Studies in Classic American Literature* (1923; reprint. Harmondsworth: Penguin, 1977), 155. Elsewhere, one encounters claims that Melville "takes man beyond history to the source of his elemental energies" (F. O. Matthiessen, *American Renaissance: Art and Expression in the Age of*

Emerson and Whitman [New York: Oxford University Press, 1941], 466), that he "darts behind all appearance to the beginning of things, and runs riot with the frightful force of the sea itself" ("'Introduction' to *Moby-Dick*," in *Melville: A Collection of Critical Essays*, ed. Richard Chase [Englewood Cliffs, NJ: Prentice-Hall, 1962], 48), and that he "put[s] us in contact with some latent rhythm of occurrence at the heart of existence" (Warner Berthoff, *The Example of Melville* [Princeton, NJ: Princeton University Press, 1962], 171). For nature-as-voracity arguments, see Daniel Hoffman, *Form and Fable in American Fiction* (New York: Oxford University Press, 1961), 270, and Michael Gilmore, *The Middle Way: Puritanism and Ideology in American Romantic Fiction* (New Brunswick, NJ: Rutgers University Press, 1977), 157–58. For nature-as-void arguments, see Paul Brodtkorb, Jr., *Ishmael's White World: A Phenomenological Reading of Moby-Dick* (New Haven, CT: Yale University Press, 1965), 114–16, and James Wood, *The Broken Estate: Essays on Literature and Belief* (New York: Picador, 2010), 53–54.

6 Robert Zoellner, *The Salt-Sea Mastodon: A Reading of* Moby-Dick (Berkeley and Los Angeles: University of California Press, 1973), 225, 135; Philip Armstrong, *What Animals Mean in the Fiction of Modernity* (London: Routledge, 2008), 126; Sharon Cameron, *Impersonality: Seven Essays* (Chicago, IL: University of Chicago Press, 2007), 182; Elizabeth Schultz, "Melville's Environmental Vision in *Moby-Dick*," *Interdisciplinary Studies in Literature and the Environment* 7 (2000), 100. Two other usefully nontraditional approaches to the subject may be found in David Trotter, "Spitting Mad: Melville's Juices," *Critical Quarterly* 39 (1997): 23–38, and T. Hugh Crawford, "Networking the (Non) Human: *Moby-Dick*, Matthew Fontaine Maury, and Bruno Latour," *Configurations* 5 (1997): 1–21.

7 Merleau-Ponty, *Phenomenology*, xx, xvii; Melville, "The Burgundy Club," in *Tales, Poems, and Other Writings*, ed. John Bryant (New York: Modern Library, 2001).

8 Berthoff, *Example*, 198. For a more extended discussion of human and nonhuman individuations in Melville's work, see my *Whipscars and Tattoos*: The Last of the Mohicans, Moby-Dick, *and the Maori* (New York: Oxford University Press, 2011).

9 Leo Bersani, "Psychoanalysis and the Aesthetic Subject," *Critical Inquiry* 32 (2006), 69; Melville, "Montaigne and His Kitten," in *Collected Poems*, ed. Howard P. Vincent (Chicago, IL: Packard, 1947), 381; Elizabeth Grosz, *The Nick of Time: Politics, Evolution, and the Untimely* (Durham, NC: Duke University Press, 2004), 11, 98, 127, 133, 110, 102, emphasis in original.

10 Wilson Walker Cowen, *Melville's Marginalia*, 2 vols. (New York: Garland, 1988), 2: 386; Shakespeare, *As You Like It*, 2.5.31–42; Merleau-Ponty, *Phenomenology*, 217; Shakespeare, *The Winter's Tale*, 4.4.105–106; Cowen, *Melville's Marginalia*, 2: 399.

2

HESTER BLUM

Melville and Oceanic Studies

Call him Tommo; call him Typee, or Paul, or Omoo; call him Taji; call him White-Jacket. *Moby-Dick*'s "Call me Ishmael" may be the line that lingers in cultural memory, but a *nom de marin* (as we might call it) is enlisted as well in *Typee, Omoo, Mardi,* and *White-Jacket.* Of the six first-person sailor narrators in Melville's first six novels, only Wellingborough Redburn – a novice on a one-time voyage, no Jack Tar – tells us his real (however baroque) name. Other notable Melvillean narrators without formal names include the anonymous sailor who sketches "The Encantadas," and, in perhaps the most extreme form, the multiply shape- and name-shifting titular character in the riparian *Confidence-Man.* What is not always clear, though, is how arbitrary the narrator's name and its meaning are supposed to be: that is, whether the sailor chooses the new name (as Ishmael seems to) or finds it imposed or picked up as a routine practice within the drift of nautical existence. There are many dozens of minor characters nicknamed according to their places of origin, nautical association, or appearance in Melville's novels, from the Manxman and the Skyeman to Selvagee and Doctor Long Ghost; these are drawn from a comic tradition of genre fiction (such as that of Tobias Smollett or Walter Scott) in which characters are reduced to types. Such is not the primary case with Melville's first-person narrators whose personhood is pseudonymized; even when they move from the center to the periphery of their own narrative, as Ishmael does, they are not types. What form of handle do these names provide for sailors – or readers – to grasp? What do the pseudonyms keep at bay? There is something about maritime life, perhaps, that invites such provisional naming.

A name change amidst a scene of comic adventure in *Israel Potter* illustrates the often cheerful haphazardness of such naming patterns. Potter had been serving aboard an American naval vessel; in an encounter with an English man-of-war, he undergoes a narrative and maritime pratfall that ends with him implausibly aboard the royal ship, rather than his original continental one. In an attempt to assimilate to the man-of-war's crew, Israel calls himself "Peter Perkins," maintopman, and jumps from mess (a sailor's organizational dining unit) to mess. His skill in the maintop and his bluff good nature win over his new shipmates; the officer of the deck, originally skeptical, notes with surprise that he does "seem to belong to the main-top, after all." The main character who has now become Peter Perkins replies, "I always told you so, sir, ... though at first, you remember, sir, you would not believe it" (141). In this scene Potter/Perkins enacts what Melville had described earlier in the novel as the sailor's illustration of the principle that "all human affairs are subject to organic disorder" and are characterized by "a sort of half-disciplined chaos" (114). The "organic disorder" he invokes is oceanic in model.

The performance of naming in Melville's writing should be understood as both a reflection of and a reaction to the largely oceanic setting of his works: the sea is a medium inherently resistant to inscription and other forms of fixity or possession. In turn, the names assumed by his narrators can be seen more broadly as an expression of his fiction's conceptual interests in incompleteness and proliferation, and the instability of monuments and testaments. The nautical environment covers over 70 percent of the earth's surface, and serves as the physical setting for roughly a similar percentage of Melville's fiction. Even though the ocean is nominally divided into seas and punctuated by ports, when venturing upon its surfaces all traces of such anchors fall away in a manner akin to the world of the biblical flood. As Melville writes in *Moby-Dick*: "The first boat we read of, floated on an ocean, that with Portuguese vengeance had whelmed a whole world without leaving so much as a widow. That same ocean rolls now; that same ocean destroyed the wrecked ships of last year.... Noah's flood is not yet subsided; two thirds of the fair world it yet covers" (273). In its vastness and motility the ocean opens up to possibility on a planetary scale, and yet also presents the risks of chartlessness or dispersion.

Going to sea as laboring sailors, as Melville's narrators do, meant a radically different form of heading off to work, as seamen could not return to families or homes at the end of a shift, as other working classes might, but instead found their entire world encompassed by the ship. It stands to reason, then, that other markers or constraints of their land-based identifications would dissolve in the space of the sea. Subject to the caprices of storms and captains, and constituted on ships of heterogeneous crews – both racially and nationally – seamen could rarely claim individual sovereignty in the late eighteenth and nineteenth centuries of Melville's fictional worlds. This uncertainty extends to the nautical environment as well, which defies Lockean conceptions of possession or improvement of self or land. A sea that disallows records could register as a medium that both generated and annihilated history, whether personal or literary. The seaman is literally outlandish: as the agent of nautical trade, transportation, and popular imagination, he experiences firsthand the dissolution of national affiliation in the space and time of the sea. As the first global travelers, mariners were imagined free from many of the constraints of social and political life – yet they faced hostile environmental conditions as well as repressive hierarchical structures aboard ship, neither of which could be mediated by the protections of statehood or citizenship.

This chapter situates Melville's work within the emerging field of oceanic studies. The field both extends and stands apart from recent transnational and hemispheric turns in literary studies, which have called attention to the limits of studying literary and cultural productions as national products or within strictly state-bound fields of circulation.[1] While oceanic studies shares with transnational work a desire to trace literary movement beyond a given political boundary, it might be seen to model itself conceptually after the fluidity of its object of study in its lack of concern with national distinctions. By casting adrift our critical position from land- and nation-based perspectives, oceanic studies helps us to develop other possible ways of understanding questions of affiliation, citizenship, economic exchange, mobility, rights, and sovereignty. If we now view history from the bottom up, or nations in terms of their transnational or hemispheric relations, or the colonizer as seen by the colonized – to gesture to just a few reorientations of critical perception in recent decades – then what would happen if we take the oceans' nonhuman scale and depth as a first critical position and principle? While transnational forms of exchange (whether cultural, political, or economic) have historically taken place via the medium of the sea, relatively little literary critical attention has been paid to that medium itself: its properties, its conditions, its shaping or eroding forces. As this chapter discusses, Melville's work exemplifies oceanic ways of being: he is invested in modes of thinking and writing that are unbounded by expected affiliations, forms, nations, mores, or doctrines. A long-established branch of Melville studies has described the importance of the maritime world to the writer's biography and textual sources; what follows builds on that history by focusing instead on his theoretical involvement with, as well as his works' contributions to, broader questions of literary representation and exchange on an oceanic scale.

Melville's writing opens itself up to the possibilities of oceanic thinking in three main ways, the latter two of which form the substance of this chapter. First, the maritime content of much of his work reflects his own experience as a sailor, as well as his broader literary and historical moment, in which the seas served (as they have for millennia) as the primary routes for the transportation of humans, goods, and ideas.[2] These have been the main terms with which Melville's relationship to the sea has been discussed in critical history to date, and these terms are revisited briefly later in this chapter. Second, his work is deeply invested in political and etiological questions whose contours shift, if not dissolve, when considered in an oceanic context: What is the source of agency in the world? Where do affiliations lie? What taxonomies and structures organize the world? And third, we might see the formal experimentation of Melville's novels as themselves oceanic in nature, if we consider his experimental play with the generic expectations of the first-person narrative, the romance, or the sea novel. The conceptual forms of his nautical fiction are as chartless as the voyages they describe.

To sketch in a couple of paragraphs the literary-historical background to Melville's oceanic thinking: maritime culture was central to the economic as well as the imaginative lives of nineteenth-century Anglo-Americans. Population centers were clustered on coasts and the majority of trade and transit took place along water routes, as it had across global millennia. Literary culture in Melville's time offered a variety of forms of nautical writing, including fiction, drama, ballads and chanteys, pirate tales, sailor-themed religious tracts, histories, poetry, and first-person sailor narratives. While the sea has ever been a figure for metaphorical reflection, nineteenth-century U.S. maritime literature became increasingly concerned with the details of shipboard life and sailor experience. The experience or knowledge of the conditions of maritime labor became a generic feature of the sea novel in its representation of nautical practices and its specialized sea vocabulary.[3] Melville's writing shares with this body of work an abiding and detailed interest in describing labor and life at sea. He was a canny reader of (and frequent borrower from) previous generations of sea writing, which in large part took forms other than the novel. Narratives of colonial encounters with the Americas – by definition sea voyages – presented the ocean as a space for providential judgment as much as for economic opportunity. From the sixteenth to the early nineteenth centuries, readers consumed tales of shipwrecks, naval contests, captivity (particularly in the Barbary states of North Africa), piracy, and nautical adventure, which reflected the conditions of maritime life, however sensationalized.

Melville had himself, as is well known, logged time before the mast, spending the better part of four years as a working seaman aboard whaling, merchant, and naval ships. At the time of his own sea voyaging in the late 1830s and early 1840s, sea novels had been popular for several decades among British and American readers, who enjoyed the picaresque novels of Tobias Smollett, the historical romances of Walter Scott, and the varied (and remarkably prodigious) nautical output of James Fenimore Cooper, in addition to cheaper and more ephemeral fictions. Melville also read and absorbed the first-person narratives of sailors and sea voyagers such as David Porter's journal of his American naval cruises (1815), Charles Darwin's *Beagle* journal (1837), and ex-Harvard student Richard Henry Dana's hugely popular *Two Years before the Mast* (1840). In his maritime fiction, Melville explored a range of possible sailor stories and figures: the jumper of ships, the rover, the romantic quester, the greenhand, the philosopher, the pirate, the slaver, the enslaved, the man of the man-of-war, the aging Jack Tar, the Handsome Sailor. All were shaped by the political, cultural, and economic conditions of the nineteenth century. Experienced with both sea labor and sea literature, Melville at every turn drew from his nautical locker in crafting his fictions. And yet as the following section on taxonomic impulses in *Moby-Dick* suggests, he recognized the inadequacy of models of containment – such as "Davy Jones's locker," the seaman's euphemism for death – for providing material or imaginative control over oceanic orders of being.

Special Levianthic Revelations

It can be argued that *Moby-Dick* is about record keeping and score keeping in the face of a maritime environment that either thwarts or is indifferent to such efforts. The sea's erasure of accounts is not always a cause for concern, however: early in *Moby-Dick* Ishmael in fact celebrates this refusal of inscription as he and Queequeg take a short passage from New Bedford to Nantucket, from which they will launch their whaling voyage. Ishmael exclaims: "How I spurned that turnpike earth! – that common highway all over dented with the marks of slavish heels and hoofs; and turned me to admire the magnanimity of the sea which will permit no records" (60). The blankness and ahistoricity of oceanic routes are preferable to the dull pedestrianism of the "turnpike earth," which Ishmael scorns for its commonness. What Ishmael seeks is not the road less traveled, but no road at all, a passage at once without a plot and untraceable. He does not wish to blaze a trail, in other words, but to find refuge in the "magnanimity" of a sea whose indifference to human passage makes the categories of the "common" or the "slavish" irrelevant. His declaration from the ship's railing suggests that, in addition to the appeal of a fresh start, there may be something along the trail of Ishmael's history that he wishes to hide. For many young men in the first half of the nineteenth century, going to sea provided a way to escape undesirable obligations (such as debt, marriage, family business) as much as it offered a change of scene or a chance for adventure. In depressive Ishmael's own case, a sea venture is his "substitute for pistol and ball" (3) – either a suicidal move or an effort to ward off a drive to self-destruction. His process of maritime transformation registers at first, and on the most local scale, with the erasure of a legal name and the adoption of a sea handle. In either event – suicide or survival – the desired end is the extinguishment of self that Melville portrays as coextensive with going to sea.

The world of the ship heaves, rolls, plunges; the presumed stability of signposts or structures of thought (much less land-based expectations and regulations) might not register at sea at all. If understood from the vantage point of the sea, how might the parameters of ontological investigation shift? The figure of Jonah in Father Mapple's sermon in *Moby-Dick* represents such equivocality. The biblical Jonah thinks the sea will put insurmountable space between him and God's unwelcome command to preach to the residents of Ninevah. In Melville's telling via the seamen's chaplain, a divine light – away from which Jonah flees in favor of the obscurity of the sea – illuminates the contingency of oceanic systems of valuation. A lamp suspended in Jonah's cabin serves as his parable:

> Screwed at its axis against the side, a swinging lamp slightly oscillates in Jonah's room; and the ship, heeling over towards the wharf with the weight of the last bales received, the lamp, flame and all, though in slight motion, still maintains a permanent obliquity with reference to the room; though, in truth, infallibly straight itself, it but made obvious the false, lying levels among which it hung. The lamp alarms and frightens Jonah; as lying in his berth his tormented eyes roll round the place, and this thus far successful fugitive finds no refuge for his restless glance. But that contradiction in the lamp more and more appalls him. The floor, the ceiling, and the side, are all awry. "Oh! so my conscience hangs in me!" he groans, "straight upwards, so it burns; but the chambers of my soul are all in crookedness!" (44–45)

Melville literalizes the way oceanic spaces force "awry" the frames upon and through which one might base an understanding of fundamental concepts such as truth, light, and place. There is no way to come to rest: Jonah's spatial dislocation from truth suggests an oceanic frame relies on relativity rather than on absolutes.

We see a similar impulse toward definitional contingency (or what we might call a relativist epistemology) in the "Cetology" chapter of *Moby-Dick*, in which whales are memorably classified by size and shape as if they were books. This chapter inaugurates a shift in the novel's setting from the land or coastal shelf to the open sea, where Ishmael and the members of the *Pequod*'s crew will remain for the rest of the novel. The chapter's first line – "Already we are boldly launched upon the deep; but soon we shall be lost in its unshored, harborless immensities" – registers the change in subject matter from port practices to oceanic "immensities," as well as what will increasingly become the formal disintegration of the novel's structural linearity

(134). As if to hedge himself and his narrative against the sea's endlessness, Ishmael sets to the precision-based task of what he calls the "classification of the constituents of a chaos, nothing less" (134). The three primary divisions of whales, as judged by size, he constitutes as Folio, Octavo, and Duodecimo volumes, from thence accorded chapters – that is, "BOOK I. (Folio), CHAPTER I. (Sperm Whale)" (137). This systemization is never complete, however, but always in "draught" form, like the narrative itself, as Ishmael acknowledges at multiple points in the tale. By describing his method of levianthic and imaginative taxonomy as a work in progress, Ishmael is alert to the lack of fixity or finality in the natural world of the sea.

And yet while the ocean appears unaccountably vast, shipboard life is itself characterized by confinement and tight regulation, as the strict bibliographic specificity of his cetological naming demonstates. Ishmael's choice to classify whales when first confronted with "harborless immensities" is wholly consistent with the usual practices of nautical labor and their literary representation. While Melville's sea writing (as well as that of his contemporaries) acknowledges the limitless prospect of the sea from a ship, its narrative content then turns its back to the vastness, as it were, to focus on the habits and internal workings of ships: their ropes and schedules, for instance, which are rendered in maritime writing in what might seem excessive detail. A contemporary whaling narrative by Nathaniel Taylor registers this shift in prospect; when first at sea, he writes: "It is certainly a great event in the life of every man when land for the first time fades from his vision and he experiences the feelings of a wanderer upon the trackless ocean.... Oh, what a throng of deep thoughts and feelings moves the heart and imagination at such a time – thoughts which find no voice, for they are unutterable." Yet Taylor is accorded little time for such reflection; beholding the sunrise a day or two later he is interrupted by the call of shipboard labor: "the sunrise at sea! 'Is not this the time to wash down the decks?' shouts the mate. 'Bring buckets and scrub-brooms. Here you, Tom, what are you skulking for? Go relieve the wheel, Dick. Up aloft two of you and mind you keep a sharp look-out for whales. Doctor, you are only in the way; won't you go and write up my log book?'"[4] A focus on the work at hand can be a calming or centering move, in many cases, when the sailor finds action a relief from the press of "unutterable" thoughts.

Another way to think of this practice of maritime accounting in the face of proliferation comes from Owen Chase's Narrative of the Most Extraordinary and Distressing Shipwreck of the Whale-Ship Essex (1821), whose story furnished Melville with source material and is retold in part in Moby-Dick. In his account, first mate Chase relates how the Nantucket whaler was rammed twice and sunk in a seemingly premeditated attack by a sperm whale while cruising in the equatorial Pacific. The survivors turned to cannibalism; the ship's captain shot his own cabin boy, recipient of the short lot, for food. Despite his later success as a captain himself, Owen Chase in his dotage secreted food in the rafters of his house as protection against starvation; we might see this act as a pathetic extension of the sailor's impulse to catalog and contain in the face of oceanic loss. In the catalog-rich *Moby-Dick*, Melville famously elaborates on Chase's tale of a malevolent and vengeful whale, and finds in the *Essex* story more than the basic plot elements of his novel.

Melville first read the *Narrative* when a copy was given to him by Chase's son, whom he met while a sailor on a gam in the Pacific in 1841 or 1842. Although the story of the *Essex* was well known among sailors, Melville had never seen a printed account before; the *Narrative*, despite Chase's hopes, found neither large profits nor large readership. In a copy he acquired much later, Melville wrote, "the reading of this wondrous story upon the landless sea, and close to the very latitude of the shipwreck had a surprising effect on me."[5] The written narrative – and its intimate circulation within the whaling community, pulled as it was from the younger Chase's sea chest – bears a charge that goes beyond maritime gossip. It has an instrumental power as well in Melville's invocation of the narrative as part of a catalog of affidavits on whaling. The loss Chase struggles to convey is in some ways best tallied by the chart found at the end of the narrative, in which Chase organizes the fate of the men, whether "shot" (i.e., those cannibalized), "left on the island," "died," or "survived." The balance of this ledger is another way to tell the story, to account for those men lost: the "horrors" lie in the failure of the chart to serve as the ship's manifest for the dead men. It is no accident, then, that the *Narrative*'s affective power over Melville is influenced by his own proximity to the site of the wreck when he first encounters Chase's story, as Melville's ship was then "close to the very latitude" where the *Essex* went down.

Melville in turn promotes Chase's history in *Moby-Dick* to underscore the experiential and epistemological stakes of narrative in his own text – and indeed, the *Essex* disaster is retold in a chapter that begins with the qualifying phrase "so far as what there may be of a narrative in this book" (203). Here, Chase's narrative becomes one of a series of affidavits for the historical existence of agency-bearing whales such as Moby Dick. Melville/Ishmael testifies: "I have seen Owen Chace [*sic*] ... I have read his plain and faithful narrative; I have conversed with his son" (206). The character's insistence on the personal narrative as a document of truth places the broader work of the novel into an economy of accounting practices, which categorize and attempt to give name to the oceanic world much as the author classifies the different types of whales into book sizes. Melville emphasizes the physical whale, the tangible, deliberate creature throughout "Affadavit," lest Moby Dick be thought "a monstrous fable, or still worse and more detestable, a hideous and intolerable allegory" (205). While this stipulation is intended to be a comic note of self-awareness – generations of readers of *Moby-Dick* may have found the white whale an intolerable allegory, indeed! – it also privileges the experiential over the metaphorical, even as it acknowledges the limitations of experience to comprehend the sea.

As the cetology chapter in *Moby-Dick* reminds us, though, book knowledge and experiential learning go hand in hand. "I have swam through libraries and sailed through oceans," Ishmael testifies; "I have had to do with whales with these visible hands; I am in earnest" (136). But for all the taxonomic detail Melville lays out in "Cetology," the chaos he attempts to constitute in the chapter becomes not antithetical to his epistemological or narrative process, but its very state of being. "God keep me from ever completing anything" (145), Ishmael expostulates in the face of his necessarily failed attempt to sort whales into books. The capaciousness of his maritime subject brings frustrations, but still presents its own model of intellectual and literary formal expansiveness. (This may be why the dim archive-pent Sub-Sub Librarian, cataloging the references to whales in the Etymology and Extracts that open the novel, is both bloodless and himself noncirculating.) Cataloging the creatures of the deep may seem analogous to other scientific processes of accounting, yet the sea offers geometric challenges in its depths, porous nature, and volume; after all, we are reminded, the sea is "an everlasting terra incognita, so that Columbus sailed over numberless unknown worlds to discover his one superficial western one" (273). A critical stance emerging from the perspective of the sea should be mindful of registering the volumes of what its geophysical properties render inaccessible.

Beyond the dimensional, there are other problems in assaying the sea. As Ishmael reveals in "Brit": "however baby man may brag of his science and skill, … the sea will insult and murder him, and pulverize the stateliest, stiffest frigate he can make" (273). And if the sea treats with ships in this way, what, then, would it do to a cabin boy? When the small Pip hauntingly is left behind in the sea – for a spell – after imprudently jumping from a whale boat with leviathan on the line, Melville writes:

> Pip's ringed horizon began to expand around him miserably. By the merest chance the ship itself at last rescued him; but from that hour the little negro went about the deck an idiot; such, at least, they said he was. The sea had jeeringly kept his finite body up, but drowned the infinite of his soul. Not drowned

entirely, though. Rather carried down alive to wondrous depths, where strange shapes of the unwarped primal world glided to and fro before his passive eyes; and the miser-merman, Wisdom, revealed his hoarded heaps; and among the joyous, heartless, ever-juvenile eternities, Pip saw the multitudinous, God-omnipresent, coral insects, that out of the firmament of waters heaved the colossal orbs. He saw God's foot upon the treadle of the loom, and spoke it; and therefore his shipmates called him mad. (414)

When Pip faces the "awful lonesomeness" of the "intolerable" open sea (414), he seems to experience an annihilation of self. His own assumed name at sea (meaning a speck or seed) registers his inconsequence, his peripheralness; the novel itself can't locate him, designating him an "Alabama boy" (121) or alternatively a denizen of Tolland County, Connecticut (412) before losing him in the pulverizing sea. And yet the reader is told that Pip gains special knowledge of wisdom and the driving presence of God – no agent, but principal – on the loom of fate. But his shipmates cannot sense "Heaven's sense" (414) in his insanity. Again the impossibility of comprehending oceanic depths recurs: the very fact of Pip having glimpsed the divine makes his superficial shipmates unable to register his knowledge as what we might perceive as oceanic sense.

Although deemed mad, Pip performs his own form of taxonomic thinking in the novel's "Doubloon" chapter, in which the mate Stubb observes how different members of the *Pequod* variously render meaning from the text and images on the Ecuadoran gold coin Ahab has nailed to the mast. But Stubb is aware of the limitations of the kinds of readings (whether of whales, tattoos, or texts) that are on display throughout the novel. "Book! you lie there; the fact is, you books must know your places," Stubb instructs; "You'll do to give us the bare words and facts, but we come in to supply the thoughts" (433). Pip provides a final reading of the doubloon and its multiple interpreters when he recites lines he picked up from Murray's Grammar: "I look, you look, he looks; we look, ye look, they look" (434). His declension works on several levels: Pip's "I," the reader's "you," and the sailors' "he" all make a reading of the doubloon. Like the taxonomies and catalogs of "Cetology" or of the "Extracts," Pip's reading seems to provide a grammar from which to build more complex meaning. Pip's chant also exposes, however, the various ways, both hopeful and hopeless, that naming or classification becomes shipboard practice when sailors are faced with the "heartless immensity" of the ocean. Yet as the next section demonstrates, shipboard order is not always produced as a response to oceanic chaos; when exercised too narrowly or tyrannically, nautical regulatory functions can shut down possibilities for oceanic orders of knowledge or resistance.

Jack of the Beach

The other side of nautical management can be seen in captaincy's absolute power. For Robert S. Levine, the "perfect sea order" of normal nautical practice (a phrase he adapts from Richard Henry Dana's sea narrative) could produce or go hand in hand with a kind of disciplinary slavery.[6] Captains had capital authority that belied the organizational structure of wage labor in the period, and yet was justified as necessary in the face of seamen's roughness and dissolution. According to stereotype, when sailors were in port – that is, off the permanent job site of the ship – they engaged in riotous behavior, dispersing their earnings on spirits, sex, and unscrupulous landlords. Such conditions are what make the land "scorching" to Handsome Sailor Bulkington's feet in *Moby-Dick*, for whom "truth" can be found in "landlessness alone" (106–107). What would it mean, though, to find sailors in rest or repose, in seeming stasis? For one answer we can turn to the becalmed, passive captains and seamen of Melville's complex, perspective-shattering story "Benito Cereno," first published in *Putnam's Monthly Magazine* (1855) and later collected in *The Piazza Tales* (1856). Among his few works to deal substantively with slavery, "Benito Cereno" describes the encounter between the *Bachelor's Delight*, captained by the bluff New Englander Amasa Delano, and the *San Dominick,* a disabled Spanish ship seemingly under the command of the diffident captain Benito Cereno and containing a cargo consisting of apparently "tractable" slaves (*PT* 104). Even though "Benito Cereno" is set in the Pacific, off the coast of Chile, the events of the story emerge from the Atlantic slave trade of the eighteenth and nineteenth centuries.

Delano's persistent inability to interpret the actions of Cereno and of the presumed servant and slave Babo has generally been read as a reflection of his racialized preconceptions, which combine with his "singularly undistrustful good nature" to disallow him from perceiving any disorder (*PT* 47). The confidence Delano places in his uninterrogated notions of race-based hierarchy is betrayed by the individual actions of Babo and his comrades in revolt. Yet more broadly, Delano's assumptions are whelmed by an oceanic world in which fixed notions of national or racial identity might find less purchase, or more opportunity for mobility. A successful slave uprising (unimaginable to him) had taken place before Delano's encounter with the ship, and he is subject to the "juggling play" (87) of the resistance's leaders in their designs on taking the *Bachelor's Delight*. Throughout "Benito Cereno," slavery (as well as the piratical activity that could be a by-product of the slave trade) haunts the story in references that range broadly to cover the first moment of European contact with the Americas, the Haitian

Revolution, shipboard slave uprisings of the nineteenth century, and other issues contemporary with Melville's 1855 adaptation of the story from the 1817 account by the real-life Amasa Delano.[7] On a structural level in the novella, too, we see the navigational triangulation of the fictional Delano's perspective; the insurrection's legal deposition; and Babo's silence in the face of Benito Cereno's restoration.

And yet it is the *non*-oceanic characteristics of the story's setting that should most give Delano (and Melville's readers) pause: the extraordinary stillness in the atmosphere, the lack of industry the American observes in the Spanish ship, the absence of nautical regulation and hierarchical behavior. The story opens portentously: "Everything was mute and calm; everything gray. The sea, though undulated into long roods of swells, seemed fixed, and was sleeked at the surface like waved lead that has cooled and set in the smelter's mould" (*PT* 46). The stasis is uncanny in more ways than one. After being told that such conditions foretell "shadows to come," the reader is then informed that Amasa Delano – through whose perspective most of the tale is filtered – is deficient in the "quickness and accuracy of [his] intellectual perception" (47). This information, however, comes to the reader in Melville's most equivocal, hedging, and litotes-strewn prose, and requires a series of interpretive commitments whose meanings become liquid underfoot. To find humanity capable of ill would align one not with the "good-nature" of Delano's ignorance, but with a post-lapsarian recognition of a world in which things may not be as they seem, a world of unstable surfaces and depths.

Delano does not comprehend, in other words, that the unnatural motion-lessness of the sea, the ship, and its actors reflect back to him the equally artificial (and equally unsustainable) prejudices and categories into which he has customarily organized his view of the world: that Africans are "stupid" (*PT* 75) and best fit for servitude, that noble blood produces good character, that an untrim ship indicates bad management, and so forth. For Delano, all actions performed by blacks – whether enslaved or free – are for the general comfort and pleasure of whites, and this belief produces his willed misrecognition of the menacing shaving scene, among other such moments in the story. Delano seeks only to satisfy his personal accounting practices; his role within the story's humming fixity is to decide to uphold presumptions when something does not fit his conception. What makes this perceptual problem potentially deadly in "Benito Cereno" is that for Delano to see "malign evil" in humans he must also be able to perceive will – and his static, racialized worldview cannot impute willed intelligence to the enslaved people aboard the ship. The very inertia with which the story begins indicates how at odds the plot will be with oceanic orders of chaos, motion, and movement. Unlike

Ishmael, for whom the results of classifying a chaos will still be a chaos, Delano shrinks from chaos and wishes only to see or will order.

His counterpart is found in Babo, the mastermind of the slave insurrection, whose actions may have evoked for Melville's readers the uprising aboard the Spanish slave ship *Amistad* in 1839 or the coastal American slaver *Creole* in 1841. Babo's itinerary has its own oceanic scale: after the revolt he seeks to navigate the *San Dominick* to "any negro countries" on the Pacific coast of South America, and when that fails he attempts a "return" to Senegal (*PT* 105). Yet Babo's mates are not the "raw" (50) Africans of Delano's imagination, fresh from the Middle and Cape Horn Passages; instead, they were being moved among South American colonial ports – from Valparaiso, Chile, to Callao, Peru. When Babo's revolution cannot be sustained, he refuses to communicate within a legal and social order that his entire being rejects. As Melville memorably writes: "seeing all was over, he uttered no sound, and could not be forced to. His aspect seemed to say, since I cannot do deeds, I will not speak words" (116). There can be nothing provisional for Babo, once his plan essentially to retrace the Middle Passage has been thwarted. Babo's intellectual being – in its subtlety and insistence on the doing of deeds as its expression – is the opposite of Delano's. In his disembodied silence Babo removes himself from both the oceanic order whose vagaries had sustained his revolutionary success for a brief time, as well as from a terrestrial order represented by Delano's dull, narrow judgment.

This Remote Chinese World of Ours

Melville's interest in oceanic figures for working through ideas of truth and valuation – whose standards are ever in flux – extends beyond his maritime-set fiction. As a closing example we can look briefly at the moment in his novel *Pierre* (1852) in which the title character finds at random in the seat cushion of the coach taking him to the city – and yet embraces as if a message in a bottle – a cheaply printed philosophical pamphlet. Written by a philosopher-bohemian named Plotinus Plinlimmon, the pamphlet proposes an oceanic form of provisional wisdom in squaring terrestrial and heavenly orders. (We can see this as akin to Pip's inability to bridge both the ship's world and the glimpse of God's heavenly order he'd received while cast away.) Plinlimmon's theory is that humans keep expedient "horological" or terrestrial time (say, eastern standard time), while God keeps idealized "chronometrical" or celestial time (in this figure, Greenwich mean time) – akin in its accuracy to the nautical chronometers that made accurate longitude readings possible. Reconciling these two contingencies, his pamphlet suggests, is like trying to keep Greenwich mean time while in China:

But though the chronometer carried from Greenwich to China, should truly exhibit in China what the time may be at Greenwich at any moment; yet, though thereby it must necessarily contradict China time, it does by no means thence follow, that with respect to China, the China watches are at all out of the way....[O]f what use to the Chinaman would a Greenwich chronometer, keeping Greenwich time, be? Were he thereby to regulate his daily actions, he would be guilty of all manner of absurdities: – going to bed at noon, say, when his neighbors would be sitting down to dinner. And thus, though the earthly wisdom of man be heavenly folly to God; so also, conversely, is the heavenly wisdom of God an earthly folly to man.... Nor does the God at the heavenly Greenwich expect common men to keep Greenwich wisdom in this remote Chinese world of ours. (211–12)

Orientation within our "remote Chinese world" is not just a matter of post-lapsarian recognition – or in other words, discovering that local or terrestrial time only becomes false in the knowledge of an ideal or celestial time. Instead, both terms – the terrestrial and celestial – are in play simultaneously in Melville's conception, and mutually constitute the grounds for the third space – call it oceanic – in which actors move in a skew trajectory, keeping the horologue at one hand and the chronometer at the other. An oceanic sense of planetarity allows for differentiation and fluidity, indeed a protean understanding of space and time alike.

China time versus Greenwich time, insular earth versus continent earth: oceanic studies adds a dimension to our standard practices of referentiality. One of the fundamental premises of the emerging field of oceanic studies is that such patterns dissolve in the space and time of the sea. To take an oceanic perspective on Melville's writing allows us not only a more profound understanding of his work on the sea, but also a refracted understanding of other recurring thematics and figures, such as his apologia for his organic, nonlinear narrative form. His frequent metaphorics of architectural incompletion, in a final example, have an oceanic cast in their investment not in some perfect futurity, but in an inevitable disintegration: "For the cope-stone of to-day is the corner-stone of to-morrow; and as St. Peter's church was built in great part of the ruins of old Rome, so in all our erections, however imposing, we but form quarries and supply ignoble materials for the grander domes of posterity," Melville writes in *Redburn* (149). Such moments take on new expansiveness or resonance when considered from the prospect of oceanic studies: Melville's challenge to the limitations of monuments lies not in their fractional state, but in their presumption of stability or permanence in the first place. Oceanic studies finds capacious possibilities for new forms of relationality – erosion, drift, dispersion, confluence, solvency – derived from the necessarily unbounded examples provided by the seas.

NOTES

1 For examples of works that treat U.S. literature and culture in a hemispheric and/or transnational context with considerable attention to the nineteenth century, see Caroline F. Levander and Robert S. Levine, eds., *Hemispheric American Studies* (New Brunswick, NJ: Rutgers University Press, 2008); Wai Chee Dimock and Lawrence Buell, eds., *Shades of the Planet: American Literature as World Literature* (Princeton, NJ: Princeton University Press, 2007); Kirsten Silva Gruesz, *Ambassadors of Culture: The Transamerican Origins of Latino Writing* (Princeton, NJ: Princeton University Press 2002); Anna Brickhouse, *Transamerican Literary Relations and the Nineteenth-Century Public Sphere* (Cambridge: Cambridge University Press, 2004); Rodrigo Lazo, *Writing to Cuba: Filibustering and Cuban Exiles in the United States* (Chapel Hill: University of North Carolina Press, 2005); and Sean X. Goudie, *Creole America: the West Indies and the Formation of Literature and Culture in the New Republic* (Philadelphia: University of Pennsylvania Press, 2006).
2 For more on Melville's personal experience at sea, see in particular Wilson Heflin, *Herman Melville's Whaling Years*, eds. Mary K. Bercaw Edwards and Thomas Farel Heffernan (Nashville, TN: University of Vanderbilt Press, 2004).
3 On maritime labor and its literary representation, see C. L. R. James, *Mariners, Renegades, and Castaways: The Story of Herman Melville and the World We Live In* (New York: Schocken Books, 1985); Cesare Casarino, *Modernity at Sea: Melville, Marx, Conrad in Crisis* (Minneapolis: University of Minnesota Press, 2002); Marcus Rediker, *Between the Devil and the Deep Blue Sea: Merchant Seamen, Pirates, and the Anglo-American Maritime World, 1700–1750* (Cambridge: Cambridge University Press, 1987); and Hester Blum, *The View from the Masthead: Maritime Imagination and Antebellum American Sea Narratives* (Chapel Hill: University of North Carolina Press, 2008). For accounts of the relationship between American literature and the sea, consult Thomas Philbrick, *James Fenimore Cooper and the Development of American Sea Fiction* (Cambridge: Harvard University Press, 1961); Haskell Springer, *America and the Sea: A Literary History* (Athens: University of Georgia Press, 1995); Margaret Cohen, *The Novel and the Sea* (Princeton, NJ: Princeton University Press, 2010); and Jason Berger, *Antebellum at Sea: Maritime Fantasies in Nineteenth-Century America* (Minneapolis: University of Minnesota Press, 2012).
4 Nathaniel Taylor, *Life on a Whaler; or, Antarctic Adventures in the Isle of Desolation* (1858; CT: New London County Historical Society, rpt. 1929), 2, 20.
5 Quoted in Thomas Farel Heffernan, *Stove by a Whale: Owen Chase and the Essex* (New York: Columbia University Press, 1981), 191.
6 See Robert S. Levine, *Conspiracy and Romance: Studies in Brockden Brown, Cooper, Hawthorne, and Melville* (Cambridge: Cambridge University Press, 1989), 168–82.
7 For the original historical narrative, see Amasa Delano, *A Narrative of Voyages and Travels, in the Northern and Southern Hemispheres: Comprising Three Voyages Round the World; Together with a Voyage of Survey and Discovery, in the Pacific Ocean and Oriental Islands* (Boston: E. G. House, 1817).

3

JENNIFER GREIMAN

Democracy and Melville's Aesthetics

In the famous celebration of "democratic dignity" in the first "Knights and Squires" chapter of *Moby-Dick* (1851), Ishmael claims the equality of all men as something of a divine right: "Thou shalt see it shining in the arm that wields a pick or drives a spike; that democratic dignity which, on all hands, radiates without end from God; Himself! The great God absolute! The centre and circumference of all democracy! His omnipresence, our divine equality!" (117). Glorying in both the divinity and the dignity of that equality which grounds his definition of democracy, Ishmael also speaks in terms that invert, with surprising symmetry, a very different remark by the narrator of *Redburn* (1849). "Hell," Redburn Wellingborough tells us, "is a democracy of devils, where all are equals." Speculating on the afterlife of a vicious fellow sailor, Redburn appeals somewhat perversely to democracy to claim that this "nameless vagabond" is "full as dignified a personage" as Tiberius, Nero, and even Napoleon, insofar as all of them should hang, side by side, from "the lofty gallows in history" (276). Hell is a democracy, Redburn reasons, but it is one without dignity because it levels all distinction between those who have sought it out with the greatest violence. By contrast, the "democratic dignity" Ishmael celebrates is that most common thing that "radiates without end from God; Himself!" to abrogate false distinctions and elevate every mariner, renegade, castaway, and nameless vagabond alike above all "robed investiture" (117) on the earth. Arriving at equality by opposite paths, Redburn and Ishmael give evidence of the astounding variety of situations and locations where Melville finds democracy in his writing; at the same time, they suggest that, wherever and whatever democracy is, not even heaven and hell can fully contain it.

Democracy is fundamental to Melville's art, and yet it is also elusive, its meaning and function changing as it tends to unsettle relations and conditions as often as it names or defines them. Thus, if hell is a democracy, and democracy is both centered on and limned by the powers of heaven, then democracy signals something more in Melville's writing than the particular terms and concepts that usually define it – self-rule, popular sovereignty, individualism, and so on. If democracy determines the relations between diabolical and divine alike, then it is nothing quite so simple as a political attitude – something with which to agree or disagree, something to approve or disapprove, even something about which to be conflicted. Still, even as democracy is something both mutable and expansive for Melville, it is by no means inchoate or amorphous for that mutability. Democracy may never be one thing for Melville, but it is always something, identified with specific figures, particular relationships, and explicit forces both within individual texts and across the body of his work.

For this reason, democracy in Melville's writing can be associated, at once, with the elevation of the "meanest" and with the attenuation of all agency, with the irreducible plurality of human life and with an unrelenting movement toward fusion. Democracy can be linked with Melville's most robust affirmations of freedom, equality, and right, and yet it can also coexist with the suspension of all of these under conditions of war and the persistence of inequality. To track the meaning and function of democracy for Melville, readers must contend with its best and worst manifestations, with its transformations and its contradictions – in short, with heaven and hell at once. But ultimately, it is because Melville never assumes democracy is stable or singular that he finds such power in it, and it is this power that fuels his aesthetic practice.

The study of democracy in Melville's writing – which all but originates with the study of Melville himself – tends to agree on little but the ambivalence with which Melville treats it. For C. L. R. James, writing in 1953, Melville was an "extreme, in fact a fanatical democrat," who understood democracy, in its best sense, as "the power of human association for a common purpose" and, in its worst, as that collaboration with tyranny in which James finds Melville's prophetic analysis of twentieth-century totalitarianisms.[1] For Michael Rogin, writing in 1983, the evidence of ambivalence indicates Melville's eroding faith in democracy during the 1840s, after which he "found slavery everywhere in the democratic future."[2] Writing in 1989, Wai-Chee Dimock emphasizes form over thematics to argue that Melville's celebrations of democracy in particular texts are complicated by the development of an authorial sovereignty across his novels that is "analogous to America's national sovereignty."[3] Reflecting on decades of such claims in 2009, Dennis Berthold argues that each generation of critics tends to find its own understanding of democracy in Melville's work. He calls for a more historicized and experiential understanding of democracy's contingent and ambivalent meanings in Melville, one rooted "in his actual experiences with nascent capitalism, aristocratic nostalgia, literary elitism, constitutional monarchies, populist economics, workers' rights, mob violence, and socialist revolutions."[4]

Building on this work and a great deal more,[5] this chapter revisits the long conversation on Melville and democracy by proposing two slight shifts in perspective. The first is to view the ambivalence of democracy in Melville's thinking, not in the way one would consider a conflicted opinion about one political question among others (like the Mexican War or the 1850 Compromise), but as part of an understanding of democracy as structural to American life, shaping practices, beliefs, institutions, and relations for better and worse. Such a perspective necessitates an understanding of democracy that is historical and theoretical at once, one that accounts for the contingencies of what Berthold calls the experiential, as well as the contradictions fundamental to democracy as a theory, a concept, even an abstraction. Such a perspective also allows us to see the ways Melville's thinking on democracy approximates – and rivals – that of political philosophy, particularly the work of the nineteenth century's most influential democratic theorist, Alexis de Tocqueville.

If Melville approaches democracy as Tocqueville does, as a mutable and conditioning force, this understanding of democracy suggests a second perspectival shift, one that seeks democracy not only in the thematics of individual texts and the attributes of particular characters, but also in the aesthetic forms and figures that develop and repeat across the entirety of his work. Melville's aesthetics intimately follow democracy's movements, its revolutions and counterrevolutions, its fusions and dissolutions, as well as the changes in conditions and relations that it brings about. Democracy shapes Melville's figures, colors his language, and drives the flow of plot and the accumulation of analogies. By tracking three such figures – circles, colors, and rivers – as these repeat across Melville's career-long engagement with democracy, I wish to show how integral democratic ideas and ideals are to his literary production. Melville puts into practice what political theorist Jean-Luc Nancy describes as democracy's resistance to representation in any one image or figure. But if democracy can never be contained in a single figure, Nancy argues, it nonetheless "allows for a proliferation of figures – figures affirmed, invented, created, imagined and so on."[6] In Melville's proliferation of figures, he hews closely to the contours of democracy's own mutations and contradictions: its egalitarian drive; its suspensions of agency; its potential complicity with violence and war; its movement toward oneness, fusion, and the collapse of all difference; as well as its transformative potential.

Alexis de Tocqueville is credited with the insight that democracy in America is not just a mode of government or a style of politics, but the very form of society itself.[7] Indeed, the two volumes of his inquiry into American democracy during the early 1830s are structured around a distinction between political institutions and civil society, which he blurs with the very first sentence of *Democracy in America*: "Of all the novel things which attracted my attention during my stay in the United States, none struck me more forcibly than the equality of social conditions."[8] Identifying "the equality of social conditions" as the foundation of everything from the shape of American government to the attitudes of the governed, Tocqueville calls equality a "generative fact" (*fait générateur*). As such, equality maintains an uneasy relationship to the real – particularly in a slave society where "the former colors of aristocracy show through" the "democratic patina."[9] Equality thus becomes less a stable condition for Tocqueville than a shaping idea whose power rests in its partial fictiveness: it generates and transforms all aspects of American society precisely because it both does and does not (yet) exist. Hence its strangely tautological function in Tocqueville's thinking: "as the factor which generated all of the others ... it represented a central focus in which all my observations constantly ended."[10] The generative fact of equality is both the beginning and the end of everything Tocqueville sees, thinks, and writes about American democracy because it is the absent yet formative thing for which he must keep looking.

And yet the generative fact of social equality does not alone define the theory and practice of American democracy for Tocqueville. To social equality he joins the principle of the sovereignty of the people, a concept equally plagued by a certain circularity: "The people reign in the American political world like God over the universe. It is the cause and the aim of all things, everything comes from them and everything is absorbed back into them."[11] Just as the equality of social conditions draws its power as a generative fact from its empirical absence, so popular sovereignty comes to create the very people whose authority it also seeks to represent. Both social equality and the sovereign people must be understood to exist, in some sense, prior to the forces that fuel them, as their own cause and end. But rather than limiting their potential influence, the circularity of both social equality and popular sovereignty generates an almost irresistible power, though in Tocqueville's analysis that power is unstable, with as much potential for tyranny as for emancipation. Proposing for democracy the shape of a circle – precisely as Ishmael does in "Knights and Squires" – Tocqueville captures the contradictions of a self-grounding authority, as well as its potential to transform itself. Rooted in and driven by an idea of equality that constantly changes social relations, American democracy is nevertheless characterized for Tocqueville by the ease with which it has also empowered majorities to act in the name of – and tyrannize over – the people.

40

Thus, where the absence of actual equality may give rise to egalitarianism as a shaping, potentially transformative force in Tocqueville's account, the absence of universal suffrage has given rise not to a sovereign people but to a sovereign majority. Metonymically empowered to act in the name of the people, but by no means identical to them, the majority appropriates to itself all the sovereign powers of a monarch and then some. (It is not for nothing that *White-Jacket*'s [1850] Jack Chase warns, "the public and the people! Ay, ay, my lads, let us hate the one and cleave to the other!" [192].) The "tyranny of the majority" outdoes the tyranny of kings because it is "endowed with a force both physical and moral, which affects people's will as much as their actions." In this, the majority retains the sovereign right to physical force while also producing a "moral" and "intellectual" violence that "leaves the body alone and goes straight for the soul."[12] At the same time, the majority's power over thought introduces another of the tendencies toward tyranny that Tocqueville identifies with democracy: namely, its eradication of diversity and freedom of thought. Assuming that "as citizens become more equal" they will also become "more similar," Tocqueville argues that the public will take on greater authority, shaping the people in its image rather than the other way around. "In equality, I see two tendencies: one which leads every man's thought into new paths and another which would force him willingly to cease thinking at all."[13] In the apparent contradiction of a tendency that "forces" one "willingly" to abandon all thinking (*qui le réduirait volontiers à ne plus penser*), Tocqueville neatly encapsulates his own thesis. Understood as a form of society, democracy generates not only relations and institutions but subjects themselves, and it does so in ways that have the potential to sever will from thought and desire from action.

The creative fact of equality, the circularity of democratic authority, the usurpation of the people by the public or majority, the fusion of democracy's diverse subjects into sameness: each of the contradictions that are central to Tocqueville's analysis animates Melville's writing on democracy as well. Though there is no clear evidence that Melville responded to Tocqueville directly,[14] the resonance between the two is mutually instructive, with Tocqueville offering ground and context for Melville's apparent ambivalence about democracy, and Melville imagining possibilities for democracy that move beyond the gloomy impasses of Tocqueville's analysis. In the remainder of this chapter, I want to show how Melville reimagines key elements of Tocqueville's theory of American democracy as problems for political and aesthetic thought at once – that is, as problems of form, staging, figuration, and analogy. Beginning with the doubleness of equality itself, as both fact and generative force, I focus on three systems of figuration to which Melville returns again and again in his work as a way to think about and through the shifting meanings and functions of democracy. Circles, colors, and rivers recur in Melville's writing as figures at once precise and mutable on which he anchors his thinking about the contradictions of self-grounding authority, the usurpation of the people, and the dangers of a relentless movement toward an all-fusing universality. Running through even the most sober of his meditations on democracy, though, is the promise of a potentially transformative equality that unites Melville's disparate meditations on democracy as the generative force of writing itself.

In the frequently cited line from his June 1, 1851 letter to Nathaniel Hawthorne, Melville describes his own "ruthless democracy" and casts it in terms that assert the absolute equality of all people as both a fact and an elusive ideal:

> So when you see or hear of my ruthless democracy on all sides, you may feel a touch of a shrink, or something of that sort. It is but nature to be shy of a mortal who boldly declares that a thief in jail is as honorable a personage as Gen. George Washington. This is ludicrous. But Truth is the silliest thing under the sun. (*L* 190–91)

At once ludicrous and true, everywhere manifest and denied by almost everyone, equality is for Melville something that simultaneously is and must always be asserted, performed, and claimed because neither the conditions nor the opinions of the world bear it out. For this reason, equality also becomes both impetus and drive to literary production. As Ishmael writes in defense of his aesthetic choices in the first "Knights and Squires" chapter:

> If then, to meanest mariners, and renegades, and castaways, I shall hereafter ascribe high qualities, though dark; weave round them tragic graces; if even the most mournful, perchance the most abased, among them all, shall at times lift himself to the exalted mounts; if I shall touch that workman's arm with some ethereal light, if I shall spread a rainbow over his disastrous set of sun; then against all mortal critics, bear me out in it, thou just Spirit of Equality. (*MD* 117)

Ishmael's succession of conditional if clauses locates political and aesthetic force at once in the contested reality of equality.[15] He poses narrative facts as conditional counter-facts, asserting the high qualities and tragic graces of his characters under the ruse of a hypothetical that is immediately made real by the "Spirit of Equality." Equality functions here as the muse of what is most common, the transcendent spirit that authorizes the elevation of the "meanest" precisely by virtue of their inherent equality and for their own sake alone.

If there seems to be some tautology in this gesture (asserting the equality of all because all are equal) and even in this understanding of equality (as that transcendent force that elevates by virtue of inherent value), it is a tautology Ishmael has already acknowledged by claiming that democracy is circular by nature. Envisioning democracy as having a "center and circumference," Ishmael not only conjures the crises and contradictions of democratic authority that Tocqueville lays bare, but he goes further, celebrating democracy's contradictions and turning them to his own narrative purposes. If democracy introduces a crisis into its own foundation by collapsing its origins and its ends, making the people sovereign through their own retroactive authority, Ishmael imagines two resolutions. On the one hand, he proposes a classically suspect solution to this crisis of self-grounding authority by positing a transcendent, authorizing "God; Himself!" as the power that "radiates" from every hand and arm. But on the other hand (or, perhaps, arm), he encloses that God in a circular figure of his own devising, and then occupies both center and circumference himself, claiming the same rights and powers of elevation ("if I shall touch a workman's arm with some ethereal light") by virtue of the "Spirit of Equality," not divine power.[16] Ishmael's circle thus highlights and mimics the self-grounding powers of democracy. Drawing alternately on the authority of God and the equality of men, he both generates a form that assures his own authorial power and asserts the access of the very "meanest" to the power of that form by demonstrating its capacity for reproduction.

What is perhaps most remarkable about the circle that Melville draws around Ishmael's celebration of democracy is its mutability as a form for thinking about the relationship of equality and authority. Ishmael is not the first of Melville's narrators to invoke a circle, nor is "Knights and Squires" the only appearance the circle makes in *Moby-Dick*. In Chapter XXIV of *Redburn*, before the narrator goes ashore with his obsolete guidebook to explore Liverpool, he pauses to describe the activities of the crew in port and ends up analyzing the social condition of sailors around the world. Where Ishmael sees in a circle the glorious abstraction of democracy, joining every arm and hand to "the great God absolute," it is for Redburn something more mundane: a muddy carriage wheel.

> There are classes of men in the world who bear the same relation to society at large, that the wheels do to the coach: and are just as indispensable. But however easy and delectable the springs upon which the insiders pleasantly vibrate ... the wheels must still revolve in dusty, or muddy, revolutions. No contrivance or sagacity can lift them out of the mire; for upon something the coach must be bottomed; on something the insiders must roll. (139)

At first glance, this passage reads as characteristic of Redburn's conflicted class rage throughout the first half of his narrative. As he alternately scorns those sailors in whose company he finds himself and rails at the forces of capital that ruined his father and family, so here he rejects the notion that sailors as a class have progressed morally by invoking a metaphor that seems at once to condemn and to rationalize their position as the burdened wheels on which society rolls. And yet, in the same gesture with which Redburn identifies the sailor with the inexorable motion of a social machine, the workings of a world already made, he also remarks that there is both mobility and power in their rolled-over condition. Not only do the wheels themselves "still revolve in dusty ... revolutions," but they also "go and come round the world" (139). These sailor-wheels are the very vehicles of culture: "they carry missionaries, embassadors [sic], opera-singers, armies, merchants, tourists, and scholars to their destinations: they are the bridge of boats across the Atlantic." More than that, without these sailor-wheels "almost everything would stop here on earth except its revolution on its axis, and the orators in the American Congress" (139). The labor of sailors, the rotation of the earth, the endless drone of political speech: all of these powers come to rival each other as driving forces of the world, suggesting that sailors need not wait on moral reformers for their "progress" but should simply step forward to claim their rightful title.

From Redburn's rolling carriage wheel to Ishmael's circle of democracy, the power of circular authority lies in the "revolutions" that it literalizes and makes visible. Shifting between narrative contexts and figurative senses, while maintaining their basic shape, Melville's circles evoke one another and accumulate meanings with their repetition. In this, they foreground a key operation of aesthetics itself in Melville's work, which Newton Arvin describes as "essentially convertative or transmutative."[17] All figuration is "convertative," of course, but these figures do more than transform the political and social meanings of democracy that unite them. Melville's figures transform each other along with the processes of figuration through which they operate. For instance, Ishmael returns to the image of the circle that he introduces in "Knights and Squires" in "The Grand Armada," a chapter-long meditation on the variety and mutability of the circle as a figure of individual and collective being. In that chapter, the circularity of Ahab's hunt ("chasing and being chased" [MD 383]) becomes literalized as the Pequod seeks to outrun a pirate ship while chasing a massive pod of whales, which the crew sees "expanding in vast irregular circles" around them. Circles begin to circle each other, as competing figures for autonomous individuality, on the one hand, and social cooperation, on the other, collide in the peaceful calm at the center of the pod. When the crew of Ishmael's boat peer into the water and discover the whales' "nursery," they find that the pod's shape is by no means arbitrary but part of a purposeful social organization to protect its most vulnerable members: "And thus, though surrounded by circles upon circles of consternation and affrights, did these inscrutable creatures at the centre freely and fearlessly indulge in all peaceful concernments, yea serenely reveled in all dalliance and delight" (388–89). Ishmael finds here an analogy for his own silent, calm center – "deep down and deep inland there I still bathe me in eternal mildness of joy" (389). But the meaning of the circle changes with its movements, so when a violent commotion at the edge reaches the nursery, the whales come "tumbling upon their inner centre." The circle collapses, brutally, under the figurative weight of what has become attached to it – the very possibility of peace, it seems, for individuals and communities alike – but because so much of its power lies in its capacity to transform, its collapse is by no means its end.

Transformative power is key to all of the figures from which Melville derives aesthetic energy for his thinking on democracy, yet transformations in and of power are not always revolutionary (even when they are circular). In one of the most intricate and sobering meditations on democracy in Melville's fiction, the narrator of *Pierre* (1852) describes – "by apt analogy" – the process by which democracy accommodates itself to aristocratic distinction and the concentration of great wealth in families like the Glendinnings:

> For indeed the democratic element operates as a subtile [*sic*] acid among us, forever producing new things by corroding the old, as in the south of France, verdigris, the primitive material of one kind of green paint, is produced by grape-vinaigre poured upon copper plates. Now in general, nothing can be more significant of decay than the idea of corrosion, yet on the other hand, nothing can more vividly suggest the luxuriance of life than the idea of green, as a color, for green is the peculiar signet of all-fertile Nature herself. Herein by apt analogy we behold the marked anomalousness of America, whose character abroad, we need not be surprised, is misconceived, when we consider how strangely she contradicts all prior notions of human things; and how wonderfully to her, Death itself becomes transmuted into Life. (9)

Where Tocqueville saw the "colors of aristocracy" showing through America's "democratic patina," the green finish of Melville's democracy more effectively masks aristocracy because, in his devious analogy, democracy is both the tint of verdigris and the agent of corrosive change that produces it. Democracy begins as that acid element which makes verdigris of copper, unleashing a chemical reaction that corrodes and transforms everything, including itself. Thus, the moment democracy becomes vinegar, copper corrodes into verdigris, which in turn converts the naturalizing claims of democracy into nothing other than a fresh coat of green paint.

Melville's analogy exploits the duplicity of the color green – simultaneously the "signet of all-fertile Nature itself" and the product of corrosive artifice – to make visible democracy's capacity to produce that which usurps it, as well as the means of concealing that usurpation. Seen for its truer, artificial color, the "marked anomalousness of America" could be understood to describe the spectacle of what Tocqueville calls "social equality" in a slave society, or even the production of majority tyranny out of popular sovereignty. But given the complexity of Melville's analogy, the passage pushes back against the very political-allegorical readings it would seem to invite. Indeed, in introducing a process of analogy whereby each term is transformed in its turn, this passage corrodes the structure of the "apt analogy" that it employs through the specific analogy of a corrosive chemical reaction that it invokes.

Thus, where circular forms stage for Melville the means by which an apparent contradiction in self-grounding authority opens up the potential for other claims to power, even for other organizations of collective life, colors provide a form for Melville's thinking about democracy's power to produce its opposite, yielding an uncertainty within the very identity of democracy. In *Pierre*, the opposite of democracy first appears as that aristocracy which "imposingly perpetuates" itself in America, but after democracy passes through the extended "verdigris" analogy, even such defining oppositions have multiplied. Once the color green shows nature and artifice, life and death, all at once, what precisely is that "democratic element" it was originally meant to reveal? Rather than assert a stable, defining identity to democracy, Melville renders democracy's deceptive transience visible through deceptions that are inherent to colors. In this way, the thinking on democracy that the verdigris passage initiates finds a strange culmination in the first paragraph of the pivotal chapter 21 of *Billy Budd* (ca. 1890): "Who in the rainbow can draw the line where the violet tint ends and orange begins? Distinctly we see the difference of the colors, but where exactly does the one first blendingly enter into the other? So with sanity and insanity" (102). So, too, *Billy Budd* suggests, with democracy and martial law, the *Rights of Man* and the *Bellipotent*. If Billy's impressment from the former ship to the latter initially suggests a stark divide between the conditions of peace and war, the story quickly blurs that line into indistinction.

As in *White-Jacket*, the condition under which everything in *Billy Budd* occurs is that of war – specifically the Articles of War and "War's Child" (*BB* 102), the Mutiny Act, which have suspended habeas corpus and rendered the "people" subject to summary judgment and corporeal punishment. For White-Jacket, the atrocities permitted under martial law appear antithetical to democracy, holdovers from the most reactionary of monarchic regimes: "They cannot be the indigenous growth of those political institutions which are based on that arch-democrat Thomas Jefferson's Declaration of Independence? No; they are an importation from abroad, even from Britain whose laws we Americans hurled off as tyrannical, and yet retained the most tyrannical of all" (*WJ* 297). White-Jacket argues that the Articles of War come from outside of democracy to overthrow the authority of the people with counterrevolutionary rage. Four decades later, however, when the narrator of *Billy Budd* considers this problem of war and democracy, he colors the question with a touch of verdigris and calls democracy's very identity into question as it takes on the ambiguity of the rainbow. The Mutiny Act severs all action from will on the *Bellipotent*, dictating Vere's judgment and Billy's punishment. But the narrator of *Billy Budd* retroactively troubles White-Jacket's belief that such a law cannot be the "indigenous growth" of democracy when the "people" of the *Bellipotent* appear to ratify both the decision and the power that dictates it, "without volition, as it were … the vehicles of some vocal current electric" (123). As the power of martial law "blendingly enters into" the power of the people's voice in *Billy Budd*, so White-Jacket's tenuous line between the democratic and the tyrannical fades into that imperceptible distinction between violet and orange. Still, it matters that Melville's narrator makes that very indistinction so radiantly visible. Like the "whiteness of the whale," what is most powerful about Melville's chromatics of democracy is the radiance with which it colors and illuminates what is simultaneously elusive and all-pervading, indefinite and appalling.

Partly for reasons of this strange radiance, all of the figures through which Melville imagines democracy must be read as something other than allegories of democracy. Not only do his circles and colors operate on levels other than the thematic, but they also refuse to remain in any stable or singular relationship to political facts or concepts. Instead, Melville allows these figures to become implicated in the political thinking that they do, foregrounding their own operation as figures and forms. Circles stage the repeating self-generation at the heart of democratic authority, but they also spin out of control and collapse. Colors render vivid democracy's self-contradictions and usurpations, blurring the line between democracy and its others (aristocracy, tyranny, war) precisely because a color can change before our eyes. Read across Melville's texts, both sets of figures highlight the work of analogy itself, specifically the ways analogical figures convert and transmute what they purport to demonstrate. As these circular shapes and shifting colors develop through Melville's extended and intricate analogies, so they also operate through the complex interplay between commensurability and lost distinction, where things quite different come together in mutual illumination, but risk their differences in the process.

Understood in this way, the aesthetic operation of analogy itself becomes an analogy for a key problem of democratic life – namely, the fear that comparison and equivalence might erase vital difference. The aesthetic and political implications of this worry become explicit in the second chapter of *The Confidence-Man* (1857), which begins with the cacophony of "many men" with "many minds" (7) debating the authenticity of the mute man in the cream-colored suit, and ends with a vision of this "many" as the Mississippi River.

> As pine, beech, birch, ash, hackmatack, spruce, bass-wood, maple interweave their foliage in the natural wood; so these varieties of mortals blended their varieties of visage and garb. A Tartar-like picturesqueness; a sort of pagan abandonment and assurance. Here reigned the dashing and all-fusing spirit of the West, whose type is the Mississippi itself, which, uniting the streams of the most distant and opposite zones, pours them along, helter-skelter, in one cosmopolitan and confident tide. (9)

the ri-.. af m.lk.., p.t

Few passages in Melville's writing convey so clearly the intimacy between his aesthetic practice and his thinking about democracy, just as few convey so concisely the proximity of threat and promise at the center of democratic power and representation. On the one hand, this passage tracks the fusion of an almost inconceivably disparate multitude into "one cosmopolitan and confident tide," suggesting that, like the movement of the river itself, the power of the multiple lies in its fusion and singular direction. On the other hand, this passage only arrives at that tide – both cosmopolitan and confident – through the accumulation of several analogies for what unites them. In this, Melville's narrator reveals the ways analogy reduces and produces difference at the same time. Just as no listing of potential passengers can really be exhaustive, so neither "Canterbury pilgrims" nor an "Anacharsis Cloots congress" nor "foliage in the natural wood" can contain the infinite varieties the river transports. But when Canterbury pilgrims join the Anacharsis Cloots congress of trees, with a "Tartar-like picturesqueness" and a "sort of pagan abandonment," and all flow into the Mississippi River, Melville proposes that fusion into one thing is also the accumulation of many and various others. The Mississippi may go by a single name, but Melville's passage makes clear that what it names is irreducibly plural.

Ultimately, the Mississippi River proposes a vision that links democratic life and aesthetic practice: both democracy and Melville's aesthetics derive power from a combination that can never be absolute because all of its momentum relies on the accumulation of more and more difference. Indeed, by the end of the passage, even the river's "one" tide is multiple: "helter-skelter," confident, and cosmopolitan all at once. Accumulating analogies for combination in this way, Melville pushes back against the assumptions of totalizing sameness that Tocqueville fears will overtake democratic social life, reducing all subjects to particular expressions of public opinion. In the Mississippi, Melville finds figural means of preserving internal differences to make an otherwise overwhelming movement both inclusive and accumulative. This startling preservation of internal difference is precisely what Redburn finds when he dips his fingers in the North Atlantic and feels the warmth of the Gulf Stream, "a sort of Mississippi of hot water, flowing through the ocean" (R 83). Here, the figure of the river "unites the streams of the most distant and opposite zones," not by blending or fusing itself with the surrounding waters, but by carrying its difference to the other side of the hemisphere. To borrow another of Melville's analogies – that of "a wind in purpose strong" – the real potential Melville finds in the Mississippi is that of a resistant, constant countermovement. There is the drive of the "all-fusing spirit of the West, whose type is the Mississippi," but everything that feeds into that fusion accumulates, retains residues of its difference, and "spins *against* the way it drives."

These lines – "I know a wind in purpose strong – / It spins *against* the way it drives" (PP 10) – come from one of the last places one might expect to find any promise for democracy in Melville's writing. "The Conflict of Convictions (1860–61)" is the third poem in *Battle Pieces* (1866), and its premise is the death of political hope, as Melville explains in a footnote: "The gloomy lull of the early part of the winter of 1860–61, seeming big with disaster to our institutions, affected some minds that believed them to constitute one of the great hopes of mankind, much as the eclipse which came over the promise of the French Revolution affected kindred natures, throwing them for the time into doubt and misgivings universal" (PP 173). But even as "the People spread like a weedy grass / the thing that they will bring to pass" (9), Melville's poem imagines a forceful model of resistant countermovement in the face of what looks like bitter certainty. The poem's two voices (one mournful, one derisive) locate war's recurrent inevitability in the deep time of ages, but when the main speaker describes the figure of a wind whose spin and drive are at odds with each other, it introduces an internal difference that pushes back against historical necessity, preserving perhaps some hope for politics and democracy.

But however ambiguous these lines are about the meaning of war, they articulate something clearly and forcefully about the work that Melville's writing does. Indeed, they name, with startling precision, a central performance of Melville's aesthetic practice. Melville's most dense and resistant writing moves like this wind, with figures and analogies blowing back on what they seem to illustrate, defying prevailing sense, and generating more

49

and different meaning. Across the entirety of Melville's work, such passages give evidence of a poetics of democracy –"in purpose strong" – which both spins against and drives the thematics of celebration, skepticism, and ambivalence that so often characterize the treatment of democracy in his work. Read this way, what Melville's art – the shape, color, and movement of his language – tells us is that the power and meaning of democracy may lie precisely in its capacity to find purpose in conflict and difference.

NOTES

1   C. L. R. James, *Mariners, Renegades and Castaways: The Story of Herman Melville and the World We Live In*, ed. Donald E. Pease (Hanover, NH: Dartmouth College Press and the University Press of New England, 2001), 75, 60, 51.
2   Michael Paul Rogin, *Subversive Genealogy: The Art and Politics of Herman Melville* (1983; Berkeley: University of California Press, 1985), 151.
3   Wai-Chee Dimock, *Empire for Liberty* (Princeton, NJ: Princeton University Press, 1989), 7.
4   Dennis Berthold, *American Risorgimento: Herman Melville and the Cultural Politics of Italy* (Columbus: Ohio State University Press, 2009), 25.
5   In particular: Nancy Ruttenburg, *Democratic Personality: Popular Voice and the Trial of American Authorship* (Stanford, CA: Stanford University Press, 1998); Jonathan Elmer, *On Lingering and Being Last: Race and Sovereignty in the New World* (New York: Fordham University Press, 2008); Maurice Lee, *Slavery, Philosophy and American Literature, 1830–1860* (New York: Cambridge University Press, 2005).
6   Jean-Luc Nancy, *The Truth of Democracy*, trans. Pascale-Anne Brault and Michael Naas (New York: Fordham University Press, 2010), 26.
7   Claude Lefort, *Democracy and Political Theory*, trans. David Macy (London: Polity Press, 1988), 14; Jacques Rancière, *Hatred of Democracy*, trans. Steve Corcoran (London: Verso, 2009), 20.
8   Alexis de Tocqueville, *Democracy in America, and Two Essays on America*, trans. Gerald Bevan (New York: Penguin, 2003), 11.
9   Ibid., 58.
10 Ibid., 11.
11 Ibid., 71.
12 Ibid., 297–99.
13 Ibid., 510–12.
14 Mary Bercaw notes a single scholar who makes a claim (unconfirmed) that Melville cited Tocqueville directly. Mary K. Bercaw, *Melville's Sources* (Evanston, IL: Northwestern University Press, 1987), 76.
15 Donald Pease – in reading C. L. R. James reading the passage from which he takes his title – details the ways these famous lines foreground aesthetic production as addressed to and guided by the "Spirit of Equality" ("C. L. R. James' *Mariners, Renegades, and Castaways* and the World We Live In," in James, xvii).
16 See Ruttenburg, *Democratic Personality*, 344–78.
17 Newton Arvin, *Herman Melville* (New York: Grove Press, 2002), 144.

4

JEANNINE MARIE DELOMBARD

White-Jacket: Telling Who Is – and Aint – a Slave

> The captain ... call[ed] out to us: "You see your condition! ... I'll flog you all, fore and aft.... You've got a driver over you! Yes, a slave-driver, – a nigger-driver! I'll see who'll tell me he isn't a NIGGER slave!"
>
> Richard Henry Dana, Jr. *Two Years Before the Mast* (1840)

> Who aint a slave? Tell me that.
>
> Herman Melville, *Moby-Dick* (1851)

In the summer of 1849, Herman Melville drew on his brief naval stint on the frigate *United States*, from August 17, 1843 to October 14, 1844, to write *White-Jacket; or the World in a Man-of-War* (1850). In the intervening years, the national antislavery movement that had effectively begun with the founding of William Lloyd Garrison's newspaper, the *Liberator* (1831–65), gained new relevance through the literary contributions of fugitive slaves. The first-person "testimony" of enslaved author-activists like Frederick Douglass corroborated arguments Garrison and other advocates for the slave presented at "the bar of public opinion."[1] Abolitionists indicted "the perpetrators of slaveholding villainy" by combining accounts of whippings and other acts of brutality with references to the laws that authorized them.[2]

My epigraphs indicate antislavery rhetoric's pervasive influence on antebellum culture. Regardless of their relationship to abolitionism, sea writers like Melville and Dana found in the slave a powerful figure for evoking the oppression and exploitation suffered by common sailors. As yeoman farms gave way to factories and other forms of mechanized capitalist production across the rapidly industrializing nation, a broader labor reform movement protested free workers' subjection to "wage slavery." From newspaper polemics to belles-lettres, invocations of the unique plight of the hereditary bondman often had the effect of redirecting attention away from the commodification of four million enslaved African Americans toward the mistreatment of normatively white wage earners on land or at sea.

The insouciant query posed by Ishmael at the beginning of *Moby-Dick* – "Who aint a slave? Tell me that" (6) – highlights the conundrum facing scholars interested in Melville's views of one of the most politically, economically, morally, legally, and socially urgent issues of his time. References to slaves and slavery abound in his writing, but portrayals of actual slaves, especially American ones, are scant. For this reason, "Benito Cereno" (1855) has become Melville studies' go-to text on slavery. Centering on a shipboard revolt led by captive Africans, the novella is Melville's most straightforward representation of slaves and slavery. But if we turn from *Moby-Dick* to its immediate predecessor, we can see how the question Ishmael poses before signing away many of his rights as citizen to ship before the mast alerts us to much more than merely how labor reformers appropriated abolitionist rhetoric.

Telling just who is and aint a slave, *White-Jacket* offers a more profound statement on American race slavery than the much more frequently studied "Benito Cereno." Admittedly, this is a provocative claim. Whereas the novella depicts a deadly power struggle between black slaves and their white captors, *White-Jacket* offers only one enslaved character, Guinea, who "though a bondman, liable to be saddled with a mortgage, like a horse," is "so fortunate as to meet with none but gentle masters," and thus, "in India-rubber manacles, enjoyed the liberties of the world" (379). Clearly, we cannot look to *White-Jacket* to expand *Mardi*'s incisive criticism of a republic whose "federal temple of freedom ... was the handiwork of slaves" (528). Quite the contrary. If Melville's neglected fifth novel is remembered for anything beyond its protest against naval flogging, it is for providing "one of Melville's few comments on the institution of slavery," in its "bitter comparison between the easy life of 'Guinea' and the 'slavery' of the ordinary seaman."[3] As with Ishmael's query in chapter 1 of *Moby-Dick*, *White-Jacket*'s numerous references to slaves and slavery – usually as metaphors or similes for sailors and their plight – constantly shift our focus *away* from these very subjects. But like the optical illusion in which two stylized facial profiles yield to a contoured vase (or vice versa), our interpretative vision depends on alternating identifications of figure and ground. Searching for slaves in *White-Jacket*, one sees only sailors. But scrutinizing the "World in a Man-of-War," one suddenly sees the figure of the slave sharply defined, front and center.

This perspectival reorientation also provides a fresh vantage on what is often seen as Melville's uncharacteristic embrace of American exceptionalism in *White-Jacket*. Urging the U.S. Navy to break from the British tradition of corporal discipline, the narrator reminds his countrymen that "the political Messiah ha[s] come ... in *us*" (151), insisting, "in things of this kind England should be ... an example to be shunned.... Escaped from the house of bondage, Israel of old did not follow after the ways of the Egyptians. To her was given an express dispensation.... And we Americans are the peculiar, chosen people – the Israel of our time; we bear the ark of the liberties of the world" (150–51). This jeremiad is prompted by the "coarse, vulgar" Jacksonian captain who, "prov[ing] a tyrant to his crew," exceeds not only his British counterparts but also the slaveholding "descendants of the old Virginians" who are likewise "more accustomed to social command" (141). Rapidly shifting registers, the narrator mingles Puritan typology and Revolutionary ideology to associate England with biblical Egypt before turning to the contemporary slavery debate to locate the modern "house of bondage" in, alternatively, the antebellum South and the American man-of-war. That it is specifically flogging that prevents the U.S. Navy from "bearing the ark" of the very "liberties of the world" that the slave Guinea is said to "enjoy" while aboard the frigate suggests how tightly interwoven are the tangled rhetorics of antebellum reform with the nationalist discourse of American exceptionalism in Melville's *White-Jacket*. To unsnarl the former is, as the following reading demonstrates, to unravel the latter.

Unfavorably comparing Northern naval officers to British elites and Southern slaveholders, the passages from *White-Jacket* cited earlier illustrate how, at a cultural moment when "the common seaman represented the democratic man" and when decades of abolitionist propaganda had made the whipping scene a set piece for race slavery, depictions of shipboard flogging kindled outrage by placing the white "free citizen" in the position of the black slave.[4] Not always as explicit as the famous scene in which Dana's whip-wielding Captain Thompson characterizes himself as "slave-driver," this strategy of racial reversal shaped antebellum sea writing and, as we shall see, was redeployed by Melville in *White-Jacket* in unexpected, even contradictory ways. Typically, a polemicist like William McNally, whose *Evils and Abuses of the Naval and Merchant Service, Exposed* (1839) is a key *White-Jacket* source, sought to channel white Americans' surging reformist zeal away from "the swarthy sons and daughters of Africa" to "their own sons, their own flesh and blood … their own free citizens," who "are daily subject to the same treatment as the slaves."[5] Subject to coerced labor and summary punishment, sailors were not consigned to the slave's hereditary lifelong bondage and property status. The comparison of sailor to slave worked by turning scrutiny from the brutal but legal practices of captains and masters (flogging, shackling, captivity) toward the tacitly racialized subjects of those practices (black slaves, white citizen-sailors). Correlating the acceptability of such treatment to inclusion or exclusion from both the polity and the white race, this rhetoric's tidy alignment of status and race did not comport with messier political realities. Such realities were evident to a working man like blacksmith Benjamin F. Cornell who, addressing New York's Constitutional Convention (the same one that deprives "Bartleby, the Scrivener"'s lawyer-narrator of his snug chancery business), wondered at Americans' "strange disposition to overlook the existence of the conditions of extrageneous alienage and the various stages of *quasi* citizenship intermediate between the condition of chattel slavery, and that of complete technical citizenship."[6] Such intermediate conditions were the norm in the world of the man-of-war, as *White-Jacket* so vividly reminds us. Sailors were not slaves, even if their torn flesh and the flying lash suggested otherwise. Neither were all blacks, even if race slavery had made African heritage a badge of involuntary servitude. And not all sailors were white, even if it was often rhetorically expedient to presume so. Nor were all naval seamen citizens of the nation they were required to defend.

We get a rare glimpse of this world in "A Sailor's Revenge" (Figure 4.1), an engraving from another important *White-Jacket* source, *Tales of the Ocean* (1840) by Hawser Martingale (John S. Sleeper). Drawn by John H. Manning and engraved by Alonzo Hartwell, the image serves as a sort of proleptic illustration for chapter 67 of *White-Jacket*, in which the narrator, unjustly "arraigned at the Mast," perceives that "a sudden rush against" the Captain "would infallibly pitch him headforemost into the ocean" (280). Aware that "he who so rushed must needs go over with him," White-Jacket decides "to drag Captain Claret from this earthly tribunal of his to that of Jehovah and let Him decide between us" (280). With a last-minute intercession sparing both men, Melville's whipping scene manqué recasts as fantasy Martingale's tale of revenge. Indeed, in Martingale the engraving captures the moment when the object of the onlookers' gaze changes from a spectacular punishment to an astonishing act of resistance. The image prominently features, on the far left, a black sailor whose blunt, racialized physiognomy does not gainsay his membership in the ship's company, as signaled by his slops, stance, and visual alignment with his shipmates.

Much as Manning's engraved illustration did, *White-Jacket*'s typeset words offered a material reminder to nineteenth-century readers that Jehovah's divine tribunal was not the only alternative to unjust earthly tribunals. Like fugitive slaves, testifying sailors could use print to gain a hearing from an adjudicative reading public. Just as indispensable, then, to the racially inverted tableau in which the lacerated white American seaman stands in for the enslaved African American, and the lash-wielding captain and his officers for the slaveholder and his drivers, are the onlooking sailors who replace the plantation slaves as "eye-witness[es] to the cruelty."[7] Thus *White-Jacket*'s chapter 33, with its thrice-repeated command, "*All hands witness punishment, ahoy!*" (134–35), focuses as much on the deleterious effects of "the naval summons to witness punishment" (135) as on the punishment itself. A turning point in the novel, this inaugural spectacle of violence recalls the

Figure 4.1. "A Sailor's Revenge," from John S. Sleeper, *Tales of the Ocean and Essays for the Forecastle* (1843). Reproduced by permission of The Huntington Library, San Marino, California.

notorious scene in the *Narrative of the Life of Frederick Douglass* (1845) in which the young slave watches his aunt's whipping. In *White-Jacket*, too, "this horrible exhibition" is "the first of a long series of such outrages, of which" the innocent narrator is "doomed to be a witness and a participant," culminating in chapter 67, and concluding with chapters 87 and 88, "Old Ushant at the Gangway" and "Flogging through the Fleet."[8] White-Jacket justifies his secondhand portrayal of the latter "shocking spectacle" with the claim that he is "only ... saying what many seamen have seen" (371). Attuned to the juridical rhetoric that distinguished literary "reformer" from "artist or romancer," proslavery writer William Gilmore Simms opened the *Southern Quarterly Review*'s seven-page discussion of *White-Jacket* by noting that "the author appears as a witness, giving his evidence."[9]

Such extralegal appeals proved effective: six months after *White-Jacket*'s publication, Congress abolished flogging on naval and commercial vessels. Yet, we cannot approach the novel as we would an antebellum slave narrative, as the documentary account of an individual's experience of a collective injustice that, transmuted into personal storytelling in print, effected radical political reform while contributing to the establishment of an autonomous American literary tradition. For one thing, however much we might like to attribute the swell of political outrage to *White-Jacket*'s protest against flogging, it is clear Melville was riding the wave of public opinion rather than creating it in his turbulent wake.[10] Extensive documentation has shown that key scenes, images, and characters derive less from Melville's own service than from sea narratives and nonfiction discussions of maritime law

the purpose of fiction

and discipline.[11] "Ordinary Seaman" Herman Melville may have witnessed 163 floggings aboard the *United States*, but as author of *White-Jacket* he is less a Douglass than a Harriet Beecher Stowe – who, as her *Key to Uncle Tom's Cabin* (1853) revealed, pieced together scraps from other printed materials to produce a powerful literary protest against legally sanctioned injustice and brutality in America.

Such improvisational stitching and padding is, of course, the creative act that gives Melville's fanciful exposé its title. "It was nothing more than a white duck frock, or rather shirt; which ... I folded double at the bosom ... slit there, [and] opened lengthwise – much as you would cut a leaf in the last new novel" (3), says the eponymous narrator, elaborating how "with many odds and ends of patches ... I bedarned and bequilted the inside of my jacket" (4). When the unavailability of "black paint" (78) for water-proofing frustrates his efforts to "change" the garment's "complexion" (78), White-Jacket himself becomes "a universal absorber" (4). If Melville's "tailoring trope ... tip[s] us off to" the novel's "compositional method," its title, commemorating his narrator's failure to turn white into black, hints at that method's inner workings.[12] Selectively bleaching and black-ening characters from his seafaring sources, Melville perverted reformers' penchant for racial reversal, subtly unsettling the logics that held "sea-citizens" (145) and slaves – as well as the United States and Britain – in political counterpoise. Surface "complexion" often obscures underlying complexities, whether the object of scrutiny is a jacket, a "novel," or a flogging scene. (Evoking a book's newly cut pages, the eponymous jacket, as "a shirt all cut to pieces" [224], also recalls the effects of the lash.) A year before *Moby-Dick*'s musings on whiteness' uncanny "essence," Melville's *White-Jacket* offered its own "dumb blankness, full of meaning" (*MD* 195).

Introducing such contradictory figures as the free black war hero and the enslaved naval sailor, *White-Jacket* does not so much resolve the competing rhetorical claims of the antislavery and sailors' rights movements as alert us to how the monochrome of racial thought could block out the full spectrum of what the narrator, along with Dana's Captain Thompson and blacksmith Benjamin Cornell, refers to as "condition" in America. If Ishmael's status as a white male citizen (however down at the heels) ensured that readers, then and now, would read his question regarding "Who aint a slave" as a flip, rhetorical one, the story told by his predecessor, White-Jacket, would be structured by the earnest effort to "tell," in the dual sense of discerning as well as recounting, just "who" wasn't a slave, especially if some seamen could not claim the full citizenship that gave Ishmael's query and contempo-rary calls for maritime reform their implicit force.

White-Jacket's gradual discovery of who is and is not a slave supplies Melville's novel with the plot that, since its publication, it has been accused of lacking. To piece together the sequence of interrelated events and characters that form this plot requires, again, that we look beyond "complexion." Such an approach departs from analyses that situate Melville's few depictions of slavery within a broader ethnographic treatment of racial difference – from Typee Valley, to the *San Dominick*'s decks, to the Spouter-Inn's "prodigious bed" (*MD* 19) – so as to ascertain the globe-trotting New York sailor-turned-author's investments in discourses of whiteness, blackness, or imperialism.[13] For, with almost nothing to say about human diversity, *White-Jacket* speaks volumes about slavery's centrality to nineteenth-century understandings of political membership. Recognizing this, historicist critics tend to read Melville's invocations of slaves and slavery as analogies for, even allegories of, America's new forms of exploited labor (such as that endured by the sailor, the factory operative, and even the hack writer), or its equally novel "total" institutions (like the asylum, the prison, and the factory).[14] Such analogical thinking is what made the "trope of the sailor-slave" so persuasive in seamen's rights rhetoric.[15] But when we scrutinize Melville's selection, coloring, and tailoring of the literary "odds and ends" he stuffed into *White-Jacket*, we see that the novel ultimately rejects the structure of analogy in favor of what the narrator himself comes to perceive as a "scale" of conditions, where one finds not analogs, but gradations. So doing, *White-Jacket* not only complicates the facile racial reversals upon which seaman's rights rhetoric sometimes turned, but also calls into question nationalist claims to an exceptional American liberty defined by its opposition to British despotism.

Not coincidentally, the novel's first sustained instance of racial reversal also introduces the phrase – "liberties of the world" – which will subsequently serve first to oppose exceptional American republicanism to outmoded British tyranny, and then to contrast the "fortunate" black slave to brutalized white citizen-sailors. One of the few characters traceable to the muster roll of Melville's own man-of-war, Jack Chase is the Briton who, as "a stickler for the Rights of Man, and the liberties of the world," deserts the frigate "to draw a partisan blade in the civil commotions of Peru; and befriend ... the cause of the Right" (17). Melville's Chase is apprehended when the *Neversink* anchors "alongside of a Peruvian sloop of war," and he is "descried, promenading the Quarter-deck" by Captain Claret, who "stared at him ... through his spy-glass" before demanding his return (18). The *United States*' log documents the diplomacy that resulted in London-born John J. Chase being "received on board a deserter" with the Peruvian admiral's request for his pardon.[16]

Recounting the capture of the noncommissioned "noble First Captain of the Top" (*WJ* 13) by his American superior, the anecdote hums with national and class tensions. But beyond the assertion that "a finer specimen of the island race of Englishmen" than Jack Chase could not be found (14), the scene's racial echoes are muffled by *White-Jacket*'s dense padding. For if Melville accurately records his shipmate's military adventure, the pivotal recognition scene originates in one of the novel's main sources, *Thirty Years from Home, or a Voice from the Main Deck, Being the Experiences of Samuel Leech Who Was for Six Years in the British and American Navies* (1843). The Scottish Leech breaks from his own experiences on H.M.S. *Macedonian* to tell the story of "a colored man whose name was Nugent," and who, like Melville's Chase, "ran away" from the man-of-war only to "be taken in a rather curious manner." One day, recounts Leech, as the officers "walked the deck with their spy-glasses," one is startled to descry "the person of the fugitive Nugent on the deck of an American vessel! Upon this, a boat was despatched, which soon returned with the crest-fallen deserter, who was unceremoniously thrown into irons" – although he too "escaped a flogging."[17]

An examination of Melville's revision of his source text reveals how *White-Jacket*'s densely compacted composition belies its surface appearance. Even before we take Nugent into account, Jack Chase's story doubles back on itself. Initially, the anecdote seems to offer a cautionary tale about what Melville (borrowing now from McNally's *Evils and Abuses*) will deplore as the "lack of patriotism" (380) among the disproportionate number of foreign seamen who enlist on American naval vessels "against the law" (378). Such misgivings seem borne out in a nationalist race against H.M.S. *St. George*, when White-Jacket suspects that the "Briton [Chase] ... perhaps favored the Englishman more than the Neversink" (270). But Chase's commitment to core American values is vindicated by his decision actively to fight for "the cause of the Right" – defending Peru's independence – rather than fulfill his peacetime duty to the United States (which, after all, "has now existed as a nation upward of seventy years" [303]). Considering how Melville filled out the historical Chase's adventures with Nugent's experiences, it is tempting to find a parallel in Chase's abortive but principled defection to "the cause of the Right" and the black British man-of-war's man's unsuccessful desertion to the "vessel" of a nation also known as "a stickler for the Rights of Man, and the liberties of the world."

This reading breaks down, however, when we realize that Melville's decision to model the fictional Chase, in part, on "a colored man" troubles any easy association of the United States with "Rights" and "liberties." Melville encountered Nugent's story in the midst of a longer passage that he would reserve for the end of his novel, stitching it into the same "Manning of the Navies" chapter that laments the oppressive labor conditions that result in mercenary foreigners protecting American interests at sea. The passage seeks to strike through the mask of the "Happy Jack" stereotype by rebutting the false impressions arising from "the revelry of the crew."[18] Abused seamen sing and dance, Leech explains, "on the same principle as the slave population in the South, to drown in sensual gratification the voice of misery that groans in the inner man – … speaking of the indignity offered to its high nature by the chain that eats beyond the flesh – discoursing of the rights of man, of liberty on the free hills of a happier clime" (74). Here the sailor-slave dyad does not so much flatten out differences in condition as identify common strategies for preserving a shared human dignity. It is at this point that the free black sailor Nugent is introduced as one of those uncommon "individuals" whose "spirits … writhe under the gripe of merciless authority" rather than enduring "the thraldom of the hated service to which they are bound" through "forced merriment" (74–75). Far from "bearing the ark of the liberties of the world," the United States is aligned in Melville's source text with the undemocratic British Navy in denying that very liberty to a select portion of its "population." If Nugent had successfully deserted the British man-of-war for the U.S. vessel, his symbolic bid for republican freedom would have been countered by what was becoming an equally exceptional American racism.

Inaudible in chapter 5's portrayal of Chase, the discordant racial strains of Nugent's story burst out in chapter 90, when Melville offers his own opposition of "Happy Jacks" (384) to "fine tars" (385) like Chase and Old Ushant, the sailor scourged and shackled for refusing to shave his beard. Such a "noble man-of-war's man," observes White-Jacket, was for "most sea-officers" as "unendurable, as an erect, lofty-minded African would be to some slave-driving planter" (385). With this lingering textual echo prompting us to look beneath mere "complexion," we see that the comparison of white sailor to enslaved African works here not by analogy, but by a stadial progression linking "the slave population of the South" first to Nugent (the seafaring "colored man" "thrown into irons" on the British man-of-war) and Chase (his English counterpart on the U.S. frigate), and finally to Old Ushant (the citizen arbitrarily flogged and imprisoned by his fellow Americans).

How, then, to reconcile this nuanced appreciation for the complex interplay of race, class, and national identity with *White-Jacket*'s participation in the nomenclature of racial caricature? For if, in his emphasis on Jack Chase's personal uniqueness ("even to a mole on his cheek" [18]), Melville registers the individuality that enables the spyglass identification of Chase's dignified "colored" original, the novel's black characters nevertheless bear names like Guinea, Tawney, Old Coffee, Sunshine, Rose-Water, and May-day. When we consider, moreover, that the most tired of these cognomens, "Tawney" (L 23), had been affixed by a twenty-year-old Herman to a fraternal letter written in "black" dialect, White-Jacket's adoption of such demeaning "poetical appellations" (58) betrays – at best – an authorial failure to take race seriously.

Significantly, however, White-Jacket's second sustained exercise in racial reversal plays out in a character "who went by the name of Tawney" (311) and who, far from embodying hackneyed expectations about African American character, upsets conventional Jacksonian alignments of race and nation, particularly those that would oppose the black slave to the white citizen-sailor. Having whitened Leech's Nugent into White-Jacket's Jack Chase, Melville now has the "old negro" Tawney (311) stand in for the presumptively white "Americans ... compelled ... to fight against their own countrymen" in Thirty Years from Home.[19] (Before and during the War of 1812, British officials "pressed" English-speaking sailors, regardless of nationality, into naval service for the crown.) Acceding to White-Jacket's untiring efforts "to draw out the oldest Tritons into narratives of the war-service they had seen" (311), Tawney recounts the historic battle that culminates in the Macedonian's surrender to their frigate. Melville's source text sympathetically recalls how one of "the Americans" offered himself up "to the captain, as a prisoner, frankly declaring his objections to fight," only to be compelled to his station.[20] In White-Jacket, the Americans' similarly unsuccessful request "to remain neutral during the conflict" yields a scene in which "side by side with his country's foes, Tawney and his companions toiled at the guns" (312). Among the "many ... stories" the "negro had ... to tell of this fight" (315) is one that attributes the American victory not to an obvious "superiority in guns" (313) but to sabotage by the Macedonian's recalcitrant, captive gunners. Citing further instances of "this maiming of the guns" by Britons on their own ships, White-Jacket asks, "is it to be wondered at that impressed English seamen have not scrupled, in time of war, to cripple the arm that has enslaved them?" (313).

At first, White-Jacket's musings on Britons' class-based acts of sabotage threaten to obscure Melville's remarkable positioning of the "old negro" as the representative American tar whose quiet heroism saves the day through a daring act of patriotic resistance. But just as, elsewhere in White-Jacket, ideas like "liberty" and "the rights of man" cannot be ripped out of one fabric (survival strategies of "the slave population of the South") and seamlessly patched into another (nationalist struggles for sovereignty), the political tyranny suffered by British seamen cannot be figured as slavery without exposing some frayed ends. *White-Jacket's* idiomatic elision of political despotism and "enslave[ment]" alerts us to how this second instance of racial reversal once again preempts the United States' definitive association with republican liberty in opposition to British tyranny. The political significance of Melville's decision to have the insistently racialized Tawney embody the valiant American patriots becomes apparent when we consider Melville's embellishment of his source's spare phrasing. In *White-Jacket*, "Tawney and his countrymen ... respectfully accosted the captain," insisting that "it was a most bitter thing to lift their hands against the flag of that country which harbored the mothers that bore them" (312). Placing this newly sentimentalized protest in the mouths of "Tawney and his countrymen," Melville offers the ironic reminder that, if the United States harbored the mothers of tawny-colored children, it also authorized their sexual and reproductive exploitation, which under the legal doctrine of *partus sequitur ventrem* perpetuated slavery in America.[21] For the millions of Tawney's "countrymen" who share his color, motherhood represented not the affective bonds of national identity but the literal bondage of race slavery.

On the *Neversink*, however, it is not Tawney but Guinea who is the "hereditary ... bondman" (378–79). Appropriately, then, it is in the portrayal of Guinea that Melville most decisively, albeit subtly, rejects the rhetorical conflation of (white) citizen-sailor and (black) slave. "A Virginian slave regularly shipped as a seaman, his owner receiving his wages," Guinea, White-Jacket explains, "belonged to the Purser, who was a southern gentleman" (378–79). Guinea's flesh and blood counterpart was Robert Lucas, whom the historical purser Edward Fitzgerald likewise "enlisted ... in the teeth of a law of Congress expressly prohibiting slaves in the Navy" (378). The legal fallout occurred upon the frigate's return to the United States. Having embarked from slaveholding Virginia, the *United States* returned to abolitionist Massachusetts. Although, as Garrison's Boston-based *Liberator* reported in the fall of 1844, the enslaved Lucas had been "received ... on board" the frigate "by written consent of the secretary of the navy," upon the ship's arrival in Boston harbor, "the writ of habeas corpus was served upon Mr. Fitzgerald" for Lucas, who was taken into protective custody.[22] White-Jacket's cryptic acknowledgment of the fictional purser's good-hearted "treatment of Guinea, under circumstances peculiarly calculated to stir up the resentment of a slave-owner" (379), would seem, then, to allude to *Commonwealth v. Fitzgerald, in the Matter of Lucas*, decided by Melville's family friend and future father-in-law, Massachusetts Supreme Court Chief Justice Lemuel Shaw. Less concerned than White-Jacket with the 1837 law prohibiting the naval enlistment of slaves, Shaw took up the more urgent legal – and political – issue of how Lucas's enslaved status was affected by the frigate's departure from the slave state of Virginia and return to the nominally "free" state of Massachusetts. Because Lucas had not run away but sailed through "a voluntary act" of his master, Shaw ruled him legally emancipated.[23] These events form the murky backdrop for *White-Jacket*'s starkest invocation of the trope of the sailor-slave.

Leading up to his introduction of Guinea, White-Jacket sardonically notes that the 1837 "law, indirectly, means black slaves, nothing being said concerning white ones" (378), adding that, "in view of what most armed vessels actually are at present, the American Navy is not altogether an inappropriate place for hereditary bondmen." Yet even as his narrator adopts the strategic identification of (and thus opposition between) oppressed seamen and enslaved African Americans, Melville marks the important difference between political rhetoric and legal reality: as commoditized "hereditary bondmen," and not merely coerced and brutalized laborers, only blacks are "slaves" under American law.

In what at first appears – but ultimately refuses – to be a third scene of racial reversal, White-Jacket claims: "Never did I feel my condition as a man-of-war's man so keenly as when seeing this Guinea freely circulating about the decks in citizen's clothes, and, through the influence of his master, almost entirely exempted from the disciplinary degradation of the Caucasian crew" (379). Even more than the "citizen's clothes" that replace the sailor's slops, Guinea is set apart from the crew by his approved absence from the flogging scene – as both victim and witness. Other than those confined to "the sick-bay" Guinea "was the only person on board ... who was exempted from being present at the administering of the scourge" (379).

Guinea's exemption from the command for "all hands ... to witness punishment" is what finally, in *White-Jacket*, demonstrates that similar treatment is irreducible to equivalent status. As the iconography of flogging illustrates, "the leading idea" of the punishment, whether staged on the plantation or in the gangway, "is to strike terror into the beholders" (371). This is the lesson White-Jacket learns when he himself is arraigned at the mast. Not coincidentally, the epiphany comes just after chapter 66's account of Rose-Water and May-day being unjustly punished for the unauthorized fighting that ensues from their participation in the brutal sport of "*Head-bumping*, as patronized by Captain Claret" (275). A reminder that it is not "the Caucasian crew" alone who are subjected to "disciplinary degradation," the chapter highlights how the captain's racism ("whites will not answer" [275]) only intensifies his despotic power over these black seamen under the Articles of War. The well-worn closing comparison of captain to "master" and sailor to "slave" gains salience from the fact that, in this case, "the negroes were flogged" (276).

Initially, however, White-Jacket finds that the "scourging of poor Rose-Water" (277) reinforces rather than collapses the racial and political binaries that assigned rhetorical priority to the plight of the brutalized, exploited seaman as free white citizen. After all, the mulatto's punishment would appear to restore the racial order that is inverted in *White-Jacket*'s inaugural flogging scene. In chapter 33, the whipping of four seamen culminates in that of Peter, a paragon of the citizen-sailor, who "often boasted that he had never been degraded at the gangway" (138). Painful as it is to "see a human being, stripped like a slave; scourged worse than a hound," White-Jacket's fascination with the victim's race careens between sentimental sympathy and gothic horror (138). Recalling how just "the day before," Peter's "cheek had worn its usual red," White-Jacket observes that "now no ghost was whiter," as the robust young seaman was "secured to the gratings, and the shudderings and creepings of his dazzlingly white back were revealed" (138). When, one-third of the novel later, the narrator counts himself "with five hundred others" as "one of the compelled spectators" of Rose-Water's flogging, his preoccupation with complexion transforms horrified identification into comforting alienation: "Poor mulatto!" White-Jacket apostrophizes, "one of an oppressed race, they degrade you like a hound. Thank God! I am a white" (277). But this paternalist reverie is disrupted by the accumulated memories of traumatized witnessing, which in turn lead White-Jacket to reflect on the spectrum of "condition" in antebellum America: "Yet I had seen whites also scourged; for black or white, all my shipmates were liable to that. Still, there is something in us, somehow, that, in the most degraded condition, we snatch at a chance to deceive ourselves into a fancied superiority to others, whom we suppose lower in the scale than ourselves" (277). Resisting the pedagogy of "compelled spectator[ship]," White-Jacket tries to misread Rose-Water's flogging as an exhibition of racial, rather than class, control. Only the lingering afterimage of previous floggings of shipmates, "black or white," affirmed by his own sudden appearance before "the dread tribunal of the frigate" (279), schools him in his "degraded condition." As Melville's repeated use of the word suggests, to be degraded is not to be ejected from one category (citizen) into its opposite (slave), but to be lowered by degrees along the scale of condition between the two.

It is through such penal spectacles, *White-Jacket* insists, that law differentially constitutes its subjects, from captains and masters, to seamen and slaves. Every sailor in the navy "knows that the same law which impels" the "entire ship's company" to "*witness punishment*" is "the same law by which the culprits of the day must suffer; that by that very law he is also liable ... to be judged and condemned" (135). For the common seaman, "the inevitableness of his own presence at the scene; the strong arm that drags him in view of the scourge ... forcing upon his loathing eye and soul the sufferings and groans of ... men of his own type and badge – all this conveys a terrible hint of the omnipotent authority under which he lives" (135). Proscribed from the ship's company and immune to the Articles of War, Guinea, a hereditary bondman "lower in the scale" than either the "black or white" crew members, cannot learn the same penal lesson from watching a sailor's flogging as that of one of his "own type and badge." Nor, as White-Jacket's initial response to Rose-Water's scourging indicates, could the slave's punishment before the ship's crew serve any disciplinary function: producing a reassuring sense of pity (or scorn) for the "oppressed race," it cannot inculcate the sailor with a terrified realization "of the omnipotent authority under which he lives." In *White-Jacket*, the very flogging scene that in antebellum America had come to identify sailor with slave becomes the site of their dissociation.

This dissociation is confirmed when the *Neversink* finally reaches the national "home" (*WJ* 159) toward which it and the novel have, from the outset, been headed. Faced with the flogging that epitomizes how the white citizen-sailor is "cast into an American frigate shorn of all rights and defences" (301), White-Jacket reflects that "in a few weeks ... I would be a freeman" (279). Not so Guinea, we must presume, notwithstanding – or perhaps because of – *White-Jacket*'s vague allusion to Robert Lucas's legal emancipation upon the frigate's "arrival home" (379). Even if Melville had wanted to pad out *White Jacket* by filling in the obscure "circumstances" of the legal proceeding, the decision to return the *Neversink* to "the innermost harbor of Norfolk" (395) – the *United States'* point of *embarkation* – rather than following its original into Boston harbor, deprives him of his material. The fictional Guinea thus lives out the grim counterfactual that Chief Justice Shaw envisioned as the alternative to Lucas's manumission: "though his service was valid in Virginia and *would have continued had the vessel returned to a port in that State*," Shaw explained, "it terminated on entering a State where slavery did not exist" (emphasis added). With the *Neversink*'s arrival in Virginia, Guinea alone is not at liberty and cannot join "the Retreat of the Five Hundred inland" (396). It may well be that, as White-Jacket maintains, cribbing from Nathaniel Ames's *A Mariner's Sketches* (1831), "the Lieutenants from the Southern States, the descendants of the old Virginians, are much less severe, and much more gentle and gentlemanly in command, than the Northern officers, as a class" (141). But, like the "Southern gentleman" who has become the latest of Guinea's "gentle masters," those same lieutenants – or pursers – would have retained "command" over their enslaved human property upon return to a slave state jurisdiction like Virginia.

By having his narrator scrupulously "adhere to my one proper object, *the world in a man-of-war*" (160) during its "Homeward-Bound" journey (6), Melville sharpens the contrast between the sailors' status as the ship's "*people*" (28) under the Articles of War and as "we the people" (399) under the Constitution. But by having his frigate return to "our Yankee nation" (388) via the "Capes of Virginia" (391) rather than what Leech's "slave population in the South" imagines – and *Commonwealth v. Fitzgerald* affirmed – to be "the free hills of a happier clime," he also heightens the disparity between the ship's one identified black slave and the rest of the crew. With no hope of emancipation, the hereditary bondman occupies a position markedly different from aliens and quasi-citizens like Chase and Tawney who, upon discharge, "scattered broadcast over the land" (396) – to say nothing of the "man-of-war's-men at home" who, as "free and independent citizens … in the public streets," regain political equality with "those who may have outrageously abused them" (190). Returning the *Neversink* to Norfolk, *White-Jacket* makes it easy to tell just who is – and aint – a slave.

Not insignificantly, White-Jacket himself returns home disencumbered of his burdensome namesake. "The Last of the Jacket" comes in chapter 92, when the narrator, having fallen overboard, cuts himself out of the waterlogged coat, only to have his shipmates mistake it for a "white shark" (394) and harpoon it "out of sight." Finally, White-Jacket is "free" (394) of the "sponge"-like (4) garment which, from the beginning, has imperiled him with its capacity to hold much more than water. Careful to sew a pair of "capacious pockets on the outside … to slip books into when suddenly started from my studies," White-Jacket initially provides "several unseen recesses" within, ensuring that the jacket, "like a confidential writing-desk, abounded in snug little out-of-the-way lairs and hiding-places" (36). Confusing as this jumble of figures may be – Is the jacket a sponge or a writing desk? Does it take the world in or keep it out? – Melville's contradictory portrayal of the titular garment represents *White-Jacket*'s composition with remarkable precision. In a cultural climate saturated with the propaganda of the antislavery and labor movements, the novel absorbs antebellum America's pervasive reform rhetoric; indeed, *White-Jacket* is sufficiently capacious to include not just books which, like *Two Years before the Mast*, we can see from "the outside" to have formed part of Melville's "studies," but also the countless passages, characters, and events that appear to emerge from the author's "writing desk," but in fact derive from texts hidden in its "recesses." Tellingly, however, we learn "Of the Pockets That Were in the Jacket" in the same chapter that the narrator, who has already compared his fabrication to "the last new novel," decides to seal the compartments and render their contents inaccessible. Given the narrator's regret for having inadvertently revealed to his shipmates (and readers?) that "the white jacket" was, in fact, "a store-house" (37), the climactic sinking of the jacket suggests an authorial desire to be similarly "free" of the layers of textuality *White-Jacket* at once comprises and conceals.

Indifferent to such desires, generations of scholars have probed *White-Jacket*'s hiding places and confirmed that it is "soaked" (4) through with others' words and images. Until now, however, critics have not examined how, by attributing the jacket's remarkable absorbency to a failed effort to turn white into black, the novel highlights the strategy of racial reversal that, in very different ways, characterized labor reformers' appropriation of abolitionist propaganda and structured Melville's own borrowings from maritime texts. In contrast to sources that beg the question "Who aint a slave?" by placing normatively white laborers in the position of enslaved African Americans, Melville in *White-Jacket* redeploys the strategy of racial reversal to demonstrate how the question's central term scuttled any claim to an American liberty defined in opposition to political tyranny.

NOTES

1 Frederick Douglass, *Autobiographies*, ed. Henry Louis Gates, Jr. (New York: Library of America, 1994), 106.

2 Ibid., 367.

3 Keith Huntress, "'Guinea' of *White-Jacket* and Chief Justice Shaw," *American Literature* 43.4 (January 1972): 639.

4 Paul A. Gilje, *Liberty on the Waterfront: American Maritime Culture in the Age of Revolution* (Philadelphia: University of Pennsylvania Press, 2004), 234.

5 William McNally, *Evils and Abuses of the Naval and Merchant Service, Exposed* (Boston, 1839), 129, 128.

6 William G. Bishop and William H. Attree, *Report of the Debates and Proceedings of the Convention for the Revision of the Constitution of the State of New-York* (Albany, 1846), 1047.

7 Douglass, *Autobiographies*, 39.

8 Bishop and Attree, *Report*, 51.

9 [William Gilmore Simms,] "Critical Notices," *Southern Quarterly Review* 1.2 (July 1850): 514.

10 Charles R. Anderson, *Melville in the South Seas* (New York: Columbia University Press, 1939), 431.

11 Anderson, *Melville*; Howard P. Vincent, *The Tailoring of Melville's* White-Jacket (Evanston, IL: Northwestern University Press, 1970).

12 Vincent, *Tailoring*, 198.

13 Samuel Otter, *Melville's Anatomies* (Berkeley: University of California Press, 1999); Christopher Freeburg, *Melville and the Idea of Blackness: Race and Imperialism in Nineteenth-Century America* (Cambridge: Cambridge University Press, 2012).

14 Carolyn Karcher, *Shadow over the Promised Land: Slavery, Race, and Violence in Melville's America* (Baton Rouge: Louisiana State University Press, 1980); Wai-Chee Dimock, *Empire for Liberty: Melville and the Poetics of Individualism* (Princeton, NJ: Princeton University Press, 1989); Robert S. Levine, *Conspiracy and Romance: Studies in Brockden Brown, Cooper, Hawthorne, and Melville* (Cambridge: Cambridge University Press, 1989).

15 Levine, *Conspiracy and Romance*, 176.

16 Quoted in Vincent, *Tailoring*, 37.

17 Samuel Leech, *Thirty Years from Home* (Boston, 1843), 75–76.

18 Ibid., 74.

19 Ibid., 127.

20 Ibid., 127–28.

21 "The offspring follow the condition of the mother. This is the law in the case of slaves and animals ... but with regard to freemen, children follow the condition of the father." John Bouvier, *Law Dictionary*, rev. 6th ed. (Philadelphia, 1856), s.v. "maxim."

22 "Important Decision," *Liberator*, October 18, 1844.

23 Ibid.

5

SAMUEL OTTER

Reading *Moby-Dick*

Despite the book's length and digressiveness, the plot of *Moby-Dick* has the concentration Aristotle recommends in the *Poetics* for an effective tragedy. Melville's story can be abstracted so that mere summary conveys its force: a young man, who asks to be called Ishmael, goes to sea to find himself, befriends the Polynesian harpooneer Queequeg, and encounters a captain obsessed with killing Moby Dick, the white whale who severed his leg in an earlier encounter. Captain Ahab lures his crew, with the exception of his reluctant chief mate Starbuck, into that quest, which results in the death of all except the young sailor, who writes the story in retrospect and to comprehend his experience. It is a tale of yearning, obsession, wreckage, and deliverance, and the archetypal captain and white whale and their inexorable fates have become part of world culture.

Whether in the mode of tragedy, comedy, or satire (and Melville mixes his genres), the outline of *Moby-Dick* is potent for those who have never read the book. But *Moby-Dick* contains much more than its plot. Its narrative is part of elaborate verbal patterns including etymology, philosophy, anatomy, cetology, theology, cartography, allegory, drama, and poetry. Some publishers have brought out editions of *Moby-Dick* that strip away what they consider its excrescences, resulting in a much slimmer volume. (For a recent example, see Orion Press's 2007 *Moby-Dick in Half the Time* and Damion Searls's 2009 rejoinder titled "; or *The Whale*."[1]) The gap between plot and pages raises questions about the form of *Moby-Dick* and, more broadly, about what we mean by "form." Raymond Williams points to the complications of the term, which historically has been used to refer to "a visible or outward shape, with a strong sense of the physical body" and also "an essential shaping principle, making indeterminate material into a determinate or specific being or thing."[2] In *Moby-Dick*, Melville examines the relationships between shape and principle, part and whole, and substance and abstraction, embodying them in both whale and book. *Moby-Dick* is distinguished by an elaborate reflexivity (and, as we shall see, a publishing history) that ties its meanings to its materiality. To read *Moby-Dick* is to consider what kind of a book it is, the magnitude of details, the weight of scholarship, the difference editors make, how plot relates to other trajectories, and a range of formal possibilities, including formlessness.

Ishmael, as narrator, draws out the analogy between books and whales in chapter 32, "Cetology," where, in response to what he views as the inadequacies of previous systems of classification, he jocularly proposes dividing whales according to magnitude and proportion into three categories based on book formats – Folio, Octavo, and Duodecimo – each of which contains several "chapters." As is often the case in *Moby-Dick*, the jokes contain jokes. This system, purporting to clarify the ambiguities in whale classification, is not only analogical, rather than empirical, but based on nomenclature that itself had become a semblance of an approximation.

In the hand-press period, until the early nineteenth century and the development of machine paper and printing, terms such as *folio*, *octavo*, and *duodecimo* referred to bibliographical format, to the relationship between the size of the original sheets of handmade paper used in printing a book and the size of the individual leaves that resulted from folding and assembling the whole sheets into a group of leaves or gatherings. When the original sheets of printed paper were folded twice to form gatherings of four pages, the result was called a *folio*, with each book page one-half the size of the whole sheet; when the original sheets were folded three times to form gatherings of eight leaves or sixteen pages each, the result was called an *octavo*, one-eighth the size of the original; when the sheets were folded into thirds and then in half twice the other way, the result was called a *duodecimo*, one-twelfth the size of the original sheet. The size of the resulting books was relative to the size of the original sheet of paper, rather than the product of a fixed measurement.

In the modern-press period, paper was supplied not in sheets but in larger or smaller machine-made pieces and books lost their bibliographical format, since there was no longer a ratio between the size of the original handmade sheet of paper and the size of the individual leaf. The terms *folio*, *octavo*, and *duodecimo* were retained to loosely designate relative size. Thus Ishmael seeks to resolve the difficulties of whale classification by introducing a system, which he confesses (and celebrates) is, like *Moby-Dick*, "but the draught of a draught" (145). Whales are defined like books, but Ishmael's bibliographical terms had become merely impressionistic by the middle of the nineteenth century. In a note, he explains that he omitted the term *quarto* because the folded pages of these volumes, unlike octavos, do not preserve the shape of folios (141). In another joke, the absence of quartos leaves out the relative size we might associate with the original

1851 publication of *Moby-Dick*, in either its one-volume American or three-volume British edition.

Ishmael's system invokes the history of printing, signals the importance of magnitude and proportion as formal categories, joins the interpretation of Moby Dick and *Moby-Dick* (as does the hyphen that distinguishes name from title), and returns us to the book we are reading. Punning, Ishmael encourages his readers "to take hold of the whales bodily, in their entire liberal volume" (140). Later, at the end of a chapter about whale physiognomy, he conveys skepticism about the possibility of deciphering the faces of whales or humans and urges those contemplating the sperm whale's brow: "Read it if you can" (347). Readers have found *Moby-Dick* a challenging book, and the narrator, anticipating such reactions, redundantly offers a challenge.

The "Cetology" chapter is not about the impossibility or absurdity of definitions and classifications but about their complexities and histories. This chapter and so many of the other chapters in *Moby-Dick* are about their topics and also about the reading and writing of the book, in distinctively involuted and material ways, recalling Laurence Sterne's eighteenth-century *The Life and Opinions of Tristram Shandy,* at least part of which Melville read in 1849. Ishmael's digression on whales in "Cetology" (the first of many) returns us to the book and suggests the ways that attending to what is on its pages involves the meanings, etymologies, circulations, and physical appearance of words. The insistent reflexivity of *Moby-Dick*, flouting the choice between form and history sometimes advanced by literary scholars, turns back on words and shows how their production is individual, social, historical, and technological.

"And some certain significance lurks in all things, else all things are of little worth, and the round world itself but an empty cipher, except to sell by the cartload, as they do hills about Boston, to fill up some morass in the Milky Way" (430), Melville has Ishmael write at the beginning of chapter 99, "The Doubloon," a meditation on perspective. Here Ishmael seems to embrace Ahab's compulsive approach to understanding the figures stamped on the Ecuadoran coin nailed to the main mast as a goad and reward for the man who first sights Moby Dick. Ishmael's pronouncement is marked by hesitancy (the specific but not explicit "certain" joined to the unspecific "some" and qualified by "else," an adverb that raises the specter of meaninglessness); intensity (the comprehensive "in all things" also appears, parenthetically, in chapter 60, "The Line," as "an aesthetics in all things" [278]); irony (imagining the world razed to fill a swamp in the Milky Way, converting quality into quantity and shoveling the mundane into the cosmic); and anxiety (that which "lurks," hidden or latent or barely discernible, may wait in ambush or present a threat). Such combinations stoke exegesis in and of the book.

One way to meet the challenge of lurking significance in *Moby-Dick* is to read the text alongside the volumes of indispensable scholarship it has generated. *Moby-Dick* was published in significantly different editions in England and America in 1851, and so readers and critics need to know which text they are talking about. Melville arranged to have his manuscript typeset for publication by Harper & Brothers in New York. The American edition, published in November 1851 under the title *Moby-Dick; or, the Whale*, was printed from these stereotyped plates. The English edition, titled *The Whale*, published by Richard Bentley in London in October 1851, was reset from the revised proof sheets taken from the plates used for the American edition. Corrections and revisions were made by Melville and also by his British publisher. The English edition is approximately two thousand words shorter than the American (many passages dealing with religion, politics, and sex were altered or removed), omits the epilogue in which Ishmael describes having survived the destruction of the ship and its crew, and places the sections "Etymology" and "Extracts," which precede the narrative in the American edition, in an appendix. In the absence of Melville's manuscript or the proof sheets he sent to England, scholars have speculated on the agents behind these changes and their effects.

The Northwestern University Press and Newberry Library *Moby-Dick* (1988), edited by Harrison Hayford, Hershel Parker, and G. Thomas Tanselle, provides a critical text in which the editors have sought to determine Melville's final intentions. They retain passages deleted from the British edition but also adopt some of the changes made and correct what they determine to be mistakes introduced by the author or his transcribers. The Northwestern-Newberry volume includes extended discussion of the adopted readings and a full list of variants between the English and American editions. Using this supplementary material, readers can identify the differences between the two original editions and also the adjustments introduced by the modern editors. The Norton Critical Edition (2nd ed., 2002), edited by Hershel Parker and Harrison Hayford, uses the Northwestern-Newberry critical text. The Longman Critical Edition (2007), edited by John Bryant and Haskell Springer, provides a reading text of the American edition on whose pages, through highlighting and notes, the differences between the two original editions are made visible. Readers of *Moby-Dick* need to consider how editors' perspectives and selections have determined the book they hold in their hands or view on their screens.

The Norton and Longman editions contain a wealth of supplementary material, including documents having to do with whaling and details about

Melville's literary, philosophical, and historical allusions. The Hendricks House edition (1951), prepared by Luther Mansfield and Howard Vincent, offers more than 240 pages of notes. For navigating the copious criticism on *Moby-Dick*, a variety of resources are available, including anthologies edited by Brodhead, Bryant, Higgins and Parker, Jehlen, Kelley, and Parker and Hayford listed in the "Collections of Critical Essays" section of the bibliography in this *Companion*.

Many critics have tended to emphasize the dialectic that joins or separates Ishmael and Ahab and the book's impressive set pieces: Ishmael and Queequeg in bed at the Spouter-Inn (chapters 3 and 4), Ahab vowing to strike through the pasteboard masks (chapter 36), Ishmael speculating on Ahab's and his own obsession with Moby Dick (chapters 41 and 42), Ishmael separating himself from the infernal quest (chapter 96), the captain and crew projecting meanings onto the doubloon (chapter 99), Ahab shedding a tear in the Pacific Ocean (chapter 132), and the final encounter with Moby Dick (chapters 133–35). Yet to read *Moby-Dick* is to be presented not only with plot, characters, and set pieces but also with an array of other information in a variety of formats, whose relationships and trajectories need to be considered. In chapter 44, "The Chart," the narrator examines Captain Ahab's methods of pursuing Moby Dick, while the author, invoking recent efforts to map and predict the movements of whales, reflects on interpreting *Moby-Dick*. To read this chapter is to become involved in textual, contextual, and critical histories and with images as well as words. The term *plot* comes under scrutiny, and a spectacular final scene is presented, whose diction and intensities will recur in unexpected ways. Melville has his narrator write that this chapter "in its earlier part, is as important a one as will be found in this volume" (203).[3]

At the beginning of "The Chart," for the first time in the book, Ishmael describes a scene below the decks of the *Pequod*, a scene that, given maritime social hierarchies and spatial discriminations, he could not have witnessed himself. It is a chapter, one of several, in which Ishmael as narrator exceeds his knowledge (sometimes, as in the chapters given in dramatic format, he seems to recede to a vanishing point) and questions arise about whether the book is narrated by a single, stable persona. Melville signals both the unprecedented access ("The Chart" follows a brief chapter, "Hark!," in which sailors discuss strange noises under the hatches) and the speculative register of the chapter:

> Had you followed Captain Ahab down into his cabin after the squall that took place on the night succeeding that wild ratification of his purpose with his crew, you would have seen him go to a locker in the transom, and bringing out a large wrinkled roll of yellowish sea charts, spread them before him on

his screwed-down table. Then seating himself before it, you would have seen him intently study the various lines and shadings which there met his eye; and with slow but steady pencil trace additional courses over spaces that before were blank. At intervals, he would refer to piles of old log-books beside him, wherein were set down the seasons and places in which, on various former voyages of various ships, sperm whales had been captured or seen. (198)

In what "might seem an absurdly hopeless task" (199), Ahab seeks to predict where Moby Dick will be, and when, in order to confront and kill him. Part of the purpose of the chapter, and part of the reason Melville signals its importance, is that he intends to demonstrate the plausibility of his narrative. He strives to convince readers that the search for one whale in the world's oceans is grounded in actual data and practice. Ahab uses stagecraft and rhetoric to sway the crew, but this performance is followed by solitary calculation, also necessary to achieve his ends.

Melville draws heavily in "The Chart" (tracing his own additional courses) on chapter 12, "Currents and Whaling," in the fifth volume of Charles Wilkes's *Narrative of the United States Exploring Expedition during the Years 1838, 1839, 1840, 1841, 1842* (1845). Wilkes, who led a major U.S. government–sponsored scientific mission in Antarctica and the Pacific, had answered skepticism about his mapping of whaling grounds by arguing for the links between ocean currents, paths along which food was borne, and seasons when and locations where whales could be found. Melville incorporates Wilkes's arguments and also evokes, in the passage I have quoted, the "various lines and shadings" in the actual fold-out migratory whale chart Wilkes included at the beginning of his chapter (Figure 5.1).

In this steel engraving, over the grid of latitude and longitude, the curved lines denote the ocean currents, with arrows signaling their directions, and the closely spaced horizontal lines, forming shaded areas, indicate regions where whales were likely to have been found. In Wilkes's map, calculation (data about currents, food, and sightings) blends into prediction, and the contours of possibility are incised. Its lines resemble the "maze of currents and eddies" that, Melville's narrator tells us, "Ahab was threading ... with a view to the more certain accomplishment of that monomaniac thought of his soul" (199). Ahab's obsessive reckoning, his tracing and retracing of lines, gives form to his monomania in the shadowed areas of his own charts.

While writing *Moby-Dick*, Melville read a circular issued by oceanographer Matthew F. Maury, who was director of the Naval Observatory in Washington. Maury described a chart in preparation, based on the data in the logbooks of whaling captains, that would show the preponderance of sperm and right whales in different locations and the best seasons in which to hunt them. Maury's circular, incorporated in his *Explanations and Sailing*

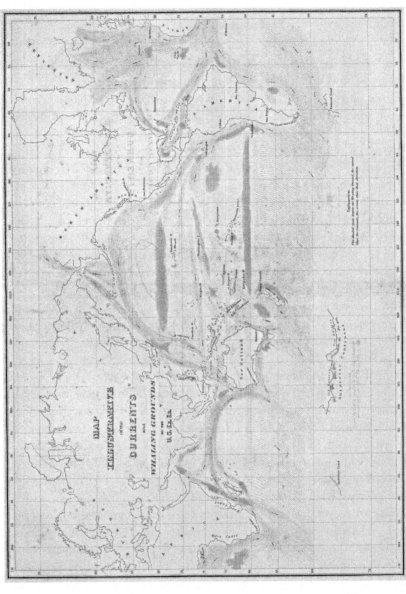

Figure 5.1. "Map Illustrative of the Currents and Whaling Grounds by the U.S. Ex. Ex." Charles Wilkes, *Narrative of the United States Exploring Expedition During the Years 1838, 1839, 1840, 1841, 1842.* Vol. 5. Philadelphia: Lea and Blanchard, 1845. Courtesy of the David Rumsey Map Collection.

Directions to Accompany the Wind and Current Charts (1851), included details about sightings of sperm and right whales but not the chart itself, which appeared after the publication of *Moby-Dick*. Melville supplies a footnote to his chapter, adducing Maury's data and forthcoming map as additional evidence supporting the plausibility of Ahab's efforts and his own plotting.

In Maury's chart (Figure 5.2), at the bottom of which he cites Wilkes, the oceanographer opts not for lines, arrows, and shading but for small icons whose shape, hue, and spout contour distinguish sperm and right whales. These icons are situated in the grid of latitude and longitude to indicate their location, season (marked by lower case initials), and frequency (with two whale icons of the same species in the same square indicating their prevalence). In many copies, colors have been applied to the steel engraving to render the particular whaling grounds more conspicuous: blue for right whales, pink for sperm, and green for areas where both are found.

Although Melville had not seen this chart when he added the footnote to *Moby-Dick*, Maury's project helped to corroborate that the fictional Ahab had historical colleagues in addition to Wilkes. (As the editors of the Hendricks House edition of *Moby-Dick* explain in their notes, the knowledge transmitted by such charts was evanescent, since the lag in receiving information and the extensive killing of whales quickly rendered these guides obsolete.) If Wilkes's map materialized possibility in tight, machine-ruled horizontal lines, Maury's chart, with its train of tiny whales pinpointing location and their cumulative mass looming over the world, made literal and instrumental the vision Ishmael describes at the end of the first chapter: "in the wild conceits that swayed me to my purpose, two and two there floated into my inmost soul, endless processions of the whale, and, midmost of them all, one grand hooded phantom, like a snow hill in the air" (7).

"The Chart," like much of *Moby-Dick*, is about how conceits are materialized and also about confidence and interpretation. Twice in the chapter, the narrator refers to the spectrum of judgment. Ahab hoped that, by combining his data and charts, his own experience and expertise as a captain, and the documented seasonal encounters with Moby Dick in one area of the equatorial Pacific, he "could arrive at reasonable surmises, almost approaching to certainties" (199). He anticipated finding Moby Dick at a particular time and particular spot: "when all possibilities would become probabilities, and, as Ahab fondly thought, every probability the next thing to a certainty" (200). Ahab seeks certainty, and "The Chart" examines the path of his confidence.

I have quoted from the Northwestern-Newberry edition of *Moby-Dick*, whose editors have corrected what they take to be a mistake in Melville's

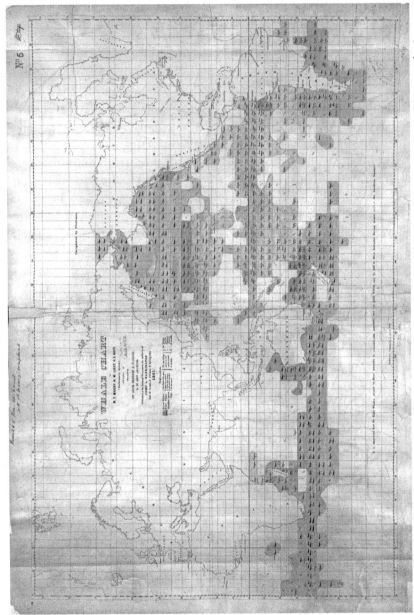

Figure 5.2. "Whale Chart" (1851); black-and-white reproduction of colored original. Matthew Fontaine Maury. Map reproduction courtesy of the Norman B. Leventhal Map Center at the Boston Public Library.

formulation in both 1851 editions of the book. Here is how the phrase reads in those first editions: "when all possibilities would become probabilities, and, as Ahab fondly thought, every possibility the next thing to a certainty" (Longman 189). The Northwestern editors argue that "the logic of progression in the terms" from "possibilities" to "probabilities" to "certainty" (867) requires the change from "every possibility" to "every probability." A logic of progression might demand the change, but as the Longman editors argue, explaining their retention of the original wording, Melville may have been suggesting in Ahab's imagined prospects a leap, rather than a sequence, from "possibilities" to "certainty." Melville describes Ahab's "thought" as "fond," that is, as overindulgent or excessive, with an echo of its older meaning, "foolish." His "fondness" may have to do with imagining that "every possibility" (rather than "every probability") is "the next thing to a certainty."

Does interpretation curve, asymptotically, toward certainty, or proceed by sudden leaps, or through its intensity risk depletion or consumption? Melville suggests the interpreter may not be sovereign. Ahab appears to be written upon as he writes, subject to fate, God, or his unconscious (and, of course, his author). Even as Ahab traces lines on his ocean charts, the narrator tells us the effect of the rocking cabin lamp that casts shadows on his wrinkled brow (an identifying feature he shares with his cetacean nemesis) makes it seem "that while he himself was marking out lines and courses on the wrinkled charts, some invisible pencil was also tracing lines and courses upon the deeply marked chart of his forehead" (198). The textual quandary in this chapter – whether a "possibility" is a "probability" – is entangled with Melville's staging of questions about interpretation. Editors, based on the charts and logbooks of their profession, seek to distinguish among possibility, probability, and certainty, and readers are asked to assess their choices.

When Ishmael envisions Ahab at his table scrutinizing volumes and marking his sea charts, the scene evokes the author composing his lines with his source books beside him, and reflects back on readers (including this literary scholar, bent over his desk) who sit before *Moby-Dick* and attempt to construe its meanings, frequently consulting reference books or the copious notes found in the various editions. *Moby-Dick* insists on multiple contexts of explication and invites its readers to examine the array of evidence on and off the page, test the qualities of their confidence, ponder their judgments, and trace additional paths on overwritten charts.

We might draw a line from chapter 43, "The Chart," to chapter 59, "Squid," based on a striking verbal repetition and on shared, but differently articulated, concerns. These chapters are not part of a pair, triad, or sequence, nor have they often, if ever, been discussed in relation. But again, we do not need to read the chapters of *Moby-Dick* in order. The diverse chapters often do not proceed in a smooth narrative arc, and so open the possibilities for a variety of connections. "The Chart" ends with a scene of eloquent vehemence, only partially explained by what precedes it. Often at night, the narrator tells us:

> Ahab would burst from his state room, as though escaping from a bed that was on fire…. For, at such times, crazy Ahab, the scheming, unappeasedly steadfast hunter of the white whale; this Ahab that had gone to his hammock, was not the agent that so caused him to burst from it in horror again. The latter was the eternal, living principle or soul in him; and in sleep, being for the time dissociated from the characterizing mind, which at other times employed it for its outer vehicle or agent, it spontaneously sought escape from the scorching contiguity of the frantic thing, of which, for the time, it was no longer an integral. But as the mind does not exist unless leagued with the soul, therefore it must have been that, in Ahab's case, yielding up all his thoughts and fancies to his one supreme purpose; that purpose, by its own sheer inveteracy of will, forced itself against gods and devils into a kind of self-assumed, independent being of its own. Nay, could grimly live and burn, while the common vitality to which it was conjoined, fled horror-stricken from the unbidden and unfathered birth. Therefore, the tormented spirit that glared out of bodily eyes, when what seemed Ahab rushed from his room, was for the time but a vacated thing, a formless somnambulistic being, a ray of living light, to be sure, but without an object to color, and therefore a blankness in itself. God help thee, old man, thy thoughts have created a creature in thee; and he whose intense thinking thus makes him a Prometheus; a vulture feeds upon that heart for ever; that vulture the very creature he creates. (202)

A chapter that begins in an isolated cabin with meticulous drawing on sea charts ends with a spectacular image of the self ablaze, fleeing from and devouring itself. Ahab's determination, kept in check during the day, escalates at night, assuming in his sleep an independence from and sovereignty over his soul. Late at night, that soul seeks to elude his will, recoiling at its proximity and dominance. Ahab becomes a semblance of himself, and his self-division is conveyed through a series of knotted allusions (to internal hells in Thomas Browne's *Religio Medici* and Milton's *Paradise Lost* and self-destruction in Shelley's *Prometheus Unbound* and Byron's *Manfred*) and jarring metaphors. The self is split and part of it is on fire; the self gives birth to a monster (with a possible echo of Mary Shelley's *Frankenstein*); the soul flees from the will, which is still encased in the body, and becomes vacant; the soul becomes a ray of light with no object to reflect it and give it substance and visibility. The allusions and metaphors culminate in the image of Ahab as a Prometheus, tortured not by an eagle sent by Zeus but by his own consuming thoughts. The narrator emphasizes the cycle of self-inflicted

78

self-division and self-destruction, repeating the already doubled phrases "created a creature" and "the very creature he creates."

What could it mean for Melville to write that Ahab's agonized spirit was "a formless somnambulistic being"? "Somnambulistic" is relatively easy to parse, since the narrator describes Ahab's soul as walking, or fleeing, while he is asleep. But "formless"? The adjective is part of a sentence whose optics hark back to the end of chapter 42, "The Whiteness of the Whale," when Ishmael worries about color as a secondary quality, not the property of objects but the product of sensation in observers. In "The Chart," his concern is that light without an object to color, or the soul without a will to give it shape, is empty, without character. But the word "formless" also looks forward to its only other appearance in the hundreds of pages of *Moby-Dick*, in chapter 59, "Squid."

One morning, which the narrator describes as "transparent blue ... when a stillness almost preternatural spread over the sea," the harpooneer Daggoo, looking out from the main masthead, discerns "in this profound hush of the visible sphere a strange spectre":

> In the distance, a great white mass lazily rose, and rising higher and higher, and disentangling itself from the azure, at last gleamed before our prow like a snow-slide, new slid from the hills. Thus glistening for a moment, as slowly it subsided, and sank. Then once more arose, and silently gleamed. It seemed not a whale; and yet is this Moby Dick? thought Daggoo. (275)

The fluctuations and indistinctness do not seem reminiscent of a whale, but the color and magnitude, and a silvery jet that had appeared before the ship repeatedly at night, suggest Moby Dick, and so Daggoo calls out to the crew, telling them the great white whale is breaching ahead of the ship.

Ahab orders a lowering, and four boats, led by the captain, approach the white mass. It sinks and then as the sailors wait, their oars suspended, it rises again:

> Almost forgetting for the moment all thoughts of Moby Dick, we now gazed at the most wondrous phenomenon which the secret seas have hitherto revealed to mankind. A vast pulpy mass, furlongs in length and breadth, of a glancing cream-color, lay floating on the water, innumerable long arms radiating from its centre, and curling and twisting like a nest of anacondas, as if blindly to clutch at any hapless object within reach. No perceptible face or front did it have; no conceivable token of either sensation or instinct; but undulated there on the billows, an unearthly, formless, chance-like apparition of life. (276)

Ahab and his crew first mistake the giant squid for Moby Dick, and then the narrator describes their astonishment at what they see instead, an astonishment that briefly eclipses the obsession with their quarry. In "Squid,"

Melville incorporates material from Thomas Beale's *Natural History of the Sperm Whale* (1839), Frederick Debell Bennett's *Narrative of a Whaling Voyage* (1840), and Francis Allyn Olmsted's *Incidents of a Whaling Voyage* (1841), but he far exceeds these sources in his rendition. He turns the squid into a portent of, but also departure from, Moby Dick.[4]

Melville's squid moves up and down with a wave-like motion detached from the ocean's rhythms; its arms grasp ("if" that is what they are doing) without sight. Like many others who reported on the giant squid (but not Thomas Beale), Melville amplifies its size, describing it as "furlongs in length and breadth" (one furlong is 660 feet, while actual giant squids, measured from tip of fin to end of tentacle, are a fraction of this length). He also alters its proportions, giving it a breadth comparable to its length. The color of the squid encountered by the *Pequod*'s sailors, not quite white but "cream," is described as "glancing," perceived obliquely, again evoking the indirect optics and superficial hues at the end of "The Whiteness of the Whale." From the sailors' perspective and in Melville's expressive terms, the squid, a cephalopod whose structure displays bilateral symmetry, appears radially symmetrical, with its "innumerable long arms" extending outward from a center, rather than down from a head (in actual squids, heads do contain eyes, "tokens of sensation"). Unlike Moby Dick, who is persistently figured as male, Melville's squid is not gendered, although its arms "curling and twisting like a nest of anacondas" resemble the hair of Medusa, changed into serpents by the goddess Athena. The narrator cannot discern evidence—or imagine—that such a creature has senses or instinct; but, in Melville's careful diction, that such attributes in the squid are not "conceivable" does not necessarily mean they do not exist. The motion detached from environment, the absence of bilateral symmetry, the apparent lack of sensation or instinct, and the sightless grasping all contribute to the narrator's depiction of the giant squid as a "chance-like apparition of life": not life as commonly understood but life, without apparent design, that balks definition (including the humorous bibliophilia of "Cetology"), a nebulous trace. The absence of any individual mental, physical, or moral qualities forecloses the portrayal of a distinct or elusive interior that would give the squid a character, whereas Moby Dick manifestly is a character. The apparitional qualities of the squid are reinforced in the dialogue, when the unnerved first mate Starbuck exclaims that he would almost rather have encountered Moby Dick than such a "white ghost" (276).

The word "formless" seems crucial to understanding the intensities behind Starbuck's apprehension and Ishmael's fascination with the squid as "the most wondrous phenomenon which the secret seas have hitherto revealed to mankind" (276). "Formless" cannot simply refer to the squid's whiteness or magnitude or facelessness or to its visibility only in parts, since these are also attributes of Moby Dick. The narrator explains more than once that the sperm whale has "no face" (346, 379). The white whale displays an excess of form: recognizable outline, awe-inspiring symmetry, vivid parts. Moby Dick (and *Moby-Dick*) is a prodigious embodiment of the relationship between the particular and the general, the concrete and the abstract, the superficial and the determining, and also a provocation: Read it if you can.

The giant squid in *Moby-Dick* not only has no face but also has "no front," unlike the sperm whale, whose "full front" is extolled by the narrator: "This aspect [of his head] is sublime" (346). Melville's giant squid, a shapeless mass, is centrally unstable, has no front or back and no left or right; it moves without direction and grasps without apparent purpose or object. The sperm whale poses a perceptual difficulty, as the narrator wonders, in chapter 74, how it takes in the world with eyes placed on opposite sides of its head (echolocation would not be understood for another century) – but at least the sperm whale has a head and that head has two sides. The giant squid in *Moby-Dick* has no head and no eyes.

Unlike whales, whose images in paint, ink, wood, and stone Ishmael evaluates in the triad of chapters 55–57, often faulting their creators for the distance between representation and reality, the giant squid appears to have goaded no artists. The narrator is not constrained by the facts, which are scarce. Ishmael reports that the men who hunt sperm whales are superstitious about the great squid; since it is rarely seen, "very few of them have any but the most vague ideas concerning its true nature and form" (276). (Melville himself may never have seen a specimen.) In the first of the image chapters, "Of the Monstrous Pictures of Whales," Ishmael introduces the sequence and heightens interest by forecasting his own verbal accuracy: "I shall ere long paint to you as well as one can without canvas, something like the true form of the whale as he actually appears to the eye of the whaleman when in his own absolute body the whale is moored alongside the whale-ship so that he can be fairly stepped upon there" (260). Melville's giant squid cannot be lashed to a ship, measured, tread upon, peeled, cut, boiled down, scooped out, and sold on the market like the body of a sperm whale, as the narrator details across the cetological chapters of *Moby-Dick*. The giant squid resists the dynamics of human projection famously outlined in chapter 41: "all evil, to crazy Ahab, were visibly personified, and made practically assailable in Moby Dick" (184). Melville's "vast pulpy mass" would seem an inadequate vessel for human desires. On the transparent blue morning of the "Squid" chapter, Ishmael confronts magnitude without proportion and a fathomless opacity that evacuates his customary approaches. His final glimpse – "as with a low sucking sound it slowly disappeared again" (276) – anticipates the climactic ocean vortex in the narrative, when the *Pequod* and its sailors, drawn into a vast whirlpool, vanish beneath the waves. Yet he finds the phenomenon of the giant squid "wondrous." Why "wondrous"?

Meditating on visual form, art historian T. J. Clark writes, "Form is a way of capturing nature's repetitiveness and making it human, making it ours – knowable and dependable.... For nature's repetitions come with a huge (cosmic, microcosmic) margin of error, and it is this fact of existence that man most wants to forget."[5] Visual form and verbal form are not identical, but Melville's pictorial interests and his linking of human and natural forms across his career lend resonance to Clark's observations for *Moby-Dick*. In "The Chart," Melville shows how Ahab seeks to capture Moby Dick by identifying the patterns of ocean currents and whale migrations; the chapter defends the reliability and effectiveness of such knowledge. But the author also reveals its limits. Nature's repetitiveness climaxes in disaster. What Clark terms "nature's uncontrollable life" exceeds human mastery despite Ahab's straining to forget this fact, and his quest renders him inhuman.[6]

At night, Ahab flees his cabin and himself and becomes "a formless somnambulistic being" (202). One morning, the giant squid rises and falls as "an unearthly, formless, chance-like apparition of life" (276). Ahab's obsessive resolve detaches his will from his soul, and he suffers a more fundamental division than that between mind and body. He becomes "but a vacated thing," lacking the "contiguity" between will and soul and the "object to color" (202) that give human beings form. He becomes a mind without vitality or direction and a spirit without the ability to act and without a substance to reflect its radiance. "The Chart" begins with the narrator imagining Ahab plotting the route from possibility to certainty and ends with "a chance-like apparition of life." Both Ahab and the squid are "formless": animated without purpose, lacking recognizable design and meaningful attachments between interior and exterior, apparently incapable of coherent sensation or agency.

The narrator gives these two instances of "formlessness" different tones and textures. Ahab is frantic and scorched, self-divided and self-consuming, immaterial; he abandons himself, and Ishmael invokes God's assistance. The squid is described as placid (rippling on the ocean), agitated (blindly clutching), excessively material ("a vast pulpy mass"), and Ishmael expresses wonder. The squid appears to embody a possibility he cannot yet grasp, a relation to formlessness or to "true nature and form" (276) that does not proceed from obsession or disintegration, but from a regard for the possibilities of extension, rhythm, and substance.

Melville's book provokes – explicitly, reflexively, redundantly, intricately – the construal of its forms. Attention is directed to words, their origins, definitions, and translations ("Etymology") and to a mixture of perspectives and genres ("Extracts"), focused on the whale. Whale and book are joined ("Cetology") as objects in the quest to understand the principles of coherence, the qualities of definition, and the relationships between parts and wholes and surfaces and depths. Interpretive confidence ("The Chart") can be sought across the narrative chapters, in the extended digressions, in the voluminous scholarship and proliferating contexts, and in Melville's enticements to read according to logics other than numerical sequence, plot, or character. Melville's narrator considers the reach of the endeavor, stressing that form is an object of sense as well as thought: "Since I have undertaken to manhandle this Leviathan, it behooves me to approve myself omnisciently exhaustive in this enterprise; not overlooking the minutest seminal germs of his blood, and spinning him out to the uttermost coil of his bowels" (455). From "seminal germs" to "uttermost coils," involving "blood" and "bowels," the pressures and pleasures of the book are bound to its injunction not to overlook and, instead, to be continuously mindful that "some certain significance lurks in all things" (430). *Moby-Dick* materializes its interpretive challenges in the spectacle of two immense ocean creatures, one the elusive epitome of form, the other undulating at, or beyond, its limits. With all this in mind, we might imagine a different title: *Moby-Dick; or, –* with the conjunction, as it often does in Melville's books, inviting but also unsettling alternatives – *the Squid*.

NOTES

1 Moby-Dick *in Half the Time* (London: Orion Books, 2007); Damion Searls, ed., "*; or The Whale*," special fiction issue of *The Review of Contemporary Fiction* 29.2 (Summer 2009): 9–345.
2 Raymond Williams, *Keywords: A Vocabulary of Culture and Society: Revised Edition* (New York: Oxford University Press, 1985), 138.
3 On "The Chart" (which has been receiving more notice from critics lately), see Bainard Cowan, *Exiled Waters:* Moby-Dick *and the Crisis of Allegory* (Baton Rouge: Louisiana State University Press, 1982), 90–112; T. Hugh Crawford, "Networking the (Non) Human: *Moby-Dick*, Matthew Fontaine Maury, and Bruno Latour," *Configurations* 5.1 (Winter 1997): 1–21; Anne Baker, *Heartless Immensity: Literature, Culture, and Geography in Antebellum America* (Ann Arbor: University of Michigan Press, 2006), 30–43; Eric Bulson, *Novels, Maps, Modernity: The Spatial Imagination, 1850–2000* (New York: Routledge, 2007), 47–58; and Maurice S. Lee, *Uncertain Chances: Science, Skepticism, and Belief in Nineteenth-Century American Literature* (New York: Oxford University Press, 2012), 57–60.
4 On Melville's sources for "Squid," see Howard P. Vincent, *The Trying-Out of* Moby-Dick (Kent, OH: Kent State University Press, 1949), 223–27. On "Squid," see Robert Zoellner, *The Salt-Sea Mastodon: A Reading of* Moby-Dick

(Berkeley: University of California Press, 1973), 37–38; Robert K. Wallace, *Melville and Turner: Spheres of Love and Fright* (Athens: University of Georgia Press, 1992), 248, 383–84, 506–507; Shawn Thomson, *The Romantic Architecture of Herman Melville's Moby-Dick* (Cranbury, NJ: Associated University Presses, 2001), 37–38; and Derek John Woods, "Knowing When You're in *Terra Incognita*: Mapping, Vision, and Orientation in Ishmael's Anatomies," *Leviathan: A Journal of Melville Studies* 14.3 (October 2012): 25–41. On issues raised by the squid in Melville's work, see Gilles Deleuze, "Bartleby, or The Formula," in *Essays Critical and Clinical*, trans. Daniel W. Smith and Michael Greco (London: Verso, 1998), 77–78; and Nancy Ruttenburg, "'The Silhouette of a Content': 'Bartleby' and American Literary Specificity," in *Melville and Aesthetics*, ed. Samuel Otter and Geoffrey Sanborn (New York: Palgrave Macmillan, 2011), 148–52. On formlessness in Melville's writings, see Branka Arsić, *Passive Constitutions or 7 ½ Times Bartleby* (Stanford, CA: Stanford University Press, 2007), 156–65. For an art historical analysis, see Yve-Alain Bois and Rosalind E. Krauss, *Formless: A User's Guide* (New York: Zone Books, 1997).

5 T. J. Clark, "More Theses on Feuerbach," *Representations* 104 (Fall 2008): 4–5.
6 Ibid., 4.

6

WYN KELLEY

Pierre, Life History, and the Obscure

Melville's seventh novel, *Pierre, or the Ambiguities* (1852), ends with Isabel, the protagonist's possible sister-wife, exclaiming over his poisoned corpse: "All's o'er, and ye know him not!" (*P* 362). Her words theatrically disclose her secret relationship with the novel's hero, but they also raise questions for the baffled reader. Know Pierre? Who is Pierre, exactly, and how would we know him? At different times he appears to be a virtuous son, sentimental lover, daring rebel, starving artist, philosophical seeker, vengeful murderer, even tottering lunatic. The seeming inconsistencies in his character have suggested to various critics that Melville had not sorted out family problems that may have included an illegitimate sister; that he reacted angrily to negative reviews of *Moby-Dick* (1851); that he was writing sentimental fiction (badly); or that he suffered temporary insanity, as one contemporary reviewer implied by headlining his article, "HERMAN MELVILLE CRAZY."[1] From most of these perspectives, the problem of knowing or understanding Pierre grows out of certain assumptions about fiction itself. Fictional characters seem knowable, not because they are real people but because they obey certain rules of a fictional world: verisimilitude, consistency, coherence, logical development, not to mention the demands of genre. In Melville's early sea novels, his characters resembled the protagonists of nautical fiction. Readers could also see that they were drawn from the author's own adventures, were "real" as projections of Melville's life. Beginning with Taji in *Mardi* (1849), and even more obviously with Ahab in *Moby-Dick*, Melville experimented with characters who could not be "real" – characters often too extreme, alien, or allegorical for conventional fiction – and he continued this trend throughout his career with such challenging figures as Pierre, Bartleby, the Confidence Man, and Claggart.

Readers tend not to like, know, or understand Melville's unreal characters, even to consider them poorly conceived and developed. But the problem may lie less with Melville's artistic failures than with his own passions and choices. As his writing became more experimental in the 1850s, Melville strongly resisted the demand that his characters be knowable or real. Such resistance to fictional authority looks Romantic, and indeed Melville acted on such impulses to some extent. But he had also learned something about "real" characters from a perhaps unexpected source: biography. Elements of plot and characterization in *Pierre* show Melville rewriting the biographies of his time in new ways to consider greatness, genius, and heroism and how these qualities emerge among the most obscure recesses of American life. Biography, indeed, may have allowed Melville to renovate his own fictional art. The result of his studying "real" people, ironically, is that he may have felt emboldened to make unknowable characters.

During the early 1850s, when Melville wrote *Moby-Dick*, *Pierre*, and his first short stories, he gave considerable thought to what he called in "Bartleby, the Scrivener" the writing of "full and satisfactory biography" (*PT* 13). In *Moby-Dick* he mentions a wide range of biographies, from Plutarch's accounts of Marius and Sylla to Eckermann's *Conversations with Goethe*, from the life of George Washington (probably an oblique reference to biographies by Mason Locke Weems or Jared Sparks) to the sensational "Life of Samuel Comstock (A Mutineer) by his Brother, William Comstock," to the whale Moby Dick himself – although "his is an unwritten life" (*MD* 205, xxv, 50, xxvii, 135). After *Pierre*, Melville addressed what the narrator of "Bartleby" calls an "irreparable loss to literature" (13) by supplying a series of obscure lives: not only "Bartleby," but also "Jimmy Rose" (1855) and *Israel Potter* (1856), as well as tales of Charlemont the "gentleman-madman" and the perpetual borrower China Aster (*The Confidence-Man* [1857]), Nathan the murdered Jewish convert of *Clarel* (1876), and the wandering exile John Marr (*John Marr* [1888]). As Melville wittily philosophized at the beginning of *Israel Potter*, biography could elevate both writer and subject to great heights: "Biography, in its purer form, confined to the ended lives of the true and brave, may be held the fairest meed of human virtue – one given and received in entire disinterestedness – since neither can the biographer hope for acknowledgment from the subject, nor the subject at all avail himself of the biographical distinction conferred" (vii).

But the form of life history Melville eventually practiced, while sometimes elevating "the true and the brave," more often featured humbler heroes than those of the popular patriotic biographies of the period: for example Mason Locke Weems's *Life and Memorable Actions of George Washington* (1800), Washington Irving's *Life and Voyages of Christopher Columbus* (1828), Jared Sparks's Library of American Biography (1834–38, 1844–47), Elizabeth F. Ellet's *The Women of the American Revolution* (1848–50), Ralph Waldo Emerson's *Representative Men* (1850), Nathaniel Hawthorne's *Life of Franklin Pierce* (1852), William Cooper Nell's *Colored Patriots of the*

American Revolution (1855), not to mention the great autobiographies of
Benjamin Franklin and Frederick Douglass.[2] With *Pierre*, Melville turned
from sea stories told by an adventurer-narrator toward a new kind of
generic hybrid: part Gothic romance, metaphysical satire, sentimental novel,
to be sure – but also in remarkable ways part life history narrated by a
biographer.

Pierre, of course, has not been thought of as biography at all, having
long been paired with *Moby-Dick* as its literary evil twin. Whereas Ahab
strikes through a metaphysical mask, Pierre seeks to pierce the mocking
social masks of family, race, class, gender, and nation. More than biography,
the plot resembles a blend of romantic love story, *künstlerroman*, fractured
family narrative, and experimental philosophical outpouring. An upper-class
youth, Pierre Glendinning, in love with an "angel" named Lucy Tartan, lives
in an ancestral country mansion with his attractive but haughty mother,
Mary Glendinning. His father, long dead, remains enshrined in their hearts
as a model of gentlemanly courtesy and decorum. Most unexpectedly, Pierre
encounters a strange dark maiden named Isabel Banford, who, in a series
of letters and nocturnal interviews, claims she is the daughter of Pierre's
revered father, who met her French mother in New York – before he married
the current Mrs. Glendinning. Puzzled as to how to acknowledge this possible sister and at the same time protect his proud mother from the unsavory
details of her husband's past, Pierre announces to the world that he and
Isabel are married. His mother throws him out of the house, Lucy collapses
in grief, and he and Isabel, with a farm girl named Delly Ulver (seduced and
betrayed by "the infamous Ned" [103]), escape to New York City. There they
live at the Apostles, a church converted into artists' studios clustered around
a grim guru called Plotinus Plinlimmon. Pierre commences writing a philosophical novel, while Isabel plays a mystical guitar and utters mysterious
pronouncements. Eventually Lucy finds the couple and moves in, painting
portraits for pennies and claiming to be some "nun-like cousin" (310) who
has joined their small band. Her suitor (also Pierre's cousin), Glendinning
Stanly, and her brother Frederick Tartan follow her to the Apostles, where
they threaten Pierre, who has also just received bad news from his editors
about his unpublishable book. Infuriated by these attacks, and distressed
by the sudden notion that Isabel may not be his sister after all, Pierre kills
Glen with a pair of pistols. Held in the Tombs Prison for his crime, he awaits
Lucy, who dies of shock upon hearing Isabel call him "brother," and Pierre
takes from Isabel the poison that will kill them both. Isabel's insensible form
falls upon the dead bodies with the final words of the novel.

As the successor to *Moby-Dick*, this story has perplexed Melville's readers. The topics of incest and family secrets have titillated some who have

wondered whether the book reflects hidden scandals in the Melville family.[3] The florid style and shifting narrative point of view have seemed signs of an exhausted and depressed author. Yet viewed as a precursor to Melville's later stories, novels, and poems and as a transitional fiction full of "the ambiguities" that characterize such experiments, *Pierre* offers fresh insights into the later work. In particular, Melville developed new modes of creating character that suggest what he learned from reading contemporary biographies.

Isabel's final comment – "All's o'er, and ye know him not" (362) – draws attention to the epistemological allure of biography as a genre: it purports to give the reader a way to know someone well. Biographies of the American nineteenth century, while not prone to the celebrity gossip of today, nevertheless evolved from the stiff hagiographies of Founding Fathers and Revolutionary heroes toward more complex portrayals of eminent but nevertheless very human beings. They suggest the wide range of Melville's resources, which may have supplied him with models for developing characters not just as recognizable people but also as emblematic of certain social, political, and ethical issues. The seemingly erratic development of Pierre's character from aristocratic youth to struggling author to cold-blooded murderer suggests Melville was interested in him not just as a "real" person but as representing – while also undermining or revising – certain characteristic American types.

Melville did not have to look far for fascinating examples of literary biography. Every American schoolchild read Plutarch's *Lives* or found it in a local library.[4] The Bible contained endless stories of kings, patriarchs, heroes, martyrs, and priests, as well as the life of one exceptional carpenter. In the period culminating in *Pierre*, Melville owned, read, or quoted Boswell's *The Life of Samuel Johnson*, Coleridge's *Biographia Literaria*, Jared Sparks's *Life of John Ledyard*, William Leete Stone's *Life of Joseph Brant*, as well as numerous whaling chronicles, voyages, naval histories, encyclopedias, and autobiographical narratives by Owen Chase, Richard Henry Dana, Charles Dickens, Goethe, Thoreau, and others.[5] He purchased Henry Trumbull's *Life and Remarkable Adventures of Israel Potter* in London in 1849 and discussed using it "in case I serve up the Revolutionary narrative of the beggar" (*J* 43) – his later novel *Israel Potter*. Although there may be little agreement on what defines *biography* over time and in different cultures, Melville would have imbibed certain standard criteria: biography was to provide didactic models for imitation, reveal American history through the lives of its patriotic heroes, explore teachable portrayals of the "inner man," and promote a heroic notion of "character" as vital in a new nation.[6] Most obviously, American biography presented character as exemplary, as representing America's best and greatest heroes.

A public debate over *representativeness*, however, complicated these worthy goals, as the examples of Jared Sparks, Ralph Waldo Emerson, and Frederick Douglass particularly suggest. American biographies raised compelling questions: Who might be said to exemplify American character, to *represent* the nation most fully? Might a figure be called representative who did not fit certain high standards of behavior and character? And perhaps most vexing of all, did great character reside in being representative or exceptional, typical or outstanding?

Jared Sparks came down on the side of biography as exemplary record of American history represented by its most remarkable men. The biographer of George Washington, Gouverneur Morris, and Benjamin Franklin, he edited the twenty-five-volume Library of American Biography, with lives of Ethan Allen, Benedict Arnold, Daniel Boone, Charles Brockden Brown, John Eliot, Robert Fulton, Anne Hutchinson, Cotton Mather, William Penn, John Smith, and Roger Williams among its many names; Melville was to include and indeed satirize a number of these figures in his works, especially *Israel Potter* (Benjamin Franklin and Ethan Allen, most memorably). As the Library grew, Sparks expanded his vision of America beyond his own New England to include the mid-Atlantic states and frontier.[7] But as this list clearly shows, Sparks's representative American was overwhelmingly male, white, and enterprising in the fields of war, invention, politics, literature, the clergy, exploration, conquest, and education.

Pierre, as we will see, owes some of his character traits to the Sparksian patriot. But as Melville later reveals, Pierre is also, curiously, a philosopher and a genius. Emerson's *Representative Men*, while not biography in the strictest sense, focuses on the central quality of genius as a vital spirit that distinguishes great men and enlightens the world: "Genius is the naturalist or geographer of the supersensible regions, and draws their map; and, by acquainting us with new fields of activity, cools our affection for the old." Emerson writes that all humans have this spark of the divine but that in certain men it shines more brightly: "Great men are thus a collyrium to clear our eyes from egotism, and enable us to see other people and their works." Yet their genius does not belong to them alone: "The qualities abide; the men who exhibit them have now more, now less, and pass away; the qualities remain on another brow."[8] Great men embody the greatness of all humans while at the same time rising above the mass; they are both typical of human behavior *and* exceptional.

Clearly Emerson departed from Sparks by suggesting that greatness is given to all, not just an exemplary few. And he differed from Sparks in another major way: his Representative Men – Plato, Napoleon, Goethe – are not American. Emersonian genius belongs to all nations, not one. Nor, except for Napoleon, do his Men all display manly strength and heroism. Emerson renders biography as philosophy, raising questions about greatness that Sparks's books do not consider. Both Sparks and Emerson agree, however, that greatness dwells in the light of fame. All their subjects occupy the highest strata of their fields. If *Pierre* is informed by these different treatments of biography, then we might expect Melville's hero to achieve great things in his chosen arenas, whether social or literary.

Instead Pierre becomes an urban laborer, "a poor be-inked galley-slave, toiling with the heavy oar of a quill" (260) at a book likely to doom him to a life of obscurity. In this sense, we might see Frederick Douglass's autobiography as another possible context for *Pierre*, not just because Douglass was a former slave, but also because his narrative might be seen as testing the models of both Sparks and Emerson. The title of his 1845 *Narrative of the Life of Frederick Douglass, an American Slave. Written By Himself* recalls titles like Sparks's *Life of John Ledyard* or Stone's *Life of Joseph Brant*. But Douglass also rewrites the Sparks model to suit his own case. In appending the phrase "*an American Slave*," Douglass calls attention to his identity as an American, a fact implicit in Founding Fathers biographies but seldom mentioned. Pairing *American* with *Slave*, of course, heightens the irony of his being a biographical subject at all, and closing with "*Written by Himself*" casts into bold relief his further status as his own biographer, unlike the heroes of conventional biography, who depended on the efforts of others.[9]

Douglass thus distances himself from patriotic biography by emphasizing his obscurity. Douglass's insistence on his slave identity implicitly takes issue with American representativeness as conceived by Sparks. At the same time Douglass's *Narrative* seems to anticipate Emerson's notion of representation in that he embodies genius and seems not to belong solely to American history. Hence he inhabits a paradox like those of other Emersonian Men. Douglass's genius makes him typical *and* exceptional, obscure *and* celebrated, at once ambiguous and yet also in bold relief. Seeing him in the context of other "representative" black leaders, as Robert S. Levine has done in placing him in relation to Martin Delany, suggests that Douglass was not the *only* representative of America's former slaves, hence not exceptional.[10] But viewing him as an Emersonian genius implies that he was, indeed, exceptional in escaping the obscurity of slavery. Thus Douglass may be seen as challenging Emersonian representativeness while also seeming to embody it.

Although we cannot be sure which if any of these authors of American (auto)biography Melville might have read, the biographical elements in *Pierre* seem to reflect contemporary debates about character, fame, and obscurity. Hence we observe Melville seeming to borrow heavily from

Sparks and other patriotic biographers in the early sections of the novel, where Pierre's status as an American aristocrat, the descendant of a general who "defended a rude but all-important stockade fort, against the repeated combined assaults of Indians, Tories, and Regulars" (6), gives him a sense of proud and patriotic dominion over the landscape. As the sole male inheritor of this Revolutionary legacy, Pierre "fondly hoped to have a monopoly of glory in capping the fame-column, whose tall shaft had been erected by his noble sires" (8). Melville's ironic narrator suggests that such dreams of glory reflect overweening class and racial pride. Nevertheless, for much of the first half of the novel, Melville's narrator sustains the image of Pierre as a perfect American gentleman, full of courtly love for women, conscious of his duties to tenants and those beneath him in status, richly endowed with manly strength, and training himself for vaguely conceived feats of heroism. As in Sparks's and Weems's biographies, his life is emblematic of virtue and impending fame. Only the sly narrator suggests that "[i]n all this, how unadmonished was our Pierre by that foreboding and prophetic lesson taught, not less by Palmyra's quarries, than by Palmyra's ruins" (8), namely the lesson of the vanity of human ambition. Otherwise, the narrator prepares the reader for a character of unimpeachable virtue and valor.

Pierre seems to assume that character consciously when he learns of Isabel's existence and adopts the extraordinary measure of pretending to marry her. Although the situation resembles nothing that Revolutionary heroes and Founding Fathers had to face, the narrator's language again brings those elevated figures to mind, as for example when Pierre contemplates Isabel's story and imagines himself preparing for battle: "He felt that what he had always before considered the solid land of veritable reality, was now being audaciously encroached upon by bannered armies of hooded phantoms, disembarking in his soul, as from flotillas of specter-boats" (49). His suffering on this psychological battlefield, when he realizes that his stainless father and mother are hypocrites, that he must live a lie in order to combat a world of lies, that he must surrender one good – his love for Lucy – to preserve Isabel's honor, compounds his heroism in terms the narrator puts in a military context: "as the vine flourishes and the grape empurples close up to the very walls and muzzles of cannoned Ehrenbreitstein; so do the sweetest joys of life grow in the very jaws of its perils" (69). Setting out for the city as the protector of Isabel and Delly, Pierre appears as the descendant not only of his courtly father and heroic grandfather, but of a whole chivalric tradition of manly and military American virtue.

Character, as conceived in Sparksian biography, is given and shaped not just by innate virtue but by national fame. Although a biographical subject like Washington or Franklin must develop from childhood into maturity, the biographer selects those fixed traits that explain the hero's adult reputation; this is no *bildungsroman*. Melville's narrator is most Sparksian in assigning to Pierre the characteristics that indicate his future achievements, seeming not to grow from within but to be bequeathed by birth and breeding, a version of destiny. Hence, "*it had been the choice fate of Pierre to have been born and bred in the country*" (13); he has "read the History of the Revolutionary War" and modeled himself on its heroes (13); he has imbibed his father's religion along with his gentlemanliness (6); he observes the "profoundest filial respect" (14) toward his mother and "feelings of a wonderful reverentialness" toward Lucy (39). Mary Glendinning seems to recognize the inherent problem in Pierre's privileged upbringing. How can he be all "sweet docility" to her and yet grow to be "an uncompromising hero and a commander among his race" like his illustrious grandfather? Only if he lives in "unwavering prosperities" will he "remain all docility to me, and yet prove a haughty hero to the world!" (20). Even Pierre's mother seems to recognize, in the early parts of the novel, that her son represents American manhood solely by virtue of his class and breeding, rather than by anything he has done. He is, like Sparks's Washington, all future potential already realized.

Yet Melville's narrator gives Pierre another character when he somewhat abruptly announces late in the novel that he is "a gentleman, a Glendinning, and a genius" (260). It appears that Pierre's genius has been assigned him by the same fate that gave him a class and a name. But in calling him a genius, indeed a literary genius who has already impressed the publishing world with his youthful sonnets, the narrator shifts from the domain of patriotic to literary biography – the realm of Coleridge's *Biographia Literaria* (1817), Henry Theodore Tuckerman's *Characteristics of Literature, Illustrated by the Genius of Distinguished Men* (1849, 1851), Emerson's *Representative Men*, and Evert A. and George L. Duyckincks' eventual *Cyclopedia of American Literature* (1856). Here fame is determined by deeds not of chivalry or patriotic courage but rather of intellect. Readers have found this shift to Pierre's literary genius puzzling, even, as in Hershel Parker's case, speculating that Melville did not intend to make Pierre a writer, that the "real" *Pierre*, composed before the disappointing reviews of *Moby-Dick*, resides in those sections in which Pierre's writing and the narrator's critique of the publishing industry do not appear.[11] To remove the implications of Pierre's genius, however, would not only excise some of the book's most acid satire but would also obliterate its experiment in Emersonian representativeness. With these sections, Melville suggests Pierre is representative or exemplary, not just as an American, but also as a writer and philosopher.

In terms of character development, this choice emphasizes that Pierre has been given traits of a different kind from those associated with class, name, and breeding. Pierre must also prove himself capable of "that maturer and larger interior development, which should forever deprive these things ['the associations of Saddle Meadows'] of their full power of pride in his soul" (6). As an Emersonian genius he will write *with* genius and as a philosopher: "Two books are being writ; of which the world shall only see one, and that the bungled one. The larger book, and the infinitely better, is for Pierre's own self" (304). Although Melville's narrator mocks the whole enterprise – "Civilization, Philosophy, Ideal Virtue! behold your victim!" (302) – it nevertheless calls forth a new kind of heroism in Pierre. In his Hamlet-like acceptance of a fate that has led him to a position "solitary as at the Pole" (338), yet still "with the feeling of misery and death in him, he created forms of gladness and life.... For the more and the more that he wrote, and the deeper and deeper that he dived, Pierre saw the everlasting elusiveness of Truth" (339); and unlike Pip in *Moby-Dick*, who experiences a similar kind of dive but goes mad, Pierre continues to grapple with the "Inferno of his Titanic vision" (347). As revealed in the image of Enceladus, the Titan trapped in stone, Pierre appears ludicrous yet heroic, wearing the demigod's "face and features ... [of] prophetic discomfiture and woe" (346).

If Pierre's principled pursuit of truth at all costs makes him seem an exceptional hero, the narrator perplexingly suggests at this point that he is nevertheless representative: he is "this *American* Enceladus, wrought by the vigorous hand of Nature's self" (346; emphasis mine). Hence even in his dedication to genius, Pierre might be seen as an American type. His character is still in some respects fixed in a national mold, even when animated by Emerson's antinationalism. The demands of biography, that a subject represent a national and ethical ideal, seem here to have been upheld, even as Pierre descends further and further away from the privileged and sanctioned status he held at the beginning of the novel.

In another context, however, that of the slave narrative, Pierre's arc represents a different life history, and a perhaps more richly conceived notion of character development. That is, like Frederick Douglass, Pierre insists on, even chooses his obscurity. He is not literally a slave, but like Douglass he labors to the point of exhaustion, and like Douglass he labors at writing. Douglass, for example, reminds his reader that he had no clothes or warmth as a child: "My feet have been so cracked with the frost, that the pen with which I am writing might be laid in the gashes."[12] This image grotesquely juxtaposes Douglass's physical and mental suffering, the privations he endured as a slave child, with the agonies of reliving his past through writing. Melville similarly blends Pierre's suffering with his writing: "A rickety chair, two hollow barrels, a plank, paper, pens, and infernally black ink, four leprously dingy white walls, no carpet, a cup of water, and a dry biscuit or two" (302) – these are his writing conditions. The grandson of a man who held slaves becomes a "galley-slave of letters" (260). Melville emphasizes that, like Douglass, Pierre is both "slave" and writer at once.

As writers, Douglass and Pierre develop quite differently from Sparks's or Emerson's famous subjects. Their obscurity and suffering instead render them invisible to ordinary readers. Pierre travels the city at night in an almost hallucinatory state, until he falls "crosswise into the gutter, dabbled with mud and slime" (341) – but no one knows or cares for him except the ineffectual women at home. Likewise, although the real Douglass had family and friends, in his *Narrative* he enjoys only the small community of fellow slaves and free blacks in Baltimore, for the most part presenting himself as acting alone. As isolatoes, Douglass and Pierre do not have the progressive, upwardly mobile character development of Sparks's heroes or Emerson's Representative Men. Indeed character seems less important over time than their condition, which represents an existential status – Douglass as self-liberating slave, Pierre as self-immolating writer. Ultimately, although both seem to travel part of their way along an ascending arc like the men in Sparks's or Emerson's narratives, they remain abject throughout their narratives, their heroism only dimly realized, in Douglass's case (though only in his 1845 *Narrative*), or swiftly snuffed out, in Pierre's.

Hence, in opposition to a notion of character development as an upward progress toward fame or achievement, Douglass and Melville seem to be experimenting with a character who develops all the more richly as he descends the social ladder into obscurity – or, to be precise, social ambiguity. Douglass by becoming free, and Pierre by becoming a writer, move from the clearly defined locations of their youth into positions more mixed, uncertain, and troubling. Douglass's freedom would seem to guarantee him success but instead cuts him off from home and community and isolates him in a hostile city. Pierre likewise frees himself from his stultifying class positions, rights the wrongs his father committed, and discovers his vocation, but instead of experiencing fame he becomes a criminal who dies shamefully in prison. Yet he has acted bravely, defied hypocrisy and conventionality, and carried out in eccentric ways the heroic potential of his forefathers.

Biography offers another generic feature Melville may have used experimentally in *Pierre*, namely its memorial function. Biography, that is, *remembers* its subject, serving as his or her monument. That monument takes the form not of granite or wood but of literary work – the book that bears the subject's name. The life once lived by a human being becomes remembered by the biographer and embalmed in verbal text. Although Melville does not present his book explicitly as biography, he occasionally and directly speaks of Pierre's life as a text. The passage quoted earlier, in which Pierre writes "a larger book ... from Pierre's own self" (304) makes the point dramatically, but the narrator has spoken of Pierre as a textual self throughout. Thus, for example, in the early pages Pierre's life is compared to a manuscript: "So perfect to Pierre had long seemed the illuminated scroll of his life thus far, that only one hiatus was discoverable by him in that sweetly-writ manuscript. A sister had been omitted from the text" (7). The image suggests not so much a character developing in a novelist's creative hands as a life taken down by a biographical scribe as events unroll before him. Isabel too describes herself as a text, the "one poor book of Isabel" (156) that Pierre has perused. In the long sections describing Pierre as a writer, Melville frequently associates Pierre's life with a book or suggests that the writer's life is encased in a book: "in the inferior instances of an immediate literary success, in very young writers, it will be almost invariably observable, that for that instant success they were chiefly indebted to some rich and peculiar experience in life, *embodied in a book*, which because, for that cause, containing original matter, the author himself, forsooth, is to be considered original" (259; emphasis added). Pierre embodies himself in a book, a book that represents him as biographical subjects were considered to represent their nation or culture. In that sense, then, *Pierre* is autobiographical – not because it tells Melville's life story but because it considers people as texts, their lives as Plutarchan Lives suitable for memory, study, and posterity.

Eventually, ironically, Pierre's book, his Life, appears to kill him. In the writing of his book and the creating of his "maturer" self, the narrator asks, "Is it creation, or destruction? Builds Pierre the noble world of a new book? or does the Pale Haggardness unbuild the lungs and the life in him?" (304). The narrator concludes that in writing, Pierre is "learning how to live, by rehearsing the part of death" (305). Novels and biography may both simulate life and death, but in biography life and death are intimately interwoven with the text itself, which typically ends with the death of a living being. To reflect on a biographical Life is to contemplate the life and death of texts too – an opportunity Melville seems to relish at this new phase in his career.

Melville went on to more years of authorship after *Pierre* and perhaps even more pages than what had come before. Curiously, while writing mostly fiction and poetry, he continued his fascination with biography. The narrator of "Bartleby" is explicitly the scrivener's biographer, though he lacks the "materials" for more than "a few passages in the life" of this mysterious man. But, through the narrator of "Bartleby," Melville provides perhaps his most cogent statement on his project of importing biography into fiction:

> I have known very many of them [scriveners], professionally and privately, and if I pleased, could relate divers histories, at which good-natured gentlemen might smile, and sentimental souls might weep. But I waive the biographies of all other scriveners for a few passages in the life of Bartleby, who was a scrivener the strangest I ever saw or heard of. While of other law-copyists I might write the complete life, of Bartleby nothing of that sort can be done. I believe that no materials exist for a full and satisfactory biography of this man. It is an irreparable loss to literature. (*PT* 13)

Without the full materials a biography requires, the narrator seems thrown back upon a less "satisfying" genre, the sketch, subtitling his tale "A Story of Wall-Street." But the narrator is nevertheless at a "loss" to supply a literary form as suitable as biography.

Melville seemed to address that loss or failure in later works as well. The narrator of "Jimmy Rose" collects stories about a pitiful man who once lived in his house, but he cannot deliver a full account of his life. Melville lifts many details in "Benito Cereno" from the autobiographical narrative of Amasa Delano's voyages but makes them into a mystery. In *Israel Potter* Melville recycled Trumbull's book, which he had bought in 1849 with the stated purpose of "serv[ing] up the Revolutionary narrative of the beggar" – then seemingly botches the job, as Israel Potter becomes a comic figure rather than a patriotic hero. *The Confidence-Man* includes a number of life stories – of Charlemont, China Aster, and John Moredock, the Indian-hater, of whom a story-teller remarks, "'How evident that in strict speech there can be no biography of an Indian-hater *par excellence*, any more than one of a sword-fish, or other deep-sea denizen; or, which is still less imaginable, one of a dead man'" (*CM* 150). Among his poems Melville includes rescued "lives," including those of Nathan and Agath in *Clarel*, the sailors John Marr and his mates in *John Marr*, and the eponymous Timoleon (drawn from Plutarch). Finally, in a poem that grew into a life, he told the life story of Billy Budd, whose Captain Vere shows his "superior mind" by preferring "books treating of actual men and events no matter of what era – history, biography and unconventional writers, who, free from cant and convention, like Montaigne, honestly and in the spirit of common sense philosophize upon realities" (*BB* 62).

Melville does not overtly appear to be writing biography in his works after *Pierre*. Even in *Israel Potter* and "Benito Cereno," for which alert readers might find a biographical source, Melville covers his tracks, presenting biography as fiction. But conversely, Melville often presents his fiction as biography, the lives of mostly forgettable men – the great exception being Hunilla, the Chola widow of "The Encantadas," a heroic woman who nevertheless, like many others, chooses obscurity and disappears unremarked at the end of her story. In that sense, then, these are hybrid works, and the presence of biography in Melville's writing seems as mysterious and fugitive as the characters themselves.

It is an important presence, however, for it helps to explain a troubling feature of Melville's oeuvre: his characters do not obey the rules of fiction. They seldom seem real or knowable in the ways readers ironically expect of fictional characters, namely in having typical human emotions and experiences.[13] Pierre, Bartleby, Jimmy Rose, Israel Potter, Nathan, and the rest appear rather as emblems of certain social or ethical conditions: poverty, isolation, rebelliousness, homelessness, artistic endeavor, religious fanaticism. In that sense they are Representative Men, characters who represent but do not act as real people. Their obscurity makes them atypical of conventional biographical subjects, but biography suits them as a genre because it does not inquire too closely into their personal lives.

Hence the very feature that makes many of Melville's characters seem alien to readers – was there ever such a person as Pierre or Bartleby? – suggests that these are not people at all, that the question is completely misplaced. Instead Melville seems to be playing with notions of character as representing itself in text, of personhood as fitly embodied in life story or memorial book. If such a concept seems to diminish the ethical importance of human life, it may point to Melville's concern with a larger temporal span and planetary scope – with the life history of human beings seen from afar.[14] Through his microscopic lens, pitiful humanity in all its obscurity becomes wondrous again. Isabel's dying words – "All's o'er, and ye know him not!" – remind Charlie Millthorpe, Pierre's childhood companion, that knowing a person – "schoolmate – playmate – friend!" (362) – ends in inevitable frustration. Only in *not* knowing the person is the reader free to consider humanness beyond the typical means of representing character. Biography, by making humans representative rather than personal, rescues what might otherwise be "an irreparable loss to literature" (*PT* 13).

NOTES

1 See Harrison Hayford, "Melville's Imaginary Sister," in *Melville's Prisoners* (Evanston, IL: Northwestern University Press, 2003); Hershel Parker, introduction to *Pierre, Or the Ambiguities; The Kraken Edition* (New York: Harper Collins, 1995), xi–xlvi; Wyn Kelley, "*Pierre's* Domestic Ambiguities," in *The Cambridge Companion to Herman Melville*, ed. Robert S. Levine (Cambridge: Cambridge University Press, 1998), 91–113; Caroline Levander, "The Female

Subject in *Pierre* and *The Piazza Tales*," in *A Companion to Herman Melville*, ed. Wyn Kelley (Oxford: Blackwell Publishing, 2006), 423–33; Cindy Weinstein, *Family, Kinship, and Sympathy in Nineteenth-Century American Literature* (Cambridge: Cambridge University Press, 2004); "Historical Note," in Herman Melville, *Pierre, Or the Ambiguities*, ed. Harrison Hayford, Hershel Parker, and G. Thomas Tanselle (Evanston, IL: Northwestern University Press and the Newberry Library, 1971), 380.

2 Scott E. Casper, *Constructing American Lives: Biography and Culture in Nineteenth-Century America* (Chapel Hill: University of North Carolina Press, 1999).

3 See Hayford, "Melville's Imaginary Sister"; Eleanor Melville Metcalf, *Herman Melville: Cycle and Epicycle* (Cambridge, MA: Harvard University Press, 1953); Hershel Parker, *Herman Melville: A Biography. Volume I, 1819–1851* (Baltimore, MD: Johns Hopkins University Press, 1996); *Volume II, 1851–1891* (Baltimore, MD: Johns Hopkins University Press, 2002).

4 Casper, *Constructing American Lives*, 25; Mary K. Bercaw, *Melville's Sources* (Evanston, IL: Northwestern University Press, 1987), 110.

5 Bercaw, 61, 69, 121, 122, 126. During the writing of *Pierre*, Melville read Stone's *Life of Joseph Brant* for information about his grandfather's exploits at Fort Stanwix (*L* 209). This material became part of the patriotic biography of Pierre's family in the novel.

6 Casper, *Constructing American Lives*, 4–7.

7 Ibid., 137–58.

8 Ralph Waldo Emerson, *Representative Men. Seven Lectures* (London: George Routledge & Co., 1850), 9, 15, 20.

9 See also James Olney, "'I Was Born': Slave Narratives, Their Status as Autobiography and as Literature," *Callaloo* 20 (1984): 46–73.

10 Robert S. Levine, *Martin Delany, Frederick Douglass, and the Politics of Representative Identity* (Chapel Hill: University of North Carolina Press, 1997).

11 Hershel Parker, introduction to *Pierre, Or the Ambiguities; The Kraken Edition* (New York: Harper Collins, 1995), xi–xlvi.

12 Frederick Douglass, *Narrative of the Life of Frederick Douglass*, ed. Houston A. Baker, Jr. (New York: Penguin, 1982), 72.

13 For a complementary perspective on Melville's characters, see Michael Snediker's essay in this volume.

14 For a complementary perspective on the planetary view of humans, see Timothy Marr's essay in this volume.

7

GRAHAM THOMPSON

"Bartleby" and the Magazine Fiction

For a few short weeks, "Bartleby, the Scrivener: A Story of Wall-Street" was a piece of anonymous magazine fiction. The first installment appeared toward the end of the November 1853 issue of *Putnam's Monthly Magazine* and was just one of the many other anonymous poems, stories, essays, and reviews making up that issue. By the time the second and final installment was published in December 1853, however, *The Literary World* had revealed Melville as the author of this "Poe-ish tale."[1] Thereafter, the lawyer and his copying clerk move beyond the bounds of the magazine world. Reprinted simply as "Bartleby" with four of Melville's other *Putnam's* stories in *The Piazza Tales* (1856), the seriality and full title of the magazine version were lost as Melville's authorship was formally instituted. Continually reproduced and anthologized as a freestanding short story in the wake of Melville's canonization during the twentieth century, "Bartleby" has become a milestone for any understanding of Melville's authorial persona. As a consequence, *Putnam's Monthly* attracts little more attention in the vast expanse of "Bartleby" criticism than the object to which the magazine compared itself in its very first editorial of January 1853: a "speck of star dust" in "the celestial dairy" of America.[2] But what would it mean to reconnect the most famous and widely read of Melville's short stories to the magazines of the 1850s? And what does it mean to read "Bartleby" as magazine fiction?

Some questions often asked of the story might become less important. Who is Bartleby, why does he "prefer not to," why does the lawyer not dispense with him more quickly, and how should Bartleby's death be interpreted? Questions of this nature have preoccupied two dominant approaches to the story. The first tries to identify the literary and historical sources on which "Bartleby" is based. Because of his preference for refusal, Bartleby has been read as the Thoreau of "Resistance to Civil Government" (1849) and often biographically as Melville himself as he became alienated from writing and publishing after the commercial failures of *Moby-Dick* (1851) and *Pierre* (1852).[3] Melville's friend and traveling companion Eli Fly, who worked as a scrivener in the office of Melville's uncle before being invalided and then dying in 1854, also bears striking resemblances to Bartleby.[4] The lawyer has been read as Melville's early supporter and later critic, journalist and writer Evert Duyckinck; as Melville's father-in-law, lawyer Lemuel Shaw; and as the Hawthorne ejected from public office just like the lawyer-narrator of "Bartleby" who loses his position as Master in Chancery.[5] Specific historical references in the story – to John Jacob Astor, the Colt and Adams murder, and the Dead Letter Office – have all been followed up as potential keys to unlock the story's ambiguities.[6] Meanwhile, the story's literary debts have been traced to Irving, to Poe, or more specifically to the legal fictions of Dickens's *Bleak House* or James Maitland's *The Lawyer's Story*, both of which were published before "Bartleby."[7]

If this first approach emphasizes biographical and literary sources, the second treats Bartleby the character and "Bartleby" the story as symptomatic of broader changes shaping mid-nineteenth-century America. This approach has dominated "Bartleby" criticism since the 1970s. The Wall Street location of the lawyer's office is invoked to establish a context of capitalism, class, and labor where the lawyer is caught between being patron and employer with Bartleby as his alienated employee.[8] The specters of capitalism, particularly the labor activism that sparked New York's Astor Place riot of 1849, are seen more generally to haunt the text.[9] Other discourses by which modernity is now understood are also seen to permeate the story. The concentration in New York City of emerging industries of cultural consumption and production re-enliven the context of Melville's writerly alienation and its encoding in his scrivener.[10] Considerations of autism and disability produce a medicalized version of "Bartleby," while the bonds of attachment between the lawyer and Bartleby can be understood in the light of the historical development of structures of gender and sexuality.[11] The hermeneutic density of the text, and the challenge this presents to the act of interpretation itself, also means that "Bartleby" frequently occupies critical theorists. In the most recent incarnation of this approach, Branka Arsić suggests Bartleby now ranks alongside Oedipus, Hamlet, and Don Quixote; all are characters who "announce a different way of thinking" and thus "remain unthinkable" within the confines of our own knowledge.[12]

If Arsić is right, then questions about Bartleby's identity, his refusal to check or copy legal documents, and the lawyer's hesitancy in dispensing with his services or his personal fate will resist definitive answers. These unanswered questions are part of the pleasure of the text and reason enough to keep readers and critics returning to "Bartleby"; but the story one now reads in the light of these critical contexts is not the story published in *Putnam's Monthly*. Both source and symptom criticism prioritize textuality over the contingencies of magazine writing and publishing. From these critical perspectives, "Bartleby" is a story one reads through the prism of its sources or a story that is itself the prism through which one reads the contextual factors shaping its form and content. That "Bartleby" was magazine fiction does not matter when it is read as parable or synecdoche because the emphasis is on revealing meaning through textual reference and allusion, and not by way of that story's coming to publication in *Putnam's Monthly*. A story, however, need not only be a text whose form and content are subject to interpretation following publication; it can also be a material object that bears witness to the circumstances by which it comes into publication. To read "Bartleby" as magazine fiction is to see meaning emerge in the connection of thinking, writing, and publication rather than through a symptomatic relation of text to source or context.

The sequence of events by which "Bartleby" became part of the magazine world can be put into relief by thinking about the matrix in which Melville's writing was embedded from the very beginning of his literary career. Although he published two short pieces in the *Democratic Press, and Lansingburgh Advertiser* in May 1839, Melville was not driven to write by long-standing literary ambition. After listening to the tales of his adventures at sea, it was his family and friends who encouraged him to write down these stories. In hindsight it may be difficult to imagine Melville not becoming a writer after this point, but this did not stop him from stumbling into print. No publisher had asked Melville for a book. When he did produce the manuscript of *Typee* in 1845, it was rejected by Harper's of New York: not as good as the most famous of castaway narratives, Daniel Defoe's *Robinson Crusoe*, it was also considered too fantastic to be true. Melville had to rely on his brother Gansevoort to secure publication. When he was posted to London as a diplomat, Gansevoort took the only copy of the manuscript with him. He found a British publisher and, after reading sections to Washington Irving during a breakfast meeting, also managed to secure American publication with Wiley & Putnam, the latter partner – George Palmer Putnam – being responsible subsequently for *Putnam's Monthly Magazine*.

Typee came to publication only when two factors were in place: first, some impetus turned ideas and stories into material form; second, a network of aesthetic judgment, special interest, and economic decision making was already established in which the manuscript could circulate. Writers have first to write before they can be read, and Melville had to translate the oral performances witnessed by his friends and family into a written narrative. The linguistic, temporal, and physical differences between telling and writing a story make this a significant undertaking. Not all good storytellers make good writers, and entertaining one's family over the course of an evening is a very different task to spending six months writing a manuscript for an unknown public. Melville also took *Typee* to Harper's in recognition of the book's imitative rather than its unique qualities. Harper's had already published, with some success, Richard Henry Dana's autobiographical sea narrative, *Two Years before the Mast* (1840), a book Melville read and admired. The generic qualities of *Typee* – "if not as good as Robinson Crusoe … not far behind it"[13] – ensured a favorable reader's report from Harper's; being too much like fiction and deviating from generic norms meant Harper's rejected the manuscript. The question of authenticity was a concern for the British publisher, John Murray, although he overcame his doubts. For George Palmer Putnam, the word of Washington Irving was recommendation enough.

Material and publishing prehistories of this sort can seem like antiquarian details alongside the gravity texts or writers assume in their later cultural existence. But in the journey of a literary text, being read by the public is just one of the events triggered by its writing and circulation. The contingencies of the events themselves – how the endeavor of writing proceeds practically following friendly encouragement; the precarious transatlantic voyage of a unique manuscript; how a well-connected brother leverages his contacts; and so on – create a very different orientation of text to meaning than would be available by prioritizing formal or contextual readings of *Typee*. Contingent events can even add to the later literary evaluations of a work. For example, Melville's representation in *Typee* of the contact between white and nonwhite, "civilized" and "savage," appears of secondary importance if one concentrates on the novel's publishing prehistory. But racial and cultural difference propel Melville to write in the first place. It was tales of exotic encounter rather than anything else about his time at sea that Melville's friends and family suggest he turn into fiction. And his British and American publishers understood there was a market for material of this kind. Even before we get to interpreting a text, the decision to write and the coming to publication of a manuscript is freighted with meaning.

The same holds true for "Bartleby," albeit in a different set of publishing circumstances. While *Typee* was written speculatively, Melville knew he was writing "Bartleby" for a magazine. In late 1852, George Palmer Putnam was on the verge of realizing his ambition to produce a quality monthly magazine on the back of his successful book publishing business. While periodicals had been a feature of literary life in Europe and America for several decades, they were growing in number in the 1840s and 1850s because of the development of a print culture taking advantage of mechanical advances in papermaking and printing, faster transportation networks, healthy literacy rates, and expanding and diversifying demand from educated urban consumers. Putnam composed a letter soliciting contributions from the authors he considered "the best talent of the country to aid us in the undertaking."[14] The list was long, upward of 200, and included Emerson, Hawthorne, Longfellow, Thoreau, and Cooper as well as Melville. In targeting writers of this stature, as well as American writers who have long since dropped off the literary radar, Putnam signaled his intention to print original, American contributions. This was in contrast to one of the new magazine's main competitors, *Harper's Monthly Magazine*, which had been running since June 1850 and was known for printing imported British material alongside pieces often reprinted from other American sources.

Harper's and Putnam's, then, took their competition in the book market into the world of magazines. Melville was already bound up in this economic market. After the success of *Typee*, Harper's published Melville's subsequent novels. So when he received the letter from Putnam, Melville found himself in a position where both of the publishers of his fiction now had magazines for which they wanted him to write. Although he had written reviews and short pieces, mainly for Duyckinck's *Literary World*, Melville had not yet taken on the tale or short story. In debt to Harper's after poor sales of his books, and following the rejection by Harper's of his now lost novel, *The Isle of the Cross*, he faced the prospect of becoming a magazine writer to stabilize his career and his finances.

In a letter to Hawthorne drafted while he was writing *Moby-Dick*, Melville famously declared that "Dollars damn me! ... What I feel most moved to write, that is banned, – it will not pay. Yet, altogether, write the *other* way I cannot" (*L* 191). This has become a convenient shorthand for identifying Melville's dissatisfaction with the demands of the literary market. But the comment should be understood in the context of his finishing the writing of that large and difficult novel. When it came to writing for magazines, Melville proved he could in fact "write the *other* way." He set himself to this task in the spring and summer of 1853 as he wrote three stories for *Harper's Monthly* as well as "Bartleby." Hershel Parker has noted that Melville "picked himself up stoutly" when faced with the prospect of writing for magazines and not with his "characteristic recklessness."[15] Melville was certainly familiar with the form and content of magazines. He subscribed to *Harper's Monthly* and even in his letter to Hawthorne mentions having read Hawthorne's "The Unpardonable Sin" in *Dollar Magazine*. Magazines were not a mystery to Melville; he understood their conventions in the same way he understood the conventions of the sea fiction and travel narratives he embraced so successfully in his early books. Having pushed the form of the novel to the point of collapse in *Moby-Dick* and *Pierre*, a task he would take up again in *The Confidence-Man* (1857), meeting the demands of writing magazine fiction required that Melville adopt a much more pragmatic approach. In his response to this challenge and the coming to publication of "Bartleby" in *Putnam's Monthly*, it is possible to see a story with qualities very different from the ones often seen by later readers and critics. Although hard to imagine now as just an ordinary story, "Bartleby" first declared itself to the world in quite an ordinary way.

The nature of this ordinariness, suggested by the anonymity of its publication and the location of the first installment toward the end of the magazine, is better understood if one pushes the story back against some of the sources often claimed as influences. The most obvious to consider is James Maitland's *The Lawyer's Story*, the first chapter of which appeared in the New York *Tribune* and *New York Times* of February 18, 1853. "In the summer of 1843," Maitland's tale begins, "having an extraordinary quantity of deeds to copy, I engaged, temporarily, an extra copying clerk, who interested me considerably, in consequence of his modest, quiet, gentlemanly demeanor, and his intense application to his duties."[16] In "Bartleby," the lawyer likewise is in need of extra help and advertises for another copying clerk; he also is taken with the sedate, gentlemanly, and industrious qualities of his new employee. Both tales are narrated in the first person by a lawyer, and Bartleby shares his melancholy disposition with the scrivener in Maitland's story. The similarities seem too particular to be the result of coincidence, although, unlike Bartleby, Maitland's copying clerk is easily put out of the lawyer's office once work dries up and the source of his melancholy is identified and resolved through the intervention of the lawyer. *The Lawyer's Story* turns into a saga of family separation and lost inheritance very different from "Bartleby." Even if Melville did read Maitland's story, or at least the first chapter, the larger question is why did Melville think the relationship between a lawyer and a copying clerk would make a suitable subject for a piece of magazine fiction?

The answer is that the particular nature of Maitland's story matters less than its generic qualities. Having a lawyer at the center of a mystery is what the stories share. And with lawyers come clerks. Dickens's *Bleak House*, serialized in *Harper's Monthly* from April 1852 to October 1853, contains numerous lawyers and clerks, and *David Copperfield* recounts David's employment as a legal clerk with Mr. Spenlow. Indeed, Dickens's first published story, "A Dinner at Poplar Walk" (1833), was the story of a bachelor clerk. Melville's sister Helen shook Dickens's hand on his 1842 trip to America, and both *Bleak House* and *David Copperfield* were family reading at Melville's Arrowhead home in Pittsfield. Anybody acquainted with Dickens's writing would know that lawyers and clerks were staple figures of Victorian fiction who served as the hinge by which characters were connected across class and status differences.

Lawyers and clerks of one description or another were also common enough in American magazine culture. The sensational "Dark Chapter From The Diary Of A Law Clerk" was published in *Harper's Monthly* in October 1852 while the same magazine also published several lawyer's tales, such as "The Gentleman Beggar: An Attorney's Story" (October 1850), "Jane Eccles; Or, Confessions of An Attorney" (April 1851), and "Reminiscences of An Attorney" (August 1851). In the same issue as the first installment of "Bartleby," clerks appear as characters in George William Curtis's "The Potiphars in Paris" and Edmund Quincy's serialization of *Wensley*, and they feature in a discussion of the characters of *Bleak House*. In an essay on Melville in the February 1853 issue of *Putnam's Monthly*, Fitz-James O'Brien looks back fondly to *Typee* in whose island paradise Tommo and Toby "spend as agreeable a life as ever [a] town-imprisoned merchant's clerk sighed for."[17] The second installment of "New-York Daguerreotyped" in the April 1853 issue, a piece about the commercial districts of Manhattan, drew attention to the architecture of the New York Custom House and how "utilitarian panes of plate glass ... let in light upon the 'attic cells,' where custom-house clerks sit at their mahogany desks."[18] Clerks and the urban world in which they worked were common currency in magazine writing. This was partly because clerking was fast becoming the most common form of employment in 1850s New York City and partly because clerks – just as they did in Dickens – served as markers of status distinction for the readers of these magazines. Young clerks were also literate, committed to self-improvement, and eager consumers of the cultural capital one found in magazines.[19] It is from "stalls nigh the Custom House" that Ginger Nut provides Turkey and Nippers with Spitzenbergs to moisten their mouths as they work at their own desks while performing the "husky" (*PT* 14) business of copying law papers. In vividly imagining the drudgery of clerks who could only daydream of exotic adventures and who were desk-bound in their ill-lit cells, *Putnam's* had imagined the world of "Bartleby" even before Melville came to write the story.

To read "Bartleby" as magazine fiction, then, means reading it alongside other tales, essays, and reports that deal in the same component parts; to read it, that is, as embedded in the magazine world as a piece of genre writing. It is a story whose specific sources matter less than the broader literary and magazine tradition of lawyers and clerks on which it draws. It also serves the aspirations of the magazine by bringing the details of New York City life to the page at the same time as it expands the reader's knowledge of a particular part of a more familiar world of work. And it gives clerks and their acquaintances a story highlighting the conditions giving rise to their daydreams rather than the contents of the daydreams themselves.

The importance of this clerking milieu is evident in the structure of the story. Bartleby does not appear in person until almost a third of the way through the first installment as it was published in *Putnam's Monthly*. Before the reader meets the scrivener, the lawyer suggests "it is fit I make some mentions of myself, my *employés*, my business, my chambers, and general surroundings" (*PT* 13). Quite why it is "fit" is not clear given the relatively minor roles played by these ancillary characters in the rest of the story. But the lawyer-narrator is painstaking in his introductions to himself and especially to the idiosyncrasies of his other clerks – the aging Turkey, the younger Nippers, and the office boy Ginger Nut. This decision makes little sense in narrative terms. The lawyer's claim that "some such description is indispensable to an adequate understanding of the chief character about to be presented" (13) shows that it makes much more sense as a way of establishing the story's generic credentials and the clerking environment with which the magazine's readers would have been familiar.

These introductory descriptions also allow Melville to establish the tone of the story in a way that fulfills one other vital aspect of *Putnam's* prospectus: "A man buys a Magazine," the first editorial announced, "to be instructed, if you please, but the lesson must be made amusing."[10] In interpretations that privilege endings, Bartleby's fate – imprisonment and death – negates the comedy of the lawyer's narration. The portraits of his clerks, though, are comic sketches or caricatures and work primarily through exaggeration. So after his morning productivity begins to wane, Turkey grows "altogether too energetic" and has a "strange, inflamed, flurried, flighty recklessness of activity about him" that causes him to "make an unpleasant racket in his chair," to spill his sandbox, and to split his pencils and throw them to the floor in a fit of passion as he tries to mend them. Of Nippers, the lawyer observes bathetically that "I deemed him the victim of two evil powers – ambition and indigestion" (*PT* 16). It is the latter of these that preoccupies the lawyer as he explains Nippers's protracted struggles to find the right height for his desk.

Turkey also shows himself to be a fluent pacifier of the lawyer in moments that work by wry comic reversal. When he complains about the blots Turkey makes on his copy, Turkey offers old age as his excuse: "Old age – even if it blot the page – is honorable. With submission, sir, we *both* are getting old" (16). And when the lawyer thinks about dismissing Turkey for "moistening a ginger-cake between his lips, and clapping it on to a mortgage for a seal," Turkey makes an oriental bow and turns the situation to his advantage: "With submission, sir, it was generous of me to find you in stationery on my own account" (19). In his dealings with Bartleby, the lawyer also shows himself to be capable of comic intent. When Bartleby refuses various other career options – a clerkship in a dry goods store, bartending, a traveling job collecting bills for merchants – the lawyer asks, "How then would going as a companion to Europe, to entertain some young gentleman with your conversation, – how would that suit you?" (41). The magazine reader is left to recognize the lawyer's irony.

The sketch-like qualities and moments of comic exchange in "Bartleby," while they fulfill *Putnam's* remit to amuse, are features more often associated with the stories Melville wrote for *Harper's Monthly* around the same time as "Bartleby" – "The Happy Failure," "The Fiddler," and "Cock-A-Doodle-Doo!" Shorter and much lighter in tone than "Bartleby," what they seem to lack to a later reader is the seriousness one finds in Melville's *Putnam's* stories, especially "Bartleby" but also "Benito Cereno," serialized in three parts from October to December 1855. At one level, *Harper's* and *Putnam's* were different kinds of magazines. *Harper's* was popular, with a circulation of over one hundred thousand, and populist. In March 1857, a piece in *Putnam's* described its rival as "a repository of pleasant, various reading, of sprightly chit-chat, and safe, vague, and dull disquisitions upon a few public questions."[21] In contrast, the circulation of *Putnam's* peaked at thirty-five thousand in the summer of 1853. The nature of the magazine's content earned it a reputation for being both more original and more intellectually demanding than *Harper's*, especially as political essays appeared with greater frequency toward the end of its existence in the autumn of 1857. Given these different qualities, Sheila Post-Lauria has argued that Melville adapted the style of his stories for each magazine, sending his stories with more complex political, social, and aesthetic themes to *Putnam's* and his more sentimental and lightweight pieces to *Harper's*.[22] The two magazines were not, however, always so easily distinguished.

There were limits to what even *Putnam's* would publish. "The Two Temples" was rejected because of the obvious attack on Grace Church in New York City. Another of Melville's diptychs, "The Paradise of Bachelors and the Tartarus of Maids," appeared in *Harper's*, but the stark examination of gender difference and female labor in a Massachusetts paper mill seems better suited to *Putnam's*. More important, though, authors other than Melville wrote for and helped shape the tenor of both magazines. The most important of these figures was George William Curtis, one of the three founding editors of *Putnam's Monthly* along with Charles Briggs and Parke Godwin. Curtis took on the role of gatekeeper for arts and literature at *Putnam's*. At the same time he also wrote the popular "Editor's Easy Chair" columns for *Harper's* each month from April 1854 until his death in 1892. Curtis's mild satires of metropolitan socialites were published as *The Potiphar Papers* (1853) and *Prue and I* (1856), after being serialized in

Putnam's and *Harper's*, respectively. There was little to distinguish them. Curtis's own response to Melville's stories was also mixed. He praised "Bartleby," and once even had the scrivener appear briefly as a character in his own fiction. He liked "The Encantadas," another story serialized in three parts, from March to May 1854, but had misgivings about "The Bell-Tower," which he initially rejected before changing his mind. He showed only grudging admiration for "Benito Cereno," telling his publisher: "take up Benito Cereno of Melville. You have paid for it. I should attenuate the dreadful statistic of the end.... why can't Americans write good stories. They tell good lies enough, & plenty of 'em." The only story Curtis accepted for *Putnam's* without question in this period was "I and My Chimney," and the terms of his acceptance indicate the criteria on which he judged Melville's stories: it was, he wrote, "a capital, genial, humorous sketch ... thoroughly magazinish."²³ This story was not reprinted in *The Piazza Tales.* Curtis's enthusiasm shows that while *Putnam's* and *Harper's* may have had different political and philosophical outlooks, their aesthetic standards were much less distinct. That Melville accidentally sent the manuscript of "Bartleby" to *Harper's* instead of *Putnam's* might indicate something similar.

Ordinary, generic, and *magazinish*: these are not adjectives often used to describe "Bartleby." They are, though, the qualities that brought the story to publication. This is not to diminish the quality of "Bartleby" but to see Melville writing "the *other* way" and to read the story as it was encountered by readers of *Putnam's Monthly* in 1853. To be sensitive to the way that a story comes into publication, however, does not mean discounting qualities that allow it to withstand the pressures of obsolescence. In fact, the capacity for a story like "Bartleby" to be transformed from ordinary magazine fiction into canonical text across 100 years may even be a consequence of the manner of its coming to publication. As well as writing within a tradition, Melville writes a story that goes beyond it. The story fulfills the remit *Putnam's Monthly* set itself of offering "a running commentary on the countless phenomena of the times as they rise,"²⁴ but the ambition of the story is to open up a new world: as the lawyer-narrator immediately suggests, "Bartleby" is about that "interesting and somewhat singular set of men, of whom as yet nothing that I know of has ever been written: – I mean the law-copyists or scriveners" (*PT* 13). Part of the story's enduring quality results from the techniques Melville deploys to subject this new world to examination.

One of the dilemmas when thinking about Melville is why a writer now so revered was so routinely ignored or undervalued when he was writing and publishing. What do we see in his work that readers did not in the 1850s? The question, though, can be usefully turned the other way: What did readers of his work in the 1850s see that we do not? Apart from the comparison to Poe in *The Literary World*, there is little evidence of any reaction to "Bartleby" as it appeared in *Putnam's Monthly*. When reprinted in *The Piazza Tales* reviewers certainly saw the humor, but one word that reoccurs in the reviews is "quaint." The New York *Criterion* described "Bartleby" as "a quaint tale, based upon living characters." The Boston *Evening Traveller* wrote of the "quaint explanation" of Bartleby's silence, while the New York *Tribune* noted a "quaintness of expression" across the collection as whole. These positive connotations of *quaint* stand in contrast to *Godey's Lady's Book*, whose disparaging review suggested Melville's "style has an affectation of quaintness, which renders it, to us, very confused and wearisome."[25]

The modern meaning of *quaint* suggests something pleasantly old-fashioned. *quaint* In all of these reviews, however, *quaint* is used in an archaic sense to indicate something elaborate, detailed, and artfully designed. This is the sense in which Melville uses the word in his own novels: "the quaint old arms on the panel" (*P* 19) of a carriage in *Pierre*, for instance, or the tattoos in *Typee* that Tommo compares to "quaint patterns we sometimes see in costly pieces of lace-work" (*T* 78). Perhaps more apparent when "Bartleby" was set alongside his other stories in *The Piazza Tales* rather than buried in the miscellany of a magazine, readers of the 1850s saw quite clearly the intricacies of Melville's writing that distinguished it – for good or bad – from other writing.

To read "Bartleby" as magazine fiction, then, also means recognizing how Melville embeds these "quaint" designs in the story's generic, or "magazinish," dimensions. So the lawyer-narrator's effort at the beginning of the story to describe Turkey, Nippers, and Ginger Nut sketches and establishes their characters; it also elaborates the characters with detail – the multiplying of their eccentricities – without making them more than supporting characters or exceeding the purpose of a sketch. The lawyer's delineation of his office space likewise locates the reader in the familiar territory of Wall Street and a white-collar working environment. It is then embellished with details – the white wall of the light shaft, the wall black with age at the other side of the chambers, the demarcation of space, and Bartleby's place behind his screen – that go beyond the information needed to position the reader but do not threaten the reader's familiarity with the scene. The brief references to John Jacob Astor and the Colt Adams murders might, in retrospect, add contextual weight to the story, but they work as topical asides for the reader of the 1850s without intruding on the central characters or the story's development. All these details reward interpretation without impeding the story's magazinish qualities.

Finally, and most wondrously of all of course, there is the design of Bartleby himself. Melville's master stroke is to keep the reader constantly at one remove from the scrivener, whose character becomes all the more mysterious and intriguing because one only ever encounters him from within the partial and retrospective imagining of the lawyer. In trying to understand Bartleby, the reader is continually confounded by first having to try and understand the lawyer. Both are revealed iteratively: through Bartleby's refrain of "I prefer not to" and his repeated refusal to work; through the lawyer's repeated descriptions of Bartleby as pallid; through the accumulation of incidents – Bartleby's eating of ginger biscuits, his locking himself in the office, his unchanging demeanor – that the lawyer struggles to understand; and through Bartleby's capacity to withstand the lawyer's attempts to be rid of him. In these recurrences the reader follows the lawyer in looking for meaning, only to have that expectation deferred or denied. Unlike the copying clerk in Maitland's *The Lawyer's Story*, and even though his profession is central to his identity and gives him his place in this generic story of lawyers and clerks, Bartleby's melancholy disposition and mysterious personality are never supplanted or explained by hard facts and family history.

In place of these, Melville brings together a series of details, actions, and observations and holds them in relation to one another in a way that provokes interpretation without telling the reader what to think. Coming at the end of the story, Bartleby's tragic death appears to be the result of prior events. And yet the causal chain is not connected for the reader by the lawyer's narration to show why Bartleby dies. The rumor of his previous employment in the Dead Letter Office tantalizes by suggesting an explanation. The lawyer himself is moved to say, "When I think of this rumor, hardly can I express the emotions which seize me" (*PT* 45). But just as the prospect of clarification seems at hand, the lawyer deepens the mystery still further in his conjectures about dead men, dead letters, and the effects they may have had on his former scrivener. What is reiterated is the partiality and incompleteness of the lawyer's perspective. The rumor about the Dead Letter Office is the final addition to the story's elaborately constructed design. Bartleby is truly *quaint* in the nineteenth-century meaning of the word, and Melville's artful design of his character (and of his character's demise) becomes part of the larger design of a story intended to function as magazine fiction.

"Bartleby, the Scrivener: A Story of Wall-Street" was written at a time when literary authorship and the cultural industry of magazines were undergoing an uneven and unpredictable development. Caught up in the midst of this process because of his need to write for money, Melville faced the problem of trying to ask the kinds of searching questions his novels explore within the confines of magazine fiction. By first taking a generic dramatic situation and then deploying his artful design, Melville makes the familiar and expected sufficiently less well known that it becomes intriguing but does not entirely confound. To read "Bartleby" as magazine fiction is to see how the magazine format disciplines and releases Melville's creative energy. As if in ratification of his own idea that "the greatest, grandest things are unpredicted,"[26] the longevity and ubiquity of "Bartleby" results from Melville managing the contingencies of his position as a reluctant magazine writer in the 1850s without abandoning his intellectual ambition. In "Hawthorne and His Mosses," Melville writes that truth reveals itself in literature "only by cunning glimpses ... covertly, and by snatches," but that when it does the reader senses "those deep far-away things" that hint at the "the very axis of reality" (*PT* 244). Melville's "Bartleby" continues to offer such glimpses to generation after generation.

NOTES

1 *Literary World*, December 3, 1853, 195.
2 *Putnam's Monthly Magazine*, January 1853, 1.
3 Michael Paul Rogin, *Subversive Genealogy: The Politics and Art of Herman Melville* (New York: Knopf, 1983), 195–99; Richard Chase, *Herman Melville: A Critical Study* (New York: Macmillan, 1949), 142–47; and Leo Marx, "Melville's Parable of the Wall," *The Sewanee Review* 61 (1953): 602–27.
4 Jay Leyda, ed., *Complete Stories of Herman Melville* (New York: Random House, 1949), 455.
5 Daniel A. Wells, "'Bartleby the Scrivener,' Poe, and the Duyckinck Circle," *ESQ: A Journal of the American Renaissance* 21 (1975): 35–39; Brook Thomas, "The Legal Fictions of Herman Melville and Lemuel Shaw," *Critical Inquiry* 11 (1984): 24–51; Walter Evans, "Hawthorne and 'Bartleby the Scrivener,'" *American Transcendental Quarterly* 57 (1985): 45–58. See also Robert Weisbuch, *Atlantic Double-Cross: American Literature and British Influence in the Age of Emerson* (Chicago, IL: University of Chicago Press, 1986), chapter 2.
6 Mario D'Avanzo, "Melville's 'Bartleby' and John Jacob Astor," *New England Quarterly* 41 (1968): 259–64; T. H. Giddings, "Melville, the Colt-Adams Murder, and 'Bartleby,'" *Studies in American Fiction* 2 (1974): 123–32; Hershel Parker, "Dead Letters and Melville's Bartleby," *Resources for American Literary Study* 4 (1974): 90–99.
7 David Jaffe, *"Bartleby the Scrivener" and* Bleak House: *Melville's Debt to Dickens* (Arlington, VA: Mardi Press, 1981); Johannes Dietrich Bergmann, "'Bartleby' and *The Lawyer's Story*," *American Literature* 47 (1975): 432–36.
8 Michael T. Gilmore, *American Romanticism and the Marketplace* (Chicago, IL: University of Chicago Press, 1985), 132–45; Louise K. Barnett, "Bartleby as Alienated Worker," *Studies in Short Fiction* 11 (1974): 379–85.
9 Barbara Foley, "From Wall Street to Astor Place: Historicizing Melville's 'Bartleby,'" *American Literature* 72 (2000): 87–116.
10 John Evelev, *Tolerable Entertainment: Herman Melville and Professionalism in Antebellum New York* (Amherst: University of Massachusetts Press, 2006), 1–21.

11 Amit Pinchevski, "Bartleby's Autism: Wandering along Incommunicability," *Cultural Critique* 78 (2011): 27–59; Graham Thompson, "'Dead Letters! ... Dead Men?' The Rhetoric of the Office in Melville's 'Bartleby, the Scrivener,'" *Journal of American Studies* 34 (2000): 395–411.

12 Branka Arsić, *Passive Constitutions or 7½ Times Bartleby* (Stanford, CA: Stanford University Press, 2007), 10.

13 Cited in Hershel Parker, *Herman Melville, 1819–1851* (Baltimore, MD: Johns Hopkins University Press, 1996), 376.

14 Cited in Ezra Greenspan, *George Palmer Putnam: Representative American Publisher* (University Park: Pennsylvania State University Press, 2000), 290.

15 Hershel Parker, *Herman Melville, 1851–1891* (Baltimore, MD: Johns Hopkins University Press, 2002), 163.

16 James A. Maitland, *The Lawyer's Story: or, The Orphan's Wrongs* (New York: H. Long & Brother, 1853), 7.

17 *Putnam's Monthly Magazine*, February 1853, 160.

18 *Putnam's Monthly Magazine*, April 1853, 353.

19 See Brian P. Lusky, *On the Make: Clerks and the Quest for Capital in Nineteenth-Century America* (New York: New York University Press, 2010).

20 *Putnam's Monthly Magazine*, January 1853, 1.

21 *Putnam's Monthly Magazine*, March 1857, 296.

22 Sheila Post-Lauria, *Correspondent Colorings: Melville in the Marketplace* (Amherst: University of Massachusetts Press, 1996), 151–209.

23 George William Curtis to J. A. Dix; July 31, 1855; MS Am 800.13 (79) and George William Curtis to J. A. Dix; September 7, 1855; MS Am 800.13 (89), Houghton Library, Harvard University.

24 *Putnam's Monthly Magazine*, January 1853, 2.

25 Brian Higgins and Hershel Parker, eds., *Herman Melville: The Contemporary Reviews* (Cambridge: Cambridge University Press, 1995), 473, 472, 479, and 483.

26 From Melville's marginalia on his copy of John Milton's *Paradise Regained*, cited in Parker, *Herman Melville, 1851–1891*, 162.

8

MAURICE S. LEE

Skepticism and *The Confidence-Man*

[I]t is the part of prudence not to place absolute confidence in that by
which we have even once been deceived.
                                                    – René Descartes

I can believe that worse things than being duped may happen to a man
in this world.
                                                    – William James

Lord knows, the paths to error are legion, and there are lots of reasons to
lack confidence. Melville seems to canvass them all in *The Confidence-Man*
(1857), a book that is crucial to the arc of his career and that has been
called his "most nearly perfect work," but one that continues to baffle literary critics, many of whom associate it with the word *problem*.[1] Problems of
epistemology, problems of language, problems of theology, aesthetics, ethics,
and politics – one reason *The Confidence-Man* is hard to read with confidence is that the book, for better and for worse, is the purest distillation of
Melville's skepticism. *Mardi*, *Moby-Dick*, and *Pierre* all explore an array of
philosophical doubts about the accuracy of perception, the foundations of
selfhood, the scope of human reason, and the bases for moral judgment. *The
Confidence-Man* pursues these lines of inquiry beyond generic boundaries
as Melville does not so much entertain skepticism in his capacity as a story-
teller but instead takes problems of knowledge, inference, and action as the
primary impetus for his book.

The Confidence-Man has been compared to picaresque novels, frontier
folklore, satire, and allegory, yet the text defies easy categorization, even
at basic levels of form. Its novel-length narrative has virtually no plot, as
scenes follow scenes with little causal logic and often perfunctory transi-
tions. The titular character may be a shape-shifting con man or we may
witness a procession of swindlers, but even if there is a single protagonist, he
lacks the kind of fully realized personality one expects in a main character.
A Mississippi steamboat provides the stage for the exits and entrances of
a host of minor players, but the *Fidéle* is not a carefully delineated setting,
especially in comparison with other Melville ships, nor does the landscape
that slides spectrally by have much dramatic presence. The entire action of

the book takes place appropriately on April Fools Day sometime after the Mexican-American War (1846–48), and scholars have made good use of nineteenth-century contexts – the growth of a speculative market economy that depended on confidence but destabilized value; the rise of swindling, hoaxing, and dissembling (from forgery and what we now call identity theft, to P. T. Barnum exhibits, to minstrelsy and makeup); the rootlessness of an American culture in which citizens and noncitizens are atomistic strangers; the spread of utopian hopes and institutionalized benevolence in a nation marked by violence, poverty, racism, and a protracted slavery conflict that would soon lead to the Civil War.[2]

We can productively situate *The Confidence-Man* within antebellum America, and the book's Western setting and frontier characters cater to generic expectations of domestic and transatlantic audiences. More subversively, the *Fidéle*'s advance on New Orleans can highlight sectional differences and reorient progressive historical narratives in which American empire takes a strictly westward course. And yet *The Confidence-Man* resists the spatial, temporal, and psychological specificities that typify nineteenth-century novels, as Melville simultaneously bridges and exploits gaps between lived experience and abstract speculation. An 1857 review of *The Confidence-Man* in London's *Literary Gazette* complained, "A novel it is not, unless a novel means forty-five conversations held on board a steamer, conducted by passengers who might pass for the errata of creation, and so far resembling the Dialogues of Plato as to be undoubted Greek to ordinary men."[3] Melville himself may not have disagreed with this and similar assessments from his contemporaries. Manuscript revisions of *The Confidence-Man* show Melville twisting his syntax and obfuscating his claims as if to frustrate the superficial skimming of readers, while chapters 14, 33, and 44 self-referentially satirize novelistic conventions of the time. Perhaps, too, the *Literary Gazette*'s reference to Plato would have tickled Melville (were he still capable of taking pleasure in reviews), for if *The Confidence-Man* sounds like a sequence of Socratic dialogues and alludes to Plato among many philosophers, the book ultimately has little faith in idealism (Platonic, Christian, or transcendental) and severely doubts that rational methods can accurately ascertain truths.

That Melville would write such an intensely privative book – one characterized by the abandonment of novelistic conventions and an absence of trustworthy knowledge – makes some sense in the context of a career that by 1857 seemed destined for commercial failure. *Moby-Dick* and *Pierre* include moments that mock novel writing, reviewing, and publishing, while *Israel Potter* (1855) and Melville's short stories from the period subvert popular beliefs in American exceptionalism. As his last work of fiction published during his life, *The Confidence-Man* can represent the climax of what Nina Baym four decades ago called Melville's "Quarrel with Fiction," though Baym's claim that Melville "drops metaphysics altogether" in his ironic debunking of literary form does not account for the philosophical seriousness of Melville's resistance to novels as such.[4] *The Confidence-Man* aggressively parodies both novelistic discourse and rational inquiry, and yet still it invites us to examine with some earnestness the relationship between fiction and philosophy, even teaching through its own privative example how literature might figure in the search for truth.

"How Unreal All This Is!"

Melville's skepticism can be taken to anticipate post-metaphysical philosophy and poststructural theory of the twentieth and twenty-first centuries, though his sensitivity to epistemological limits looks backward as well as forward, especially as he becomes in the late 1840s and 1850s increasingly committed to the history of ideas. The story of Melville's skepticism might start with Descartes, the so-called father of modern philosophy, who admitted the power of skeptical arguments even as he sought to refute them. In the first section of his *Meditations* (1641), "Concerning Those Things That Can Be Called into Doubt," Descartes reasons that one cannot have "absolute confidence" in methods that have "even once been deceived."[5] Commencing with skepticism in order to erect on first principles an infallible metaphysical system, Descartes sets aside imperfect knowledge derived from the senses and trusts instead his own God-created mind: the senses of the self may be fooled, but to be fooled, the thinking self must first undoubtedly exist. In *The Confidence-Man* and elsewhere, Melville shares with Descartes a (relatively straightforward) mistrust of the senses, but he departs from Descartes's (more complicated) claims for unchanging, absolute selfhood, leaving little – though not exactly nothing – on which philosophical confidence might rely.

If *Moby-Dick*'s allusion to "Descartian vortices" (159) has more to do with physics than epistemology, it nonetheless underscores Melville's abiding concern that our sense perceptions are subject to deceit.[6] Ishmael repeatedly mistakes dreams for reality, a danger Descartes emphasizes, while Ahab suspects the object world is in reality a facade. Pierre is another disastrous dreamer whose senses are often misguided, while "Bartleby" suggests how perceptions can fail to connect individuals to each other and the world, a problem suffered by Amasa Delano of "Benito Cereno," who is beguiled by both conspiratorial performances and his own self-interested misprisions. The threat of misperception begins for Melville in the cultural register of *Typee*, but by the 1850s the problem was increasingly inflected by skeptics he was reading, including philosophers such as Pyrrho (through Diogenes Laertius), Michel de Montaigne, David Hume, Pierre Bayle, and Ralph Waldo Emerson.[7]

Melville's engagement with skepticism culminates in *The Confidence-Man*, a book that imagines – and encourages – its readers to exclaim, "How unreal all this is!" (*CM* 182). Words such as *appear* and *seem* abound in the text, as do references to deafness, blindness, dreams, counterfeiting, dissimulation, and masquerades. When accusing the crippled beggar Black Guinea of being an able-bodied white man, the man with the wooden leg insists, "Looks are one thing, and facts are another" (14). Characters accuse each other of being misled by their perceptions, as when Charlie Noble and Frank Goodman argue over their wine. And after buying stock from the stranger in a snuff-colored coat, the tubercular miser cries, "[C]an't trust my senses any more, since trusting him!" (102). *The Confidence-Man* everywhere plays on potential differences between appearances and reality, a main preoccupation of skeptical philosophers – from Pyrrho ("[I]f appearances are deceitful, then they do not deserve any confidence"), to Montaigne ("Man cannot avoid the fact that his senses are both the sovereign regents of his knowledge, and yet, in all circumstances, uncertain and fallible"), to Hume (see his chapter "Of Scepticism with Regard to the Senses" in *A Treatise on Human Nature* [1740]), to Emerson ("Dream delivers us to dream, and there is no end to illusion").[8] Just as Descartes in *Meditations* worries that dreaming and demons might mislead our perceptions, the devilish con man (or men) aboard the dreamlike *Fidéle* undercut the authority of the senses and the foundations of social trust.

One response to this quandary is to willfully believe in the object world as we experience it – to abjure the idealist's desire for deeper truths, to bracket the skeptic's doubts about perception, and to practice a looser, more charitable, more communal epistemology that relieves confidence from the burden of certitude. The word *confidence* (like *trust*, *faith*, and *belief*) should not connote absolute certainty so much as a willingness to proceed *as if* something were true, even if – and sometimes precisely because – that something cannot be rationally guaranteed. After eating, playing backgammon, and making merry with his friends, Hume finds experience sufficient proof of itself, rendering his skepticism (if only for a time) "cold, and strained, and ridiculous."[9] Emerson in certain moods of his essay "Experience" (1844) also leaves off the quest for certainty and its attendant doubts: "Let us treat the men and women well: treat them as if they were real: perhaps they are."[10] An alternative to disbelief is a realist epistemology that does not suffer from naïve positivism insofar as sense-based knowledge is understood as provisional and self-consciously arrogated as such.

Yet *The Confidence-Man* makes it hard to maintain even this modest sort of trust. Just as the possible diddlers aboard the *Fidéle* ask their interlocutors to believe in stories sure to induce suspicion, readers may find it difficult to willfully suspend their disbelief about a book that displays its own artifice. If many of Melville's ocean novels intimate deep foundational truths, *The Confidence-Man* is more like the Mississippi River. Shallow, muddy, and mature (in the potamological sense of running slowly, being fed by multiple tributaries, and growing wider rather than deeper), the book encourages readers to dwell on its surfaces, even as the untrustworthiness of those surfaces renders the fictional world less credible. Unlike romantic texts that aspire to feel real by inhabiting self-generated, self-contained universes, *The Confidence-Man* with its metacritical asides purposefully punctures verisimilitude. And unlike realist novels that aspire to feel real by corresponding with material and cultural conditions, *The Confidence-Man* is not committed to finely textured settings and intricate social relations. The steamboat may be named the *Fidéle*, but Melville ironizes mimetic fidelity as pursued by most nineteenth-century novels. Just as Descartes in *Meditations* wonders whether he is sitting in his dressing gown next to a fire with a body that is really his own, *The Confidence-Man* casts the shadow of doubt over everything from settings to appearances to bodies.

More stubbornly than any Melville text, the uncertainties of *The Confidence-Man* remain unresolved, severely complicating critical attempts to ascribe ethical or political order. Hypocrisies in the book are evident enough: cynical characters refuse to trust in appearances but are quick to judge Black Guinea by the color of his skin; wealthy characters adopt skeptical stances that help them shirk the moral duties they proclaim. Despite much critical attention, scholars still disagree as to whether the four chapters on "The Metaphysics of Indian-Hating" are more about philosophy or politics. As with other episodes in *The Confidence-Man*, the contest between charity and misanthropy is abstracted (touching on such issues as the prejudice of deduction, the mystery of iniquity, and the untrustworthiness of secondhand narrative), to the point that the historical reality of American genocide threatens to fade into the background. At the same time – and to read the "Indian-Hating" chapters ironically – the sheer prolixity of the philosophizing can make the chapters feel evasive to the point of self-willed denial. In general, the last few decades of scholarship on *The Confidence-Man* have largely focused on political content, but the epistemological ambiguity of the book erodes the ground for ideological claims. If Babo's performance in "Benito Cereno" is ultimately recognizable as such, and if Delano's perceptual confusion is revealed as a symptom of his racism and an excuse to avoid moral action, the masquerade of *The Confidence-Man* is never unmasked. We never learn whether characters are crooks or not, whether decisions to give or withhold trust are wise or foolish, ethical or wicked. The moral of the book, if there is one at all, is that skepticism can preempt moral judgment.

"Vindicating One's Self"

It is no coincidence that Melville refers to Descartes in *Moby-Dick* at a moment when Ishmael nearly "loses his identity" (159). A curious dynamic in Melville's career is that the more committed he becomes to philosophical explorations of identity, motive, and agency, the more he suspects that human psychology and character lie beyond the reach of philosophical explanation. As Baym has documented in the antebellum period, and as Amy Kaplan has argued regarding realist fiction after the Civil War, novel reviewers and readers across nineteenth-century America possessed a wide range of aesthetic preferences but tended to value characters for their depth, transparency, credibility, and consistency.[11] By these standards, the more Melville ruminates on character, the less successful his characters become, at least in the case of *The Confidence-Man*'s shifty, flat players, who caused an 1857 reviewer to wonder "whether the characters were intended ... not for actual living beings, but for philosophical abstractions."[12] Melville's philosophical imagination and artistic ambition frequently impel him toward limit cases, and his commentaries on character in *The Confidence-Man* suggest that any deficiencies in this regard are intentional. What characterization there is in the book is largely accomplished through eccentricities of body and dress, demographic stereotyping, as well as long dialogues that, given the ever-present potential for dissimulation, cannot be trusted to indicate deeply held feelings or thoughts. *The Confidence-Man*'s impersonal characters do follow from perceptual skepticism, though they also entail a more fundamental critique of Cartesian selfhood.

Descartes's epistemology, and by extension much modern philosophy, is built upon trust in the self. After taking his duped-but-thinking self as a response to the problem of fallible perceptions, Descartes momentarily retreats from confidence toward doubt when he wonders, "I am, I exist – that is certain. But for how long?"[13] Descartes responds to this existential threat by arguing that the self continuously thinks and therefore continuously exists. But lest such thinking be mistaken for the autonomous creation of one's own selfhood, he finds in the desire of the self to prove itself evidence of the existence of God. That is, the Cartesian subject's need to demonstrate its existence indicates that it did not author itself (otherwise it would not feel the need for such demonstration). Melville, however, does not find epistemological reassurance in an absolute identity underwritten by God; or as he puts it in *The Confidence-Man* when defending the inconsistency of his characters, "[E]very one knows how bootless it is to be in all cases vindicating one's self" (183).

The Confidence-Man is hardly Melville's first text to take a skeptical view of personal identity. From Babbalanja's distrust in *Mardi* ("I keep an eye on myself, as I would on a stranger" [456]), to the reinvention of selves in *Redburn* and *White-Jacket*, to Babo's opaque and Pierre's untraceable identities – Melville doubts that absolute selfhood can provide a basis for absolute knowledge. In *The Confidence-Man*, characters play roles, lack proper names, and are defined by their clothing and comportment, as if identity is a disguise or performance to be shuffled on and off. It can be tempting to try and penetrate appearances to get at some core or foundational self. If we read carefully enough, might we – like some kind of detective – trace the true identity of the confidence man and make sense of his motives and machinations? Some literary critics have attempted to do so using allegorical approaches (for instance, the con man as Satan), biographical contexts (Melville or his associates as the con man), and historical coordinates (the con man as the forger and plagiarist Thomas Powell, the crook William Thompson, or any number of antebellum figures).[14] Source study has enriched critical understandings of *The Confidence-Man*, though many scholars take Melville to be actively denying that selves can ever be confidently known as anything more than social, literary, and linguistic fictions.[15]

One reason why selves may be so difficult to know is that they are irreducibly unstable, a point emphasized by skeptical thinkers from Montaigne (see his essay "On the Inconstancy of Our Actions" [1580]), to Hume ("[T]he characters of men are ... inconstant and irregular"), to romantic contemporaries of Melville.[16] Stanley Cavell has argued that writers such as Emerson, Edgar Allan Poe, and Henry David Thoreau leave behind Descartes's claims for absolute selfhood, though they do so without taking up the radical position that the self literally thinks itself into being. Rather, such writers depart from Descartes by taking the self to enact its own becoming: thinking is a determinative (but not originating) act; selves are malleable and have agency; humans can participate in the always unfinished project of moral perfectionism. Focusing on Emerson's essay "Self-Reliance" (1841), Cavell reads Emerson as a champion of the inconsistent self. The Emersonian genius must reclaim language as an inheritance common to all readers in order to teach both himself and his audience confidence in their upwardly motile selves. Cavell writes, "'Self-Reliance' as a whole presents a theory – I wish we knew how to call it an aesthetics – of reading.'"[17] And this thought, generative like so much of Cavell's work, can instigate a discussion of how *The Confidence-Man* dramatizes both the claims and limits of post-Cartesian identity.

Scholars have long noted that *The Confidence-Man* continues a commentary on American transcendentalism that Melville begins around 1850. In *Moby-Dick*, Ahab can be taken to represent the imperial potential of Emersonian selfhood, while Plotinus Plinlimmon of *Pierre* suggests how transcendental idealism can authorize a risky moral relativism. Emerson and Thoreau appear in *The Confidence-Man* lightly disguised as Mark Winsome and his disciple Egbert, and the most blatant target of Melville's satire is the idealized vision of friendship set forth in Emerson's essay "Friendship" (1841) and Thoreau's *A Week on the Concord and Merrimack Rivers* (1849). Melville also levels the related charge that beneath the vatic idealism of transcendental philosophy lies a selfish, materialistic individualism, which we see when Winsome dismisses a Poe-like character described as a "crazy beggar" with "a disheveled mass of raven curls," leaving Egbert to explain why transcendental philosophy precludes helping friends in financial straits (194–95). Here Melville anticipates political attacks on transcendentalism's complicity in liberal individualism, though more central to the epistemology of *The Confidence-Man* is its engagement with Emersonian inconsistency.

When Winsome blithely declares, "I seldom care to be consistent," Melville not only echoes "Self-Reliance" – where Emerson writes, "With consistency a great soul has simply nothing to do" – he also makes explicit a skeptical concern that appears throughout *The Confidence-Man*.[18] Within the first dozen chapters of the book, characters are possessed by sudden "wayward mood[s]" (12), the failure of memory suggests that "the mind is ductile" to the point where past and present selves are discontinuous (20), and a "Protean easy-chair" with its "endlessly-changeable accommodations" symbolizes the ease with which people adjust the moral convictions often regarded as sources of selfhood and the very foundations of character (38). At one point, a merchant praises benevolence only to voice the sudden conviction that charitable inclinations are delusional. It may be his wine talking, but *The Confidence-Man* goes on to defend as an aesthetic principle "the queer, unaccountable caprices of [the] natural heart" (68).

For a novelist whose calling was taken to be the creation of believable characters, Melville finds personal inconsistency a challenge for both his epistemology and art, a dynamic apparent in one of the most commented upon chapters in *The Confidence-Man*. The very title of chapter 14, "Worth the consideration of those to whom it may prove worth considering," satirizes circular methods of proof and dismisses potentially censorious readers, even as it logically mounts a defense of the characters in *The Confidence-Man*. An authorial voice admits that most "sensible" readers feel that "consistency

should be preserved" in novels, for they prefer "fiction, where every character can, by reason of its consistency, be comprehended at a glance" (69–70).
Nonetheless, the authorial voice rhetorically asks, "[I]s it not a fact, that, in
real life, a consistent character is a *rara avis*?" – that is, a "rare bird." The
characters of *The Confidence-Man* support this radical assertion, including
the Missouri bachelor Pitch and his unaccountable caprices of the heart.

Pitch demonstrates how hard it is to live a consistent life. The pun with his
name is that despite his repeated insistence, "I stick to what I say" (117), he
proves as unpredictable as the "pitch-penny game" that passengers earlier
play by tossing coins at Black Guinea's mouth (11). Pitch initially seems a
figure of absolute certitude: he withstands the sophistry of the herb doctor;
his misanthropy covers all cases; and he is associated with Cicero's *Tusculan
Disputations*, a book that equates legitimate philosophizing with consistency. Such absolutism is tested, however, when a probable con man posing
as an agent for the Philosophical Intelligence Office recommends a boy to
work on Pitch's farm. Having hired thirty-five boys over a fifteen-year period
and finding each to be a "rascal," Pitch objects on the principle that "[a]ll
boys are rascals," an axiom he repeats no less than six times (126). Pitch
also assumes that all boys will stay bad ("All boys are rascals, and so are all
men"), syllogistically defending a belief in absolute consistency across all
individuals and through all time. In response, the P.I.O. agent – who claims
to view the subject "scientifically" – rejects Pitch's deductive logic, pointing
out that experience is not always predictive and that inferential reasoning is
never absolute (120). The agent is correct that no amount of evidence and
induction can ever rule out good boys, black swans, and other phenomena
inconsistent with prior experience, though he goes too far when invoking
the gambler's fallacy: "If hitherto, sir, you have struck upon a peculiarly bad
vein of boys, so much the more hope now of your hitting a good" (127).
Like Winsome but arguing in a scientific mode, the P.I.O. agent divorces
consistency from the traditional office of philosophy, ultimately persuading
Pitch to put down a deposit for a boy.

If for Emerson the becoming, inconsistent self holds always the promise
of improvement, *The Confidence-Man* takes inconsistency as a fact of experience that remains impossible to judge. Inconsistency in the book can be a
sign of hypocrisy and can lead to seemingly imprudent decisions, as when
Pitch and the barber at the end of the book stray from their supposed principles. At the same time, to quote the P.I.O. agent, inconsistency can be seen as
a kind of "flexile gracefulness" marked by open-minded, generous hope and
an understanding of inferential reasoning (126). Thus inconsistency may be
foolish or wise, self-interested or charitable, irrational or scientific. Which is
to say that the meaning of inconsistency is contingent, provisional, and – in

a word – inconsistent. Whatever the case, it gives the lie to novelistic conventions of character and Cartesian accounts of the self.

An Outside Narrative

Whether a third-person novel is the best form for Melville's critique of Cartesian subjectivity remains a difficult question that bears on how much a reader might value and enjoy *The Confidence-Man*. In *Meditations,* Descartes's persona appropriately assumes a consistent, coherent, transparent "I," and even when romantic writers explore the possibilities of post-Cartesian identity, they tend also to adopt first-person perspectives, thus offering relatively stable purchases from which to describe the breakdown and becoming of selves. Such is generally the case with William Wordsworth's unfolding reflections, Poe's helter-skelter narrators, Walt Whitman's perennially dissolving identities, Emily Dickinson's disjointed selves, and Emerson's "Experience," an essay that stands simultaneously as his most skeptical account of identity and his most intimate text. Romantic speakers – almost despite themselves – can arrogate a confidence in identity-based knowledge, even while enacting post-Cartesian identities that generate dialectical tension. This is part of the irony of Mark Winsome's claim taken at face value, for to say, "I seldom care to be consistent," assumes the existence of a coherent self able to announce from the "inside" its characteristic inconsistency.

By contrast, *The Confidence-Man*'s distant third-person perspective represents inconsistent selfhood from an "outside" position that offers no trustworthy referents. The cosmopolitan can defend the obstreperous Pitch by reassuring Charlie Noble: "You do not know him, or but imperfectly. His outside deceived you.… His outside is but put on" (156). The trick is that without reliable access inside the cosmopolitan's dubious character, readers have no basis on which to trust him. This is not to say that third-person narratives cannot credibly trace changes in character. Sentimental novels, *bildungsroman*, and many realist fictions are premised on such changes, though they are typically justified through generic morphologies, psychological transparency, and explanatory social contexts, particularly when the mechanisms of personal growth and devolution are central to moral structures and plots. In *The Confidence-Man*, however, changes in character are mainly driven by abstract arguments when they are driven by anything discernible at all. For a book that thematizes human suffering, moral dilemmas, political injustice, and personal transformations, *The Confidence-Man* remains strangely, stubbornly detached – as if Melville is unwilling to treat his characters as if they were real, as if his resistance to *a key problem with the book*

novelistic conventions precludes deep social engagement and courts a kind of aesthetic failure.

"Charity never faileth" is the final message of the mute at the start of *The Confidence-Man* (5). Melville's writings during the 1850s turn increasingly to the subject of failure, and *The Confidence-Man*, more than most Melville texts, may require some charitable reading. How can one identify with a novel whose characters lack identity? What is at stake – dramatically, emotionally, morally – in a narrative that defends the realism of its characters while flaunting how unreal they must seem? Melville knows how to write engrossing characters and scenes, but *The Confidence-Man* seldom does so. Its refusal certainly harmed the book's reception, though by violating his audience's expectations, the book manages to suggest how difficult it is to take seriously a world full of post-Cartesian selves. The becoming self can reflect on itself with trepidation, hope, and surprise, but from the outside – from a distant third-person view – such selves are hard to trust, befriend, and care deeply about. This may be why American transcendentalists struggled with friendship, intellectually and personally. It may help explain why Emerson and Thoreau did not write fiction (or read much of it), why Whitman and Dickinson wrote in lyric more than dramatic forms, and why Poe, so attuned to post-Cartesian identity, performs best in the first person.

The Confidence-Man can be read as a bold experiment attempting to novelize post-Cartesian identity, and its failure to meet aesthetic and ethical expectations while succeeding as philosophical provocation not only suggests how nineteenth-century novels assume Cartesian frameworks, but also points toward a tense dynamic between novelistic and philosophical traditions of the time. What if literature in general and novels in particular tend to be more sensitive than philosophy to the threat skepticism poses to moral, emotional, and intersubjective life? Cavell's self-relying Emerson models one way a newly invigorated common language can help us encounter skepticism. *The Confidence-Man* presents a related though negative example in which the abandonment of novelistic conventions, particularly regarding character, exposes how post-Cartesian thinking, particularly regarding identity, makes better sense as a philosophical argument than as a description of experience with which a reader on the outside might identify and trust. The common language of genre can allay skepticism, even if the feeling of realism is "merely" conditioned by habits of literary expression and response. Such habits no longer work toward realism when their artifice becomes apparent – when conventions become too well worn, or when literary experiments are so unfamiliar as to call attention to themselves as such. Melville knew the costs and benefits of both copying and originality.

The Confidence-Man errs on the side of the latter while showing brilliantly what is aesthetically lost and epistemologically gained when the novelist and, with him, the reader lose faith in fictions of the self.

The seriousness of Melville's quarrel with the novel is suggested by his thirty-year turn to poetry after *The Confidence-Man*, as well as by his long return to fiction with *Billy Budd*, subtitled *An Inside Narrative*. It makes sense that *The Confidence-Man* is regularly taken as a turning point in Melville's career, for not only is it the last novel he published, but in the absence of credible characters, Melville remains the most compelling personage in the book. *The Confidence-Man* expresses Melville's waning faith – not only in God, democracy, capitalism, and some imagined ideal readership – but also in the novel as a mode of philosophy, as one genre of what Melville calls in "Hawthorne and His Mosses" (1850) "the great Art of Telling the Truth" (*PT* 244). This waning faith is not quite a lost one. Melville writes at the end of chapter 14 of *The Confidence-Man*, "[T]he more earnest psychologists may, in the face of previous failures, still cherish expectations with regard to some mode of infallibly discovering the heart of man" (71). A mode of infallibly knowing the self is the ambition of Descartes and his legacy, and though Melville recognizes this Descartian dream as such, he cannot regard it without some earnestness.

The final chapter of *The Confidence-Man* may seem much like the rest. Satanic allusions, dubious deployments of the Bible, self-interested calculations, fallible perceptions, quandaries of hermeneutics and identity – all are arranged within a familiar dialectic of cynical skepticism competing with foolish-seeming trust. Parody is rampant, culminating in an old man mistaking a toilet for a life preserver. Yet even today, and maybe more so for Melville's contemporaries, one might sympathize with a "clean, comely, old man, his head snowy as the marble" who believes in the Bible, cares about lost children, does not pretend to have all the answers, and has little choice but to trust a stranger when faced with his own frailty and the onset of night (241). The chapter is titled, "The Cosmopolitan increases in seriousness." Generic conventions are visible enough and irony everywhere threatens, but like some readers across the decades, and of course to speak personally, I cannot believe here at the end of the book that Melville's skepticism goes all the way down. Perhaps it is an old habit, the desire to care about characters and find meaning, pleasure, and even goodness in the texts we read. Whatever the case, to take *The Confidence-Man* seriously at its end is to feel that utter doubt is more easily thought than lived, even if, as the faithful old man admits, "I don't know what else to think" (248). Perhaps, then, there is a moral to a book that only seems to set literature and philosophy at odds: fictions of the self are hard to abjure in reading as in life.

NOTES

1 For selected studies of *The Confidence-Man* that use the word *problem* in titles and section headings, see Tom Quirk, *Melville's Confidence Man: From Knave to Knight* (Columbia: University of Missouri Press, 1982); John Bryant, "*The Confidence-Man*: Melville's Problem Novel," in *A Companion to Melville Studies*, ed. John Bryant (New York: Greenwood Press, 1986), 315–50; Gustaaf van Cromphout, "*The Confidence-Man*: Melville and the Problem of Others," *Studies in American Fiction* 21:1 (1993), 37–50; and Gavin Jones, *American Hungers: The Problem of Poverty in U.S. Literature, 1840–1945* (Princeton, NJ: Princeton University Press, 2008). H. Bruce Franklin, who calls *The Confidence-Man* "nearly perfect," writes that the book "tries to define every important ethical problem known to man; it tries to dramatize man's epistemological problems; it tries to provide a voice for each way of looking at these problems" (*The Wake of the Gods* [Stanford, CA: Stanford University Press, 1963], 153–54).

2 For historicist criticism of *The Confidence-Man*, see, for instance, Michael Paul Rogin, *Subversive Genealogy: The Politics and Art of Herman Melville* (Berkeley: University of California Press, 1983), 236–55; Susan M. Ryan, *The Grammar of Good Intentions: Race and the Antebellum Culture of Benevolence* (Ithaca, NY: Cornell University Press, 2003), 46–77; Jennifer Greiman, *Democracy's Spectacle: Sovereignty and Public Life in Antebellum American Writing* (New York: Fordham University Press, 2010), 192–222.

3 Anonymous review of *The Confidence-Man*, *Literary Gazette* (April 11, 1857), 348–49, rpt. in *The Confidence-Man: His Masquerade*, ed. Hershel Parker and Mark Niemeyer (New York: W. W. Norton, 2006), 273.

4 Nina Baym, "Melville's Quarrel with Fiction," *PMLA* 34 (1979): 909–23, 921.

5 René Descartes, *The Meditations and Selections from the Principles of René Descartes*, trans. John Veitch (Chicago, IL: Open Court, 1913), 22.

6 Melville also mentions "Descartian vortices" in *Pierre* (267).

7 For Melville's background in skeptical philosophy, see Maurice S. Lee, *Uncertain Chances: Science, Skepticism, and Belief in Nineteenth-Century American Literature* (New York: Oxford University Press, 2012), 47–88.

8 Diogenes Laertius, *The Lives and Opinions of Eminent Philosophers*, trans. C. D. Yonge (London: George Bell and Sons, 1901), 415; Michel de Montaigne, *An Apology for Raymond Sebond*, in *The Complete Essays*, trans. and ed. M. A. Screech (1580; New York: Penguin, 1987), 669; Ralph Waldo Emerson, "Experience" (1844), in *Essays and Lectures* (New York: Library of America, 1983), 473.

9 David Hume, *A Treatise of Human Nature* (Oxford: Clarendon Press, 1888), 269.

10 Emerson, *Essays and Lectures*, 479.

11 Nina Baym, *Novels, Readers, and Reviewers: Responses to Fiction in Antebellum America* (Ithaca, NY: Cornell University Press, 1984), 82–107; Amy Kaplan, *The Social Construction of American Realism* (Chicago, IL: University of Chicago Press, 1992), esp. 23–25.

12 Anonymous review of *The Confidence-Man*, *Illustrated Times*, April 25, 1857, rpt. in *The Confidence-Man*, ed. Parker and Niemeyer, 282.

13 Descartes, *Meditations*, 33.

14 For satanic, biographical, and cultural contexts, see the supplementary materials in *The Confidence-Man*, ed. Parker and Niemeyer, 293–503. See also Hershel Parker, *The Powell Papers: A Confidence Man Amok among the Anglo-American Literati* (Evanston, IL: Northwestern University Press, 2011); and Helen Trimpi, *Melville's Confidence Men and American Politics in the 1850s* (Hamden, CT: Archon Book, 1987).

15 Peter Bellis, "Melville's *Confidence-Man*: An Uncharitable Interpretation," *American Literature* 59:4 (December 1987), 548–69; Sharon Cameron, *Impersonality: Seven Essays* (Chicago, IL: University of Chicago Press, 2007), esp. 180–81; James B. Salazar, *Bodies of Reform: The Rhetoric of Character in Gilded Age America* (New York: New York University Press, 2010), 36–62. For language-based skepticism in *The Confidence-Man*, see Cecelia Tichi, "Melville's Craft and Theme of Language Debased in *The Confidence-Man*," *ELH* 39:4 (December 1972), 639–58; Peggy Kamuf, *The Division of Literature; or the University in Deconstruction* (Chicago, IL: University of Chicago Press, 1997), 167–83; and Elizabeth Renker, "'A – !' Unreadability in *The Confidence-Man*," in *The Cambridge Companion to Herman Melville*, ed. Robert S. Levine (New York: Cambridge University Press, 1998), 114–34.

16 David Hume, *An Enquiry Concerning Human Understanding and Selections from A Treatise of Human Nature* (1740; London: Open Court, 1907), 91.

17 Stanley Cavell, "Being Odd, Getting Even (Descartes, Emerson, Poe)," in *Emerson's Transcendental Etudes*, ed. David Justin Hodge (Stanford, CA: Stanford University Press, 2003), 83–109, 94.

18 Emerson, "Self-Reliance," in *Essays and Lectures*, 265.

9

ELIZABETH RENKER

Melville the Poet in the Postbellum World

FOR DOUGLAS ROBILLARD

Herman Melville presents one of the strangest – and most intriguing – cases in the history of American poetry. His status as one of our greatest authors is widely acknowledged, but few know that he was primarily a poet. While he published novels for eleven years, from the best seller *Typee* in 1846 through the marketplace failure *The Confidence-Man* in 1857, he then turned nearly exclusively to writing and publishing poems until his death in 1891. For more than thirty years, he pursued a career as a poet. An 1860 volume (which does not survive) failed to find a publisher; he went on to publish four additional volumes, all of which experimented with techniques and genres, with aims and aesthetics, and with concepts of audience. When he died, he left on his desk another volume of poems nearing completion, as well as an extensive array of short and longer poems and groups of poems. Many of these poems remain mostly unknown to students and general readers, and unfamiliar even to many scholars.

Melville lived in a world in which poetry was a lively part of daily life for people across social spheres – not just cultural elites. Even illiterate people created and participated in cultures of poetry in the forms of recitation and song. Unlike today, songs and poems were widely understood to be permeable genres, with poems frequently also serving as song lyrics. Such other common fare as newspaper verse, books of poetry (widely reviewed as volumes of common interest), church hymns, sea shanties, labor union songs, long narrative poems (wildly popular in a way readers today can barely imagine), and broadside ballads suffused the culture. People routinely quoted familiar poems in all forms of speech, both public (political orations, school exercises, civic ceremonies) and private (conversations, letters – the primary forum in which Emily Dickinson circulated her own poems).

When scholars rediscovered Melville's work in the 1920s, a phenomenon that literary history calls "the Melville Revival," their central text was

Moby-Dick. These early scholars, often mystified by the poetry that was marginal to their interest in Melville's prose, judged the poems to be the failed efforts of a burned-out genius. Pioneering Melville scholar Raymond Weaver designated Melville's later years "the long quietus," and his concept stuck.[1] To call all those years of writing many thousands of lines a "long quietus" is to treat those many volumes and many unpublished poems as if they had never been written. And that is mostly how literary history treated them thereafter. Melville the poet became a disaffected "isolato," a hermit alone in his room. Bitter, disappointed, a failure, he withdrew from the world and lived in his own head, in his books, and on his pages. He communed with artists of the past, creating a private art because the marketplace of his time had rejected him. Stanton Garner, who situates Melville in what he calls "the Civil War world," aptly challenges the myth that Melville was detached from his own culture and lived instead in a "philosopher cave."[2]

For much of the twentieth century, Melville's only postbellum text to receive significant attention was the unfinished novella *Billy Budd*, typically hailed as the last flowering of his creative genius after decades of silence and retreat. This entire account can only stand if we erase Melville's decades-long investment in poetry. The writing process for *Billy Budd* began with a short poem, "Billy in the Darbies," which Melville eventually placed at the end of the novella. "Billy in the Darbies" has gotten more attention than most of Melville's other poems *because* it appears in this final work of fiction – not because it is inherently better than the other poems. In addition, the language of poetry infuses *Billy Budd* in ways crucial to the tale. For example, when Captain Vere is about to mandate Billy's execution, he invokes "measured forms" (128), an artistic term for poems; Vere's nickname, "Starry Vere" (61), comes from Andrew Marvell's poem "Upon Appleton House." Counter to the prevailing image of *Billy Budd* as Melville's last flowering in fiction after his unfortunate detour into poetry, in generic fact the novella qualifies as one of an array of verse-prose hybrids with which Melville experimented during his long career as a poet. Few of the other hybrid texts unpublished in his lifetime (for example, "Rip Van Winkle's Lilac" and the unfinished "Burgundy Club" materials) have received sustained attention by scholars.[3] None of these complex works has entered American literary histories more broadly as examples of extended generic innovation that Melville pursued well before modernism's later, kindred experiments.

Indeed, Melville the poet is chronically missing from larger narratives of postbellum American literary history as written by the twentieth century. Standard accounts portray the decades following the Civil War as an era of bad poets, with only Emily Dickinson and Walt Whitman worthy of attention, as well as a few late-century glimmers of poetic hope like Edwin Arlington Robinson and Stephen Crane. This tired account holds that only the fresh air of modernism cleared out the genteel and other bad poets who held cultural sway during this time. These two faulty narratives – Melville was a negligible poet; postbellum poetics was a dead zone – feed one another. It should be stressed that the circulation of these stories often does not involve actually reading the poems in question; instead, the familiar (erroneous) tale itself is what recirculates and thereby retains its status as reliable, implying as it does that the poems are not *worth* reading. In 2011, on the date of Melville's birthday, August 1, *The Atlantic* posted an Internet story with the headline, "Herman Melville's Mediocre Civil War Poetry."[4] No one had read any of Melville's poems for that story, either; *The Atlantic* simply reprinted a bad review of *Battle-Pieces* by William Dean Howells from 1867. And so the myths continue to circulate.

It would be exceptionally wise to remember that most scholars judged *The Confidence-Man* to be a "failure" for decades after *Moby-Dick* had been claimed as a masterwork. A handful of scholars countered the generally clueless, negative, perplexed responses to this deft and complex work, but the consensus on Melville's achievement would not change dramatically until a postmodern sensibility redefined the novel's effect on readers. Today, *The Confidence-Man* is hailed as a dazzling, metafictional performance puzzle. Melville's many poems are no more difficult than *The Confidence-Man*, although many are its equal. Here we need to note a larger reception problem germane to the problem at hand: poetry does not have as wide an appeal as prose. If as many tales by Melville were sitting at the Houghton Library of Harvard University unread, as is the case with the poems – even if we simply changed the lineation of these very same poems and rewrote them *as* tales – they would have been widely published and discussed long ago.

My single largest corrective claim in these pages to our culture's stubborn tale of Melville's negligible poetry is that he was not a recluse, hermit, or isolato, and he was certainly not quiet. He was an active poet engaged in the vital culture of poetry circulating at all levels of literacy in the world he lived in. Melville painstakingly crafted a poetics of difficulty, but his difficult poems were nevertheless part of their own time and responded actively to its poetic energies. As William C. Spengemann points out, Melville "seems never to have entirely abandoned hope of reaching a public with his poems," or he would not have relentlessly published them.[5] He paid for publication of three of his four poetry volumes, two in small private editions of twenty-five copies. We must remember that, while perhaps privately paid for, such publications were hardly "private art." The poetic marketplace of the time was highly heterogeneous, including amateur and coterie niches designed for limited, specialized audiences. Melville's imagination of his poetry's relation to the public sphere includes an awareness of changing and variable readerships.[6]

Two energetic trends in twenty-first century literary studies are creating a new climate in which Melville the poet can at last claim a more accurate and ample place in literary history. First, recent studies situating Melville's poetry in relation to broader cultural phenomena (such as Civil War discourse, the fashion of Holy Land travel, and niche markets for poetry) represent an important step in bringing Melville the poet into history. These studies are mostly by Melville scholars, often published under the auspices of the Melville Society, such as special issues of *Leviathan*, the Melville Society journal. Institutionally speaking, publications affiliated with author societies tend to remain somewhat insular in influence, no matter how excellent the scholarship. Thus, one of the immediate challenges to Melville scholars, from a purely pragmatic standpoint, is to bring Melville the poet into the essential fabric of larger accounts of literary history in general, and postbellum history in particular. I use the term *pragmatic* here deliberately, since pragmatism itself was one of the philosophical discourses that emerged in the postbellum age to grapple with the meaning of uncertainty in a new world traumatized by the legacies of Darwin, the Higher Criticism, and the Civil War. That list of crises will resonate with any reader of Melville's poems; they are three of his most enduring preoccupations.

Second, one of the most productive avenues for integrating Melville the poet into his postbellum world will be by way of rethinking the history of poetry itself. Scholars are now working toward a new history of the stunning range of poetic genres in the long nineteenth century, by poets well known, little known, and unknown, circulating in a range of forms and media at all levels of literacy. One of the core premises of this new history of poetry is to challenge the long-standing legacy of the New Criticism. An overriding critical investment in the lyric as the quintessential form of poetic expression, as Virginia Jackson argues in her influential *Dickinson's Misery: A Theory of Lyric Reading*, effectively reduced a vast range of poetic practices to a severely restricted field of cultural production. By contrast, one of the most exciting things about the new poetry studies is its focus on a truly immense, untapped, heterogeneous archive of poems, creating an opportunity to rethink Melville's poems within a much more ample world of poetry than we have known. For example, the essays in Meredith McGill's edited collection, *The Traffic in Poems: Nineteenth-Century Poetry and Transatlantic Exchange*, address the transatlantic circulation of poems, both current poems and poems from the (perhaps distant) past circulating in the present.[7] The issue of "sources" comes up repeatedly in Melville scholarship, typically chronicling what Melville bought or borrowed, on what date, and then tracing his marginalia. Now is the time for a new approach to his use of sources, situated within the broader world of copying, citation, allusion, and circulation.

Beginning with his first published volume of poems, *Battle-Pieces and Aspects of the War* (1866), Melville wrote with full awareness of the many other war poems circulating in the United States and abroad, published in such sources as *Harper's Weekly* and *The Rebellion Record*. His prefatory note indicates that he wrote most of the volume after the fall of Richmond. This time line accentuates the sheer *number* of Civil War poems already circulating across the culture by the time he composed his volume. While esteemed poets of the past like Milton and Keats were also crucial to this volume, they too were transmitted through the lens of his own era and its recirculations. His prefatory note says he has taken "but a few themes" from larger "events and incidents of the conflict." This idea of selection is crucial: it reminds us of how carefully Melville chose particular "aspects" of the war. He also worked carefully with issues of poetic craft, creating seventy-two poems, often in forms of his own creation, and without repeating the same form twice.[8]

Melville the poet has long been accused of formal ineptitude, as if all those carefully wrought forms were not the index to a perhaps fresh and unfamiliar poetic project. These long-noted formal blocks and stumbles have their corollary in his sometimes bewildering use of perspective. Poems in *Battle-Pieces* are often refracted through obscured, blocked, muddy, oblique, mediated, or hidden scenarios of vision. Lookouts, scouts, moonless nights, apparitions, housetops, wildernesses, photographs, and storms: the perspectival challenges abound. The obliquity of perspective is tied to the effect he frequently creates whereby we cannot identify who is speaking, from where, or even why. Since voice, especially in relation to the contested history of the lyric, is forming a cornerstone of the new poetry studies, Melville's very complex work in this regard can offer an overlooked but key instance in this new history. For example, while Melville studied Wordsworth seriously, Hershel Parker convincingly argues that Melville defined himself against Wordsworth, partly on the grounds of the egotism of the romantic lyric focused on personal voice and personal feelings.[9] In Jackson's reading of the opening poem in *Battle-Pieces*, "The Portent," she observes that "one of the weirdest things about the poem" is that "it can't be said to represent anyone's subjective experience." Here we find, once again, not a flaw but an innovative countercurrent in the history of poetics.[10]

Amidst its many purposeful difficulties, *Battle-Pieces* also offers a relatively accessible group of beautifully crafted poems that offers a good place to start for those new to Melville's work, and that repay rereading for longstanding admirers. This thematic group includes "The March into Virginia, Ending in the First Manassas. (July, 1861.)," "The College Colonel.," "Shiloh. A Requiem. (April, 1862.)," and "Ball's Bluff. (A Reverie.) October,

1861)."[11] The clear relation of these poems to a pressing historical context – something Melville's many ahistorical, placeless, sceneless, and disembodied poems do not provide – can open the door for readers inexperienced with his intimidating and obscure poetic voices. Each of these poems depicts young men motivated by their idealistic visions of heroism who march off instead to "Perish, enlightened by the vollied glare," as in "The March into Virginia" (l. 34). In "The College Colonel," the injured title character comes home, "stunned," after two years at war (l. 8). "Shiloh" presents a paradoxically peaceful scene of young men stretched on the field, dying after the battle has ended. A single parenthetical phrase, "(What like a bullet can undeceive!)" (l. 16), presents what Michael Warner calls the "climactic burst of recognition" – formally, a textual bullet.[12]

"Ball's Bluff" serves as an excellent example of Melville's skilled and careful sense of craft and of his vital engagement with the culture of poetry in his own day. Geographically speaking, Ball's Bluff is a 100-foot bank on the Virginia side of the Potomac River. A Confederate brigade rebuffed a poorly planned Union assault, sending the Union soldiers over the bluff and into the river, where many were either shot as they tried to swim away or drowned. As historian James M. McPherson puts it, Ball's Bluff was a "humiliating disaster."[13] Melville's title serves as an historical marker, a monument to a place of disastrous loss. But Melville's interests here exceed mere historical referent, as they do in the entire volume. The gap between the historically specific names in this volume and what we discover them to designate – or to fail to designate – is crucial to Melville's larger engagement with what Rosanna Warren calls "dark knowledge."[14] Throughout *Battle-Pieces*, Melville invokes persons, places, events, and, crucially, their representations – the filters for the facts. His repeated incorporation of such media forms as photographs, dispatches, and news bulletins stresses the equivocal position of information about the war with respect to knowledge.

Despite its title, the poem is not set at Ball's Bluff, nor does it record the actual events there. These transpire entirely off camera. Such deflections and gaps, typical of Melville's poems, are only two of the many distancing mechanisms that tend to perplex readers. His persistent concern with blockage and distance takes us to one of this poem's particular interests: the word *bluff*. A *bluff* is a "cliff or headland with a broad precipitous face," a term that emerged in North America and was used mostly for American landscapes.[15] I reproduce the poem in full:

> One noonday, at my window in the town,
>   I saw a sight – saddest that eyes can see –
>   Young soldiers marching lustily
>   Unto the wars,

With fifes, and flags in mottoed pageantry;
  While all the porches, walks, and doors
  Were rich with ladies cheering royally.

They moved like Juny morning on the wave,
  Their hearts were fresh as clover in its prime
  (It was the breezy summer time),
    Life throbbed so strong,
How should they dream that Death in a rosy clime
  Would come to thin their shining throng?
Youth feels immortal, like the gods sublime.

Weeks passed; and at my window, leaving bed,
  By night I mused, of easeful sleep bereft,
  On those brave boys (Ah War! thy theft);
    Some marching feet
Found pause at last by cliffs Potomac cleft;
  Wakeful I mused, while in the street
Far footfalls died away till none were left.[16]

The idea of the bluff serves not only as a concrete historical and geographical allusion. The word connotes deception, and the poem teases out the
threads of this connotation. *Bluff* denotes posturing, boastful language or
demeanor. The soldiers march "lustily," for example, showing off for the
cheering girls watching from their doorways. For boys with restricted access
to female sexual partners, and for girls with severely restricted cultural permission for sexual contact with boys, males here perform their march to
war for a female promise of sexual reward. In another usage emerging at
this time, *bluff* also denotes a card game strategy for deceiving an opponent;
however, the game evoked by the word *bluff* in the poem is not a game of
cards, but of mating. Part of what the speaker sees as "sad" is the sexual
pageant that redirects natural physical drives into a manufactured, violent,
culturally sanctioned outlet. Too often, its result will not be reproduction,
but death.

The sexual dynamic that the speaker calls a "saddest sight" is one that
other poems of the time record enthusiastically. It is thus tactically important that Melville's speaker stands as an observer, distanced from the spectacle – of war and of war poetry – by his window. Elaine Showalter points
out that poets and songwriters, male and female, in both the North and
the South, urged women to urge men to enlist. One example from the
South, an 1861 poem that originally appeared in a New Orleans newspaper, was reprinted in the *Rebellion Record* of 1861. There it, and poems
like it, would have fallen within Melville's reading. Titled "Song for the

Times (Written for the Ladies' Military Fair, New Orleans)," by the otherwise unidentified "L.F.," the poem's voice is that of a female speaker who repeatedly promises sexual approval for males who return from battle. She exhorts men with this call: "To arms, who have fair lady woo'd!/ To arms, if you would know the joy/ Of her esteem, without alloy" (lines 16–18).[17] The dynamic of "joy" in this poem is Melville's "saddest sight," both at the level of content and of poetic ideology. Lucy Larcom's popular war verse, "A Loyal Woman's No," published in *The Atlantic Monthly* in December 1863, provides a Northern example. Larcom (1824–93) was a popular Massachusetts poet and writer well known for her accounts of working as a child in the Lowell mills. Her female speaker passionately rejects her lover because he will not oppose the evil of slavery by fighting for the Union: "Not yours, – because you are not man enough/ To grasp your country's measure of a man!" (lines 29–30).[18]

The bluff in Melville's poem operates at levels beyond sexual posturing. To bluff in poker meant not simply to show off, but "to bet on a worthless hand as if it were a good hand, and force your antagonist to back down in fear."[19] The first motive – a form of deception in which one bets on a worthless hand – is not one the poem attributes to the boys. They posture, but they don't bluff in this sense. Their "[y]outh feels immortal" (line 14). Here we find another layer of the poem's pathos, because the boys don't know (yet) that their pageantry is a put-on whose swagger will be pulled out from under them. In this sense, the heart of the poem is a bluff in which the boys are not the deceivers but the deceived. They march toward an opponent, yet the Confederates as such appear nowhere in this poem. There is no battle scene in this poem named after a battle. The opponent they imagine – the Rebels – is not the opponent they in fact meet: "How should they dream that Death in a rosy clime/ Would come to thin their shining throng?" (lines 12–13), What they can't yet imagine or "dream" in stanza 1 is what they have implicitly learned by stanza 3.

In a volume of poems characterized by relentless formal experimentation and poetic self-awareness, the "marching feet" (line 18) in this predominantly iambic poem metapoetically evoke poetry itself. Stanza 1 opens with two end-stopped lines of iambic pentameter. The trochaic inversion in the third foot of line 2 emphasizes the word "saddest," and so temporarily disrupts the march, metrically and emotionally. The enjambed iambic tetrameter of line 3 leads into line 4's dimeter line "Unto the wars." The enjambment, the sudden metrical truncation from four feet to two, and the indentation emphasize that the lusty marching will also be cut off. (Melville was scrupulous about indentation and other matters of poetic layout throughout his career as a poet.) When the marching feet recur in the

134

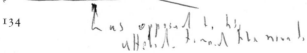

last stanza, they are now the footfalls not of "lusty" but of dead boys. They "pause" as the poem itself falls silent in elegiac kinship.

In stark contrast to the national occasion of *Battle-Pieces*, Melville's next volume, *Clarel: A Poem and Pilgrimage in the Holy Land* (1876), a colossally ambitious narrative poem in four parts and eighteen thousand lines, was published in the centennial year with Melville's own funds (a gift from an uncle). As Lawrence Buell observes, "Very little at first sight marks it as an American work," and indeed little about it appealed to scholars working within frameworks of American exceptionalism.[20] Recently, however, scholars have become engaged by its global perspective. Its plot follows the title character, an American divinity student, through a pilgrimage in what was then called the "Holy Land," now Palestine, during which he meets an array of characters marked by various national, ethnic, religious, sexual, and philosophical identities. The backdrop is the drained legacy of Western Christianity after the convulsive nineteenth-century crisis of faith caused by theories of evolution and the Higher Criticism. The epilogue opens: "If Luther's day expand to Darwin's year,/ Shall that exclude the hope – foreclose the fear?" (*C* 498). A Victorian epic of faith and doubt in recognizable keeping with such (British) works as Tennyson's *In Memoriam A.H.H.*, poems by Arthur Hugh Clough and Matthew Arnold, and George Eliot's translation of *Das Leben Jesu*, its marginal place in American literary history reminds us that the category of "Victorian" literature has artificially cordoned off British from American writers. *Clarel* insists on heterogeneous and global matrices for meaning, offering a Holy Land setting, a troubled but simultaneously expansive engagement with ancient and with non-Christian history, a catalog of travelers from across the globe, and an array of ethnic, regional, national, sexual, and religious identity positions.

The traumatized loss of orientation that frames the poem catapults the protagonist into a simultaneously ancient and modern world of stony resistance. Clarel's predicament in this hardened and inhuman landscape is much like that of the reader trying to make his or her pilgrimage through the poem – notably also named *Clarel*. Scholars have pointed out that its iambic tetrameter form served as a prison-like set of formal constraints mirroring Clarel's struggle to find meaning in the material world. Samuel Otter demonstrates how the poem's thematic interest in stones speaks to the way Melville meticulously crafts his word and line arrangements, including his rhymes and extended metaphors, to invite and resist the desire for meaning.[21] Only a single review of the time (from among the admittedly minimal number it received) indicates more than hasty skimming beyond this resistant surface. That single review, in the London *Academy*, described the poem's "rugged inattention to niceties of rhyme and metre" as "rather deliberate than

careless," and suggested that the poem, reminiscent of Clough's work, war-
ranted the study and attention it would be unlikely to receive from an age
that "craves for smooth, short, lyric song."[22] This lone review represents one
end of an historical trajectory that is gaining energy today, in which the largest single challenge is to overturn the erroneous cliché of Melville's poetic
ineptitude and to bring this formidable long poem into the wider world with
which it was intensely engaged.

What happens if we approach *Clarel* as a significant Victorian epic of faith
and doubt instead of a clunker? Defenders of Melville's poetry have often
called him a "protomodernist" to stress the poetics of difficulty that Melville
pursued and that the modernists later introduced more widely as a poetic
ethos; however, since his techniques and experiments were chronologically
prior to those of the modernists, defining his poetic practices by way of
modernism assumes ideologically that the greatest value lies with modernism – at the expense of Melville's chronologically prior innovations. A key
polemic in the new poetry studies is to challenge the long-reigning assumption that modernism was a dramatic, definitive, or even actual (rather than
ideologically constructed) break with the poetry of the nineteenth century.
One quick example will have to serve in this short chapter. Robert Penn
Warren pointed out long ago that *Clarel* is a precursor to *The Waste Land*;
in its search for renewal in a ruined Promised Land, he argued, it presents
the "same basic image, the same flickering contrasts of the past and the
present, the same charade of belief and unbelief."[23] Warren's insight about
Clarel's wasteland world is one we would do well to bear in mind as we
interrogate the relationship between early-twentieth-century poetry and its
predecessors. Melville's works were enthusiastically passed around among
a circle of radical, iconoclastic readers in late Victorian Britain, including
poet James Thomson.[24] Melville read Thomson's work as well, including
The City of Dreadful Night (1880), which a correspondent from that British
group of admirers, James Billson, sent him. Melville acknowledged the gift
in January 1885, commenting: "Your friend was a sterling poet, if ever one
sang. As to his pessimism, altho' neither pessimist nor optimist [sic] myself,
nevertheless I relish it in the verse if for nothing else than as a counterpoise
to the exorbitant hopefulness, juvenile and shallow, that makes such a blus-
ter in these days."[25] Since T. S. Eliot consistently acknowledged Thomson for
his influence, we needn't look far to see the clear ties between Melville the
poet and the post-Melvilleans – a term I adopt here polemically to replace
the habit of calling Melville "protomodernist."[26]

An example from Melville's next published volume, *John Marr and Other
Sailors with Some Sea-Pieces* (1888), reveals additional liabilities arising
from the "protomodernist" lens that tends to lift Melville out of history

and thus to seriously distort his relation to his own age. The last poem in the volume, "Pebbles," is an epigrammatic work in seven numbered sections voiced by a range of speakers. To an eye trained to appreciate modernist poems, this one looks protomodernist indeed. But consider "Pebbles" in its own time. The New York Congregational weekly *The Independent* printed a long-running miscellany column called "Pebbles." (The paper also reviewed Melville; in other words, it was a newspaper in his world.) *The Independent* ran "Pebbles" for decades, until well after Melville's death, offering bits of information, jokes, riddles, puzzles, witticisms, wisdom – and poems, strung into newspaper column form. The June 25, 1874 "Pebbles," for example, included Walt Whitman's poem "A Kiss to the Bride," followed by literary gossip and jokes.[27] From this postbellum perspective, what looks anachronistically like the radical "modernist" fragmentation of "Pebbles" becomes a form recognizable in Melville's own day, and titled by him in a way that emphasized the poem's place in the wider public sphere of contemporary print forms. (William Dean Howells went on to publish a string of poems in *Harper's* in 1895 that he also titled "Pebbles.") Melville's tone and his content differ from the newspaper column, and here they mark their distance in ways that deserve careful parsing; but these differences are to be measured by their conversation with forms legible to the age, not their utter seclusion from them. The conversation cannot be ignored without dehistoricizing Melville's poem.

   Timoleon, Etc. (1891), Melville's last published volume, evinces a thematic interest in worlds geographically and temporally distant: historical characters (the eponymous Timoleon); texts ("Fragments of a Lost Gnostic Poem of the 12th Century"); periods ("The Age of the Antonines"); geographies ("Venice"); religions and philosophies ("Buddha"); and works of art and architecture (such as "The Parthenon," "Greek Masonry," and "The Great Pyramid"). The volume's thematic concern with remoteness, distance, and, simultaneously, with art objects to be looked at, finds its largest occasion metapoetically, that is, in Melville's vision of his poems as works of visual art. From this vantage, he imagined his poems as a set of objects carefully constructed on the page for (presumed) readers to encounter visually, a conception related to his long-standing interest in the visual arts more generally. During Melville's lifetime, architects made the stunning discovery that the apparent perfection of the Parthenon was an optical illusion, that is, that its architects had used techniques of curvature and inclination to make the temple's columns appear to be straight lines.[28] His poem, "The Parthenon," depicts looking at the (optically complex) Parthenon from greater and lesser distances and shifting perspectives, necessitating a hermeneutic approach that Melville's own poems also require. Here we should recall the perspective "problems" in *Battle-Pieces*. (The title term of that volume is itself borrowed from the arena of painting.) Part of what *Timoleon* ponders is what presumed readers would, could, or might try to see, or not see, in relation to the craft of the poem-objects themselves.

We find a meditation on the status of art objects again, for example, in *Timoleon's* highly resistant "Disinterment of the Hermes." Likely responding to the 1877 discovery of a marble statue of Hermes at Olympia, this actual, historical discovery raises the notional prospect of artworks literally or figuratively buried, and then found or rescued from oblivion.[29] I reproduce the poem in full:

> What forms divine in adamant fair –
> Carven demigod and god,
> And hero-marbles rivalling these,
> Bide under Latium's sod,
> Or lost in sediment and drift
> Alluvial which the Grecian rivers sift.
>
> To dig for these, O better far
> Than raking arid sands
> For gold more barren meetly theirs
> Sterile, with brimming hands.[30]

The "adamant fair" of line 1 is, like the Hermes disinterred, an emblem for this poem itself. *Adamant* as a noun designates a stone of impenetrable hardness, or any unyieldingly hard substance. The hardened, chiseled language of the poem is difficult to parse, "buried" or obscured to the eyes of the skimmer-readers that Melville elsewhere derided.

We find a quite classic conundrum here for the reader of Melville the poet, and part of the reading challenge is *not* to read past the difficulty, or to falsely simplify what's in front of you, but to understand its resistance *as part of* the poetic project. Space limitations here allow only a quick summary. The speaker ponders "forms divine" hidden (under the "sod") that might be "dug for." The effort to dig for these would be "better far" than to seek gold. OK ... but. The syntax remains clear through the word "gold" ("It is far better to dig for divine forms than to rake sands for gold"), but here the syntax hardens – like adamant. Even granting the archaic "meetly" for "properly," the arrangement of words blocks the flow of reading. What is the syntactic function of "meetly"? The arrangement of words offers multiple plausible options, rendering none obvious or clear. Words pile up like stones, as if words are either missing or they no longer function according to conventional grammar.

At the level of concepts, we can see that "gold" is likely to be "more barren" than the "forms divine," because the speaker already told us that digging for divine forms is "better" than more superficial "raking" for gold. "Barren" also repeats the aridity of the sands. OK ... but. Perhaps "more barren" instead (or also) modifies what follows, that is, the mysterious "they" who now implicitly enter the poem. In this option, the barren "they" deserve the barren ("sterile") treasure they misread as truly valuable. "They" do not realize that their brimming hands are barren, that their presumed treasure is, paradoxically, nothing. In sum, we cannot understand this tale about the dynamics of finding great works without some very serious interpretive digging. The poem's historical context of the literal disinterment of the Hermes serves as a figurative allegory of reading. Melville crafts a poem that hardens before the reader's eyes. Engaging this poem on the page poses the question directed at you: Will you read, or will you not read? The distant, lost, hidden world of such artworks – biding, waiting to be disinterred – is the world of *Timoleon*.

I have briefly discussed the published poems, but let me close with a note as to how genuinely shocking it remains that a vast body of unpublished poetry by Melville remains mostly out of more general sight. The very idea that many unpublished works by one of our most canonical authors are lying, (mostly) unread, among his (mostly) unpublished papers, is almost incredible – except that it's true. The very serious problem of textual access to the unpublished poems should be partially remedied by the pending final volume of the Northwestern-Newberry edition, projected to include *Billy Budd* and the other late manuscripts. As one clear institutional indication of how little studied these unpublished projects of Melville's have been, it remains the case that two of the best places to go (aside from the Houghton Library itself) to begin to grapple with these complex, often hybrid-genre texts are dissertations written long ago: Robert Charles Ryan's "*Weeds and Wildings Chiefly: with a Rose or Two* by Herman Melville, Reading Text and Genetic Text, Edited from the Manuscripts, with Introduction and Notes" (PhD dissertation, Northwestern U, 1967) and Robert Allen Sandberg's "Melville's Unfinished *Burgundy Club* Book: A Reading Edition Edited from the Manuscripts with Introduction and Notes" (PhD dissertation, Northwestern U, 1989). Some individual unpublished poems are available erratically, in editions by various scholars; some manuscripts are not available in any edition at all. The state of Melville's handwriting and revisions would make it difficult, in some of these cases, to establish a reading text. Color digital facsimiles of all the manuscript pages would be a great boon to scholarship. A few individual pages are currently available on the

Internet by courtesy of the Houghton Library, and the Melville Electronic Library is working toward a related, urgent goal. To end with one tantalizing tidbit among many that emerges from working hands-on with these unpublished manuscripts is the fascinating fact that Melville assembled handmade books for some poems, with cut-out pages for covers, in the manner of Emily Dickinson's fascicles. An absolute revolution in Dickinson scholarship in recent years has demonstrated that the famously reclusive Dickinson was actively engaged with the world outside her room. Many such fascinating aspects of Melville the poet "bide" – awaiting their readers.

NOTES

1 Raymond M. Weaver, *Herman Melville: Mariner and Mystic* (New York: George H. Doran, 1921).

2 Stanton Garner, *The Civil War World of Herman Melville* (Lawrence: University Press of Kansas, 1993), 389.

3 "Rip Van Winkle's Lilac," in Robert Charles Ryan, "*Weeds and Wildings Chiefly: With a Rose or Two* by Herman Melville, Reading Text and Genetic Text, Edited from the Manuscripts, with Introduction and Notes," PhD diss., Northwestern University, 1967, 26–34; Robert Allen Sandberg, "Melville's Unfinished *Burgundy Club* Book: A Reading Edition Edited from the Manuscripts with Introduction and Notes," PhD diss., Northwestern University, 1989.

4 Eleanor Barkhorn, August 1, 2011, theatlantic.com, accessed July 28, 2012.

5 William C. Spengemann, "Melville the Poet," *American Literary History* 11.4 (1999): 569–609, 583.

6 Matthew Giordano, "Public Privacy: Melville's Coterie Authorship in *John Marr and Other Sailors*," *Leviathan: A Journal of Melville Studies* 9.3 (2007): 65–78.

7 Virginia Jackson, *Dickinson's Misery: A Theory of Lyric Reading* (Princeton, NJ: Princeton University Press, 2005); Meredith L. McGill, ed., *The Traffic in Poems: Nineteenth-Century Poetry and Transatlantic Exchange* (New Brunswick, NJ: Rutgers University Press, 2008). Other important recent work in the new poetry studies includes Paula Bernat Bennett, *Poets in the Public Sphere: The Emancipatory Project of American Women's Poetry, 1800–1900* (Princeton, NJ: Princeton University Press, 2003); Mary Loeffelholz, *From School to Salon: Reading Nineteenth-Century American Women's Poetry* (Princeton, NJ: Princeton University Press, 2004); Eliza Richards, *Gender and the Poetics of Reception in Poe's Circle* (Cambridge: Cambridge University Press, 2004); and Angela Sorby, *Schoolroom Poets: Childhood, Performance, and the Place of American Poetry, 1865–1917* (Durham, NH: University of New Hampshire Press, 2005).

8 William H. Shurr, *The Mystery of Iniquity: Melville as Poet, 1857–1891* (Lexington: University Press of Kentucky, 1972), 16.

9 Historical Note, *PP* 484.

10 Virginia Jackson, "Who Reads Poetry?" *PMLA* 123.1 (2008): 181–87, 184.

11 All citations to *Battle-Pieces and Aspects of the War* in this chapter refer to the facsimile edition, intro. Lee Rust Brown (New York: Da Capo, 1995).

12 Robert Penn Warren (Introduction, *Selected Poems of Herman Melville* [New York: Random House, 1967], 3–88) and Michael Warner ("What Like a Bullet Can Undeceive?" *Public Culture* 15.1 [2003]: 41–54; the quoted phrase appears on 42) have published magisterial readings of two of the poems in this cluster, "The March into Virginia" and "Shiloh," respectively.

13 James M. Mcpherson, *Battle Cry of Freedom: The Civil War Era* (New York: Oxford University Press, 1988), 362.

14 Rosanna Warren, "Dark Knowledge: Melville's Poems of the Civil War," *Raritan* 19.1 (1999): 100–21; Faith Barrett, "'They Answered Him Aloud': Popular Voice and Nationalist Discourse in Melville's *Battle-Pieces*," *Leviathan* 9.3 (2007): 35–49.

15 www.oed.com, accessed June 25, 2012.

16 *Battle-Pieces*, 28–29.

17 Reprinted in *The Rebellion Record*, ed. Frank Moore, v. 1 (1861), Section 3, "Poetry," p. 64. The reprint indicates the original printing appeared in the *New Orleans Picayune* on April 25, 1861.

18 Elaine Showalter, *A Jury of Her Peers: American Women Writers from Anne Bradstreet to Annie Proulx* (New York: Knopf, 2009), 132; Garner cites Larcom to exemplify the broader sexual dynamic of "Ball's Bluff" (119); "A Loyal Woman's No," http://www.gutenberg.org, accessed September 25, 2012.

19 This sense of the word originated in the United States around this time. See www.oed.com and John Russell Bartlett, *Dictionary of Americanisms: A Glossary of Words and Phrases Usually Regarded as Peculiar to The United States* (Boston, MA: Little, Brown, and Company), second edition (1859) and fourth edition (1877).

20 "Melville the Poet," *The Cambridge Companion to Herman Melville*, ed. Robert S. Levine (Cambridge: Cambridge University Press, 1998), 147.

21 Samuel Otter, "How *Clarel* Works," *A Companion to Herman Melville*, ed. Wyn Kelley (Malden, MA: Blackwell, 2006), 470.

22 Walter E. Bezanson, Historical and Critical Note, *C* 545–46; the *Academy* review as quoted by Bezanson.

23 Warren, Introduction, 36.

24 Parker, Historical Note, *MD* 735–40; Paul Giles, "'Bewildering Intertanglement': Melville's Engagement with the British Tradition," *Virtual Americas: Transnational Fictions and the Transatlantic Imaginary* (Durham, NC: Duke University Press, 2002), 47–48.

25 Herman Melville to James Billson, January 22, 1885, *L* 485–86.

26 On Eliot's citation of Thomson, see Peter Brooker and Simon Perril, "Modernist Poetry and its Precursors," in *A Companion to Twentieth-Century Poetry*, ed. Neil Roberts (Malden, MA: Blackwell, 2001), 24.

27 *The Independent*, June 25, 1874 (8), American Periodical Series, Web, accessed July 4, 2012.

28 Elizabeth Renker, "Melville's Poetic Singe," *Leviathan* 2.2 (2000): 28.

29 On the historical disinterment, see *The Poems of Herman Melville*, ed. Douglas Robillard (Kent, OH: Kent State University Press, 2000). Robillard concludes that "Melville probably read stories of the discovery in newspapers" (343).

30 "Disinterment of the Hermes," *Timoleon*, by Herman Melville, facsimile edition, ed. Charles Habserstroh (Camden, NJ: Rutgers University Press, 1976), 65.

IO

GREGG CRANE

Judgment in *Billy Budd*

After *The Confidence-Man* (1857), Melville stopped writing fiction. For decades, he focused his creative energies on his poetry. However, near the end of his life, Melville returned to prose. His final major literary work, *Billy Budd, Sailor (An Inside Narrative)*, began as a headnote to a ballad Melville had written about a sailor sentenced to hang for mutiny, "Billy in the Darbies." As Melville worked on the prose explanation of the condemned man's situation, the headnote grew into a novel, and the poem became a coda.[1]

Unfinished at Melville's death in 1891 and first published in 1924, *Billy Budd* tells the tale of a handsome young sailor falsely accused of mutiny. We meet Billy aboard "a homeward-bound English merchantman" (44–45), the *Rights-of-Man*, where he is adored by officers and crew alike. The *Rights* is boarded by a naval lieutenant from a British warship, the *Bellipotent* (a Latin compound meaning warpower), seeking able-bodied seamen to impress into service aboard the warship (*impressment* refers to the act of forcing men, usually merchant sailors, to serve in the British Navy). The captain of the *Rights* protests that the lieutenant mustn't take Billy, his "best man" (46), his "peacemaker" (47). In physique and personality, Billy embodies a particularly unsullied kind of perfection. He has only one physical defect, a stammer that worsens when he's under pressure. His character is simple and unspoiled. On taking up his new duties as foretopman on board the *Bellipotent*, something about Billy's beauty and innocence provokes the master-at-arms, John Claggart, who as a type of shipboard chief of police helps to maintain order and watches for signs of mutiny. Claggart schemes to frame Billy, instructing subordinates to implicate him in mutinous conversation. Claggart levels a charge of mutiny against Billy to Captain Vere. When the incredulous Vere arranges to have Claggart repeat this accusation in Billy's presence, Billy's stammer prevents him from answering. Unable to speak, Billy strikes his accuser, killing him with one blow. Vere immediately convenes a shipboard trial – the drumhead court. Acting as chief witness, prosecutor, and judge, he orchestrates Billy's conviction and execution.

Melville's story of the doomed sailor is one of his most prominent and frequently read works, and, in recent decades, it has become an iconic text for scholars interested in the intersections of law and literature (for instance, the first number of *Cardozo Studies in Law and Literature* [1989] was devoted to *Billy Budd* because, in the words of Richard Weisberg, Melville's "text has come to 'mean' Law and Literature").[2] One clue to *Billy Budd*'s appeal to jurisprudentially oriented readers lies in the fact that the novel offers a legal and ethical drama that seems simultaneously historically particular and yet transhistorical, even universal.

Melville's novel is very much a creature of history. The narrative is set in 1797 during the Revolutionary-era war between Britain and France, a period of widespread unrest in the Royal Navy. Mounting frustration with impressment, poor living conditions, inadequate pay, and the protracted war with France fueled mutinies at Spithead and Nore (two anchorages in England) as well as a number of smaller incidents in the Mediterranean in 1797. In addition, Melville drew aspects of *Billy Budd*'s storyline from the shipboard trial and execution of suspected mutineers aboard the USS *Somers* in 1842. This event had personal significance for Melville as his first cousin, Guert Gansevoort, was a first lieutenant aboard the *Somers* and participated in the mutiny investigation. Finally, *Billy Budd* was composed during an era of considerable economic turmoil and labor unrest in the United States, epitomized by the Haymarket riot and the subsequent trial of eight anarchists for conspiracy (1886–87).[3] Taken together, these conflicts between the ruled and their rulers form a multilayered historical backdrop to Melville's narrative.

However, Melville's novel also aspires to universality. Asking us to weigh the competing claims of morality and law, feeling and reason, *Billy Budd* feels as archetypal as Greek tragedy (it has often been compared to Sophocles's *Antigone*). Even the specific, historically located issues, such as the necessity of strict military discipline during the Revolutionary era or nineteenth-century views of capital punishment, push us toward larger jurisprudential questions: (Is the law capable of justice?[4] Are *we* capable of justice?)

The processes of judgment are fundamental to such questions. It is hard to imagine weighing the justness of any decision or ruling without working through the deliberation process oneself and comparing one's conclusion to that of the decision maker. One's sense of the injustice of any legal decision probably implies a contrary result derived from different imperatives, principles, or facts or from an alternative version of the decision process. *Billy*

Budd has become an essential text for people interested in jurisprudence because it so compellingly focuses the reader's attention on judgment. As Barbara Johnson rightly notes, "Judgment, however difficult, is clearly the central preoccupation of Melville's text, whether it be the judgment pronounced *by* [Vere] or *upon* him."[5]

The scholarly conversation on *Billy Budd*'s representation of judgment and its conception of justice is heated and sharply divided; indeed, few other literary works have produced such a polarized critical reception. One line of *Billy Budd* criticism emphasizes a change in the temper of Melville's time from the antebellum period's romanticism and idealism to a particularly skeptical form of realism predominant in the waning decades of the nineteenth century. Such accounts find a biographical correlative to this generational shift in the downward turn of Melville's personal fortunes. Failing in his youthful dream of making a living as a writer, Melville had to come to terms with the humble position of customs inspector, a job he held from 1866 to 1885.[6] Chastened by his personal difficulties, the horrific sacrifices of the Civil War, and the general failure of reform to improve American society in any marked fashion, Melville, these critics argue, came to a deep and abiding skepticism about idealistic schemes for the world's betterment. As a valediction to what he had called in *Pierre* the "beautiful illusions of youth" (218), Melville's last work of fiction is thus best read, for these critics, as a "testament of acceptance" that nothing higher than the will of the king (i.e., the state) prescribes one's duties to others. Moral abstractions and idealized notions of justice have to yield to society's need for secure and predictable forms of organization. From this perspective, Captain Vere, despite his sympathetic feelings for Billy and his sense of Billy's essential innocence, must choose head over heart, law over moral feeling, professional duty over private conscience. These readings make Vere Melville's alter ego and portray both Vere and Melville as closely resembling Justice Oliver Wendell Holmes, Jr., who, having witnessed the sacrifice of the nation's "best citizens" in the Civil War, accepted the disjunction between law and morality and came to view the reformer's appeal to conscience as a delusional and potentially destructive form of sentimentalism.[7]

In contrast to the "testament of acceptance" reading, the "testament of resistance" line of *Billy Budd* criticism approaches the narrative ironically, separating Vere from Melville and finding a continuity between the author's younger and older selves, such that his final work continues to manifest the younger man's "fierce commitment to everything in the world that resists confinement and oppression and opposes injustice."[8] Vere's supposedly noble commitment to the letter of the law and professional duty is, these critics argue, ignoble, comparable to the immoral legalism of Northern judges enforcing the fugitive slave law despite their ethical and religious objections to the institution of slavery and the law itself.[9] Like such earlier works as "Benito Cereno," *Billy Budd* is, these critics argue, subversive of the authoritarianism and exceptionalism underwriting unjust domination at home and abroad, and Vere's choice of professionalism and legal form over sympathy and moral feeling is Melville's way of attacking the entire legal system as an instrument of class oppression.[10]

Refashioning an apt comment by Andrew Delbanco, one might say that for those scholars with "regard for constituted authority" in difficult times, "Vere tends to come off as a heroic figure who, with tragic awareness of his responsibilities, sacrifices an innocent for the sake of the state," but for those who tend to be suspicious of "established power," Vere is "a despot whose callous commitment to the letter of the law, 'however pitilessly' it grinds the innocent, is ultimately no different from Ahab's doctrinaire will."[11] Despite their apparent mutual exclusivity, however, these divergent perspectives agree on a key point – one *must* choose between the tale's various oppositions (either head or heart, law or morality). Vere chooses the wrong side for those who want to see Melville as attacking the idea of law unchecked by morality, or he makes the right choice for those who either see Melville as accepting the impracticability of moral conceptions of the law or who laud the legal professional's stoic, Holmes-like adherence to his role despite the misgivings of his private conscience.

In what follows, I contend that Melville's tale ultimately pushes us to reject such either/or choices between competing values when it comes to handling an exceptional moral or legal dilemma. Vere fails morally and legally not because he makes the wrong choice but because he thinks he must make a choice between opposed values when the most difficult and best form of judgment in this case requires that he balance these ostensibly contrary ideals – both the law and morality, both mind and heart. To choose, as Vere does, is to abbreviate the protracted, uncertain, ad hoc, and often messy and compromised nature of judgment. This chapter intrudes on the Vere-centered studies of the novel the presence of a different reasoner, that of the reader. To look at the way the novel focuses the reader's attention on judgment is to pay as much attention to our own reflections as to Vere's. By positing evidence and support for both sides of any given opposition or by blurring the line of distinction between contrasting terms, Melville's narrative keeps his readers, if not Vere, in the middle of a matrix of various competing values, interests, and facts. The tale stirs us to imagine replacing Vere's precipitous, single-minded, and altogether too certain conclusion with a more deliberate, complex or "many-minded" balancing of concerns and norms. A particular type of intuition proves crucial to working through this less sure process of sustaining the many values and interests in order to arrive at the best possible decision.

From the outset, the tale involves the reader in a process of balancing various oppositions or contradictions. For instance, with Billy's impressment, the story asks readers to compare and weigh the competing claims of an individual's natural rights and the societal interest in a system of law and order, embodied in the British Navy that protects "free" society from the "red meteor of unbridled and unbounded revolt" (54). Each position has appeal. We sympathize, I think, with Billy's (unironic) farewell to the "*Rights of Man*" (49) *and* with the narrator's description of the British Navy as the last defense to the spread of the French Revolution's chaos and destruction (55–56). Any argument that Melville is ultimately a revolutionary Paineman or a counterrevolutionary Burke-man cannot adequately address the fact that the narrative offers support for both positions.

As readers, we are asked not only to balance such competing values as the individual's claim to fundamental natural rights and society's need for stability and order, but also to struggle with the narrative's many epistemological ambiguities and contradictions. For instance, the story both posits and withdraws evidence of the threat of mutiny. The narrator tells us that "anxiety" about a recurrence of mutiny was natural given the closeness in time of the Nore mutiny and notes that "precautionary vigilance was strained against relapse" (59), but he also tells us that on the *Bellipotent* "nothing obvious ... would have suggested that the Great Mutiny was a recent event" (60). Apparently, there is and there isn't reason to worry. A legitimate general anxiety about the possibility of mutiny can realistically coincide with a sense that there doesn't seem to be any imminent threat. Such allowance for contradiction must extend to individuals who possess divergent personality traits. Vere is "intrepid to the verge of temerity" (60), but he is also dreamy and meditative. Vere's love of reading includes "unconventional writers like Montaigne, who, free from cant and convention, honestly and in the spirit of common sense philosophize upon realities," suggesting a genuine open-mindedness, even an experimental outlook, yet Vere's reading and reflection have led him to "settled convictions," forming a "dike" against "novel" social and political opinion (62).

As Eric Sundquist's landmark reading of "Benito Cereno" suggests, Melville was intrigued by the suspension of opposed ideas in an unresolved tension, a dialectic without synthesis. "Unlike irony, which by deception, insinuation, or bald presumption revolts against the authority of one meaning to proclaim the authority of another, [Melville's] tautology," says Sundquist, "asserts the virtual equivalence of potentially different authorities or meanings," "by bringing two meanings into such approximation as to collapse the distinction between them without literally doing so."[12] In a similar vein, Sharon Cameron argues that the power of *Billy Budd* derives from the contradictory imperative to maintain and erode lines of distinction.[13] In determining whether Vere's intensity in rushing Billy's trial and predetermining its outcome is a sign of sanity or insanity, the reader is expressly given a task comparable to distinguishing the colors in a rainbow: "Who in the rainbow can draw the line where the violet tint ends and the orange tint begins? Distinctly we see the difference of the colors, but where exactly does the first one blendingly enter into the other? So with sanity and insanity" V. W. (102). For Cameron, the figure of the rainbow suggests that "opposites – sanity and insanity and honor and ignominy – are ... indistinguishable."[14] But this gloss misses an ambiguity in the passage and consequently pushes the interpretation too far in one direction. Does the phrase "the colors" refer to violet and orange or the other colors of the rainbow? When looking at an actual rainbow or color spectrum of light refracted through a prism, there really isn't any problem seeing that violet and orange are markedly different. For one thing, violet and orange are on opposite ends of the spectrum; other colors stand between them. But maintaining that clarity of distinction while moving from violet to orange is a different matter. That is to say, while it's not hard to see the opposed extremes, it is impossible to mark a clear and absolute barrier between any of the intervening colors, which do enter "blendingly" into each other. So that, while violet and orange (or sanity and insanity) are clearly at opposite ends of the gradient, Melville's figure suggests there is no unambiguous line of demarcation between the colors though the two are visibly different. Differentiation and indistinguishability are thus *both* present in Melville's figure, which suggests thereby how the reader who must judge Vere's mental state has to keep in mind both the difference between opposites *and* the way one can subtly and imperceptibly meld by degrees into the other.[15]

The deliberative process is both categorical (good is good, evil is evil) and noncategorical (some things can be, despite logic, one thing and the opposite at the same time). For example, while we know Billy is fundamentally honest, we also know that he is not above lying so as not to be a snitch (when asked by the drumhead court whether he has any awareness of "aught savoring of" mutiny, Billy answers in the negative rather than play the part of an "informer" [106]). We reject, I think, the categorically rigorous judgment that Billy is dishonest because he is not wholly forthcoming with the drumhead court. While such a conclusion might be true in the world of logical exclusions, it is not particularly useful in the compromised world of human existence. Billy's honesty meets our pragmatic expectations. We can depend on him to be generally truthful though not without exception.

At several points in the narrative, Melville suggests that the comprehension of characters and events necessary to the deliberative process requires something more than or different from mere analytic reason: we're told, for instance, that "something else than mere shrewdness is perhaps needful for the due understanding of such a character as Billy Budd's" (90). And, by way of explaining what seems inexplicable, the hatred motivating Claggart's scheme against Billy, the narrator says that "to pass from a normal nature [such as the reader's] to him [Claggart] one must cross 'the deadly space between'" (74). The phrase, "the deadly space between," is a quote from "The Battle of the Baltic" by Thomas Campbell (1777–1844), a poem commemorating one of Nelson's famous sea victories. In Campbell's poem the warring ships rush over "the deadly space between" to engage in battle. Here the spatial image is turned into a figure for inquiry and deliberation, but one that retains the war-like sense of conflict and uncertainty as one moves between antitheses (such as sanity/insanity, right/wrong, just/unjust).

To amplify how one navigates this uncertain and hazardous "space between" so as to understand a difficult character or a mystifying act such as the master-at-arms's false accusation, Melville quotes an "honest scholar" "now no more" (74). The scholar opines that "in an average man of the world, his constant rubbing with it blunts that finer spiritual insight indispensable to the understanding of the essential in certain exceptional characters, whether evil ones or good" (75). By "spiritual insight," Melville means something akin to the "intuition" he attributes to Shakespeare in "Hawthorne and His Mosses": "But it is those deep far-away things in him [Shakespeare]; those occasional flashings-forth of the intuitive Truth in him; those short, quick probings at the very axis of reality; – these are the things that make Shakespeare, Shakespeare" (*PT* 244). According to *Billy Budd*'s narrator, to know a difficult or disguised human nature requires a form of insight deeper than the lawyer's diligent study of "Coke and Blackstone" (75). By intuition, rather than mere professional expertise, one can penetrate Claggart's apparent rationality to find the contradictory irrational impulse in the man, the "natural depravity" that works with reason to achieve an "atrocity" that "would seem to partake of the insane" (76). Working in an ad hoc and holistic fashion, intuition is open to impressions and feelings as well as to contradiction, perceiving while not necessarily being able to explain the fact that Claggart can be simultaneously rational and irrational.

Like Melville, several noted American philosophers and jurists in the late nineteenth and early twentieth centuries were interested in the hard-to-define, amorphous power of intuition. William James, for instance, also turns to Shakespeare for an illustration of this kind of insight: "Why, for instance, does the death of Othello so stir the spectator's blood and leave him with a sense of reconcilement." James speculates, "Shakespeare, whose mind supplied these means, could probably not have told why they were so effective." For James, the authority of intuition appears to be discerned by the subject as deriving in part from its mysterious nature – it astonishes and seems to come from some "deeper level" than mere rationality. In intuiting something, our "thought obeys a *nexus*, but cannot name it." "[A]sk your most educated friend," says James, "why Beethoven reminds him of Michael Angelo, or how it comes that a bare figure with unduly flexed joints, by the latter, can so suggest the moral tragedy of life," and you will receive no adequate answer.[16] Citing James, Judge Joseph C. Hutcheson, Jr. and Justice Benjamin Cardozo candidly admit that, in certain difficult cases, judicial reasoning has to proceed "by feeling" rather than "by calculation." The judge accepts the novel legal question in its confusing entirety, trying "to feel, or hunch out a new category into which to place relations under his investigation," a concept capable of fully addressing the particular circumstances of the case while serving the normative goal of establishing and/or modifying rules in light of an always developing sense of justice.[17] Even Justice Holmes's deference to his professional role, his willingness to be "the supple tool of power," did not blind him to the "avowed or unconscious" intuitions, moral feelings, biases, and customs that inevitably lie behind and animate the process of judgment.[18] As Holmes famously observed, "The language of judicial decision is mainly the language of logic. And the logical method and form flatter that longing for certainty and for repose which is in every human mind. But certainty generally is illusion, and repose is not the destiny of man. Behind the logical form lies a judgment as to the relative worth and importance of competing legislative grounds, often an inarticulate and unconscious judgment, it is true, and yet the very root and nerve of the whole proceeding."[19]

Vere himself is not averse to the intuitive form of judgment Holmes describes as the unseen foundation of legal decisions. The narrator tells us that "something exceptional in the moral quality of Captain Vere made him, in earnest encounter with a fellow-man, a veritable touch-stone of that man's essential nature" (96). However, when confronted with Claggart and his accusation, Vere's intuition fails: as to "what was really going on in [Claggart], [Vere's] feeling partook less of intuitional conviction than of strong suspicion clogged by strange dubieties" (96). It is important that Vere's response to Claggart and later his conduct of the official inquiry into Billy's act comes after the tale tells us that doubts and fears have occluded Vere's better intuitive sense. As Sharon Cameron and others have rightly observed, the temporal proximity of the events on board the *Bellipotent* to the Nore mutiny is critical to making Vere's behavior "intelligible."[20] The potential threat of mutiny makes Vere less "starry" and more fearful, less intuitive

and more rigidly rationalistic, more likely to seek the comforting security
of bright-line rules and either/or choices because nuanced judgment and ad
hoc flexibility require a degree of confidence and security – something Vere
implicitly acknowledges is missing as he urges the drumhead court that the
threat of mutiny militates against any fine moral reasoning (110–12).

We have now come to the critical moment of the tale: Do we accept Vere's
account of the case, in particular that the only issue before the court is
whether Billy struck Claggart? As Andrew Delbanco puts it, "Every reader
of *Billy Budd* asks, Why? Why must Billy die?" Considering the volume
and intensity of the critical disagreement over Vere's judgment, one could
reasonably conclude that Melville intended to provoke precisely this kind of
reflection in his readers, to make them struggle with the question before the
drumhead court for themselves. Clearly, Melville does not assume his readers are intimately familiar with military or criminal law but rather assumes
they will independently ponder and attempt to think their way around the
facts of the case and the law as it is summarized by Vere. Accepting Vere's
account of the case and feeling that Melville "sides" with Vere, Delbanco
finds his answer to the question of why Billy must die "in the crystal clarity
of the Royal Navy's Articles of War."[21] As Vere puts it, merely to strike one's
"superior in grade" is, "according to the Articles of War, a capital crime"
(111). However, if Melville solely or even primarily wanted his readers to
side with Vere, it seems unlikely he would compose the narrative so as to
arouse passionate disputation of Vere's account.

The questions inspired by the narrative, while not necessarily condemning
Vere, prevent the reader from simply acquiescing in his handling of Billy's
case. Indeed, much of the power of Melville's novella derives from the forceful manner in which it induces the reader to reflect on Vere's judgment. *Billy
Budd* is more than a dry courtroom report on an actual case; it is an "inside
narrative" of Vere's reasoning, vicariously engaging us in that process and
simultaneously spurring us to question it. While sympathizing with Vere
and the difficulty of his situation, yet impelled by the question "why must
Billy die," the engaged reader makes further inquiry. Perhaps the first thing
that comes to mind is that if one accepts Vere's account of the case there is
no need for deliberation at all. Once one had determined the objectionable
act, nothing would remain for reflection – the law, by Vere's account, would
be practically self-executing. Why convene a court and institute a trial proceeding if the law is as simple and unyieldingly strict as to be automatic in
such a case? Yet the members of the drumhead court and Vere himself admit
that this is a difficult and even harrowing case to try – Vere calls it "exceptional" (110). Also if the law is perfectly clear that the mere act of striking
an officer is a capital offense, as Vere says late in the proceeding (111), why

does he earlier seek to "confine [the court's] attention to the blow's conse-quence" (107)? Why repeat the fact that Billy's blow killed Claggart if that fact is immaterial and yet bar evidence as to Billy's lack of homicidal or mutinous motivation as immaterial? Is Vere really saying that the law would automatically without any further reflection or inquiry require executing a sailor who struck a superior while having a seizure or spasm of some sort (a condition not dissimilar from Billy's)?

In addition, the court's questions about Billy's and Claggart's respective motivations suggest further lines of inquiry, such as whether Claggart can be said to have been acting as a superior officer when he knowingly made a false charge of mutiny against Billy, an act that Vere warns Claggart is itself a capital offense (95–96). How can Claggart's illegal calumny against Billy be an act in the execution of his office as a "superior in grade"? If Billy violently rejected an order from Claggart that he steal from the ship's stores, would he be liable for a capital crime under this statute? Also, while the average reader is not versed in military law, still something about Vere's participation as chief witness, prosecutor, and judge raises a question as to whether this procedure meets the standards for a court-martial in a capi-tal case. Other than Billy, Vere is the sole witness to the event in question. Wouldn't the fact that he, of necessity, must be the chief witness in any trial of the matter require that the matter be deferred to later trial by the admi-ralty, the preference of his junior officers, to avoid the apparent impropriety of serving in different roles?[22] The novella does not unambiguously answer these questions, but it does insistently engage the reader in such interro-gation, and that process is precisely the type of deliberation that Vere, not Melville, wants to avoid or truncate.

Vere rejects the balancing of opposed values and the observation of both differentiation and indistinguishability manifest in the two intuitive alterna-tives offered by members of the drumhead court. For instance, holding Billy until he can later be tried by the admiralty adheres to the law yet respects the moral qualms about the case felt by the drumhead court. Vere's reflex-ive argument against that option, that it would increase the likelihood of mutiny, is not convincingly explained. Why would according Billy Budd, who, unlike Claggart, is a well-liked member of the ship's crew, fair play and due process increase the chances of mutiny? Is instilling in the crew a fear of imminent execution the only way to achieve loyalty? The exam-ple the novel offers of Admiral Nelson suggests just the opposite (59). Or, in the alternative, convicting Billy but mitigating the penalty in light of Claggart's malign and Billy's innocent motives, while conceptually messy (Billy, in effect, would be treated as both guilty and not guilty in such a rul-ing) and lacking the smooth, well-oiled quality of the automatic imposition of a straightforward and unambiguous rule, feels like a more just result than executing an innocent man.

Even if we allow hypothetically that the condemnation and execution of a sailor in Billy's circumstances may as a matter of historical fact have been mandated by a tyrannical and patently unjust law (obviously unjust because, under predominant ideas of criminal responsibility both now and when the work was composed, it requires the death penalty without any inquiry into the mental state of the defendant, punishing an unintentional or reflexive act with the same unyielding severity as an act of premeditated and malign intent), we are nonetheless pushed by the novella to question Vere's conduct of Billy's trial. Melville's tale grips us in proportion to the degree to which we are engaged in both closely observing and judging Vere's judgment of Billy. While we recognize the difficult spot the case puts Vere in, we are impelled by the narrative to stand apart from him, his conclusion, and his justifications. The tension of the story, its drama, derives in large part from the reader's discovery that Vere's reasoning process is overdetermined by circumstances. That is to say that, while Vere is capable of better judgment and intuition, something about the array of factors in this case will drive him inevitably to a decision that will haunt him, the decision to take an innocent man's life. As a meditation on judgment, *Billy Budd* illustrates the necessity of both serving established rules and norms yet also attending comprehensively to the particular facts of a given case in light of our broader conceptions of justice.

Vere's positing of an essential and unavoidable conflict between morality and law is self-justifying and hyperbolic. It is a way of avoiding judgment, which is, of necessity in difficult cases, an uncertain, ad hoc process combining the rational weighing of facts, the careful reading of relevant rules and consideration of the policy behind those rules, and an intuitive sense of the just outcome in a more complex and far less absolute fashion than that suggested by Vere's formulation, "Struck dead by an angel of God! Yet the angel must hang!" (101). The best form of judgment, whether occurring in a literary representation or a judge's chambers, requires something more. Of course, Melville was well aware that what passes for intuition can lead one disastrously astray. As Samuel Otter observes, *Pierre* relentlessly demonstrates that "feelings are a treacherous ground for moral action."[23] However, different Melville tales center on different weaknesses. Where one might fault Pierre or Ahab for being too credulous of what they take to be intuition, Vere's mistake is expressly described as a failure of intuition. A refusal of intuition is no wiser, for Melville, than a positive certainty that such beliefs will prove apt. To refuse the force of intuition is to commit the error of Vere, which is a kind of inversion of the error of Ahab. Or to

152

put this point in *Billy Budd*'s terms, judgment requires navigation of the uncertain and hazardous "space between" options, the place where opposed concepts blend into each other, and intuition (whether dependable or not) is indispensable to this process.

NOTES

1 For an excellent account of this period in Melville's life, see Andrew Delbanco, *Melville: His World and Work* (New York: Knopf, 2005), 288–322.
2 Richard H. Weisberg, "Editor's Preface," *Cardozo Studies in Law and Literature* 1 (1989): vii.
3 For a reading of *Billy Budd* in relation to the Somers Mutiny, see Michael Paul Rogin, *Subversive Genealogy: The Politics and Art of Herman Melville* (Berkeley: University of California Press, 1983), 288–316. On the relation of *Billy Budd* to the Haymarket affair, see Alan Trachtenberg, *The Incorporation of America: Culture & Society in the Gilded Age* (New York: Hill and Wang, 1982), 203.
4 See, for example, H. Bruce Franklin, "Billy Budd and Capital Punishment: A Tale of Three Centuries," *American Literature*, 69 (1997): 337–59.
5 Barbara Johnson, "Melville's Fist: The Execution of *Billy Budd*," in *Herman Melville's* Billy Budd, *"Benito Cereno," "Bartleby the Scrivener," and Other Tales*, ed. Harold Bloom (New York: Chelsea House, 1987), 72.
6 Rogin, *Subversive Genealogy*, 288, 292.
7 See, for example, Rogin, *Subversive Genealogy*, 293, 299–300; Trachtenberg, *The Incorporation of America*, 201, 205; Michael T. Gilmore, "'Speak, man!': *Billy Budd* in the Crucible of Reconstruction," *American Literary History*, 21 (2009): 495, 507; Delbanco, *Melville*, 312; Robert A. Ferguson, *Law and Letters in American Culture* (Cambridge, MA: Harvard University Press, 1984), 288–90; John P. McWilliams, "Innocent Criminal or Criminal Innocence: The Trial in American Fiction," in *Law and American Literature: A Collection of Essays* (New York: Knopf, 1983), 74.
8 William V. Spanos, *The Exceptionalist State and the State of Exception: Herman Melville's* Billy Budd, Sailor (Baltimore, MD: Johns Hopkins University Press, 2011), 33. See also, Franklin, *"Billy Budd* and Capital Punishment," 357–9; Philip Loosemore, "Revolution, Counterrevolution, and Natural Law in *Billy Budd, Sailor,*" *Criticism*, 53 (2011): 99–126; Joseph Schiffman, "Melville's Final Stage, Irony: A Reexamination of *Billy Budd* Criticism," *American Literature*, 22 (May 1950): 128–36; and Karl E. Zink, "Herman Melville and the Forms – Irony and Social Criticism in 'Billy Budd,'" *Accent*, 12 (1952): 131–39.
9 Robert M. Cover, *Justice Accused: Antislavery and the Judicial Process* (New Haven, CT: Yale University Press, 1975), 1–6.
10 See Spanos, *The Exceptionalist State and the State of Exception*, 7, 24, 32–33; Brook Thomas, *Cross-Examinations of Law and Literature: Cooper, Hawthorne, Stowe, and Melville* (Cambridge: Cambridge University Press, 1987), 212.
11 Delbanco, *Melville*, 313.
12 Eric J. Sundquist, "Suspense and Tautology in 'Benito Cereno,'" in *Herman Melville's* Billy Budd, *"Benito Cereno," "Bartleby the Scrivener," and Other Tales*, ed. Harold Bloom (New York: Chelsea House, 1987), 83, 91 (reprinted from *Gylph: Johns Hopkins Textual Studies*, 8 [1981]: 103–26).

13 Sharon Cameron, *Impersonality: Seven Essays* (Chicago, IL: University of Chicago Press, 2007), 183.

14 Ibid., 185.

15 Noting the fact that violet and orange appear at the opposite ends of the spectrum, Thomas Claviez reads the rainbow as a figure for the clear demarcation of Vere's madness – a "pronounced case" ("Rainbows, Fogs, and Other Smokescreens: *Billy Budd* and the Question of Ethics," *Arizona Quarterly: A Journal of American Literature, Culture, and Theory* 62.4 [2006]: 36). In my view, the figure of the rainbow does not support a choice between indistinguishability (Cameron) or exact demarcation (Claviez), but insists on the coexistence of both concepts as essential to judgment.

16 William James, *The Principles of Psychology* (Cambridge, MA: Harvard University Press, 1981), 985–86, 988.

17 See Gregg Crane, "The Art of Judgment," *American Literary History* 23 (2011): 754–55.

18 Yosal Rogat, "The Judge as Spectator," *University of Chicago Law Review* 31 (1964): 249–50 (quoting Holmes); Oliver Wendell Holmes, *The Common Law* (Boston, MA: Little, Brown, and Company, 1881), 1.

19 Oliver Wendell *Holmes*, "The Path of the Law," in *The Essential Holmes*, ed. Richard Posner (Chicago, IL: University of Chicago Press, 1992), 167.

20 Cameron, *Impersonality*, 186.

21 Delbanco, *Melville*, 309.

22 Richard H. Weisberg condemns Vere's multiple breaches of the legal procedure under the relevant British naval laws, *The Failure of the Word: The Protagonist as Lawyer in Modern Fiction* (New Haven, CT: Yale University Press, 1984), 131–76. Richard Posner defends Vere's actions as consistent with precedent and appropriate in the exigent circumstances of threatened mutiny; Posner, *Law and Literature: A Misunderstood Relation* (Cambridge, MA: Harvard University Press, 1988), 155–65.

23 Samuel Otter, *Melville's Anatomies* (Berkeley: University of California Press, 1999), 238.

II

MICHAEL D. SNEDIKER

Melville and Queerness without Character

While queer studies has extended the ways readers think about the import of same-sex desire in Melville's writings, much of the scholarship conducted under the name of queer studies more accurately reflects the earlier critical focus and interests of gay studies. This latter field has helped us think more rigorously about the ways same-sex desire informs relationships among some of Melville's characters. An emphasis on character, however, risks overstating the extent to which Melville's characters resemble actual persons with whom we can identify in terms of internal and external motivation. We wish for Melville's characters to function enough like erotic subjects that their predicaments speak not only to the interests of the text at hand, but also to Melville's lived experiences and our own; more often than not, however, Melville's characters fall short of this basic criterion.[1] If gay and lesbian studies has enriched our understanding of how same-sex desire shapes and impels a character's thought and action, queer studies complicates what we mean by thought and action, and challenges where and how we understand agency and affect beyond gay and lesbian studies' understandings of sexuality and identity.

As articulated by a range of critics, notably Leo Bersani, Judith Butler, and Eve Kosofsky Sedgwick, queer theory traces the ways desiring subjects fall short of (or overreach) erotic, epistemological, political, and affective stability. In the fluctuation of these categories, same-sex desire illuminates but does not resolve the terms by which queer identity both comes into being and resists its crystallization as such. At its most vibrant, queer theory encourages us to think about the often surprising ways that desire either undoes or recalibrates even our most spacious understandings of personhood and relationality. Analogously, queer literary criticism has moved from gay studies' attention to the desires of textual characters to considerations of desire extricated from character, and of characters who only sometimes operate as we implicitly think characters ought. Queer literary criticism speaks to a strangeness in Melville's writing that exceeds questions of homoeroticism;

even more queer in Melville than characters informed by same-sex desire are characters that barely function like characters at all.[2] Differently put, Melville's foiling of the insights of gay studies can illuminate what in his work is most queer-theoretically resonant.

This chapter considers some of the ways the erotic interactions of Melville's characters vex the interpretive expectations of other characters, as well as the interpretive expectations of readers. Gay criticism calibrated to the feelings and actions of people lacks a vocabulary for the extravagance with which Melville's characters seem oblivious to erotic contexts that strike readers as flagrantly sexual, or negotiate desire as though not even they (as opposed to readers) could decide if desire were a literal or figurative phenomenon. Such extravagance and indiscriminateness, in exceeding the parameters of analysis predicated on gender and sexuality per se, calls for a queer (as opposed to gay) understanding of characters as aesthetically promiscuous rather than mimetically faithful. Melville's texts are most queer in their treatment of characters as irresolvable aesthetic problems. In texts like *Moby-Dick* and *Pierre*, Melville cultivates an aesthetic whose lavish vitality overshadows the plots and characters it supposedly describes.

In the past two decades, queer literary criticism has emerged from the earlier fields of gay and lesbian studies, which had provided new ways of thinking about literary representations of same-sex desire. In the case of Melville, whose short stories and novels often focus exclusively on men, gay literary criticism articulates the erotic valences of his works' many male-male relationships. The earliest wave of gay literary criticism faced the challenge of pointing out the obviousness of these relationships' erotic contours – for instance, the conjugal language in which Melville describes Ishmael and Queequeg's sharing of a bed. Before gay literary criticism, Melville scholars might have discussed such a scene in terms of the metaphors of marriage or romance, but the conversion of bed sharing into a vehicle for something metaphorical obscured and lessened the significance and implications of this homoerotic turn. Subsequent work in gay literary criticism has elaborated on and complicated these first gay-attuned readings. For instance, feminist theory illuminates the ways marriage relations between men and women consolidate and conceal cultural discourses about subordination and power. Ishmael and Queequeg's "marriage," then, raises questions of homoeroticism that are inseparable from certain gendered codifications of agency. Gay Melville criticism likewise has benefited from the scholarship of postcolonial theorists for whom Ishmael and Queequeg represent not only two men temporarily inscribed in the convention of marriage, but also, in terms of power relations, two men occupying nearly opposite positions in an imperial narrative. That Ishmael is a New Englander and Queequeg a Polynesian further complicates how we think about the characters' union. These sorts of complications don't necessarily make Melville's already difficult texts more difficult to read; rather, they help us do justice to a wide range of characters and scenes against which we'd otherwise perhaps come up short.

The insights of gay and lesbian studies most saliently speak through characters to the lived concerns of both Melville's and our own world. In doing so, these insights are predicated on a belief that Melville's characters function as proxies for persons, which at the very least requires our being able to take characters for granted as people. And yet Melville himself reminds us throughout his career of the limitations inherent to this mode of reading, and alternately evokes an arguably queer reading practice that takes his characters' inconsistency and confusion as interpretive openings, rather than as problems. In an aside to readers, the speaker of *The Confidence-Man* puzzles over why we require that "fiction based on fact should never be contradictory to it," when "in real life, a consistent character is a *rara avis*" (69). Conventionally speaking, a character's inconsistency corresponds to an erraticism in feeling or action nonetheless consistent with how we imagine persons as potentially erratic. Here as throughout his writing, however, Melville signals a far more radical "unraveling" (70) made even more disorienting by the fact that Melville's speakers and characters so often are in on the game. Newton Arvin – like F. O. Matthiessen a gifted, closeted critic of the 1950s – notes that at best a few of the characters in *The Confidence-Man* "have a jerky, marionettish, rather ghastly semblance of vitality. They have no more than that, and for the most part the others have not even so much."[3] Even more ghastly, however, than characters that seem jerky to a critic are characters whose ghastliness becomes the subject of other characters' scrutiny, as well as characters who seem unaware of their own defining implausibility when the latter seems their most defining trait.

In much of his fiction, Melville challenges how we normally think about characters and desire, both within a text and in readers' relations to the text. By "normally," I mean that we often do not think about characters *qua* characters at all. Our wish to make interpretive sense of Melville sometimes cozens us into not adequately recognizing the degree to which we share Arvin's sense that Melville's characters are jerky, that they are too thinly or exorbitantly conceived for us to "believe in them" enough to fall into their story. As early as his first novel, *Typee*, Melville experiments with the "more and less" of characters who *nearly* seem like characters, and whose desire for other characters, concomitantly, only nearly seems like desire. Like *Moby-Dick*'s Ishmael, Tommo is too much a character to function seamlessly as a narrator, but too much a narrator to seem sufficiently embodied as a character. Throughout *Typee*, Tommo observes the loin clothed bodies of

Polynesian islanders: he notes that Marnoo's "unclad limbs were beautifully formed; whilst the elegant outline of his figure, together with his beardless cheeks, might have entitled him to the distinction of standing for the statue of the Polynesian Apollo" (135). Although it is possible to interpret this Hellenizing of Marnoo as erotic, such a reading too quickly collapses the observation's aesthetic logic, in which Marnoo subjunctively "might" stand for a sculpture that is only absurdly, fictively canonical. Our hypothetical attraction to a classical sculpture's own "elegant outline" presumes that the original who stood for it no longer exists, even as the original stands right there. But what is standing here in this passage invariably differs from what the passage becomes in the hands of critics (including Tommo, whose reading of Marnoo we read). Sensitive to the simultaneously Westernizing and exoticizing gestures of nineteenth-century ethnography, critics tend to speak of both Tommo and Marnoo as though they were actual people, when in fact we're encountering a barely sketched character struck by another barely sketched character who flickers between aesthetic and ontological categories without inhabiting either.

While Tommo's attention to nearly naked male bodies conjures something like a homoerotic gaze, Tommo's affective response to the islanders is less desirous than astonished – as is their response to him. In the moment of perception, neither seems to believe in each other enough to cultivate a relation that approaches erotic:

> I was somewhat astonished to perceive that among the number of natives that surrounded us not a single female was to be seen. (*T* 14)

> Every item of intelligence appeared to redouble the astonishment of the islanders, and they gazed at us with inquiring looks. (70)

> As soon as Kory-Kory comprehended from my motions that this was to be the extent of my performance, he appeared perfectly aghast with astonishment. (89)

> I was thrown into utter astonishment. (136)

> For a moment I was overwhelmed with astonishment. (139)

Robert K. Martin, who has written insightfully on sexuality in Melville, suggests the novel's "evocation of a place of apparently unbridled and polymorphous sexuality" contributes to "a reorganization of erotic activity" in Melville's work "to a greater range of possibility."[4] It seems as likely, however, that *Typee* flirts with the island's erotic possibilities as a principal version of the text's flirtation with the more general dangers of interpretive significance. After all, the novel is named – *perhaps* haphazardly – after one of two tribes. "Thus it is that they whom we denominate 'savages' are made to deserve the title" (26). It is not that one tribe practices cannibalism and the other does not, but that of both cannibal tribes, one is hostile and the other friendly. Tommo doesn't know which tribe he has encountered; analogously, we cannot entirely know if we are reading a "friendly" text that readily supports our interpretive impulse or a more guileful one that solicits interpretations it simultaneously problematizes (similar interpretive tensions inform "Benito Cereno").

While gay studies has illuminated numerous ways of reading Tommo's relation to the potentially eroticized islanders, it does so at the risk of under-articulating the uncanny imbrication of Tommo's reading practices with our own. In this imbrication, the differences blur between desiring bodies and desiring textual meaning, as do the broader and only deceptively straight-forward differences between persons and characters. These blurs, no less erotically dense than the bodies and texts that impel them, give way to what in Melville is most queerly striking. *Typee*'s conjuring of tropical capers might, as Martin claims, signal on some level a wishful reprieve from the increasingly taxonomizing discourse of nineteenth-century sexuality. At the same time, Melville's early novel, like his later work, treats the strenuous-ness of interpretation as its own erotic enterprise.

In *Typee*, we encounter a surfeit of nominally homoerotic bodies, all of which lack an interiority capable of erotic complexity or motivation; the text circuits between an astonishment that precludes observation to obser-vations incapable of interpretation beyond superficial significance. *Pierre*, by contrast, spins for its eponymous protagonist an irresolvable heterosex-ual imbroglio that is saturating to the point if not of incredulity than sheer exhaustion. This weariness is suggested in the *New York Herald*'s laconic 1852 précis: "desperate passion at first sight, for a young woman who turns out to be the hero's sister, &c., &c., &c. It is conceded that Mr. Melville has written himself out."[5] More and less: the review's "&c." typographically figures Melville's aesthetic as simultaneously so excessive as to require not one but three "et ceteras," and so impoverished as to be typographically truncated to ampersands.

Martin writes that "the best future for the study of sexuality in Melville's texts" will require "a queer model that proposes contingency instead of certainty."[6] In his influential "cruising" reading of *Pierre*, James Creech makes good on a certain version of Martin's proposal in speculating that Pierre's incestuous contretemps obfuscates and is energized by an even ear-lier, stickier proscription against desire for his father. In his father's absence, Pierre's queer desire for his father is mediated by an alluring portrait of his father that Pierre keeps in his closet. The "streams" of Pierre's clos-eted, portrait-centered "reveries" signify, for Creech, the fruits of Pierre's masturbatory labor, arising from a queerness that echoes Melville's as much as it refracts Creech's own. Creech avers, after all, that his gay reading of *Pierre* is made possible by his own intuitions as a gay critic.[7] Such a reading indeed relies on the contingency of connections between character, author, and critic. This collation of Pierre, Melville, and Creech as a trio of nesting dolls – &c. &c. &c. – asks us to take Pierre, literally closeted with his father, as a character whose closetedness to himself and other characters could correspond to lived duress. Such a correspondence, however, is made impossible by the unctuous language in which *Pierre*'s characters drown.

The fulsome style of *Pierre* is more queer than Pierre is gay. Before turning to this style, it is helpful to consider Melville's posthumously published novella(*Billy Budd*), which of Melville's texts comes closest on the level of character and plot to staging the difficulty and dangers inherent in investing a given character with gay meaning. At the same time, even the most assiduous critics of homosexual desire in Melville's novella will come up short if they take character, conventionally understood, as their principal unit of analysis. Influential queer theorist Eve Sedgwick models a reading that takes character as point of departure, but brings us to the brink of wondering what remains in a character's wake. Sedgwick tracks our inclination to read Claggart and not Vere as a homosexual, to the extent that Claggart's preoccupation with Billy resembles in its ambivalence and ardor the impacted desire of a closeted homophobe. "In contrast to Claggart's toilsome enmeshments," Sedgwick writes, "Vere's eye sees in Billy a clean-cut stimulus to his executive aptitudes, the catalyst of a personnel-management project to get the magnificent torso hoisted up to 'a place that would more frequently bring him under his own observation.'" In this sense, Vere's public display of potentially homosexual desire, like Poe's purloined letter, is less detectible than Claggart's, in that the latter strikes us as visually arresting *because* it is concealed.[8]

The novella extends a model of desire scaled to an axis of ever-diminishing visibility: as readers, we descend from Billy's irresistible scopic beauty, to Claggart's inability to communicate ostensibly private feeling, to Vere's translation of ostensibly private feeling into seemingly nonsexualized juridical discourse. Following this logic, *Billy Budd* ultimately imagines the descriptively void narrator as the "character" with greatest erotic viability. Sedgwick notes the narrator's intrusions, but only in passing (a phrase all the more telling in this context), in the spirit of the narrator who only barely calls attention to himself. "[T]he narrative," Sedgwick writes, "itself ostentatiously suspends judgment on the question" of Vere's sanity. This extravagant reticence suggests an intensification of Vere's own affective modus operandi: as Sedgwick observes, "We know 'Vere suffers in private' because

Vere suffers in private in public." As an alternative to the erotic nesting dolls of Pierre/Melville/Creech, Vere's gaze holds Claggart's delectation of Billy, but the narrator's own gaze hold's Vere's delectation of Billy and Claggart. Vere's orchestration of "a theatrical ritual around the liminal sufferings of not only Billy's body but his own" turns Vere himself, Sedgwick argues, into "an object of view – for his officers and men, but most of all for the narrative itself – the Nixonized Vere becomes subjected, in a way that he cannot, after all, bring under single-handed control." This proprietary narrative, mobilized by an invisible narrator, improves upon Vere's own barely perceptible erotic strategy.[9]

While myriad critics of *Billy Budd* note that the narrator describes Claggart as a "nut not to be cracked by the tap of a lady's fan" (*BB* 74), less attention is paid to the narrator's subsequent description of Claggart's "unobserved glance" as it "happened to light on belted Billy rolling along the upper gun deck" (87). Unobserved, that is, by everyone except the narrator, this look "would have in it a touch of soft yearning, as if Claggart could even have loved Billy but for fate and ban. But this was an evanescence, and quickly repented of, as it were, by an immitigable look, pinching and shriveling the visage into the momentary semblance of a wrinkled walnut" (88). Claggart's face momentarily becomes a walnut if only so the narrator can rub in our own faces that his description cracks the earlier nut that couldn't be cracked. Interrupting the "immitigable" story of Billy, we might well say that the narrator cracks himself up. The narrator has his way not only with Vere, but with us – his affectively overdetermined manipulation of the text rests on the knowledge that without his narrative, there is nothing to read at all. However we are inclined to describe this particular arrangement of power and desire is a subject less for gay studies than for queer theory. Put differently, gay studies can perhaps crack the nut of Claggart's "soft yearning," but not the nut of a narrator who takes pleasure in turning yearning into a walnut. The insights of queer theory, on the other hand, help us make sense of a textual longing more particular than the deconstructive play of *differance*, but too vague to approximate the contours of any single or shared psychical desire, on either conscious or unconscious register.

The effulgences of narration in *Billy Budd,* coming at the expense of characters and readers alike, return us to the question of character and description in *Pierre*. Characterological bias, I suggest, leaves inexplicable the rococo floridity of *Pierre*'s narrative style. To read, as Creech does, Melville's streaming reveries as analogs for Pierre's masturbatory practices neither speaks to nor clarifies the astonishing extraneousness with which those reveries are described. If the erotics of the following lines are cloying, their excess belongs less to character or author than to the text itself, to the narrative that, like that of *Billy Budd*, takes the vulnerability of its own character as "object of view":

> Thus sometimes in the mystical, outer quietude … either when the hushed mansion was banked round by the thick-fallen December snows, or banked round by the immovable white August moonlight; in the haunted repose of a wide story, tenanted only by himself; and sentineling his own little closet; and standing guard, as it were, before the mystical tent of the picture; and ever watching the strangely concealed lights of the meanings that so mysteriously moved to and fro within; thus sometimes stood Pierre before the portrait of his father, unconsciously throwing himself open to all those ineffable hints and ambiguities, and undefined half-suggestions, which now and then people the soul's atmosphere, as thickly as in a soft, steady snow-storm, the snow-flakes people the air. Yet as often starting from these reveries and trances, Pierre would regain the assured element of consciously bidden and self-propelled thought; and then in a moment the air all cleared, not a snow-flake descended, and Pierre, upbraiding himself for his self-indulgent infatuation, would promise never again to fall into a midnight revery before the chair-portrait of his father. (*P* 84–85)

Are we facing the blindness of a snowy whiteout, or the luminous insight of an August moon? The distinction, somewhat like Tommo's attempt to distinguish one cannibal tribe from another, is moot, insofar as the "light banks" of the moon seem as immovably opaque as snow (if not more so). Significance – for Tommo, Pierre, and Melville's readers – doesn't illuminate ambiguity so much as constitute it ("strangely concealed lights of the meanings"). The text equivocates between materiality and dissolution with dizzying speed: thought populates a soul like snow, and snow populates the air like people, designating both the landscape Pierre himself inhabits ("in the haunted repose of a wide story, tenanted only by himself") and an analogy for his own mindset as he watches meaning move as though from within. This implosion of recognition and visibility suggests that what Melville in *The Confidence-Man* describes as an "unravelling" of character corresponds to an erotic willfulness of words in the service neither of character nor plot. If desire (queer or otherwise) usually is understood in relation to an absent erotic object, then writing such as this seems motivated less by desire than self-motivating, objectless pleasure.

The text's own pleasure in itself brings to mind Foucault's distinction between pleasure and desire. Foucauldian pleasure, writes Arnold Davidson, "is related to itself and not to something else that it expresses, either truly or falsely. There is … no primacy of the psychological subject in the experience of pleasure. Structures of desire lead to forms of sexual orientation, kinds of subjectivity; different pleasures do not imply orientation at all, require no theory of subjectivity or identity formation."[10] That this pleasure beyond the representational fields of sex or character is aesthetically compelled (in that the text privileges its absorption in its own beauty over its comprehensibility to readers) calls to mind Christopher Looby's recent articulation in Melville of pleasure's imbrication with aesthetics. "In the early nineteenth-century ... when 'sexuality' had not yet been categorically discerned as a particular variety or construction of bodily experience, never mind an 'identity,' '[b]odies and pleasures' and 'aesthetics' ... begin to look a lot alike; they are both terms for 'the whole of our sensate life together.'"[11] Melville's queer aesthetics are most disorienting in those instances when aesthetics and pleasure inspire textual verve in the absence of characters or characters' bodies, beholden to no one and nothing so much as itself.

My reading of *Pierre*'s weather[12] in the passage cited earlier admittedly is a far cry from other critical efforts to locate homosexuality or homosexual characters in Melville's writing. And yet, there is something importantly queer at stake in the pleasure Melville's malapropisms seem to take from themselves. *Pierre*'s grandiloquent figurations spoil the novel's erotic strain, even as they are prompted by an aberrant willfulness that corresponds to the sexual vagaries they sometimes superficially describe. If the confusions constitutive of *Pierre*'s incest plot depend on an unmooring of relationality – nominal designations of the maternal, sororal, or spousal alternately exceeding and falling short of what they describe – a similar set of relational confusions informs the novel's more local figurative logistics. Melville's figurations threaten to empty out whatever meaning they produce, not only because they are clumsy or indulgent, but because their particular sinuousness is conceptually self-consuming. They all but dare us to read over (rather than over read) them, as we attempt to distill their largesse into some significance directly linked to character or plot.

A queer sensitivity to the pleasure Melville's language takes in itself – rather than to the pleasure Melville's characters take in other characters – illuminates a power dynamic as slyly animated as that which informs dialectics of gender and sexuality. *Pierre*'s demanding descriptive voice often disregards the hierarchy that usually governs a metaphor's vehicle and tenor. Even when the text's metaphorical vehicles at least nominally exist as material objects and not abstractions, there is no guarantee that they will remain any more empirically real than the abstract tenors to which they sometimes give rise. There is likewise little guarantee that Melville's metaphorical vehicles, after dubious expansion and figurative transformation, exist at all. *Pierre* further undermines the logic of tenor and vehicle in the incredulity that its metaphorical vehicles consistently solicit. There is nothing in *Pierre* that isn't already saturated in if not altogether constituted by a nonliteral, credulity-straining register. Thus, when Lucy enters Saddle Meadows "carrying a little basket of strawberries" (57), she for all intents and purposes already is as rosy cheeked and nubile an allegory of innocence as any allegory of innocence. Even Pierre, outrageously incredible in his own right, "almost thought she could only depart the house by floating out of the open window, instead of actually stepping from the door" (58). Eerily, it's difficult to say whether Pierre would even be surprised if Lucy sprouted wings. As a reader, I'd be nearly unsurprised, and would only somewhat care, to the extent that Lucy-in-the-sky would register as a logical, metonymic extension of Lucy's "rosy-snow[ed]" essence. What would elsewhere operate as allegory (relation between woman and angelic purity as two disparate objects) operates as mere intensification or protraction of a single thing. The lack of distance between Lucy-as-character and Lucy-as-allegory suggests a discomfiture that is at least structurally analogous to the incest plot to which it is adjacent; in both cases, a couple is close in jarringly uncanny ways. The queer propinquity of Lucy and her allegorical self is inseparable from the unsettling velocity with which we "know" how to read her from the first moment on.

As an allegory for herself, Lucy paradoxically functions as a freshly minted cliché, and thus inspires on a smaller scale a version of the epistemological anxiety Bartleby inspires in many readers, including the lawyer who employs him. Our relation to her induces a literary nausea that corresponds to the queasiness Pierre himself feels in the face of his own ontological catastrophe: "The cheeks of his soul collapsed in him: he dashed himself in blind fury and swift madness against the wall, and fell dabbling in the vomit of his loathed identity" (171). Melville further explicates this characterological disorientation in Pierre's enchanted survey of Lucy's bedroom, her "secret inner shrine":

> Now, crossing the magic silence of the empty chamber, he caught the snow-white bed reflected in the toilet-glass. This rooted him. For one swift instant, he seemed to see in that one glance the two separate beds – the real one and the reflected one – and an unbidden, most miserable presentiment thereupon stole into him. But in one breath it came and went. So he advanced, and with a fond and gentle joyfulness, his eye now fell upon the spotless bed itself, and fastened on a snow-white roll that lay beside the pillow. Now he started; Lucy seemed coming in upon him; but no – 'tis only the foot one of her little slippers, just peeping into view from under the narrow nether curtains of the bed. Then again his glance fixed itself upon the slender, snow-white ruffled roll; and he stood as one enchanted. Never precious parchment of the Greek was half so precious in his eyes. Never trembling scholar longed more to unroll the mystic vellum, than Pierre longed to unroll the sacred secrets of that snow-white, ruffled thing. (39)

Melville's insistence on the snow-white roll subliminally extends the possibility of the roll's being *unrolled*, in its becoming a vellum scroll. The passage barely avoids the silliness of such an inadvertently punny formulation by ultimately revising the roll as a "thing." This swerve from an unrolled roll performs the extent to which even Melville's facetiousness might have a limit; nonetheless, the narrator's clumsily legible avoidance of the pun (which would ruin his already jeopardized depiction of Pierre's solemnity) serves to underscore rather than deflate the scene's fustian. The passage's joke, while constellating around the word "roll," already is operative on a more general level: were Pierre to be the "trembling scholar" unrolling his love's mystic vellum, it is implied that the vellum, like everything else in the room, would be a snow-white blank. Like Lucy, who is less a perfect nullity than an accretion of earlier textual nullities – we think we know who she is on account of vaguely recalling having come across versions of her in other texts that make us similarly flinch – this blank is more a palimpsest of whitewashes than a *tabula rasa*. Even as there is little here of decided erotic import, this bedroom's melodramatic vertigo is queerly teeming.

While Pierre imagines a difference between the vellum and the roll, there effectively is none. Similarly, although Pierre registers the difference between the two beds – one is "real" and the other is "reflected" – that difference is itself elided in the spatial confusion with which he misperceives Lucy's slipper as "Lucy coming in upon him." If his eye "is [falling] on the spotless bed itself," the bed putatively is in front of him. But if the slipper indicates to him that Lucy is approaching from behind, then the bed and its slippers are not in front at all. It would seem that Pierre's surprised start originates not only in the animation of the slipper, but in the indistinction for him of the real and the reflected. In this sense, the roll already is unrolled before it figuratively becomes something else: the roll fails to exist in either an actual register (because it already is too much of a figuration, a bolster in need of bolster) or a figurative one (because its figuration embarrassingly is too propinquitous to what it originally is). This failure deprives it of any tenable status at all. Limply toggling simultaneous registers of legibility and illiteracy, the roll isn't unrolled so much as undone. In being turned into a thing, the cliché – its own intractable thingness – performs a failed retreat from discernibility of any sort. The drama unfolding from this bedroom scene takes on a life of its own, and the more it does so, the more ghastly (to return to Arvin's word) it becomes. I've lingered in this play of epistemological and aesthetic limbo as it speaks to the queer extremities we find in the wake of Melville's characters. We might well take Pierre's detective work as a model for queer reading: a barely plausible character entranced and nearly undone by what in a bedroom isn't there.

What would it mean to imagine this bedroom scene, rather than that between Queequeg and Ishmael, as Melville's queer point of departure? This pornography-without-people ("Pierre longed to unroll the sacred secrets of that snow-white ruffled thing") serves as a caveat against too quickly thinking we'll know Melvillean desire when we see it. A case in point is the more famous bedroom scene at the start of *Moby-Dick*: "Upon waking next morning about daylight, I found Queequeg's arm thrown over me in the most loving and affectionate manner. You had almost thought I had been his wife" (25). We don't as readers almost take him for Queequeg's wife, and yet trying to coax these lines into homosexual meaning feels nearly as challenging as trying to make an argument for Lucy's innocence: it's so *there*, it may as well not be. The scene's interpretive obviousness is confounding not because it takes the work out of our own hands, but because the interpretation accrues to characters that strain our credulity as characters.

After all, Ishmael himself is unnerved at the outset by Queequeg's arm thrown across him, because at first it doesn't seem real even to Ishmael. The "awful fear" of a nonexistent embrace slowly materializes for Ishmael into "the comical predicament" of sharing a quilt with a Polynesian harpooner. Although the scene eventually materializes for its readers in like fashion, I wish to hold onto the queer sensation of encountering a character who is potentially spooked because his bedmate strikes him as no more real than either of them strikes us. In place of the character we will come to know as Queequeg, Ishmael senses – or rather, *almost* senses – the presence of a phantom: "Instantly I felt a shock running through all my frame; nothing was to be seen, and nothing was to be heard; but a supernatural hand seemed placed in mind. My arm hung over the counterpane, and the nameless, unimaginable, silent form or phantom, to which the hand belonged, seemed closely seated by my bed-side. For what seemed ages piled upon ages, I lay there, frozen with the most awful fears, not daring to drag away my hand; yet ever thinking that if I could but stir it one single inch, the horrid spell would be broken" (26). Leo Bersani notes of this scene that "far from representing either unequivocal homosexuality or surfaces of heterosexual desire troubled by repressed homosexual impulses, Melville's characters have no sexual subjectivity at all.... Ishmael's marital metaphors reveal nothing about him because there is nowhere in the novel an Ishmael about whom such metaphors can be revealing."[13] Were we to concede that Ishmael is as "unimaginable" a phantom character as Queequeg, the erotics of this scene would grow to resemble less that of an intelligibly gay coupling than that of an unintelligibly queer meeting of hands, ours included, as we turn the page.

While certain arguments about desire might require at least temporarily that we believe in *Moby-Dick*'s characters, the future of queer Melville criticism may well require at least temporarily that we admit we do not believe in them. That it seems less heretical to make such a claim about Lucy Tartan than it does about Ishmael says less about Lucy or Ishmael than it does about the deference with which we hold *Moby-Dick*, although the sooner we suspend the notion that characterological deficit is only always pejorative, the sooner we might realize that Melville's greatness not only doesn't lie in his characters, but may have something to do with his brilliant, queer dismantling of them. Queer theory complicates our understanding of sexuality's shifting constellation of identity, power, and desire. At the same time, it frees us to think about pleasure separate from bodies as its own deep aesthetic condition. In its turn from desire as the exclusive province of characters, Melville's writing resonates with what is most vitally challenging in queer theory, and likewise anticipates it.

The rapture of queerness without character can be heard in "A Squeeze of the Hand." A chapter of *Moby-Dick* usually read as a utopic dream of homoeroticism, this section ebulliently recounts the labor of turning the lumps of a whale's sperm back into liquid. "I found myself," Ishmael declares, "unwittingly squeezing my co-labourer's hands in it, mistaking their hands for the gentle globules. Such an abounding, affectionate, friendly, loving feeling did this avocation beget" (416). *Sperm? Same-sex hand squeezing? Surely*, readers ejaculate, *this must be gay!* The pleasures of the passage, however, exceed and elude such vocabularies as quickly as the vocabularies are drawn. It is in the joyous first contact between text and us that our shared pleasure is most acute. "My fingers," Melville writes as Ishmael, "felt like eels, and began, as it were, to serpentine and spiralize" (415). Like Lucy's nearly unrolling roll, these eels point to a queerness in Melville's writing – beyond desires attributed to characters too flimsy to sustain them – that is as electrifying as it is slippery.

NOTES

1 Critics wishing to align homoeroticism in Melville's writing with Melville's biography usually cite his friendship with Nathaniel Hawthorne. See *Hawthorne and Melville: Writing a Relationship*, ed. Jana L. Argersinger and Leland S. Person (Athens: University of Georgia Press, 2008).

2 Nina Baym makes a related but less theoretically inflected claim about Melville's more general disenchantment with fiction's generic features in "Melville's Quarrel with Fiction," *PMLA* 94.5 (October 1979): 909–23.

3 Newton Arvin, *Herman Melville* (Westport, CT: Greenwood Press, 1950), 250.

4 Robert K. Martin, "Melville and Sexuality," *The Cambridge Companion to Herman Melville*, ed. Robert S. Levine (Cambridge and New York: Cambridge University Press, 1998), 186, 190.

5 *Herman Melville: The Contemporary Reviews*, ed. Brian Higgins and Hershel Parker (Cambridge and New York: Cambridge University Press, 1995), 419.

6 Martin, "Melville and Sexuality," 200.

7 James Creech, *Closet Writing/Gay Reading: The Case of Melville's* Pierre (Chicago, IL: University of Chicago Press, 1993), 130–46.

8 Eve Kosofsky Sedgwick, *Epistemology of the Closet* (Berkeley: University of California Press, 1990), 108–109.

9 Ibid., 123, 115–16, 124.

10 Arnold I. Davidson, *The Emergence of Sexuality: Historical Epistemology and the Formation of Concepts* (Cambridge, MA: Harvard University Press, 2001), 212.

11 Christopher Looby, "Strange Sensations: Sex and Aesthetics in 'The Counterpane,'" in *Melville and Aesthetics,* ed. Samuel Otter and Geoffrey Sanborn (New York: Palgrave Press, 2011), 66.

12 This account of Melvillean weather is indebted to Eve Kosofsky Sedgwick's essay "The Weather in Proust" (*The Weather in Proust,* ed. Jonathan Goldberg [Durham, NC: Duke University Press, 2011], 1–41).

13 Leo Bersani, *The Culture of Redemption* (Cambridge, MA: Harvard University Press, 2000), 146.

12

ELISA TAMARKIN

Melville with Pictures

At thirty-seven years old, Johann Wolfgang von Goethe traveled to Italy, drew pictures of what he saw, and then etched them on metal plates. But, since he was a limited draftsman, he also wrote about Italy in his correspondence and notebooks, dipping a pen in the sepia ink he used for etching so that even his writing would have the warm, washed-brown tone of the prints he made when he was there. The sepia helped Goethe remember the atmospheric effects of Italy, especially when, at dawn or dusk, its broad umber light blurred edges and harmonized surrounding forms. The landscape, filtered through the tinted air, looked like it was pulsing and glowing from within. Nothing was clear at these times of day, but the reduction of colors and details to a simpler scale of tones (for Goethe, mist, clouds, or smoke had a similar effect) created the same kind of synthesis he also saw in picturesque paintings, especially when an artist worked from memory. It was here that Goethe says he started "looking at the world with the eyes of painters," which meant for him that his firsthand experience of Italy had more of the qualities of an "after-image," or mental picture, or maybe that Italy up close looked more like a sepia-toned picture of Italy, already aging. Watching the contours of the coastline through a Sicilian haze, Goethe writes, "I no longer saw Nature but pictures." Why would he want nature to look like pictures, and not the other way around?[1] Goethe returned to Germany and became an avid collector of prints.

Herman Melville was thirty-seven years old when he went to Italy, and liked to remember that Goethe was, too. Melville read Goethe's *Autobiography* and *Travels in Italy*. He also read essays on art by Charles Eastlake, who had translated Goethe's *Theory of Colors* into English in 1840. We know now that Melville himself had a pictorial turn after his 1857 trip and, if not "changed to the very marrow," as Goethe claims to have been (Melville marked the passage in *Travels*), at least pictures became increasingly significant to him.[2] For the next thirty-four years, Melville stopped publishing fiction and only published poetry and thought deeply about the correspondence between poetry and painting. He read essays on Charles DuFresnoy's treatise on painting, *De Arte Graphica* (1668), which begins, with Horace, "Let poetry be like painting, and painting like poetry." He very seriously collected prints, over 400 by the time he died, and many very late, in the 1880s, after an inheritance from his wife's family made buying them much easier. We also know that he bought or borrowed a range of books on the history of art and art criticism, on theories of art, design, and painting, and on the material practices of painting and etching especially.[3]

Was there an author in the nineteenth century more invested in the visual arts, except for Goethe? Melville spent the last three decades of his life studying and collecting pictures that then became the basis of his poetry and late writings either explicitly, in poems about pictures, or else in the way his words reproduced the effects of the pictures he liked as a way of envisioning the world. Certainly Melville's interest in pictures dates before 1857, but, after he returned from traveling, his dedication to the way they teach us to see differently – to frame experience through images of it – became primary to his writing, including his turn to poetry. Collecting and studying pictures in this period also helped crystallize earlier ideas, in *Moby-Dick*, *The Piazza Tales*, and elsewhere, about the perspectives we gain on nature when it gets filtered through the mirror of art. So while Melville was almost always concerned with pictures, he became, between 1857 and 1891, something of a theorist of vision whose late work reflects the visual logic of the prints that he collected in these years with the same commitment as Goethe.

Recent discussion of Melville and the visual arts tends to emphasize his "undiscriminating eclecticism": there is scholarship on Melville and landscape painting, history painting, genre painting, and sculpture, with reference to Raphael, Rembrandt, Guido Reni, Giovanni Piranesi, Nicolas Poussin, Claude Lorrain, Pieter Bruegel, J. M. W. Turner, and Elihu Vedder, on texts ranging from *Typee* to *Billy Budd*. There is "much ... to be done," says Robert K. Wallace, "before a full synthesis can be achieved of the literary uses to which Melville put his experience with art."[4] Indeed the studies we have, attempting to find a category for Melville's aesthetics in a particular case – the sublime, for example, in *Moby-Dick* or classicism in *Billy Budd* – are not broadly illuminating in the way that, say, the diffusing light Goethe sees in Italy imbues a field or the radiating sunlight in Turner's *Regulus* (a print of which Melville bought [Figure 12.1]) colors the full picture at once. Critics tend to reflect prismatically: each facet of Melville's aesthetic shines in its own right, like individuated pieces of stained glass or the articulated colors of a Pre-Raphaelite painting or an early Hudson River School painting, except that these happen to be the only kinds of

Figure 12.1. S. Bradshaw after J. M. W. Turner, *Regulus Leaving Carthage*, engraving, 1859. Courtesy of Berkshire Athenaeum, Pittsfield, Massachusetts.

paintings Melville never seemed to find a way to like. "Who in the rainbow can draw the line where the violet tint ends and the orange tint begins?" Melville writes in *Billy Budd* (102). In another passage Melville marked, William Hazlitt admires the way a rainbow, by Rubens, creates a scintillating film through which we only get the essence (an "air") of everything else built up in coruscating form: our "imagination is lost, in hopes to transfer the whole interminable expanse at one blow upon the canvas."[5] So I'll try, in this short chapter, to consider Melville and pictures at one blow, since his interest in pictures, at least after his 1857 trip, lies in part in the synthetic effect they still have even thirty years later, when so many of them reappear in the poems he calls "Fruit of Travel Long Ago" (1890), or in the many prints he collected over the same years, which themselves transfigure the pictures he saw through the reduction of details to a suggestive register of tones and values – his ink engravings as "inklings" (a favorite word of his) of paintings.

In Italy, Melville saw many of the sculptures and antiquities that Goethe had, and also paintings by Michelangelo, Leonardo, Raphael, Titian, Poussin, Reni, and others. But his favorite was Claude Lorrain, whose pictures at the Sciarra Gallery in Rome made the light and air their subject. "All their effect is of atmosphere," Melville writes. "[Claude] paints the air." In the best of Claude, solid forms and figures seem to shimmer and float in a translucent space, while the softening light on all of them – "the gloaming ... of a scene between dusk and dawn," as Melville writes in his journal – shifts focus away from particular elements and onto the relations between them (*J* 109). The viewer experiences these objects not absolutely, but relatively; chiaroscuro highlights create a vibratory movement in the picture that harmonizes its parts into tonal arrangements. Under the glittery haze, "unlike things must meet and mate," to quote Melville's poem "Art" (*PP* 280). John Burnet, whose essays on art Melville read, describes how Claude's "aerial perspective" or "interposition of air" produces a "harmonious communication" between the separate parts that shine through in varying degrees of distinctness and depth. The atmosphere "imbues every object with its just proportion" and then, as Hazlitt writes, the general connectedness and composure we sense in front of a Claude painting also "softens and harmonizes the mind."[6]

Melville bought or borrowed several books on the practice of painting and engraving that included prints after Claude Lorrain: Burnet's *A Treatise on Painting* (1834–37), George Duplessis's *The Wonders of Engraving* (1871), and Owen J. Dullea's biography of Claude (1887) are a few of them. Melville saw Claude's paintings both in Italy and, on his way home, in London, at the Vernon and Turner Gallery, having seen others in London earlier, in 1849. Now, thanks to the immense archival work of Robert K. Wallace, we have a rich account of the etchings of Claude's paintings that Melville accumulated at his home in New York, and sometimes framed.[7] In a mezzotint by Richard Earlom, after Claude's *Embarkation of the Queen of Sheba* – a painting Melville saw at the National Gallery and one of three seaport scenes he owned – the etched lines in sepia ink look more like watercolors, preserving the washed incandescence of the original painting (Figure 12.2). The sun rises through a vapor, while Earlom's use of resin creates fine dots that soften the lines and diffuse the light in indistinguishable tones and halftones. The loss of detail in the shadows of the picture gives it a dream-like quality. Melville had discovered the same "great gorgeousness of effect" in the Venetian light where ships and islands seemed to float, "mirage-like," in the air and also in the "shading" and "middle tint" of an aerial view of Tivoli that Melville likens to images of Claude (*J* 119, 113).

So many of Melville's poems about his travels in 1857 – to Italy, but also Turkey, Greece, Palestine, and Egypt – recall this pictorial effect of a fluid image suspended in space. Poetic visions flicker phantasmally through mist, vapors, clouds, smoke, dust, sand, and haloes of light at sunrise and twilight. In "After the Pleasure Party" (*Timoleon*), an aerial view of the "star-lit

Figure 12.2. Richard Earlom after Claude Lorrain, *Embarkation of the Queen of Sheba*, no. 114 of the *Liber Veritatis*, published by John Boydell, 1775. Courtesy of The Bancroft Library, University of California, Berkeley.

Mediterranean Sea" offers a moment of composure between a sexual awakening and the pain of isolation; the "white marbles" of the house or cliff gleam through patches of trees, while the corrugated rhythms of the poem take us, gradiently, to the water – "terrace by terrace, down and down" (*PP* 259). Wallace nicely suggests the poem's resemblance to Melville's engraving, *The Enchanted Castle*, after Claude (Figure 12.3). Elsewhere in *Timoleon*, the "airy spires" of the Milan Cathedral glimmer "through light green haze, a rolling sea" over the Lombardy plains. In "Magian Wine," amulets "adown in liquid mirage gleam," while rays of light through the wine and gems give rise to "sybilline inklings" (*PP* 296, 269). So attached is Melville to all atmospheric effects that he even includes a poem on tobacco, in which the magic of the smoky air – "stems of Herba Santa hazed / In autumn's Indian air" – makes us feel almost as weightless as the weed would (*PP* 288). We find our mediums for enchantment where we can. The picture hanging in the Spouter-Inn in *Moby-Dick* is also "thoroughly besmoked," but it is finally the grime that gives "unaccountable masses of shades and shadows ... floating in a nameless yeast" a sort of "unimaginable sublimity." If we

Figure 12.3. F. Vivares and William Woolett after Claude Lorrain, *The Enchanted Castle*, published by S. Vivares, 1782. Courtesy of Fogg Art Museum, Harvard University Art Museum.

look long enough at the "portentous, black mass" hovering in the middle of the "boggy" picture, it finally comes to resemble a whale (*MD* 12–13). Melville likely read Charles Eastlake's remarks on the *sfumato* of painters – from *sfumare*, meaning "to tone down" or "to evaporate like smoke" – who apply a smoky tone of paint across their pictures to dim their lines and enhance their depth. An artist may have a "spirited touch," writes Eastlake, but only the hazy obscuration of a picture, "its more or less *sfumato* nothingness, shall give the touch value."[8]

 What kind of value inheres in paintings or poems that are difficult to make out? Why not make their focus immediately known? For Burnet, the chiaroscuro flickering, from under the haze of Claude's paintings, produces a meditative state that affects the eye exactly as the formal harmony and rhythms of poetry affect the ear. Melville also saw the light and shade in Claude's pictures from a "poetic point of view," since his poems similarly obscure their main focus just enough for us to take notice of their formal patterning and overall rhythms. In poetry and in Claude, we see nothing clearly but the phantasmic, scintillating glimpses of a visionary world made possible only when things appear differently than they would in the light of day. Melville's poems act like the haze, mist, and clouds that Goethe calls "turbid mediums" and that give our visions value only by changing the forms through which we see them. His poems lie between us and lucidity or bare knowledge, but only in exchange for the contemplative rewards of softer, subtler – more forgiving – perceptions, dynamically blurring the lines at some remove.

It may seem surprising how attached Melville became to Claude, whose picturesque aesthetic he often seems to mock, along with the Victorian art critic John Ruskin. In "I and My Chimney" (1856), when objections to the narrator's outsized chimney are signed "Claude" in the village paper, we know that Claude represents a popular style as trendy and bourgeois as the home improvements with which his wife schemes to replace it. The chimney is a "blemish" to the landscape in a culture where "the picturesque yields to the pocketesque" and where mercenary contractors satisfy a relish for rusticity and quaintness that seems to trifle with the hardships of rural life (PT 376, 357). But Melville's writings suggest an alternative possibility for the picturesque than the one the nineteenth century usually pursues and that Melville otherwise devalues as touristic vignettes of nature ("pretty as a picture") or else as the "povertiresque" in *Pierre*, a sentimental scopic framing of squalor and ruin. John Bryant proposes that Melville "modified a tradition that was by the 1850s essentially passé" and that, if he criticizes the picturesque, "it is only to clarify its ethical and aesthetic potentials." We see its potential in the logic of Melville's print collection, even in the many prints that are not after Claude, and also in the books and passages Melville annotated relating to the picturesque and in the disproportionate number of his own writings after 1857 that address it. Bryant evocatively finds in Melville's picturesque an aesthetics of "repose positioned amid despair," but most critics who read Melville's "At the Hostelry," for example, or "Rip Van Winkle's Lilac," which are explicit meditations on the picturesque, have trouble explaining why such a degraded aesthetic worked so nicely for him now.[9]

It may help to know – or else continue to surprise – that Melville's contemporary, Friedrich Nietzsche, also became increasingly obsessed with one painter, Claude Lorrain, in the last decades of the nineteenth century before he died. He had encountered Claude's paintings in galleries much earlier, so his attachment was to copies of the pictures in print or to the memories of seeing them. Nietzsche, like Melville, had read Goethe's *Italian Journey*, and describes a similar experience of Claude's evanescent light and shadows and also of the atmosphere of Italy, in this case Turin, as resembling "a Claude Lorrain projected into the infinite." Nietzsche's philosophical response to Claude can help us articulate Melville's poetic response, since the Claude that inspired Nietzsche's "Claude Lorrain-like raptures" (in which he "continually broke into heavy tears") is also not the one most familiar to us for his historic use of linear perspective, for example, or for framing a field of vision from a single and elevated point of view.[10] Critics often claim the picturesque gives the impression of a rationalized and controlled visual experience, but, for Nietzsche, looking into the deep fog of Claude's paintings feels more like standing on the edge of an "abyss." If the world in the painting is spread out before the viewer, who sees it from above and at a distance, then it induces not a sense of mastery, but vertigo. We see little solid ground on which to stand – it's all vapor – but the endless depth of vision, and the glimpses of light flickering though the mist, at least make us think about the nature and limits of our visibility. In *The Gay Science*, Nietzsche says that we should learn from artists, "To distance oneself from things until there is much in them that one no longer sees and much that the eye must add *in order to see them at all* ... or to place them so that each partially distorts the view one has of the others and allows only perspectival glimpses, or to look at them through colored glasses or in the light of the sunset, or to give them a surface and skin that is not fully transparent."[11] In a similar way, *Moby-Dick* teaches us that our vision is thoroughly perspectival. Ishmael, for example, sounds just like Nietzsche (and Goethe, too), when he suggests that we only see the world well – its subtle values – if we look through "colored or coloring glasses" or other mediums that half shade or tint our view, "else the palsied universe lies before us a leper," colorless and blank in itself. A "wretched infidel" will gaze directly at the bleak prospect around him, but if our vision is cloudy, we at least come to believe in the provisionality of our perspective and in alternative points of view (195).

Melville, like Nietzsche, was afraid of going blind; as early as 1857 in Italy he complains in his journal that his eyes are "troublesome" and sometimes prevent him from "doing or seeing much" (*J* 110, 109). Perhaps Melville found the same elegiac tone in Claude's hazy images that one critic links to Nietzsche's own decayed sight during the late years of his life when the only pictures he was able to see well were the mental pictures of things he had seen before. After all, Claude's pictures themselves were a synthesis of what he actually saw in nature, blurry "after-images" of distant things shaped from memory in his studio. Melville's poem "In a Garret" (*Timoleon*) suggests that art is not some great monument, but rather the dissolving vision that we have at some remove, in our garrets: "Gems and jewels let them heap – / Wax sumptuous as the Sophi: / For me, to grapple from Art's deep / One dripping trophy" (*PP* 275). Art does not "wax" sumptuously, but asks us to grapple with ideas that melt like wax the moment we try to grasp them. Melville's poem is likely based on Friedrich Schiller's ballad, "The

Diver," in which a young page responds to his king's challenge to retrieve a golden goblet from the "dark waves" of the sea (once successfully, then tragically). Art, then, is the reward and risk of immersing ourselves, half-blindedly, in turbid waters – of losing definition while we swim in obscurity. Like the absent-minded youth in *Moby-Dick*, who "takes the mystic ocean at his feet for the visible image" of his soul, our most transfiguring visions – indeed our deepest aesthetic visions – acknowledge the antifoundationalist proposition of "every strange, half-seen, gliding, beautiful thing that eludes [us]; every dimly-discovered, uprising fin of some undiscernible form" (159). In Schiller's poem the goblet is a glistening vision founded on a black gulf.

In the story "The Piazza" (1856), Melville's narrator finds, in his picturesque view of the Berkshires, "one spot of radiance, where all else was shade," and chases it. The "picture" from his piazza is "a very paradise of painters" and the narrator's description of it reads like an ekphrasis of a Claude painting. "In most states of atmosphere," the mountains appear as irregular shapes and masses that "effacingly" touch on other masses, playing "hide-and-seek." The glittery spot appears under certain "conditions of light and shadow": in late autumn when the woods, "having lost their first vermilion tint," are covered in "smokiness" from forest fires, and, then, in May, through "misty seas of sunshine" and a rainbow. Setting out on his boat to look for the "golden window" (assuming the shimmer comes from glass), the narrator floats through the landscape in the picture from his piazza, traveling on a picturesque stream past zigzag paths, jagged hills, and overgrown ruins (*PT* 1, 4–5, 6). But finally, what he sees when he arrives at the spot is another single spot of radiance, glimmering in "the mirage haze" of the distance (*PT* 9). It is the light of his very own window, filtered through the "golden window" (finally, a grimy window inside a woman's house) that he had spotted from way back there. From here, his house shines as her house had. The golden window – which becomes a surrogate for the picturesque view he had from the piazza – is a kind of reflective mirror that lets the narrator see how such enchanting visions might be had from a reverse perspective. "Now I know how, have the know-how, to *reverse perspectives*," Nietzsche writes in *Ecce Homo*, where he also remembers his Claude-like visions of Turin: this is the "reason why a 'revaluation of values' is perhaps possible for me alone."[12] The tale's reflections suggest a kind of polarized vision as "combining, and subtle" as that of the whale who, we learn in *Moby-Dick*, has eyes on opposite sides of his head so that "he can at the same moment of time attentively examine two distinct prospects" – one on the one side and the other in the reverse direction (331).

Inside the house, the narrator also finds a sad woman, Marianna, suffering from poverty and loss, which is why critics tend to read "The Piazza" as a tale of disillusionment with picturesque aesthetics that idealize at a distance. Up close, we find ruin. But Marianna is, in her own way, only a reverse perspective on the narrator that his "picture" from the piazza makes possible. Her mirages in the haze reflect back on his. Her visions may be visionary, since she perceives her dead dog, for example, in the shadows of the clouds, and to her, "shadows are as things." But the narrator also believes in shadows, imagining a gilded "fairy-land" through the vapor of his lookout. When we learn that he is convalescing from an illness that has made him "sensitive," we wonder whether he has been hallucinating too (*PT* 11, 7, 6). Even Marianna herself? Up close, the narrator also may be delusional and sad. Marianna suggests the dark flipside of the narrator's picture-making habit, but their two visions are not self-canceling. They are two sides of the picture we get from the piazza, flickering back and forth. In this sense "The Piazza" is no different than Melville's other stories in the form of diptychs – "The Two Temples," "Poor Man's Pudding and Rich Man's Crumbs" – which admit diametrical views of the same subject within a single, unifying tale. In "The Piazza," the irony is not in spite of the picturesque, but in the nature of it.

The picturesque was accused of artifice because it wrenched things from their natural places – also from their original places of function and use, which is why ruins are so central to it – and brought them together for contemplation in a picture. How else could we see so wide a prospect of nature, at its most sublime and beautiful, in the geometry of a single glance? The picturesque "posture of contrast depends on a condition that ... is reaching, might reach plenitude," writes Sidney K. Robinson. It "does not convey nature directly," but "straightaway engages in representation." It is obviously an artistic arrangement, but the great freedom of the picturesque is that, within its form and gauzy medium, it can accommodate everything. The balance between parts and the whole is maintained by the atmospheric effect that links incongruous elements through median grades of color or tone, breaking down, in Burnet's words, the "harsh asperities" of extremes. Differences become tolerable. All the elements of the picture retain their distinctiveness, but when their limits and boundaries are hard to see, our attention shifts away from the separate parts and onto "the structure of relations" between them.[13]

For Melville, the formal work of the picturesque amounts to a political proposition, as it did for its eighteenth-century theorists, Uvedale Price, Richard Payne Knight, and others. Its spirit of accommodation suggests a classical ideal of "balanced interests" that might apply as much to the goals of a republican society as to its own heterogeneous aesthetic. The picturesque might even serve as an aesthetic model for the principle of connection in a civil society or for the kind of open-mindedness to difference that allows us to acknowledge conflicting perspectives at once. For "unlike things" to "meet and mate," in pictures and more, we adjust our frames of reference to see relative values. This means that the "grace" of the picturesque can be a creative challenge to absolutism of all sorts.[14] Melville's poem "At the Hostelry" – an extended and "inconclusive debate as to the exact import" of the term *picturesque* – begins and ends with an account of the Risorgimento, Italy's struggle for unification and independence from "tyrant powers." Why? In the poem, the Marquis recounts liberator Giuseppe Garibaldi's victories in Sicily and Naples where, freeing a "cut up, divided" Italy from a "predatory band" of foreign princes, he confederates the principalities and "[frames]" a nation. "Effecting a counterturn," the Marquis then opens the debate on the picturesque, but, of course, he already has given us a picturesque image of Italy, in which all its distant parts are brought into peaceful relation – and in fact the seeming incongruity of the poem's political frame only enhances the sense in which the aesthetic it debates is never totalizing, but contains multitudes. Famous painters from different centuries and countries join together in a dynamic conversation in a tavern, all proving, "Vain here to divide – / The Picturesque has many a side." Meanwhile, the artists who, for Melville, best represent the spirit of the picturesque remain distanced and composed – absorbing everything – like Claude who "smile[s] in thought" or Leonardo who, "lost in dream," watches rays of light sparkle through a glass of red wine.[15]

It is striking, in the poem, how many artists have some claim to the picturesque in its many forms, besides Claude, Poussin, Salvator Rosa, and its better known practitioners. The poem attributes the dark, subtlizing tone of Rembrandt paintings, for example, to the same picturesque grime that we see in *Moby-Dick*'s painting from the Spouter-Inn: Rembrandt "believe[s] in smoke" (and his "sooty stroke" creates an "umberish haze"). Several painters in "At the Hostelry," including Poussin and Herman van Swanevelt, also figure in Melville's print collection where, beside many prints that are explicitly picturesque – of English topographical views, for example, or after Claude, Aelbert Cuyp, or Richard Wilson – they suggest a more pervasive logic of picturesque values and tones. This logic also extends to the illustrated volumes Melville acquired, probably in the 1880s, by John Mollett on the French Barbizon painters, including Jean-Baptiste-Camille Corot and Jean-François Millet, who influenced American Tonalist painters and who, with them, emphasized the "relation of the part to the whole by means of coordinated tonal vales" in chiaroscuro (clear-obscure) landscapes painted from memory. Tonalist paintings often have titles like *Twilight*, *Early Moonrise*, and *A Rainy Day*.[16]

For Melville, the alternative aesthetic to the picturesque aesthetic is an unremitting attachment to clarity that he sometimes associates with the "blinding brightness" of Egypt's desert (when there was "too much light and no defense against it") and that he often associates with power and dogmatism. In "The New Zealot to the Sun" (*Timoleon*), the "sun" of religion has spread "delirious screeds" and empire, but the "light" of science, which can elucidate even the sun, is a total "power" that may be worse (*PP* 271–72). The problem with the pyramids in Egypt is that their "transcendent mass & symmetry & unity" is "all or nothing." "[Their] simplicity confounds you" (*J* 74–76). In Melville's poem "The Great Pyramid," the pyramid stands "unmoved" by the eroding effects of time and nature and gathers no moss. If Poussin paints "nature through the glass of time," as Hazlitt writes, the great pyramid will never adjust its frame of reference.[17] Its builders "Usurped on Nature's self" with an art form whose self-insistence and abstraction – "this dumb I AM" – is also linked to those systems of absolute power, Pharaoh and God, to which it pays tribute (*PP* 315–16).

In *Billy Budd*, a story about the stern necessity of the law, the narrator inserts an ekphrastic description of Lord Nelson's dilapidated battleship at Portsmouth, the *Victory*. It is a digression, or "by-path," from the main narrative and apropos of nothing in it, except that the "decaying" old boat offers a "poetic reproach, softened by its picturesqueness," to the ironclad, "utilitarian" hulks that float elsewhere. Of course, it also may be the case that it offers a picturesque reproach to the "ironclad" policies of Captain Vere, whose absolute code of law leaves no shady, gray areas in which to exonerate Billy Budd and save his life, especially since we know, as the narrator reminds us, that truth "will always have its ragged edges" (56–58, 128). The neoclassical serenity of the *Victory* is not unlike the classical beauty of Billy himself, who is compared with a Greek sculpture and whose musical voice is expressive of a "harmony within" that is also "organic" – except when he stutters (128, 53). Billy stutters when he needs to assert himself, but such acts of insistence amount to an aesthetic violence on the usual composure of a sailor whose "non-intent" and "will-power" (or power over his will) distinguish him from the willfulness of the master-at-arms, who conspires against him, and from "Starry Vere," whose system of precepts betray a "mind resolute to surmount difficulties even if against primitive instincts strong as the winds and the sea" (112, 125, 109).

While writing *Billy Budd*, Melville collected the works of Arthur Schopenhauer, who claims that, when we look at a work of art, we become receptive to seeing for its own sake rather than for the demands of our "will," with its insistence on motivations, reason, and utility. When, that is, we reflect on art – or on the world as a "representation" rather than a natural fact – we are released from our own wills into a metaphysical contemplation of "will" itself as the unitary force behind a world in which all our competing desires and interests "correspond to each other." We leave our wills behind and see into the "essence" of things and, once in a while, Schopenhauer (who was influenced by Goethe) compares this subtle vision we gain to an experience of the *picturesque*, and also of poetry: "It is precisely this [vision] that makes a perceived object seem *picturesque*, an event of actual life *poetic*, in that only this spreads that magic shimmer over the objects of actual reality."[18] In Melville's novella, Billy's willlessness provides a picturesque alternative to Captain Vere's reason that rules absolutely, seeking over-clarity and enlightenment in an ethically murky case. But Billy's repose and "grace" make us aware of different, more subtle shades of value and so teach us a lesson we also learn from Nietzsche who, following Schopenhauer, wants us "to see" by "habituating the eye to repose ... letting things come to it; learning to defer judgment, to investigate and comprehend the individual case in all its aspects ... *the essence of it is precisely* not *to 'will'*" (italics mine).[19] If only Captain Vere had received his poetic reproach and, deferring judgment of Billy, considered the full picture at once in all its nebulous truth. If only Starry Vere actually had had his head in the clouds.

When there are no clouds, says Ishmael in chapter 118 of *Moby-Dick*, the "unrelieved radiance" of the "unblinking Japanese sun" is insufferable as it reflects off the ocean: "Well that Ahab's quadrant was furnished with colored glasses, through which to take sight of that solar fire" (500). We cannot tolerate the "nakedness" of the sun, so J. M. W. Turner shows how Regulus is burned to death, after failing to carry out his orders in Rome, since the Carthaginians had cut off his eyelids as punishment before exposing him directly to the light (Figure 12.1). On the steps at the right of the painting, Regulus is as incapable of blinking as Melville says the sun is "unblinking." We also might go blind since Turner's effulgent sun throws off terrible beams along the water and the solar glare feels more like it might without the quadrant that Ahab finally destroys for making the light all too easy to see. As viewers, we can only make out, for example, Regulus's small white figure on the steps if we manage to squint like he cannot. Turner's late paintings are so brilliant, they mystified their audience, and even Ruskin, Turner's greatest fan, called them "nonsense pictures" of masses and blots with the white scumblings of sunlight dissolving everything else in view. Ruskin preferred Turner's earlier, less glaring attempts to paint the effects of light, but not Melville, who saw *Regulus* in London in 1857 on his way back from Italy and liked Turner's late style best. Melville eventually bought an engraving after *Regulus*, and several others – *The Golden Bough*, for example, which critics called "almost dim through excess of brightness," but which Melville framed.[20]

Critics suggest that the painting at the Spouter-Inn, for one, owes much to Turner's "indistinct" aesthetic, while anticipating the expressive potentials of modernism in art.[21] But Turner's style is also nostalgic for the Claude paintings they honor and sometimes outshine in a rivalry for picturesque effects that William Cosmo Monkhouse describes in his 1879 biography of Turner, a book Melville owned. *Regulus* derives directly from Claude's *Seaport* in the Uffizi, which looks almost identical to other seaport scenes in Melville's collection (Figure 12.2). Turner bequested his paintings to the National Gallery but only on the condition that they hang, side by side as pairs, with those of Claude. We see Claude's chromatic light in Turner's many watercolors for his *Picturesque Views of England and Wales* and also for his series of mezzotints published from 1807 as *Liber Studiorum*, based on Richard Earlom's mezzotints of Claude's own *Liber Veritatis*, or the drawings of his paintings. Turner's late paintings, then, do not suggest an intensification of light, so much as our enabling ability to see it only through Claudean mediums—the diffusing mists and fogs of sunrise on the water or else, in Turner, the miasmic smoke and pollution of industrial Britain (see *Rain, Steam and Speed* [1844], a print of which Melville owned), and also, of course, through the medium of pictures themselves, which can only reflect indirectly, especially when they are rendered from memory.

Nineteenth-century efforts to transfer the intense luminosities of light to canvas led to the use of the "Claude glass": a black or silver-gray convex mirror that was also the object of several studies we know Melville read, including those by Roger de Piles who, in his *Principles of Painting*, says that because we cannot represent the brightness of the sun even on the whitest paper, we need to tone it down by painting it as it first appears in a black convex mirror. When we do, the tinted glass makes us sensitive to relations between relative levels of brightness. The mirror does not attempt to reproduce the light, but to translate its force into another scale, so that we perceive tonal variations of light and dark. At the same time, the darkened Claude glass, washing over the image, harmonizes the composition into a single shimmering pattern or form. The removal of detail, de Piles reminds us, is a classical principle that gives us the "effect of the whole together," and it also brings forth an abstraction, an essence, that transforms the optical instrument into a symbolic instrument.[22] It makes a space for reverie and contemplation, in much the way Leonardo, looking through a glass of wine, gets "lost in dream." "I must tone down the green," says the artist in Melville's poem "Rip Van Winkle's Lilac."[23]

I would like to add just two, abbreviated, observations about the Claude glass, in light of Melville: one is the analogy nineteenth-century critics make between the role of the Claude glass and the role of etchers and engravers more generally. William Makepeace Thackeray, for example, says that, "As one cannot look at the sun but though a blackened glass, it has seemed to us that the most dazzling of Turner's fancies have often been improved by the ... graver." Turner may have agreed with Thackeray, since he worked to perfect the art of etching as much as painting, and so, very famously, did Claude whose own etchings were considered unsurpassed in their technique (except perhaps by Turner), a fact Melville would have learned from his copy of George Duplessis's *The Wonders of Engraving* (1871). Claude's etchings, Duplessis writes, "have all the qualities of his paintings. He distributed the light and diffused the air ... with unrivalled success."[24] De Piles suggests that etching, just like a Claude mirror, enables one to judge both the "clair-obscur" and the correspondence of the forms within an image by reducing everything to light and shades and a coherent scale of values. We could say, with Thackeray, that Turner or Claude paintings are improved by the engraver, but we could just as easily say that the tonal effect of their paintings works on the *principle* of engravings and that Melville's interest in these artists was also, primarily, an interest in the formal work of the engravings he collected.

Second, Melville would have known that our only real chance to reproduce the tone and effect of a Claude or Turner painting is not, again, by looking directly at nature, which is raw and blinding, but through a darkened mirror, which offers a reflection of the light, a secondary light. The Claude Glass, in this sense, was likened not to the sun but to the moon, and the effects it achieved were like those of a lunar eclipse (Elihu Vedder, to whom Melville dedicated *Timoleon*, painted the one pictured here [Figure 12.4]). A lunar eclipse is the kind of event which, like Turner's painting of Regulus in Carthage, lets us look directly at the sun without actually blinding us. We can achieve a similar effect by squinting. One theorist of the picturesque writes that when we squint "we see only the general effects of objects" and not the objects. As a secondary light, the Claude mirror suggests that the image it creates for us is not a transcription of nature, say, but a metaphor for it; some go so far as to suggest that the image in a Claude mirror and, by extension the painting that derives from it, are more like an ekphrasis (a verbal description of a picture) than a picture.[25]

Much of Melville's work after his visual turn is itself ekphrastic, writing about pictures, yes, but also the mediated description of things we can't manage to tolerate or see except in smaller reductive forms that make us aware of forms and patterns mostly – not unblinkingly like Turner's Regulus, but more like Nietzsche's *Augenblick* or "blink of the eye" in which we mainly see an essence or effect.[26] Through the disillusionment Melville felt in these late decades – his despair in religion and politics of all sorts, and also in the

Figure 12.4. Elihu Vedder, *Luna*, study for the cover of *Harper's New Monthly Magazine* (Christmas Issue, 1882), pastel and watercolor on paper. Courtesy of St. Augustine Historical Society, Florida.

vision of the public that neglected him – his poems and his prints are like the mitigating reflections of a Claude mirror, giving value to anything that falls within their frames. In the last poem of *Timoleon*, "The Return of the Sire de Nesle," a tired traveler returns home because "terrible is earth"; but his *return* is also the misty mirror of the poem itself reflecting back on a world he once saw (*PP* 317). Melville's "Fruit of Travel Long Ago," offering images of Italy, Greece, and Egypt in the exact reverse order of his own travels in 1857, is a mirror image of a journey that was disillusioning in its own way, but that we finally see reduced and softened in the harmonizing tones of his poems – the "I AM" of the great pyramids as an iamb, a reverse perspective.

NOTES

1 Johann Wolfgang von Goethe, *Italian Journey* (1786–88), trans. W. H. Auden and Elizabeth Mayer (New York: Penguin Books, 1970), 228, 304, 236.
2 See Walter Cowen, *Melville's Marginalia*, 2 vols. (New York: Garland Publishing, 1987), 1:572.
3 In 1870, Melville acquired an edition of Sir Joshua Reynolds's *Literary Works*, which includes William Mason's verse translation of DuFresnoy's *The Art of*

Painting, along with Reynolds's notes on the treatise, and John Dryden's preface to his own prose translation titled, "A Parallel of Poetry and Painting." Melville also likely read a translation of Roger de Piles's *The Art of Painting*, including notes on DuFresnoy (London: Payne [1754?]). See Merton M. Sealts, Jr., *Melville's Reading*, revised edition (Columbia: University of South Carolina Press, 1988).

4   See, for example, Christopher Sten, ed., *Savage Eye: Melville and the Visual Arts* (Kent, OH: Kent State University Press, 1991), especially pp. 224, 213–214; Robert K. Wallace, "Melville's Prints and Engravings at the Berkshire Athenaeum," *Essays in Arts and Sciences* 15 (June 1986): 63; and Douglas Robillard, *Melville and the Visual Arts: Ionian Form, Venetian Tint* (Kent, OH: Kent State University Press, 1997).

5   William Hazlitt, *Table-Talk* (1821–22), ed. Catherine Macdonald Mcclean (London: Dent and Sons, 1959), 7–8, and Cowen, *Melville's Marginalia*, 1:649.

6   John Burnet, *Practical Essays on Art* (New York: Edward L. Wilson, 1888), 1.7, 2.44, 3.22–25, 3.56; William Hazlitt, *Criticism on Art; and Sketches of the Picture Galleries of England* (London: John Templeman, 1843), 122.

7   Robert K. Wallace's many invaluable essays on the prints include "Melville's Prints: The Ambrose Group," *Harvard Library Bulletin* 6.1 (Spring 1995): 13–50, and "Melville's Prints: The Melville Chapin Collection," *Harvard Library Bulletin* 11.2 (Summer 2000): 5–54.

8   Charles Lock Eastlake, *Methods and Materials of Painting of the Great Schools and Masters*, 2 vols. (New York: Longmans, Green, and Company, 1869), 2:316. According to Sealts, Melville probably borrowed an earlier edition in 1848.

9   John Bryant, "Toning Down the Green: Melville's Picturesque," in Sten, *Savage Eye*, 147.

10 Quoted in Gary Shapiro, *Archaeologies of Vision: Foucault and Nietzsche on Seeing and Saying* (Chicago, IL: University of Chicago Press, 2003), 42, 54.

11 Friedrich Nietzsche, *The Gay Science*, ed. Bernard Williams (New York: Cambridge University Press, 2001), 169–70.

12 Friedrich Nietzsche, *Ecce Homo*, trans. Walter Kaufman (New York: Vintage Books, 1989), 223.

13 Sidney K. Robinson, *Inquiry into the Picturesque* (Chicago, IL: University of Chicago Press, 1991), 120, 93; Burnet, *Practical Essays on Art*, 2.3; Robinson, *Inquiry into the Picturesque*, 105.

14 Robinson, *Inquiry into the Picturesque*, 133–35.

15 Herman Melville, "At the Hostelry" in *Collected Poems of Herman Melville*, ed. Howard P. Vincent (Chicago, IL: Hendricks House, 1947), 314, 315, 317, 319, 331, 332.

16 Ibid., 323–24; Eliot Clark, *History of the National Academy of Design, 1825–1953* (1954), as quoted in David A. Cleveland, *A History of American Tonalism: 1880–1920* (Manchester and New York: Hudson Hills Press, 2010), 148.

17 Hazlitt, *Table-Talk*, 169.

18 Arthur Schopenhauer, *The World as Will and Presentation*, 2 vols., trans. David Carus and Richard E. Aquila (New York: Pearson Longman, 2011), 1:205, 2: 420.

19 Quoted in Shapiro, *Archaeologies of Vision*, 24.

20 As quoted in Robert K. Wallace, *Melville and Turner: Spheres of Love and Fright* (Athens: University of Georgia Press, 1992), 51, 49.

21 Ibid., 68, 514–18, and throughout.

22 See de Piles, *The Art of Painting*, and Arnaud Maillet, *The Claude Glass: Use and Meaning of the Black Mirror in Western Art*, trans. Jeff Fort (New York: Zone Books, 2009); as quoted in Maillet, *The Claude Glass*, 108.

23 Herman Melville, "Rip Van Winkle's Lilac," in *Collected Poems of Herman Melville*, 289.

24 Thackeray is quoted in Wallace, *Melville and Turner*, 331; George Duplessis, *The Wonders of Engraving* (New York: Charles Scribner, 1871), 255.

25 William Gilpin, as quoted in Maillet, *The Claude Glass*, 214, where Maillet also discusses the relationship between the Claude Glass and ekphrasis.

26 See Shapiro, *Archaeologies of Vision*, 51.

13

TIMOTHY MARR

Melville's Planetary Compass

Nineteen-year-old Herman Melville's father had been dead for six years and his family was low in resources when he enrolled in a course in surveying during the fall of 1838, hoping to develop skills to find a job on the Erie Canal. Unable to procure a position, he fled to New York City to seek employment as a sailor. The peripatetic circuits of Melville's travels for the next five years – out from the "Narrows" of New York to Liverpool and back in 1839; up the Erie Canal to the broad prairies following the Mississippi and Ohio rivers the following year; and then in 1841 round Cape Horn into the vast Pacific on a whaling ship before doubling back three years later on a U.S. naval ship – revolutionized his perspectives on the planet. Melville's odyssey through open oceans, expansive prairies, frozen extremes, and verdant islands exposed him to a "*realizing sense*" (R 128) of the immense power and terror of the material earth in space and time. "Hug the shore, not new is seen" (M 556) and "Nations are but names; and continents but shifting sands" (638), he averred in *Mardi* (1848). The expansive natural (and transcultural) worlds Melville discovered taught him lessons that nourished the roots of a radical religious sensibility, leading him to proclaim on the lyceum circuit in 1859–60 that "travel to a large and generous nature is as a new birth" (PT 423). Spurning parochial convention and reordinating scriptural word as fonts of inspiration, he posited in *Pierre* that "The visible world of experience is that procreative thing which impregnates the muses" (259). Melville devoted his career to courageously worlding his experience through the literary latitudes of his "sea freedoms" (L 56).

Melville's planetary ordinations drew on the geometrical knowledge he had studied in his surveying course. Jeremiah Day's textbook on *The Mathematical Principles of Navigation and Surveying* (1817) expanded, as Melville's experience had, from surveying the land to navigating the sea. As there were no stable milestones on the plane of the open ocean, the most reliable method of locating a ship's position required the "celestial trigonometry" of angular measurements between the meridian of the sun, moon, or pole star and the visible horizon.¹ Melville's artistic explorations similarly sought to position the (r)evolving planet in vertiginous space and time. His extravagant reckoning stretched across geographical latitudes into new hemispheres, but it also expanded along a vertical axis connecting the immensity of the stars above with the abyss of the oceans below. In his 1850 review of Hawthorne's *Mosses from an Old Manse* (1846), Melville described genius as a complementarity between "humor and love ... [which] soar[s] to such a rapt height, as to receive the irradiations of the upper skies" and "a great, deep intellect, which drops down into the universe like a plummet" (*PT* 242). Melville's art embodied a magisterial mingling and melding of these altitudes and depths. During the half century when Melville was traveling and writing, scientific developments in geology, astronomy, and natural history quickened the Copernican dissolution of earthly fixity, reconceiving the earth as, in effect, a "loose fish" in deep time (*MD* 398).² Melville's works charted how the planet lived out its Greek etymology as an abandoned "wanderer" bewilderingly astray in an unknowable cosmos, a spinning and orbiting outpost shaken by the chaotic flux of its own fluid depths and eruptions.

The voyage of the whaler was among the longest ocean journeys ever made by humans, equivalent perhaps to today's excursions to outer space. Melville figures the ship – with its masthead aspiring toward the stars, and its roots in the kelson astride the sea – as a microcosm of planetary transit through "an endless circumnavigation of space" (*WJ* 398). In *Mardi* and *White-Jacket* in particular, Melville equates the ship's sea circuit with the earth's having "slipped from the stocks at Creation" (*WJ* 398) and somersaulting around the sun at exorbitant speeds. Melville's sage Bardianna of *Mardi* voices the vertigo of this unsettling chiasmus: "'There is neither apogee nor perigee, ... what tonight is our zenith, tomorrow is our nadir; stand as we will, we stand on our heads'" (460). In his sea fictions, Melville improvises a literary cosmogony that intermingles the oceanic with the astronomical by figuring islands as planets, oceans as lagoons, and archipelagos as constellations. He mischievously materializes the ascent to heaven as a pagan voyage into a cosmic ocean. The coffins of both Queequeg and a warrior chief in *Typee* are featured as canoes floating beyond "mild, uncontinented seas, [to] interflow with the heavens; and so form the white breakers of the milky way" (*MD* 478; and see also *T* 173). Conversely, Melville reckons cosmic evolution as a galactic shipwreck whose debris formed the planet itself: "Shoals, like nebulous vapors, shoring the white reef of the Milky Way, against which the wrecked worlds are dashed; strowing all the strand, with their Himmaleh keels and ribs" (*M* 367).

The creative implications of Melville's planetary perspective are perhaps most clearly on display in his evocation of Ahab before he even appears – a description that also encompasses Ishmael's enterprise of narrating *Moby-Dick* and Melville's art of writing it. The unnamed Ahab, Ishmael remarks, is:

> a man of greatly superior natural force, with a globular brain and a ponderous heart; who has also by the stillness and seclusion of many long nightwatches in the remotest waters, and beneath constellations never seen here at the north, been led to think untraditionally and independently; receiving all nature's sweet or savage impressions fresh from her own virgin voluntary and confiding breast, and thereby chiefly, but with some help from accidental advantages, to learn a bold and nervous lofty language. (*MD* 73)

The conjunction of genius, solitude, remoteness, and chance – amidst nature's primal and contrary forces – charged the "bold and nervous" energies of Melville's errant expressivity. Melville's renegade peregrinations exposed him to the "sweet and savage" phenomena of the terraqueous globe circling in space in ways that displaced the ultimate lessons from scriptural texts to an imaginative reading of the "books" of nature that he witnessed through his expansive travel.[3]

This chapter charts Melville's conversion of his intimate encounter with diverse material worlds into forms of literary expression. Melville's exposure to pristine natural beauty offered him a redemptive glimpse of a celestial paradise fresh in its unspoiled creation. But earthly extremes also dramatized the chaotic and changing material forms that marked the planet as fallen, a kind of "Tartarus" or hell (*PT* 323). Melville's writings oscillate between a pantheistic merging with the cosmos and a fatal encounter with forces of heartless materialism. Yet Melville also found through his writing a repose centered in a sustaining connection with the vital energies embodied by the capacity of material forms to regenerate and evolve new life. By pointing to and holding together radically different and changing poles, the planetary compass of Melville's infidel creativity bodied forth a living language that linked the abstracted certitudes of religion to dynamic material processes that were paradoxical and provisional – what he called "the mingled, mingling threads of life" (*MD* 492).

Paradise

Sailors' experiences as "ocean wanderers" (*WJ* 76) plowing the sea and reckoning by the stars provided Melville and his characters with sublime moments of transcendental unity though which they became "diffused through time and space" (*MD* 159). Melville describes White-Jacket climbing aloft "to study the stars upon the wide, boundless sea," asserting that such practice is as "divine as it was to the Chaldean Magi" (*WJ* 76). In his long poem *Clarel* (1876), Melville hails the ancient stargazers of India and Ur as autocthonous visionaries: "Earth's first spectators, the clear-eyed,/ Unvitiated, unfalsified/ Seers at first hand –" (279) who "first, with mind austere,/ Arrived in solitary tone/ To think of God as One – alone" (194). Again and again in his writings, Melville celebrates a pantheistic merger with the constellations rather than devotion to the singular star that beckoned the Magi to the manger in Bethlehem.[4] When set upon the strange sea for the first time, Redburn writes of becoming "lost in one delirious throb at the center of the All," responsive "to all the wild commotion of the world" and "reeling on and on with the planets in their orbits" (*R* 66). Melville's star-gazing sailors imagined themselves a community of castaways who "expatriate ourselves to nationalize with the universe" through a cosmic naturalization that "fuses us into the universe of things" (*WJ* 76). Melville expounded on Goethe's ecstatic "All-Feeling" and its intimation of an organic vitalism in a June 1851 letter to Hawthorne: "Your legs seem to send out shoots into the earth. Your hair feels like leaves upon your head," exulting about "the tingling of life that are felt in the flowers and the woods, that are felt in the planets Saturn and Venus, and the Fixed Stars" (*L* 193).

Melville relished his renegade freedom of "vagabondizing" (*L* 199) equipped with only a hammock and a carpet bag. Like Moses atop Pisgah (or Balboa from Darien), Melville sought an earthly panorama from which he might survey the freshness of creation. Melville/White-Jacket's extensive description of Rio's verdant "Bay of All Beauties" from the naval masthead offers one of his most extravagant exaltations of celestial sublimity: "A new world to my ravished eyes, I felt like the foremost of a flight of angels, new-lighted upon earth, from some star in the Milky Way" (*WJ* 212). Such moments in Melville's journeys uncovered a primordial vision of "virgin freshness" (*PT* 415) whose pure energies infused Melville's writings. Melville describes his escape into Nuku Hiva's interior vales – "one unbroken solitude" seemingly "untenanted since the morning of the creation" (*T* 44) – as a ravishing "glimpse of the gardens of Paradise" (49). Melville's figures of Eden were in fact pagan in their primitive animism, evoked in his writings by a variety of legendary locations such as Arcadia, Circassia, the Vale of Tempe, Sabaea, and Elysium. He celebrated in *Clarel* an unfallen golden age "Of cordial joy in Nature's sway … / When life was innocent and free" (199) and "Power was love" (338). In an unpublished poem about his Pacific truancy, Melville reminiscences about roaming "Pantheistic ports" and "Authentic Edens in a Pagan sea" from which he "breath[ed] primeval balm."[5] When the sailor Rolfe in *Clarel* recollects the vernal fertility of the South Seas islands, he announces what Melville had noted in the margins of his Holy Land journal: "J[esus]. C[hrist]. should have appeared in Taheiti [*sic*]" (*J* 154; see also *C* 445).

The "insular Tahiti" (*MD* 274) is but one of the pantheistic intimations of natural beauty that captivated Melville with the promise of redemption. For Melville violets were the angelic vouchers of paradise: Fayaway's blush (*T* 85), Lucy's face (*P* 33), and the primeval forest (*M* 359) all share their redolence, as does the "uncontaminated aroma" of the spermaceti that Ishmael proclaims is "literally and truly, like the smell of spring violets" (*MD* 416). The language of *Moby-Dick* reveals a wondrous white whale that breaches – beyond both Ahab's malignant attacker and Ishmael's empty sign – to offer a momentary visitation of the living majesty of its ungraspable beauty.

Tartarus

For Melville, losing one's self in a mystic merger with the swells of creation was nonetheless a perilous enterprise. If the mystic sailor avoided falling from his perch of pantheistic promise, he still had to descend and engage in the toil of the hunt. That any peep into paradise was transient was dramatized by the crucifixion of Christ, the "second Adam" (*C* 20), by those he came to save, as well as by Melville's documentation of the submission of the "smiling bosom" of the South Seas to the "fatal embrace" of colonialism (*T* 26, 64). The earth might hold out the pretense of retaining the primordial energies of paradise, but its own dark forces also evinced its ironic fate as a fallen mess of matter: a pandemonium of strife, destruction, and death perhaps made so by the penalty of its creator. Melville remained transfixed by what he called "blackness, ten times black" (*PT* 243) – the sorrow of a species that retained a link with a celestial source from which it had been ousted into both earth and dearth – and he struggled to find peace with the inheritance of such indifference.

Many of Melville's narrators and characters are figured as rovers and wanderers, exiles and orphans. Melville arrogated the transgressive perspective of outcasts to locate an alternative to the hypocritical pieties of "snivelization" (*R* 100). Melville embraced primitivism to vitalize his heretical cultural critique. "Long exile from Christendom and civilization inevitably restores a man to that condition in which God placed him, *i.e.* what is called savagery," explained the tattooed Ishmael in one brazen recital of this heterodoxy, exulting, "I myself am a savage, owning no allegiance but to the King of the Cannibals; and ready at any moment to rebel against him" (*MD* 270). Melville's latitudinarianism rendered him into a nonconformist who embodied the apostate dissent of Protestantism. Melville distinguished clearly between credulity and faith, writing that "the undoubting doubter believes the most" (*M* 339) and "dissenters only assent to more than we" (*M* 296). For Melville, the unvanquished infidel and the downtrodden alien were the most noble inheritors of humanity's condition because they both raged against earthly fatality and endured its penalty. As Melville remarked in his journal in the Holy Land, "Hapless are the favorites of Heaven" (*J* 91).

While Melville figured superstitious imagination as a form of "moonshine" (*P* 205, *PT* 246), he also enlisted the moon at key moments in his fiction.[6] Figuring the planet as an unredeemed wilderness, Melville slyly supplicated: "Are there no Moravians in the Moon, that not a missionary has yet visited this poor pagan planet of ours, to civilize civilization and christianize Christendom?" (*WJ* 267). Melville depicted the alien moon, with its influence on the ebb and flow of earthly tides, as an inhuman purveyor of the "feline Fate" (*PT* 156) that toyed indifferently with mundane lives. He employed its outsider optics to highlight the sublunarian provinciality of the world's heathen strangeness, with its parallax light revealing no promised land but rather a realm of chaos devoid of benevolence. One of Melville's most revealing uses of this exotopic distancing is his satanic staging of the famous Revolutionary naval encounter between John Paul Jones's *Bonhomme Richard* and the HMS *Serapis* in *Israel Potter* (1855). Melville seems literally to lift the face of the Man in the Moon up "from the trap door of the sea" to illuminate the lunatic strife between warring Englishmen. Here Melville reverses projections that see faces in the "seas" of the moon to reveal "Mephistopheles prompter of the stage" who leeringly casts a "dubious, half demoniac glare" and announces "Gentlemen warriors, permit me a little to light up this rather gloomy-looking subject" (*IP* 123). Elsewhere, Melville characterizes the colossal force of chaos as the "Cosmic Jest or Anarch blunder"[7] of the "eminent Jugglarius" (*P* 262) who diddled with the fortunes of "that multiform pilgrim species, man" (*CM* 9).

In Melville's figuring of what James Joyce would call the "chaosmos,"[8] any prospect of an earthly paradise was transformed into a tableau of wretchedness in which green plenty had been dislodged by a barren wasteland. One of Melville's fullest inversions of the masthead's transcendent vision is the sketch of "Rock Redondo" in "The Encantadas" (1854). This solitary and deserted volcanic rock in the Galapagos provides perches for the screaming seabird species that slime its surface, while its grottos below "afford[ ] labyrinthine lurking places" for strange fish (*PT* 136). Melville's narrator ascends this rock for a "Pisgah View" (*PT* 134) but can see only the "grim and charred" (139) desolation of "an archipelago of aridities, without inhabitant, history, or hope of either in all time to come" (142). In *Clarel*, Melville

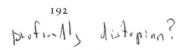
profoundly distopian?

describes the steep mountains overlooking Jericho, including Quarantania –
the Mount of Temptation from which the Devil offered the world to Christ
during his forty days in the wilderness – as a "sum of blights" representing
Calvinistic gloom: from its altitude one "everywhere/ Descries but worlds
more waste, more bare" (C 178). From Jericho, the actual Mount Pisgah is
seen in the distance, and Rolfe scornfully asserts that Moses' panorama of
the Promised Land had looked upon the same dearth and may have made
him long for the Egypt he had left behind. Far from providing the manna,
milk, and honey of salvation, the stony desiccation of the Holy Land testifies to a fallen world where celestial grace devolves into a dead zone of
dust so "blanched" and "leprous" that "Blisters supplant the beads of dew"
(C 387).

Melville's portrayals of the naturalistic hell he witnessed on earth negated
any naïve belief in the benevolence of creation or the promise of redemp- ⅄
tion. Melville's journeys around the icy extremes of Cape Horn altered his
sense of the vast range of the planet's inhuman power. Melville had read
the geological theories about the earth's ice age of Harvard geologist Louis
Agassiz, who directed Harvard's Museum of Comparative Zoology, which
Melville's father-in-law served as trustee.[9] In *Moby-Dick*, Melville writes
of "those Polar eternities; when wedged bastions of ice pressed hard upon
what are now the Tropics" (457). He views the polar seas as "deathful, desolate dominions … freighted with navies of icebergs – warring worlds cross-
ing orbits," dramatizing a world in the process of breaking up and leaving
in its wake "cemeteries of skeletons and bones." The heartless destruction
of such mobile havoc is intimated in the crash of this fatal sentence: "White
bears howl as they drift from their cubs; and the grinding islands crush
the skulls of the peering seals" (366–67). Melville's haunting poem "The
Berg: A Dream" (1888) narrates a wreck of a naval ship that founders after
striking the "dead indifference" of an iceberg, which instead of forming a
floating island that can be pushed aside is composed of a "vast" "preci-
pice" of "stolid" "inertia" that descends far down below the surface (*PP*
240–41, 605).

Melville frequently deployed the unforgiving horror of polar desolation
to dramatize the limits of human knowledge and to register the frigid fate of
human abandonment. As ground zero of the planet's longitude and latitude,
the pole is that outpost where the compass's needle indicates no true north
but rather "indifferently respects all points of the horizon alike." Pierre's
quest for truth leads him into "hyperborean regions" where "all objects are
seen in a dubious, uncertain, and refracting light" (*P* 165), leaving him "solitary as at the Pole" (338). Like Pierre, Nathan in *Clarel* finds himself "Alone,
and at Doubt's freezing pole" where "He wrestled with the pristine forms/

Like the first man" (*C* 60). "Polar citadels" (*MD* 461) possess pinnacles and peaks that mirror in ice the soaring spires of cathedral minsters, yet they simultaneously spell out the congealing of the living faith that produced and inhabited them. In this light, it is not surprising that Clarel's own eclipsed faith becomes further disoriented when his pilgrim's vision of Jerusalem reveals only "blank, blank towers ... Like the ice bastions round the Pole" (*C* 5).

If the frozen poles were one extreme in Melville's writings, another centered on the slides, quakes, and eruptions of lava from molten magma that undermined the earth's solidity. The geological cataclysms of the planet's chaotic evolution rendered destruction and waste as the formative processes of the earth's own foundation. "Andes and Appalachee tell," Melville writes, "Of havoc ere our Adam fell,"[10] and he playfully asserts in *Typee* that "the whole continent of America had ... been formed by the simultaneous explosion of a train of Etnas, laid under the water all the way from the North Pole to the parallel of Cape Horn" (155). In *Moby-Dick*'s chapter "The Street," Melville renders the opulence of New Bedford as an artful veneer of wealth dragged from the ocean and "superinduced" over "scraggy scoria" made up of "the barren refuse rocks thrown aside at creation's final day" (32–33). When *Mardi*'s philosopher Babbalanja reads the "hieroglyphic molds" of the "Isle of Fossils," he irreverently asserts that "All Mardi's rocks are one wide resurrection" of "tombs burst open by volcanic throes; and hither hurled from the lowermost vaults of the lagoon" (415). Melville presses heavenly resurrection and intelligent design back into the materiality of the tomb as the earth is constituted by a chance reformation of its own dead forms. Babbalanja's proverbial truth reflects the morbid side of Melville's cosmic perception: "Thus Nature works, at random warring, chaos a crater, and this world a shell" (*M* 417).

For Melville, volcanoes were revolutionary forces that upend complacency with their hellacious explosions of unpredictable force. European revolutions were as a "sulphureous Hill/ Whose vent far hellward reaches down!"[11] The fullest eruption of the volcano in Melville's writing is "The Apparition: A Retrospect" from *Battle-Pieces* (1866), a poem William H. Shurr suggests is "the most concise statement of Melville's philosophy to be found anywhere in his writings."[12] In this poem Melville charts earth's subterranean capacity to blast any illusion that it is a tropical paradise where "all is green."[13] "Convulsions came," the poem begins, as if the poem itself is a verbal convulsion that explodes into the midst of *Battle-Pieces*, unsettling – like war itself – its ordered verse with its rude awakening. Its ponderous diction evokes melded magma: "Marl," "slag," and "clinkers" ravage the ravine – the site in Petersburg where Union soldiers in 1864 detonated a mine shaft dug under Confederate forces – propelled through some black magic from the "unreserve of Ill" (*PP* 116). The ground's seeming solidity is merely an unstable surface (like Ahab's "pasteboard masks" [*MD* 164]) temporarily containing a volatile fluidity that humans can neither control nor comprehend. Thus "The Apparition," instead of revealing the supernatural presence of a saint, concludes with a grim warning:

> So, then, Solidity's a crust –
> The core of fire below;
> All may go well for many a year,
> But who can think without a fear
> Of horrors that happen so? (*PP* 116)

While cataclysm on land – the wildfire, the avalanche, the earthquake, the volcanic eruption – destabilized the very grounds of life, for Melville it was the fluid and unfathomable abyss of the ocean that most embod- *Ocean,* ied matter's cannibalistic power to devour human lives. "[T]he masterless ocean overruns the globe," he asserted, "No mercy, no power but its own controls it" (*MD* 274). Melville's fullest images of annihilation centered on those who "placelessly perished" by being whelmed in the ocean's depths, as the "live sea swallows up ships and crews" and is "ballasted with bones of millions of the drowned" (*MD* 36, 274, 311). Melville dramatized the forsaking of humans in the oceanic desertion of Pip and the orphan Ishmael in *Moby-Dick*, and in his description of Bartleby, "absolutely alone," as "A bit of wreck in the mid Atlantic" (*PT* 32) – an abandonment syntactically performed in the center of that story by its own half-sentence with no verb. Drowning in "the deeper midnight of the insatiate maw" (*MD* 311) materialized for Melville the fall into hell, a reversal of resurrection when "the grim despot at last interposes; and with a viper in our winding-sheets, we are dropped in the sea" (*M* 619).

The "universal cannibalism of the sea" (*MD* 274) was not only manifest in its ingestion of dead sailors but more specifically incarnated in the ravenous creatures that dove in its depths.[14] Melville describes the fury beneath the ocean's skin as a "tiger heart that pants beneath it," averring that "this velvet paw but conceals a remorseless fang" (*MD* 491). In *Mardi*, Melville spins tall tales of the terrible "Devil Fish" (*M* 39), which he further elaborated for his lyceum lectures on "The South Seas." This "Satanic fishship" "has horns, huge fins, cloven hoofs," and "dives to the profoundest abyss and comes up roaring with mouths as many and as wide open as the Mississippi" like "the belching of a Vesuvius" (*PT* 414, 765).

The real devil fish in Melville's works was the sinister shark that incarnated the immanent forces of destruction manifest in nature. Sailors dreamt of the "crunching teeth of sharks" (*MD* 127) and used these teeth to tattoo themselves with crucifixes for superstitious protection. For Melville, the shark's horror is magnified by the ghastliness of its "smooth, flaky" skin, the "mildness" of its gliding pursuit (*MD* 189), and its "mouth-yawning" maw (*WJ* 295). The shark embodies the viscera of transcendentalism – manifesting by its appetite for flesh that the oversoul also has its underfangs. The black cook Fleece in *Moby-Dick* positions "Gor" (God) as "Massa Shark" (297), the owner of a plantation planet who runs a predatory system of insatiable consumption. Queequeg concurs that the God that created the shark must be "one dam Ingin" (302). Even Celio in *Clarel* asserts that the Prince of Peace taught a hypocritical ideal when he questions why "The shark thou mad'st, yet claim'st the dove" (42). One of Melville's most anthologized poems, "The Maldive Shark" (1888), puns on the depth of the shark's evil. The adjectives with which Melville describes the shark – "Pale," "phlegmatical," "lethargic and dull" – remove all passion from the predation of this "ravener of horrible meat" (*PP* 236). Melville writes in other works how, "with body lean/ And charnel mouth," the shark "Glides white through the phosphorous sea" (*PP* 161, 136), a living embodiment of how "hate … prowls" under the surface of life "with horrific serenity of aspect" (*M* 41). Melville makes clear that Ahab projects this sharkishness to refashion the mammal Moby Dick into a malignant monster against which he crusades with defiant rage.

The Vernal Sense

Melville's accounts of transcendental bliss and heartless destruction resonate with the dualist belief in the hope of resuming a celestial paradise out of the material doom of a "Tartarus" or hell. Over the course of his writing career, Melville regularly engaged the changing forms of earth's material reality by moving beyond scriptural notions of redemption and damnation to center on matter's immanent capacity to generate continuing life in the midst of the fatal embrace of earthly destruction. As in Whitman's "This Compost," in which the "foul meat" of decay is calmly and chemically transformed into the sweetness of leaves of grass, Melville celebrated nature's capacity to germinate anew after devastation and disaster.[15] The elms growing around the graves of Civil War battle in "Malvern Hill" seem naturally to know that "sap the twig will fill/ Wag the world how it will, leaves must be green in spring" (*PP* 50). Indeed it was the sustenance released from moss and mold – what Ishmael called the "cheerful greenness of complete decay" (*MD* 193) – that ironically fertilized the life that continues beyond decease and desolation.

One of the theories of Melville's age was that Pacific atolls emerged from the accretive labor of coral insects building up matter from the bottom of the sea to which they contributed the carapaces of their own bodies. Victorian writers celebrated how the persistent exertions of the polyp naturally modeled the steady sacrifices of the meek that promised the glorious fruits of evangelical success. Lydia Sigourney, for example, ended her poem "The Coral Insect": "Ye slumber unmarked 'mid the desolate main,/ While the wonder and pride of your works remain."[16] In *Typee*, Melville voiced his skepticism of these theories: "indefatigable as that wonderful creature is, it would be hardly muscular enough to pile rocks one upon the other more than three thousand feet above the level of the sea" (155). In other of his writings, however, he mustered the tiny coral insects into ceaseless agents of assemblage, signifying the unthinking forces of material creation rather than affirming orthodox Christian faith. The polyp itself is a hybrid holobiont: an invertebrate that combines the augmentative growth of the plant with the animal agency of the zoophyte to generate creative processes neither human nor divine. Melville depicted scenes of confounding emergence beneath the sea, such as when "among the joyous, heartless, ever-juvenile eternities, Pip saw the multitudinous, God-omnipresent, coral insects, that out of the firmament of waters heaved the colossal orbs." The primordial creative urge – "God's foot upon the treadle of the loom" – is not bestowed divinely from above but rather is accreted out of the "firmament of waters" (414). Melville's fullest dramatization of the materialist engine of coral concrescence is his poem on "Venice," stimulated by his gondola journeys down its aquatic avenues in 1857 and not published until the "Fruit of Travel Long Ago" section of *Timoleon* (1888). In this poem Melville celebrates the energetic "little craftsman of the Coral Sea" whose elemental ejaculations, "Evincing what a worm can do," underlay the "shallower" architecture of the Renaissance (*PP* 291). Melville's own poetic process identifies with the worm's instinctive vitalism, dedicating twice as many lines to the accretive materialism of the polyp than to the human accomplishments of civilization. Here Melville pays homage to "the world without us,"[17] as in the much earlier lament in *Omoo* (1846) chanted by aged Tahitians: "The palm tree shall grow,/ The coral shall spread,/ But man shall cease" (*O* 192).

Melville early viewed the palm as the apex of the vegetable world, standing stately erect with its diadem of fronds, shooting up in a tuft and then bowing down, generating a nut that was also a fruit. Melville's youthful vision of the palm tree as oasis persisted from the "soft shadows" (*T* 172) of the coconut palm in *Typee* to the solitary date palm clinging to a cleft in *Clarel*'s remote monastery, a cynosure to the pilgrims whose fertile fronds symbolize the precarious nourishment of life despite desolation (book 3, cantos 25–30). "In all times past, things have been overlaid; and though the first fruits of the marl are wild and poisonous," Melville writes in *Mardi*, "the palms at last spring forth; and once again the tribes repose in shade" (500). The resilient instinct of flora to sprout shoots, tendrils, plumes, tufts, and blooms embodied Melville's own creative urge to continue writing in the face of eruptions of doubt. Melville's wondrous vision in *Moby-Dick* of the "weaver god" on the island of Tranque figures the "ceaseless industry" of the earth's "living sap" looming forth tapestries of palms and "ground vine tendrils" wound through the warp of a dead sperm whale's skeleton (449–50).

Melville's struggles bore the fruit of wisdom that the passionate energies of ambition were often themselves causes of misery and illusion. In "Fragments from a Lost Gnostic Poem of the Twelfth Century," Melville asserts that since "Matter in end will never abate/ His ancient brutal claim," then "Indolence is heaven's ally here,/ And energy the child of hell" (*PP* 284). Melville promoted the Greek virtue of *ataraxia* – quietude in the presence of uncertainty – by accepting the little that was evident with what he called "downright good feeling" (*L* 454). He voiced in *Mardi* that although sadness was "universal and eternal," it also embodied tranquility, which was "the uttermost that souls may hope for" (*M* 636). Alignment with the instinctive urge of nature itself sustained the freshness of creativity in the "dust, dearth, and din" of the earth.[18] "Let us revere that sacred uncertainty," he wrote in *Battle-Pieces* (*PP* 185); and in *Moby-Dick* he called those who attained this counterpoise the "choice hidden handful of the Divine Inert" (148).

For Melville, the natural aristocracy of the "Divine Inert" owed a good deal to the primordial being that preceded civilized craft or the wiles of conceptual calculation. He explores this type most fully in his characters Queequeg and Billy Budd. Queequeg's "pagan piety" (*MD* 86) enables him to remain serene and his "calm self-collectedness of simplicity" leaves him "always equal to himself" (50), content with "that immortal health in him which could not die or be weakened" (477). The orphan Billy Budd attracts attention as "Handsome Sailor" because his Adamic beauty embodies the "off-hand unaffectedness of natural regality" (*BB* 43). His "pristine and unadulterate" (53) virtues render him "an upright barbarian" (52) radically unfit to make sense of the mundane machinations in which he is enmeshed. His simple frankness and cheerful gaiety are unimpeded expressions of the fresh source of vital freedom that buds forth from his natural being; as Melville's narrator relates: "The bonfire in his heart made luminous the rose-tan in his cheek" (76). Similarly, in *Clarel's* remarkable canto "Of Rama," which tells the Indian saga of a "god" "puzzled at the wrong/ Misplacing him in human lot," Melville describes how, despite all his difficulties, Rama's pristine vigor shines forth as "The patient root, the vernal sense/ Surviving hard experience/ As grass the winter" (C 103, 104).

Throughout his writing, Melville addresses the heroism of patient persistence in older men who have endured the struggles of life. One such character is the very old mainmast man in *White-Jacket* whose saber-seamed face looked as if it had been "blown out of Vesuvius" and "burned almost black by the torrid suns that shone fifty years ago"; nevertheless, this tar still shows in his eye "the fadeless, ever infantile immortality within"(*WJ* 284). Melville's story "Jimmy Rose" celebrates a destitute nobleman who mysteriously survives his "nipping winter" with "undying roses which bloomed in his ruined cheeks" (*PT* 342, 344). *Moby-Dick*'s Father Mapple, like the sap of the tree to which he is linked, also experiences a "second flowering youth" "in the hardy winter of a healthy old age." After entering the church wet with "melting sleet," blooms gleam forth "among all the fissures of his wrinkles," which Ishmael equates with "the spring verdure peeping forth even beneath February's snow" (38). Spring blooms being fed with the thaws of winter, what Melville called "a fresco/ Of Roses and snow," was a persistent motif in his poetry that enacted his theory of art as the mixing and mating of "unlike things."[19] Rolfe even calls Christ "Our earth's unmerited fair guest/ – Pure as the sleet – as roses warm – " (C 199).

Melville found "cheerful" and "charmful" vitality in the "simple grace" of unassuming plants such as catnip, aloe, hardhack, lilac, ivy, asters, and rosmarine – lowly groundlings averse to ephemeral display that naturally retained the freshness of life "in spite of the Worm."[20] Melville's fine unpublished poem "Pontoosuc" personifies this pagan wisdom through the visitation of a wood nymph who counters Solomon's wisdom that "All dies" with her own generative truth: "End, ever end, and forever and ever begin again!" She represents the world's lesson that death and life revolve into each other like night and day, like light dimpling shade. She embodies death in her "cold ... rootlets" and "humid clinging mould"; yet the kiss of her "warm lips" engenders the "fragrant breath" of life.[21]

Melville's own tombstone in Woodlawn Cemetery in the Bronx announces the generation that emerges out of annihilation, not by the Christian cross of his wife's Lizzie's stone planted next to him after her death in 1906, but rather by a blank scroll devoid of any words, with only his name and the dates of his birth and death inscribed beneath it. Its material form embodies the final lesson Melville learned from life – not only that "The last wisdom is dumb" (M 620), but also the continuing presence of the "vital sap" that allowed him to "centrally disport in mute calm" in the midst of decay (MD 389). The living ivy growing today at the foot of Melville's stone has its monumental counterpoint in the sturdy vine whose main branch stretches in relief across the stone – its two stems with twelve leaves (one of which slightly overlaps the empty scroll) both topped with tendrils pointing upward at different heights on each side of the scroll. Beneath the empty scroll embossed over the vine are patches of live green lichen watered from tricklings from the unraveled curl at the base of the roll. Melville's final repose posthumously generates his expressed will that he "be urned in the trunk of some green tree, and even in death have the vital sap circulating round me, giving of my dead body the living foliage that shaded my peaceful tomb" (*WJ* 316).

NOTES

1 Wilson Hefflin, "Melville, Celestial Navigation, and Dead Reckoning," *Melville Society Extracts* 29 (1977): 3. Melville took the persona of a professor of celestial trigonometry in "The New Planet" (*PT* 445–46). For Melville's planetary ordinations, see Robert T. Tally, Jr., *Melville, Mapping and Globalization: Literary Cartography in the American Baroque Writer* (London and New York: Continuum, 2009) and Charles Waugh, "'We are Not a Nation, so Much as a World': Melville's Global Consciousness," *Studies in American Fiction* 33:2 (2005), 203–28.

2 Richard Dean Smith, *Melville's Science: 'Devilish Tantalization of the Gods'* (New York: Garland, 1993); Bruce Harvey, "Science and the Earth," in *A Companion to Herman Melville*, ed. Wyn Kelley (Oxford, UK: Blackwell, 2006), 71–82.

3 Studies of Melville and religion have traditionally examined the influence of scriptural teachings in his fiction. See, for example, William Braswell, *Melville and Religion* (Durham, NC: Duke University Press, 1943); Nathalia Wright, *Melville's Uses of the Bible* (Durham, NC: Duke University Press, 1949); T. Walter Herbert, *Moby Dick and Calvinism* (New Brunswick, NJ: Rutgers University Press, 1977); and Ilana Pardes, *Melville's Bibles* (Berkeley: University of California Press, 2008).

4 See Richard Hardack, *Not Altogether Human: Pantheism and the Dark Nature of the American Renaissance* (Amherst: University of Massachusetts Press, 2012).

5 Herman Melville, *Poems: Containing* Battle-Pieces, John Marr and Other Sailors, *and Miscellaneous Poems* (London: Constable and Company, 1924), 238–39.

6 For a broader view of this exorbitant perpectivism, see Nigel Clark, *Inhuman Nature: Sociable Life on a Dynamic Planet* (London: Sage, 2011).

7 Melville, *Poems*, 257.

8 See Umberto Eco, *The Aesthetics of Chaosmos: The Middle Ages of James Joyce* (Cambridge, MA: Harvard University Press, 1982).

9 This line of inquiry was inaugurated by Tyrus Hillway's 1944 Yale dissertation "Melville and Nineteenth-Century Science."

10 Melville, *Poems*, 433.

11 Ibid., 387.

12 William H. Shurr, *The Mystery of Iniquity: Melville as Poet, 1857–1891* (Lexington: University of Kentucky Press, 1972), 42.

13 Melville, *Poems*, 419.

14 Randall Bohrer, "The Living Mirror: Melville's Vision of Universal Process," *Research Studies* 50:1 (March 1982): 46–91.

15 "This Compost," in *The Collected Writings of Walt Whitman* (New York: New York University Press, 1980), III, 341.

16 Michelle Elleray, "Little Builders: Coral Insects, Missionary Culture, and the Victorian Child," *Victorian Literature and Culture* 39 (2011): 223–38; Lydia Sigourney, *Select Poems*, third edition (Philadelphia: Greenough, 1838), 244–45.

17 The phrase is taken from Alan Weisman's popular postapocalyptic book, *The World without Us* (New York: Thomas Dunne, 2007).

18 Melville, *Poems*, 415.

19 Melville, *Poems*, 312, 270. Compellingly, this image signified transgenerational regeneration to Melville as it was drawn from Oliver Wendell Holmes's 1830 poem celebrating his paternal grandfather, Revolutionary War veteran Major Thomas Melvill. The poem celebrates Melvill both as a young man when "his cheek was like a rose/ In the snow," and as an old man when he is "The Last Leaf," which Holmes later described "finds itself still clinging to its bough while the new growths of spring are bursting their buds and spreading their foliage all around it." *The Last Leaf* (Boston, MA: Riverside, 1895), 7, 52.

20 Melville, *Poems*, 335.

21 Melville, "The Lake: Pontoosuce," *Poems*, 431–34.

14

JOHN BRYANT

Wound, Beast, Revision: Versions of the Melville Meme

Melville's reputation looms large in the popular imagination. As of this writing, people can attend at least three *Moby-Dick* "marathons" throughout any given year, listen online to celebrities reading chapters of that book in what is called the "Big Read," glimpse images from and of the book in subway poster art and television ads, or hear Melville lines in popular song, performance art, and protest rallies as well as stage, film, and opera. Melville, it seems, is everywhere. Or rather, everywhere we find *Moby-Dick*, and often a *Moby-Dick* reduced to the icon of a one-legged man and a white whale. This synecdochal image has captured the popular imagination in ways that images of Hamlet and Yorrick's skull, or Huck and Jim on their raft, or Sancho Panzo and the Don on their respective mounts were, for a time, immediately recognizable and somehow viscerally meaningful for citizens who may never have read *Hamlet*, *Huckleberry Finn*, or *Don Quixote*. How rare it might seem that a select literary work might ever penetrate into the popular culture. And yet this kind of iconic distillate linking highbrow and low is a recurring phenomenon: St. George slaying his dragon in stained glass; Frankenstein and his creature in mutual pursuit; Dracula attending high school. We keep our monsters close to us and compressed. But why has *Moby-Dick* achieved this status of cultural icon? Why Ahab and the whale?

In today's online digital world, this cultural phenomenon would be called a *meme*. But to grasp how the "Melville meme" can help us explain the interactions of self, text, and culture, we need a critical approach that comprehends biography, revision, and adaptation, one that acknowledges literary works as fluid texts. A fluid text is a work that exists in multiple sequential versions, generated first by an originating writer (call him Melville), then by revisionary writers (Melville again, but also family, editors, and publishers), and eventually by adaptors, who extend the fluid text in the form of extra-authorial versions, such as translation and adaptation.[1] Although the manuscript of *Moby-Dick* does not survive to show us Melville's precise revisions, scholars surmise that Melville revised his novel through various stages and that British editors expurgated it in critically meaningful ways.[2] Versions of *Moby-Dick* began to appear in film as early as 1928. The power of adaptation to shape critical thinking about a literary work should not be underestimated. Often enough, our first access to iconic literary works is through memorable adaptations of those works: I saw Gregory Peck as Ahab before I ever read *Moby-Dick*. Rather than eschew such secondhand experiences, we must recognize, as Linda Hutcheon reminds us, that adaptation is an interpretive creation, extending the originating author's fluid text.[3]

But the Melville meme is not the announced adaptation of *Moby-Dick* by a creative interpreter. Anonymously conceived and openly shared, it is a unit of compressed meaning transmitting a culture's anxieties. And because this phenomenon is a version of Melville's fluid text, we might use it critically like any meaningful revision not only to investigate our culture but also to read Melville's original text more fully. And if the Melville meme is an extension of *Moby-Dick*, how might we edit Melville's work to include adaptive versions so that readers may navigate the full course of that fluid text's sequential versions, from manuscript and edition to adaptation and meme? Fittingly, given the digital environment in which the meme flourishes, the pragmatics of editing the Melville meme are best realized through digital means.

But what is so compelling in *Moby-Dick* that it generates a meme in the first place? Granted, the ability to invoke the Melville meme, to claim one's intimacy with a national epic, connects us to a knowing collective: we read; we read together; we are we. But something less solipsistic is at play. To the extent that survival in a democratic culture of perpetual revolution requires a perpetual redefinition of identity, the casualties of life are inseparable from the anxieties of social change and personal growth that emerge as one seeks relation to the shiftings of one's being, class, gender, sexuality, and ethnicity. Inherent in the instability of democratic life is the trauma of self-transformation, and *Moby-Dick* replays such traumas: Ahab, Ishmael, Pip act out their transformative wounds. In the Melville meme, wherever it emerges, trauma and transformation are wedded.

To get at the dynamics of this phenomenon, some further diving will expose the lure of the Melville meme. Let's say that the whole of Ahab reduces to his absent part, the leg that is not there. Ahab's scars are the material remnant of the absent leg so that Ahab further reduces to one irreducible part of him: his wound. For Ahab, the wound exists as the phantom leg he never stops feeling; it is an immaterial vestige of a former consciousness, still present. We can submit the whale to a similar reduction. Moby Dick's whiteness represents absences that go beyond the trauma of

Ahab's wound to a metaphysics of nothingness that negates consciousness altogether. Paradoxically, Ishmael's exposure to this animal nothing – this beast – allows the also wounded Ishmael to revise himself by poetically transforming the whale into new anatomized notions of consciousness. If this monstrous mass of flesh is a conscious being, other than ourselves, then what is the mix of material and immaterial selves that constitutes consciousness and being? What is the relation between the wound that shapes that being and the beast we seek to transform?

Surely, *Moby-Dick* cannot be reduced to two words, but *wound* and *beast* represent a thread of logic, concerning trauma, transformation, and revision that hides out in the Melville meme and suggests new ways we may read Melville biographically, textually, and culturally. But to get at the transformative dynamics of the Melville meme and its challenge to editing Melville, we first need to ground wound and beast in biography.

Wound and Replay

Literary biographers invariably look for wounds. Melville biographers have located two. In 1832, when Melville was twelve, his father, Allan, died suddenly of an aggressive, undiagnosed illness that left him raving at the end. In the wake of this sudden disaster, Herman and two siblings – Gansevoort and Augusta – struggling differently through adolescence, became a domestic coterie of gifted writers.[4] The second great wound of Melville's life came in 1867 when the wounded son Herman, now a father, broke into his son Malcolm's bedroom and found the body of the adolescent, the victim of a self-inflicted gunshot wound. Already having failed to make a career out of his prose writing or to establish a reputation as a national poet, Melville devoted his last twenty years to poetry, including a poem that became the novella *Billy Budd*. Because they have a story to tell, biographers look for narrative arcs as well as wounds, but with Melville's life, the geometry is more like the figure of an ellipse, a double centered curve that arcs around but never touches its two foci, which are these two wounds: the son who lost a father; the father who lost a son.

While these two father-wounds can never explain the totality of Melville's evolving consciousness, they are necessarily a significant grounding for our thinking about Melville's creativity and the personal appeal of cultural adaptation. Drawing on the vocabulary of trauma theory, expounded in the work of Cathy Caruth and Dominick LaCapra,[5] enables us to integrate the traumas of Melville's life with the dynamics of his creativity and to expand that focus to include the Melville meme. My claim is that elements of Melville's writing process – his replay of ideas, silences, and scenes; his transformations of self and symbol; his breakdown of form and deferral of meaning, his relentless revision in manuscript and print – coincide with various ways of voicing trauma. Melville's acting out and working through his wounds is not entirely pathological; it is also a rhetorical strategy designed to engage readers in the anxiety but necessity of transformation.

Wounds and disabilities proliferate in Melville's writing, beginning with his adolescent "Fragments from a Writing Desk, No. 2" (1839). In it, an amorous student woos dream-like "Inamorata," who in the story's final sentence is revealed to be "Dumb and Deaf!" (*PT* 197, 204). This Poe-ish extravaganza was written while Melville's brother Gansevoort was recuperating from an undiagnosed swelling in his ankle that had kept him an invalid for fifteen months. Unavoidably, Gansevoort's invalidism seemed, for his family, a worrisome version of the father in the form of Allan Melvill's stress-related illness and death. Since that traumatic event, Gansevoort had been the head of the family business and surrogate father to his siblings. Herman was the only other lad in the house strong enough to carry his invalid brother from bedroom to parlor to privy. Because Gansevoort proctored all of his siblings in their writing, the layabout brother was free to "correct" or possibly to revise Herman's sexy, gothic "Fragment." The story's fixation on female disability seems only remotely connected to Gansevoort's leg wound (harbinger of Ahab) or the latent anxieties of rival brothers forced into each other's arms, testing their social and masculine viability in the absence of their father. But fuller voicings of the father-wound were to come.

In 1845, no longer lame, Gansevoort vetted Herman's early draft of *Typee*, three chapters of which show pencil editing in Gansevoort's hand. In *Typee*, protagonist Tommo suffers a leg ailment: its cause is unknown, but its pain waxes and wanes in relation to Tommo's resistance to or acceptance of Polynesian sexual customs. Kory-Kory – brother of Tommo's paramour Fayaway – carries invalid Tommo around the valley. To be sure, Tommo's leg wound is a critique of colonialism: the white colonizer, debilitated by the clash of Victorian and Polynesian cultures, is infantilized by the native, as Tommo becomes a tribal fetish and, ironically, the colonized black man's burden. And yet this early rehearsal of Ahab's leg is a fuller acting out of Herman's masculine and family dynamics: wounded son is carried throughout the tribe's domestic terrain just as Herman carried surrogate father Gansevoort about their mother's house. At the same time, Fayaway – who expresses sympathy for Tommo in wordless moans ("Awha! awha!" [*T* 100]) – is no more articulate than the "dumb and deaf" Inamorata.

Such rewriting of trauma and disability not only responds to a line of conditions traceable to the death of Allan Melvill but also finds expression in what Caruth calls "a voice that is paradoxically released through the wound."[6] In fact, the episode in *Typee* seems to exhibit more release than voice. But if Melville's father-wound represents an absence, it is perhaps best voiced through dramatized silences. Squatting before Tommo, chief Mehevi stares into Tommo's eyes, and Tommo gazes back. Tommo can only voice his bafflement: "Never before had I been subjected to so strange and steady a glance; it revealed nothing of the mind of the savage, but it appeared to be reading my own" (*T* 71). The lame Tommo might look at the "savage" other, but he cannot see into this alien father figure, an emblem of asymmetric cultural interaction muted in this acting out of a dimly conceived personal wound.

The father-wound is more fully announced in *Redburn*. This self-probing *bildungsroman* picks at the wound with incomparable pain while it experiments with narrative strategies that presage *Moby-Dick* and *Pierre*. The modulations of voice between the angry boy (then) and the older, still boy-like man (now) are evident when Melville earnestly defends the adolescent mind as it contemplates the "blights" of life: "they strike in too deep, and leave such a scar that the air of Paradise might not erase it" (*R* 11).

The passage plays out the ineradicable scar as adult Redburn channeling the adolescent proclaims that no one should have to endure such blights until "the stout time of manhood" when we are "veterans" of life's war, not its "green recruits" (*R* 11). Redburn's trauma refuses healing: his adolescent acting out occurs moments later when he aims his rifle at shocked passengers, leaving the boy ashamed of his anger. Instances of his posttraumatic stress recur in later moments of anger and resentment in New York and Liverpool, never fully resolved, only transformed into subsequent characters: Jackson, Harry, and Carlo.

According to Caruth, the play upon the "then" and "now" of one's identity is a voicing of "otherness" in the "acting out" of trauma. LaCapra further identifies a "middle voice" (situated between subject and object) that enables a more therapeutic "working through" of trauma that "resists closure" and perpetuates "undecidability."[7] These necessary oscillations of then and now, self and other, emerge in aestheticized versions of the wound evident in one of Melville's narrative strategies, or what I call "replay." The acting out in *Redburn* adumbrates Melville's working through of trauma in *Moby-Dick*.

Moby-Dick's replay of the father-wound is more symphonic than repetitive. Ishmael's "dim, unsuspecting way" in trying to understand Ahab's anger in the chapter titled "Moby Dick" is explicitly reenacted in the "dim random way" Ishmael follows in the next chapter to investigate "The Whiteness of the Whale" (*MDL* 178, 179). The self-quotation in the *unsuspecting way* → *random way* revision is an incremental replay that calls attention to Ishmael's self-transformations. The novel's subsequent cetological chapters can also be taken as a series of replays. Each chapter essays the whale; each is seemingly "random" and "unsuspecting" of revelation, and yet each repetitively begins with anatomy and ends with an appeal to readers to look for the whale within them. These digressive chapters seem designed not so much to forestall plot but to deny plot its conventional confidence in putting a merely circumstantial period to Ahab's acting out of his wound so that Ishmael – randomly, unsuspectingly – may more successfully and perpetually transform his own wound. For all the iron-rail linearity of the Ahab plot, and for all its tricked-out prophecies prolonging anticipation of denouement, Ahab's death is contrived to come so quickly that we hardly notice it in the flurry of the final pages. "The drama's done" (*MDL* 500), but the trauma's not. Circling the vortex of the *Pequod*'s whirlpool, Ishmael cycles back to his beginning and his famous self-renaming to replay the traumatic wreck and begin again to work it through. Ishmael's necessary circularity figures a different kind of line from Ahab's.

Ishmael replays himself in various versions of manhood: lover, singer, killer. Projecting onto Queequeg, Ishmael turns into a wife and redefines male love. A singer turned gibbering mystic, wounded Pip is a brilliant black version of Ishmael contrived to heal Ahab's wound. His plea to Ahab to "use poor me for your one lost leg" (*MDL* 466) is an attempt to transform himself into Ahab's cure. What befalls Pip is the "like abandonment" (367) that befalls Ishmael, who bumped from the boat, as was Pip, is now empowered to sing, as does Pip, his versions of the traumatic tale. Abused and abusive Ahab is Ishmael's grandest replay, not just a histrionic projection of his adolescent, pistol-and-ball "hypos" but a cathartic voicing of the father-wound as a destroyer, which achieves its most eloquent replay in "The Gilder" (chapter 114).

Here, Ishmael's cyclic and Ahab's straight-line voices seem to merge, like "mingling threads," in a speech that has no clearly designated speaker.[8] Ishmael/Ahab identifies six stages of life from unconscious infancy and boyhood faith through versions of doubt, skepticism, and disbelief, to "manhood's pondering repose of If." For Ahab, these stages are fatally cyclic not resolvently linear; we relive them daily, hourly, in a split second; there is no "steady unretracing progress" (*MDL* 430) that ends them, just unwilled posttraumatic oscillations among them. The speech blends its precedents: Stubb's comic twelve ages of man based on the zodiac in "The Doubloon" (chapter 99), and Jaques's mordant "seven ages of man" speech in *As You Like It*. But lacking any repose in this damning cyclicity of "Ifs," Ahab (or rather Ishmael's self-transformative projection into Ahab) agonizes on a cause of the repetition: "Where is the foundling's father hidden? ... the secret of our paternity lies in [the] grave, and we must there to learn it" (*MDL* 430). Is death the transport to some fantasy afterlife where foundling and father congregate? Or is death itself the "secret" of paternity: fathers die, and death is father's message. Learn the message; act it out; take the ironic, self-slaying option of the survivor of trauma. But instead, Ishmael's cyclic replaying is his substitute for pistol and ball.

To boil *Moby-Dick* down to Melville's father-wound would be a mistake. Granted, the novel's popular appeal – its iteration of the Melville meme – has its fundamental source in the fact that all readers have fathers, and you do not have to be an orphan to feel a father's distance. Plenty of twelve year olds lose fathers, in ways other than death. Still, only wounded son Melville wrote *Moby-Dick*, or felt the need to, and the lure of the book lies not in the wound but in the energy Melville expends in voicing that wound through replays of himself, each version a rewriting and a revision. Eventually, I want to claim that Melville's process of revision can help us see how our need for self-transformation is played out in our need to revise Melville. But not before we consider a second version of Melville: the beast.

Beast and Revision

Earlier I said that Ahab is Ishmael's grandest replay of himself, but let me revise myself. The whale is Ishmael's fuller self-transformation. Whereas Ahab is Ishmael's self-projection into a histrionic character that can act out his rage, the whale is that same angry consciousness replayed aesthetically into other versions of himself. With this remarkable transformation of father-wound into symbolic beast, the complex necessity of Ishmael's ludic self-projections into the whale frames Ahab's revenge. After *Moby-Dick*, Melville let go of sea adventure but continued to transform further versions of the beast into modes of consciousness other than himself: scrivener, raped widow, rebel slave, confidence man, slain collegians, painter of the picturesque, Handsome Sailor, scheming master-at-arms, formalist captain. And these transformations into the other are fundamental to our grasp not only of the political Melville but also of the necessity of revision in grasping at human consciousness.

The transformation of beast into other is not just a repetitive reenactment of trauma; rather it is a textualized rewriting of the self, borne out of trauma yet simulating other modes of consciousness. The ontological grounding for this revisionary Otherness is best articulated in a line Ahab delivers when contemplating Queequeg's empty coffin sealed tight for a lifebuoy: "Oh! how immaterial are all materials! What things real are there, but imponderable thoughts?" (*MDL* 367). Taken as an "ungraspable phantom of life"

(22), this ineffable consciousness occurring in material things, Ahab argues, cannot be perceived as Thing; it can only be apperceived as Idea. Hence, Ahab gestures toward the "imponderable thought" of the coffin/lifebuoy to grasp what is "real" beyond the carved hieroglyphics on its lid. Such is the philosopher Ahab. But here, too, is the artist Ishmael who, rather than striking through the mask of materiality, pursues the Idea of Queequeg by replaying his surfaces: the coffin carvings are a version of Queequeg's tattooing, which are a rewriting of his identity, and these replays are versions of an otherness within Ishmael. This rewriting of consciousness extends to various modes of otherness – male, female, black, white, straight, gay. Ishmael's transformations elevate replay to an imperative of democratic survival: the discovery of otherness within ourselves is a transformative self-regeneration that enables us to work through the comedy of liberty and diversity. They also relate to Melville's habits of textual revision.

Melville's uncanny sense of the immateriality of materials is manifested in an early expression of the impenetrability of matter found in the heavily revised manuscript version of *Typee*. In describing the Happar attack on Toby, Melville struggles to voice Toby's panic, and in revising the scene, he excised dialog that was too prolix to express the urgency of Toby's escape.[9] In manuscript, we read: "Suddenly a terrific howl burst upon my ear, & almost in the same moment I instantly shrunk to one side from a fearful whizzing noise. A heavy javelin darting past me as I fled … stuck the next moment into a tree beyond where it hung quivering with the sudden resistance it had met."[10] Toby's close call with the "fearful whizzing" of spears is most compelling for the last spear left "quivering with the sudden resistance" of the materiality of a tree. The near miss brings Toby and tree into sudden relation: self and other unexpectedly redefine each other. However, these manuscript lines and ideas never appear in print. The deleted passage is readable only if we recover Melville's manuscript wording as it unfolds in the process of revision. It is an abandoned replay of otherness.

But the manuscript version also reads as a "regenerative" revision. Let me explain. Typically, we think of revision as "asymptotic." This mathematical term describes a curve that approaches but never intersects its asymptote, usually an x- or y-axis. Applied to the writing process, asymptotic revision conceives of revision as bringing a text closer to an intended but unachievable wording. It tries to get the text as close to "right" as possible. But revision is also invention; it generates unexpected thoughts out of the writer's original. In *Typee*, Melville was not adequately achieving the immediacy of Toby's language when he first wrote of the spear, and by removing the image, he rode the asymptote to a closer rendering of Toby. But with Queequeg's coffin in *Moby-Dick*, Melville revisited the "imponderable thought" that he never fully expressed in the quivering spear, replayed this encounter of self and other differently, and regenerated a new version of the thought in a revised form. Melville's regenerative revisions – the traces of invention – alter material words in order to find a different otherness within. Given the impenetrability of the Other and the inability of one consciousness to know another, the writer's option is a perpetual replay of regenerative revision, not to come closer to the other but to try out otherness in unsuspecting ways.

Ishmael's regenerative "essaying" of the whale – its eyes, brow, cavities, ribs, spine, tail, skin, and spout – is a "trying out" of the imponderable thought embedded in the material whale. Melville's extraction of human consciousness from this alien beast not only critiques the superficial sentimentality for animals emerging in his increasingly industrialized society but also suggests a consciousness in animality.[11] Comprehending consciousness in its variant human versions – its sexualities, genders, classes, ethnicities, and races – was no less of a challenge for Melville. In addressing these seemingly more accessible others, he adopts a strategy of what I call the "distant view," in which an unspeaking other becomes a distanced version of the beast.

Hunilla, the *chola* widow in "Sketch Eighth" of "The Encantadas," is emblematic of Melville's distant view. Abandoned on Norfolk Island, she witnesses from a promontory in mute horror the drowning on the shores below of her husband and brother in their attempt to get help. Framed by branches pulled aside for better viewing, the scene is self-consciously picturesque, but the effect is more like Brueghel: "no sound of any sort was heard. Death in a silent picture; a dream of the eye" (*PT* 154). Much later, Hunilla is rescued, but only by "feline Fate" (156). Waving her unraveled turban at a departing ship, her form, diminished by distance, is read as a flash of white, caught in the corner of the eye of a drunken sailor, just as his ship turns out to sea, just as he turns his bleary sight away from shore. Half-Indian, half-Spanish – a *mestiza* or what Peruvians call a *chola* – Hunilla is mixed, castaway, widowed, female, and thoroughly "other" in this sailor's distant eye. And, we discover, through the guarded indirections of Melville's shamed narrator, that she has been raped and abandoned, repeatedly, by the crews of passing ships.

How does a writer presume to "know" the other sex, a different ethnicity, a mixture of races, or the trauma of sexual abuse? How does one voice the abandonment, despair, and fear of raped Hunilla's risk in hailing yet another passing crew? Melville does not presume to speak it. Because he is not the other, he cannot write the other's trauma. Instead, he adopts a twofold strategy to engage readers in the unvoiceability of otherness.

First, by aestheticizing Hunilla's tragedy in painterly terms as "a dream of the eye" (*PT* 154), he converts the death-in-Arcadia trope of the pastoral to an anti-picturesque of our inability to see; he "mutes" the picture to show its frame of vision. Second, Melville allows his narrative to break down. "Against my own purposes a pause descends upon me here," he writes in hinting at the matter of rape. Moments later, he replays that breakdown. Invoking "feline Fate," he interrupts himself again: "Unwittingly I imp this cat-like thing, sporting with the heart of him who reads; for if he feel not, he reads in vain" (156). Here, Melville admits to playing us like a mouse, challenging the reader – who is figured as male – simply to "feel" and thus to make our way to the feminine heart within the male. These replayed breakdowns that refuse to mention rape deprive the male reader of easy narratorial mediations. Once cognizant that rape is the epicenter of these quakes, the reader is left on his own to contemplate, through shock and shame, the fated plight of the other.

In "Hawthorne and His Mosses," Melville speaks of the writing process as "the great Art of Telling the Truth." But his more honest admission is that truth is a "scared white doe" (*PT* 244). Democracy, marketplace, and language presumably facilitate expression, but instead, fragile truth flits away into the woodlands. The power of Melville's art is not in its truth telling or even in its deferral of truth so much as in the energy of its transformations. In transforming wound to beast to other, Melville confronts the impenetrability of these material things in order to strike at the imponderable thoughts they harbor: he replays breakdowns and makes regenerative revisions. His strategy of replay permits a widow's otherness to be a version of Melville's unrecoverable father. But how are these distanced transformations of trauma into other communicated through the Melville meme?

Revision and Adaptation: The Melville Meme

In *A Theory of Adaptation*, Hutcheon argues for the critical legitimacy of adaptation by calling adaptors "interpreters and then creators." And in defining this cultural phenomenon as "repetition without replication," she opens adaptation to notions of replay and transformation, of revision, and of wound and other.[12] From a fluid text perspective, adaptation is also a form of "cultural revision" driven by impulses other than creative reinterpretation. Moreover, when adaptors revise another writer's work, they seek to possess that work. They remake it in their own image. In traditional textual scholarship, adaptations have no bearing on the integrity of the source or on the editing of the originating text. But in the broader conception of a work as a fluid text, an "adaptive revision" of a work is the adaptor's version of that work, representing an attempt to regenerate the text and thereby have ownership of the work. As a form of revision, adaptation is an extension of the originating work and, even though it is not created by the originating author, it is worth editing alongside the original. But a further challenge to the theory of fluid-text editing is the status of the more elusive Melville meme as an adaptive version of the text. Theoretically speaking, we may edit a work, its sources, versions, and adaptations to establish a field of intertextuality. But practically, how does one edit a meme?

A *meme* (short for *mimeme*, rooted in *mimesis*) is a representative unit of cultural transmission derived from one moment within a culture that is meaningfully adaptable to other moments of expression within that culture. Controversial sociobiologist Richard Dawkins proposed the term in *The Selfish Gene* (1976) as a unit of measure parallel to the gene for tracking cultural evolution. More recently, the term has been co-opted to track the life of an image as it travels and morphs online, and *Internet meme* now denotes snatches of expression extracted from one source and inserted, often ironically, into another context, and then another. As with more self-consciously conceived forms of adaptation, one's use of an online meme demonstrates one's knowing relation to a shared moment in the culture, and invoking a meme not only replays the originating moment that triggered it but also participates in the regeneration of a new version of the meme. In this regard, the user of a meme engages the feeling of laying claim to, possessing, owning a culture that is otherwise ungraspable. As a kind of "adaptive revision," the meme is critically useful in describing how Melville has evolved from text to cultural phenomenon.

Generally, we think of cultural revision in terms of "announced adaptation," that is a fully realized enactment of an originating source, often in some other genre or media. Thus, *Moby-Dick* has resurfaced in children's books, plays, films, and opera. But "adaptive revision" is a fragmentary borrowing from the source text. Quotation, for instance, samples the text, reinserts it into the tissues of another discourse, and thereby revises the meaning of the original text by setting it in the context of the new discourse: quotation, too, is a kind of textual possession. In Tommo's rant against money in chapter 17 of *Typee*, Melville echoes Gonzalo's speech in *The Tempest*, which Shakespeare lifted from Montaigne's "Of Cannibals." This series of quotations is one strand in the intertextual fabric of the transcultural discourse on savage and civilized humanity. In *Star Trek II: The Wrath of Khan*, an inversion of *Moby-Dick*, the widower Khan quotes Ahab directly and repeatedly in his vengeful attack on the Ishmaelean Captain Kirk. In each case, one work's quotation is an adaptive revision of another work;

it is a replay of language that identifies the course of a fluid text within a readership and culture. Such literary appropriation operates much like the online meme. *Music, too*

Other adaptive revisions do not quote a source text but represent moments of creativity that regenerate the source. Sculptor Frank Stella, songwriter Patrick Shea, and artist Matt Kish have created works inspired by chapters or pages from *Moby-Dick* not to illustrate the book but to engage with the idea of Melville's creation and creativity. In popular culture, still more adaptive revisions are manifested in *Moby-Dick* marathons, t-shirts, restaurant names, menu items, a card-and-dice game, and water taxis, and in myriad other visual instances registered in a Flickr site called "Signifying the Whale," hosted by the New Bedford Whaling Museum.[13] In 2011, Bartleby's "I would prefer not to" became the motto of the Occupy Wall Street movement. These varied adaptive revisions of Melville appearing unsuspectingly and randomly in the culture contribute to the Melville meme. They compress Melville, reduce him to an audio, visual, or textual image, adapt him to circumstance, regenerate his meaning, and revise his work. But whereas we acknowledge that announced adaptation is an interpretation of its originating source, can the more fragmentary and yet pervasive Melville meme effectively inflect our reading of Melville's text?

One telling instance is *The Amazing Spiderman* (2012). This superhero film is by no means an announced adaptation of Melville's novel, nor does it make any explicit reference to *Moby-Dick*, or even whales, and yet it surely plays the Melville meme. Our hero, an introspective, thrice-orphaned adolescent – he loses his father and is complicit in the deaths of two surrogate dads, his uncle and his girlfriend's father – acquires (through science!) the agility and web-shooting power of a spider and battles the one-armed scientist Curt Connors, who (through science!) has transformed himself into a giant vengeful lizard. Spidey converts the beast back to human form, and, reclaiming his own humanity, the wall-climber saves the doomed city, restores civilization and civility, gets the girl, and converts himself from an obsessive proto-Ahab into a lover. It is a far cry from *Moby-Dick*. But, in *The Amazing Spiderman*, we readily detect elements of the Melville meme, which are meaningfully distorted and dispersed throughout the film, linking its narrative to *Moby-Dick*: the father-wound and trauma, the beast and transformation.

Placing *Spiderman* beside *Moby-Dick* reveals provocative similarities. In the film, the energy of Spidey's personal despair is transformed into romance and a magical sense of uplift for a democratic culture teetering (as ever) on the brink of catastrophe. We might deride the domestic happy ending especially in light of *Moby-Dick*'s paucity of women and tragic conclusion, unless our exposure to this popular version of the Melville meme reminds us that Ahab's tragedy is framed within an Ishmaelean comedy: the novel also ends in uplift. The sailor's comic salvation on the brink of the maelstrom initiates his transformation into a writer, calling himself Ishmael, who is ready now to write out, again, his aesthetic transformations of his wound into figurations of the beast. And whereas the cyclicity of Ishmael's reinventions of self remains sealed within the confines of *Moby-Dick*, the cyclicity of *Spiderman* is evident in the mass media presumption of a sequel: the action hero shall return to generate more versions of the film, more engagements between wound and beast set within an ever collapsing culture.

But while a comparison of film and novel might serve as a critique of mass culture, my aim is to explore how the film's deployment of the Melville meme actually resituates our rereading of the novel. At issue in both works is the dynamic of wound and beast, in particular not only the risk but also the necessity of transformation. Generally speaking, the assumption is that adaptive revision dilutes the meaning of its source, but in this case the film's interspecies transformation of men into spider and lizard offers more than Melville himself could say in his day. In effect, the adaptive energy of the meme regenerates its source, allowing us to read the source differently.

Melville sensed this transmedial critical potential in his own relation to Shakespeare. In an 1849 letter to Evert Duyckinck, Melville claims that in Elizabethan times, Shakespeare was forced to wear a "muzzle." "I hold it a verity," he wrote, "that even Shakespeare, was not a frank man to the uttermost." But, Melville optimistically concludes, "the Declaration of Independence makes a difference" (C 120). Presumably, Shakespeare would have written more dangerously in Melville's liberal democracy, and in his own way Melville's writing of Ahab as a more resistant Lear is an adaptive revision of Shakespeare that regenerates a more truly Shakespearean Shakespeare. But why must Melville play the Shakespeare meme? And why do we replay the Melville meme? What is the interpretive use of memic transformation in adaptive revision?

Although Melville parodies scientific classification in *Moby-Dick*, he nevertheless engages empirical methods to essay the whale, and he relies on technological precision to lend credibility to the improbabilities of his whaling narrative. Science is not a threat. But *The Amazing Spiderman* is laden with science anxiety in the form of a fear of genetic transformation, and of transformation itself. To paraphrase Melville on Shakespeare: the human genome map makes a difference. Just as lizards regrow tails, the film's obsessed scientist prepares a genetic distillate of lizard that when injected into his tissues will regrow his lost arm. Science will cure the wound. But Connor's experiment goes horrifically wrong, and his total being is transformed into a giant lizard: his wound becomes the beast. Here, the Melville meme comes into play: Connors's arm is Ahab's leg; the lizard is his whale. But the crucial difference in this pop culture replay is that whereas Ahab's wound and beast are separable, and whereas Ishmael transforms both wound and whale into aesthetic versions of otherness, Connor converts wound directly into beast. In the film, self becomes other.

Just as (in Melville's view) the freedom to speak truth to power on the Elizabethan stage had not been available to Shakespeare, the conventions of Jekyll and Hyde transformation and the possibilities of cloning evident in *The Amazing Spiderman* were not available to Melville. Melville might have imagined his Ahab becoming his whale, but he could not have executed it with any degree of credibility in ways that today's film can. My point is not that the film improves upon *Moby-Dick*. Rather, in seeing the film as a regenerative replay of the Melville meme, we recognize novel and film as equally valid versions of a conversation about the anxiety of transformation in a multicultural democracy. Ahab, Ishmael, and Spiderman are orphans seeking fathers in a culture that bids them to forget and instead make progress in a culture that values industry, corporation, and cash more than mind, family, and home. Their recourse is to explore otherness within their fatherless selves and to project it angrily against a resistant culture. In his own work, Melville was frequently "muzzled" (by editors or himself) in addressing the anxieties of belief, loss, multicultural integration, masculinity, and personal transformation. In replaying the Melville meme, *Spiderman*'s adaptive revision reduces the scope but extends the discourse: it confronts disability, mingles desire and fear over regeneration, removes a muzzle, and, in ways Melville might have only randomly suspected, rewrites *Moby-Dick*.

Editing Melville, Digitally

If we are to know the broadest reaches of Melville's work and measure culture through the lens of the Melville meme, we have to be able to visualize the immaterial process that connects one revision to another, from versions of Melville in manuscript and print to announced adaptations on stage and in film to adaptive revisions in quotation and meme. To visualize, we must gather texts and images, ensure their reliability, and provide ways to access and compare them. That is, we must edit.

Such an editorial project requires a digitized, fluid-text approach that represents the full revisionary process involving author, editors, and adaptors. We cannot "read" this process unless we can track the changes made by and to Melville, not just in writing but in all media. When fully realized, the *Melville Electronic Library* (MEL) will include a database of the transmedial versions of Melville.[14] Currently, MEL's model text for displaying the full range of revision, from manuscript to meme, is *Billy Budd*.

Melville's second wound was the suicide of his son Malcolm. Written twenty years after that event, *Billy Budd* – the tragedy of a father-like captain who orders the execution of an innocent, son-like sailor – seems like a working out of this second wound. In fact, Harrison Hayford and Merton M. Sealts (as well as F. Barron Freeman before them) have shown through manuscript evidence that the novella's initial impetus was no more than a version of the poem "Billy in the Darbies," which now concludes the prose fiction.[15] But they also show that Melville replayed his story through several stages of revision that expanded on the Handsome Sailor type and on Billy and added new characters (first Claggart then Vere).

With MEL's digital tool TextLab, users can track Melville's manuscript revisions through each compositional stage. They can visualize "revision sites," sequentialize revision steps, and compose "revision narratives" that explain these "revision sequences." With TextLab, they can isolate the pattern of Melville's deletions of the word *beauty* or the substitution of black for white in describing the race of an exemplary Handsome Sailor, an eleventh hour revision during an eleventh hour stage of composition. If evidence is to be found of Melville's transformation of his father- and son-wounds into the otherness of Claggart's homosexual self-loathing, or into Billy's beauty and beauty's race, or Vere's severity, or Melville's aesthetics of ruggedness and indirection, that evidence will likely be lurking in the still unexplored dynamics of Melville's revisions.

Melville never submitted *Billy Budd* for publication; he left the manuscript unfinished. Had Melville lived longer, he would surely have continued to tinker asymptotically and perhaps revise regeneratively. Instead, his unpolished text reached print only through scholarly transcription: first Raymond Weaver's (1924, 1928), then Freeman's (1948), then Hayford and Sealts's (1962). MEL will provide its own transcription as part of its scholarly digital edition, titled *Versions of Billy Budd*. That MEL edition will also include the four twentieth-century transcriptions, each version different from the other. With the collation tool called Juxta added to TextLab, users can identify print-text revision sites and compose revision narratives that track Melville's revision from manuscript to print. And with a link to *Melville's Marginalia Online* – a separate site edited by Stephen Olsen-Smith, Peter Norberg, and Dennis C. Marnon that digitizes and indexes Melville's annotations of books – users can add Melville's appropriations of source books to their revision narratives.[16] Thus, readers will be able to follow versions of *Billy Budd* from source to manuscript to print.

But the looming challenge for digital scholarship in the field of fluid-text editing is developing tools and strategies for following the process of revision across genre and media boundaries into such cultural versions as adaptation, adaptive revision, and meme. *Billy Budd* has been revised into such announced adaptations as Louis Coxe and Robert Chapman's 1949 play, Benjamin Britten and E. M. Forster's 1951 opera (revised in 1960), and Peter Ustinov's 1962 film. Clair Denis's 1999 film *Beau Travail* is an adaptive revision set in an African outpost of the French Foreign Legion. The problem in comparing these versions of *Billy Budd* to the manuscript and modern transcriptions is that technologists and scholars have yet to devise ways to digitize the process of linking "asymmetric" modes of expression, that is, a textual passage and, say, a camera shot, musical theme, or aria. MEL's development of Annotation Studio (designed by MIT's HyperStudio), which will allow editors to compare and annotate transmedial works, will go some distance to address the problem of composing revision narratives of asymmetric versions.

To pose the problem of how we might digitize Melville is already to imagine a future that contains as yet undiscovered versions of Melville and new ways of reading them. These versions lurk in heretofore inaccessible or undetected places, like manuscripts and memes. Likely as not, writers of a future *Companion to Melville* will be reading Melville's texts differently because they will have more versions to compare. And in writing their *Companion*, they might ask their readers, as I here ask you: Why read Melville? Why did he revise? What is the meaning of his transformations? Why do we rewrite Melville? What is our wound?

NOTES

1 My theoretical and critical speculations on fluid texts are in *The Fluid Text: A Theory of Revision and Editing for Book and Screen* (Ann Arbor: University of Michigan Press, 2002), and *Melville Unfolding: Sexuality, Politics, and the Versions of* Typee (Ann Arbor: University of Michigan Press, 2008).

2 See Harrison Hayford, "Unnecessary Duplicates: A Key to the Writing of *Moby-Dick*," in *New Perspectives on Melville*, ed. Faith Pullin (Kent, OH and Edinburgh: Kent State University Press and Edinburgh University Press, 1978), 128–61. For discussions of British expurgations, see John Bryant and Haskell Springer, eds., *Moby-Dick: A Longman Critical Edition* (New York: Pearson, 2007). All future page references to this edition (*MDL*) will be cited parenthetically in the main body of the text.

3 Linda Hutcheon, *A Theory of Adaptation* (Oxford, UK: Routledge, 2006).

4 These family dynamics are evident in several documents – Melville's *Typee* manuscript and Augusta's high school essays, all with penciled editings by Gansevoort – located in the Gansevoort-Lansing Collection at the New York Public Library.

5 See Cathy Caruth, *Unclaimed Experience: Trauma, Narrative, History* (Baltimore, MD: Johns Hopkins University Press, 1996) and Dominick LaCapra, *Writing History, Writing Trauma* (Baltimore, MD: Johns Hopkins University Press, 2001). I have also benefited from recent works on Melville and trauma: see, for example, Ralph J. Savarese, "Nervous Wrecks and Ginger-Nuts: Bartleby at a Standstill," *Leviathan: A Journal of Melville Studies* 5.2 (2003): 19–49.

6 Caruth, *Unclaimed Experience*, 2.

7 Ibid., 3; LaCapra, *Writing History*, 20, 22, 42.

8 The novel's historical editions assign the speech to Ishmael; whereas an editorial emendation in the Northwestern-Newberry *Moby-Dick* reassigns the speech to Ahab. See "*Moby-Dick* as Revolution," in *The Cambridge Companion to Herman Melville*, ed. Robert S. Levine (New York: Cambridge University Press, 1998), 65–90.

9 See Bryant, *Melville Unfolding*, chapter 8.

10 John Bryant, ed., *Herman Melville's Typee: A Fluid-Text Edition* (Charlottesville: University of Virginia Press, 2006) http://rotunda.upress.virginia.edu/Melville.

11 Kyla Schuller, "Specious Bedfellows: Ethnicity, Animality, and the Intimacy of Slaughter in *Moby-Dick*," *Leviathan: A Journal of Melville Studies* 12.3 (October 2010): 3–20. See also Geoffrey Sanborn's chapter in this *New Companion*.

12 Hutcheon, *A Theory of Adaptation*, 18, xvi, 7.

13 http://www.flickr.com/groups/signifying-the-whale/.

14 The URL of the Melville Electronic Library is http://mel.hofstra.edu/.

15 Herman Melville, *Billy Budd, Sailor (An Inside Narrative)*, ed. Harrison Hayford and Merton M. Sealts, Jr. (Chicago, IL: University of Chicago Press, 1962).

16 For *Melville's Marginalia Online*, see http://melvillesmarginalia.org/front.php.

15

CHRISTOPHER CASTIGLIA

Cold War Allegories and the Politics of Criticism

That Melville has been the object of numerous "political" readings is not news. Melville is credited with perpetuating, reflecting, or subverting a host of ideological structures, among them imperialism, slavery, national expansion, market capitalism, anticolonialism, and heteronormativity. Reading Melville politically is also not new. In the mid-twentieth century, as Americans came to terms with the collapse of what had seemed to some the utopian promise of the leftist activism of the 1930s, Richard Chase, an eminent literature professor at Columbia University, turned to Melville to formulate a new version of liberalism. Chase is best known as the author of the influential study *The American Novel and Its Tradition* (1957), one of the earliest "myth and symbol" studies often criticized for forming a "consensus" around American "character" through the establishment of a canon of "great" American literature. Although less well known, his earlier monograph, *Herman Melville: A Critical Study* (1949), a foundational text in Melville's Cold War "revival," is more important for Melville studies, which gained in breadth and sophistication following the end of World War II.

The Cold War brought radical changes to understandings of citizenship, politics, global relations, and social dissent, as well as to the practices of literary criticism. As Gretchen Murphy observes, Melville became the most contested author in critical debates over many of those changes, particularly in disagreements over the meaning of *liberalism.*[1] Chase's *Herman Melville: A Critical Study* offered one of the most provocative positions in those debates, creating a Melville who staunchly criticized the tendencies in American culture that led to Cold War conformity and who depicted a nuanced view of human nature that could account for, and thus avoid, the betrayals and disappointments that ended the political idealism of the thirties. Far from eschewing idealism, however, Chase saw Melville as a visionary who created allegories that repair as well as critique the previous generation's faults. No longer operating under the progressive assumptions that, in Chase's view, led critics like Vernon Parrington and Granville Hicks to condemn a bourgeois Melville and others like F. O. Matthiessen and Newton Arvin to celebrate Melville's elevation of the common man, Chase's Melville both criticized America's capital-inspired conformity and offered tempered ideals of what visionary readers could make of their world. In rescuing Chase's *Herman Melville* from the obscurity into which it has fallen, I show how and why our political Melville came into being, why he was hotly debated in Chase's day, and how Chase's Melville might lead us to a post–Cold War, socially engaged criticism.

To speak of "Chase's Melville" is to assert that readers, in interpreting Melville's texts, create a composite entity, "Melville," shaped by the assumptions readers bring to the texts (even as an engagement with particular texts leads readers to reconsider and modify those assumptions). Since readers' assumptions are shaped to a large degree by the beliefs of their age, we can say that every generation needs a new "Melville" suited to that generation's assumptions and needs. In reading Melville criticism, then, we can learn as much about the critic's place and time as we can about Melville's. Engaging a work like *Moby-Dick* with assumptions shaped by the Cold War, one may well create a Cold War Melville. If, however, one continues to construct a Cold War Melville after the Cold War has ended, a certain melancholic gap opens between the critic's Melville and the methodological needs of the critic's day. Much criticism today starts with an unimplicated critic's suspicion that nefarious ideologies operate beneath a text's surface and may be unmasked by astute analysis, a strategy informed not only by the New Historicism but also by the residues of the Cold War state, which encouraged citizens to search for and report hidden and threatening ideologies in seemingly innocuous places, remaining themselves free from ideological motives. Such assumptions are well suited for producing a Cold War Melville, but is he the Melville for a post–Cold War world?

As the following discussion shows, critics like Chase who wrote *during* the Cold War, who had not yet fully incorporated its assumptions into their methodologies, propose a Melville who, paradoxically, might be better suited to the post–Cold War world. Before exploring that paradox, however, we need to understand how Melville criticism written toward the end of the Cold War retained Cold War state strategies that are perhaps less fitting, methodologically, for criticism in a post–Cold War world. Taking Donald E. Pease's brilliant and highly influential essay "*Moby Dick* and the Cold War" as an example, we can see how a Cold War–inflected methodology creates a Cold War Melville. Pease astutely analyzes how the United States/ Soviet Union opposition absorbed "everyday life into a 'battlefield' arena the Cold War threatens to make universal." In so doing, "the complications, doubts, and conflicts of modern existence get a single opposition that then clears up the whole mess and puts everybody back to work: 'Us against them.'"² Giving the will to get "back to work" without a local object for action, modern life, in the form now of the Cold War, generates what Pease calls *boredom*. Citizens in that state require a decisive action, although not their own, to relieve boredom and at the same time to rationalize inaction, since all acts in this scenario result in destruction. Bored inaction, because it *doesn't* end badly, comes to seem like appropriate *opposition to* the agent who does act, and that now-heroic inaction (what Pease calls "indetermi-nacy") takes the more palatable form of the equally immaterial promise of an effective inactivity, a heroism that doesn't call for heroic action, or what Pease calls "possibility."

Moving then to *Moby-Dick*, Pease reminds us that Ishmael begins his narrative by announcing his boredom ("hypos"), which disappears once he becomes absorbed in the epic conflict between good and evil represented by Ahab and Leviathan, which absorbs other local doubts or conflicts in the crew members' everyday lives. In absorbing and apparently resolving those conflicts, Ahab relieves the crew members of the need to act, but he also inspires their *will* to act. Left with a motivation without any outlet, the crew becomes bored. Yet noting that the narrative *begins* with boredom, Pease asserts that Ishmael creates Ahab as the decisive actor who relieves Ishmael of his boredom. That Ahab's actions are destructive then does a double ser-vice. Not only does he relieve Ishmael's indecisive boredom (a result now of the alienating effects of modernity), he rationalizes that inactivity because decisive action, in Ishmael's construction, leads to catastrophe. Indecision is not a failure to act, then, but a heroic resistance to action, an opposition without any need to oppose.³

Pease offers this persuasive reading of *Moby-Dick*, a 1985 milestone in the New Historical redefinition of American studies, in opposition to what he posits as the totalizing reading of the novel presented by Cold War critics, in which Ishmael represents a heroic (American) opposition to the totali-tarian (Soviet) Ahab. In Pease's reading, by contrast, there are no heroes. Ishmael creates the Ahab who effectively murders his crew simply to justify Ishmael's inactions. What we might consider a saving grace – "possibility" – turns out to be a translation of bored inaction into perpetually deferred and indeterminate "freedom." Only Melville comes out well, since he, having discerned the operation of boredom, inaction, and destruction, reveals it to astute readers. Melville unmasks without being implicated, presenting a clear opposition between the nefarious operations within the text and the pure intention of depicting those actions.

Yet in this regard Melville stands in for Pease and, by extension, other New Historicists, who similarly discern and reveal. In presenting himself as contesting the axioms of Cold War critics, Pease renders himself as an Ishmael opposing the tyrannical power of an absolute Other. Yet as Pease shows, Ishmael *creates* that other to relieve his boredom. Similarly, Pease, whose narrative we're reading, creates a monolithic entity, "Cold War critics," whose dangerous actions (perpetuating their misreading) resolve and rationalize what can be understood as Pease's boredom. (Pease frames his essay in relation to his personal "failure" to be persuaded by "Cold War critics; as opposed to "refusal," "failure" implies the inaction Pease names as the source of boredom.[4]) The collective entity "Cold War critics" thus becomes the Ahab to Pease's Ishmael, and Pease's heroic boredom becomes potential un-misreading, or possibility. Pease is not alone in the Cold War strategy of presenting an ideological structure in the text as an absolute and abstract "other" revealed by an unimplicated (bored) critic. In such readings, there is often no middle ground between critic and ideology, which often remains monolithic, unconflicted, abstract, and with no points of connection with the contemporary world that might implicate the critic. Such criticism, more troublingly, focuses on critique without remedy, leaving readers with no possibilities beyond "revealing" except boredom. Criticism thereby takes on a Cold War cast, even (especially) when aimed at the forms of nationalism and power that war necessitated.

My point is not that such readings are wrong, but rather that at the end of the Cold War, some critics created a Cold War Melville readable through a Cold War methodology. The Cold War's end calls for a new Melville, however, who might be found, paradoxically, in the past. Some of the terms currently used with discomfort or viewed with suspicion – *imagination, personality, idealism, vision* – emerge around the edges of Cold War reading, and might become components of a post–Cold War methodology and the Melville it would produce. Without surrendering the power of critique, Chase's criticism was motivated as much by idealism as by suspicion. Indeed, no critique is possible without an ideal. Ideals are the standard against which we measure the past and present and find them lacking, leading to critiques. Too often, however, those ideals remain closeted, visible only in the negative form of critique. The result is a criticism that says no! in thunder, but yes only in mist. Chase saw Melville as a visionary who could teach others to become visionaries as well. Chase therefore urged readers to develop ethical distinctions rather than maintaining disinterested objectivity. What Chase shows us, in short, is a criticism that critiques, often stringently, but also names its ideals, that articulates the consequences of those ideals, and that makes ethical distinctions along the way. In his allegorical readings, Chase created a Melville to reflect those values. And in reading "Richard Chase" allegorically, I believe we might find that his Melville is, in important ways, a Melville for our time.

In a February 1950 letter to fellow Melvillean Newton Arvin, Richard Chase professed his confusion about "just what we have been at logger-heads about,"[5] referring to a two-year dispute between the two critics in private and in the key New York intellectuals' journal *Partisan Review* over Chase's interpretation of *Billy Budd*. Chase's disingenuousness not-withstanding, a great deal was at stake in their disagreements, especially changing definitions of *liberalism* in the first years of the Cold War and the divergent Melvilles those disagreements produced. Chase drew on Melville to show what he believed to be the failure of Progressive liberalism, which he defined as a naïve faith in historical progress brought about through the liberation of the common man's innate nobility, and to advocate for a so-called New Liberalism. That "new" liberalism, for Chase, involved a more complex view of human nature (or what he called "personality") and a view of history that accounted for failure, destruction, and betrayal, as well as halting progress. Critics, depending on their allegiance to older Progressive models or to Chase's New Liberalism, found in Melville allegories of col-lective brotherhood in opposition to unrestrained capitalism (represented, for instance, by Billy's innocent resistance to a tyrannical Claggart), or of Stalinist tyranny and anti-Stalinist naïveté (as in the reading Chase offered of Ahab, discussed later in this chapter, whom he regarded, in Murphy's words, as "both a totalitarian despot and an evacuated mass man willing to sacrifice his individuality for an abstraction").[6] Asserting the need for a "good deal more inclusive" understanding of American liberalism, Chase accused Melvilleans like Arvin of taking up "a 19th-century rationalist view of history and politics" that restricted liberals to "such a small category that no strong and fulsome and rounded discussion can any longer go on within its confines." In contrast, Chase tried to "enlarge the scope of 'liberalism'" so that its practitioners can "admit that all men, including liberals, are in some range of themselves like Iago and like Claggart."[7] Melville's critical champions from the generation of progressive socialists – including Arvin and F. O. Matthiessen – supported the Soviet elevation of the masses based on a rational, scientific program of historical progress. A younger genera-tion of Melvillians like Chase, however, wrote after the stunning disillusion-ment following Stalin's nonaggression pact with Hitler, his establishment of hierarchies of privilege and power, purges of dissenting intellectuals, and the violent Soviet colonization of Eastern Europe. The development and deployment by the United States government of atomic weaponry resulting in mass death added to the disillusionment that divided the American left, moving intellectuals like Chase toward a more centrist, psychological, and skeptical liberalism.

By 1949, what Chase called "personality" became perceived as a crucial force for historical change, and the history of that change, far from being uniformly progressive, looked – like human nature – uncertain, halting, and death-driven, but also full of possibility. If Marxist revolution was discredited, so too were scientific rationalism and Enlightenment values more broadly. These could no longer liberate the masses from enslavement, as science had enabled the nuclear arms race, while rationalism had failed to alert Soviet sympathizers to the coming disillusionments. Chase's concept of "personality" – and the New Liberal Melville it enabled – paralleled the work of his thesis advisor and Columbia colleague Lionel Trilling, who, in works such as his landmark 1950 *The Liberal Imagination*, popularized the "darker" Freud of *Beyond the Pleasure Principle* and *Civilization and Its Discontents* to create a psychologically complex – often unsavory and self-destructive – picture of the individual psyche and of social relations. Trilling's work suggests the ways New Liberalism, rather than wholly abandoning a previous generation's utopian politics, translated those politics into the cultural terms of postwar America, enabling in turn a New Liberal Melville who, although skeptical, was far from cynical. In a period of increasing social conformity, Trilling showed how social conventions function as a restrictive superego, suppressing libidinal instincts. While this theory individualized socialism, it also rendered resistance to conformity necessary for a "healthy" psyche. As universities underwent unprecedented social diversification that rendered a one-size-fits-all political philosophy impractical, Trilling placed individual comprehension and resolve at the heart of social responsibility, allowing politics an adaptability foreclosed by externally imposed dogma. In so doing, Trilling decollectivized politics but also made them more inventive and participatory.

Chase similarly found that Melville's complex and often bleak depictions of "personality" contradicted the idealized and inflexible faith in human nobility that doomed progressive liberalism. When earlier liberal critics did allow human nature its brooding unpredictability, they nevertheless maintained, Chase claimed, an unwavering faith in man's progressive betterment. This discrepancy turned critics into hypocrites like F. O. Matthiessen who, Chase complained, "loves Melville and Hawthorne, has a tragic view of life, believes, even, in original sin, and *nevertheless* commits himself to the most childish, shallow, and unexamined political liberalism." Such critics maintained their progressive optimism by drawing a sharp line between literature and politics, since the former would complicate the latter. Maintaining that line, critics like Matthiessen end up in Chase's account very much like Ahab who, reeking of "the odor of sanctity," was for Chase "the type of the liberal-progressive American."[8]

By contrast, Chase used Melville's fiction to debunk progressive idealism in favor of a broody and secluded individualism. For Chase's Melville, however, seclusion was more than alienation and brooding was more than cynicism. Chase conceived of a liberalism enlivened by literature's defining feature, imagination, which thrived only in seclusion. Romanticism's strength, for Chase, came in its depictions of heroes who withdrew from society to imagine other realities and better social relations. Socialists of Arvin's generation relied on the external imposition of what Chase called "dogma," but for Chase politics are impossible without vision. That such visions are necessarily individual did not detract from their efficacy for Chase, as the diversity of vision loosened the stranglehold of convention and allowed for the free play of imagination.

A literary imagination like Melville's became political for Chase through its relationship to the affects responsible for and responsive to the Cold War, which, as John Lewis Gaddis argues, was a war of dispositions, of the struggle between hope and fear, exhilaration and anxiety, resentment and inspiration. Unlike the Second World War, which required active participation from citizens at home (through rationing, knitting, factory work, etc.), the Cold War required nothing except dispositions that could be manipulated for "immediate psychological benefits."[9] In American schools, "duck and cover" exercises produced not safety measures during nuclear attack (no protection would be offered by wooden desks) but the anxiety that rationalized nuclear proliferation as an equally illogical "protective measure." Right up to the final years of the Cold War, with the exhilaration attendant on "the victory of democracy," politics were recognizable not by what governments asked citizens to do, but what they instructed them to feel.

For Chase, no author more than Melville expressed the combination of visionary imagination and intense, unpredictable emotion. Rescuing Melville from what he saw as the pious oversimplifications of naïve progressives, Chase faulted Granville Hicks, who "brought [Marxist critic Vernon] Parrington's earlier strictures up to date and attacked Melville," and F. O. Matthiessen, who "added an unresolved religious strain to the earlier progressivism."[10] In reducing themselves "to a stance of rectitude, a bondage to the absolute, or a mechanism for denying the necessity to think and feel,"[11] progressive liberals, according to Chase, were guilty of "a most culpable underestimation" of Melville (*HM* 209).

Building on D. H. Lawrence's insight that "the superhuman struggle toward civilization would have abstracted man from his own emotions" (*HM* 99),

Chase created a Melville who navigated "the dark center of the twentieth century which, whatever our cultural wreckage and disappointment, now begins to ransom liberalism from the ruinous sellouts, failures, and defeats of the thirties" (v). Melville could help modern readers resist such ruin, Chase asserts, by presenting "a vision of life capable, by a continuous act of imaginative criticism," of countering "the facile ideas of progress and 'social realism,' the disinclination to examine human motives, the indulgence of wish-fulfilling rhetoric, the belief that historical reality is merely a question of economic or ethical values, the idea that literature should participate directly in the economic liberation of the masses, the equivocal relationship to communist totalitarianism and power politics" (v). Lacking that vision, Chase warned, all liberals would go the way of Ahab, "a man slain because so easily bemused by a silly and impossible ideal."[12] For Chase, "Melville was a humanist," but with "less that was vague, utopia-aspiring, and fuzzily ethical." Melville's "tragic vision of life" had "hardened him and clarified his vision" (283), freeing him from "the mild and infantile utopia of the 'common man,' whose dangers Melville was concerned to warn us against" (33). Claiming Melville's legacy, Chase asserted, "I have the conviction that if our liberalism is serious about its new vision of life, if it has the necessary will to survive, it must come to terms with Herman Melville" (v).

Melville allowed Chase to develop the paradigm of withdrawal and return at the heart of his New Liberalism. Withdrawal, in Chase's account, is physical and metaphysical, antisocial and socially transformative, material and aesthetic. As a physical phenomenon, withdrawal involves removal from society into an isolation that allows meditation upon conventions and communion with the desires, affects, and beliefs those conventions foreclose. Physical removal is less necessary, however, than its metaphysical corollary, refusing proscribed "realism" in order to enter the "unreal" where new ideals sharpen the moral imagination. Fantasy, emotion, desire, lyricism all became, through withdrawal, cartographies of dissatisfaction and reinvention legible only to "the mind which is *more* 'spiritual, wide-seeing, conscientious and sympathetic' than other minds" (*HM* 292).

Just as important as withdrawal, however, is responsible return, in which the lessons learned outside society enable a more visionary life. As Melville showed, however, three dangers impede return. Because of withdrawal's allure, Chase explained, some refuse to return or, having returned, maintain a nostalgic longing for their lost utopia (as in *Typee* [1846]). More irresponsible are those who learn nothing from withdrawal, having refused to adapt their ideals to the truth of human personality (as in *Pierre* [1852]). For Chase, progressive liberals commit both errors, either holding tenaciously to utopian communism or refusing in the face of betrayal and failure to adapt their beliefs to present needs. With that refusal, liberals generate cynicism, the refusal to believe in the possibility of a visionary and transformative return (as in *The Confidence-Man* [1857]).

Melville's last five novels (omitting *Israel Potter*) become, in Chase's handling, allegories of withdrawal and return, of liberalism's failures and (new) liberalism's promise. For Chase, Ahab is "a 'good progressive American,'" who is "slain because so easily bemused by a silly and impossible ideal."[13] What starts as idealism ends, for Chase, as power "set free from the fallible responsibilities of human morals and emotions" (*HM* 63), a "freedom" that is finally only alienation, "man rejecting all connection with his family, his culture, his own sexuality even ... for a vision of spotless purity and rectitude attainable only in death, drifting into the terrible future, ... a catastrophe which annihilates a whole world" (vii). In that "terrible future," the "common man" becomes "mindless, heartless, unsexed, ... a dummy already dead and wonderful in his righteousness – in the midst of historical catastrophe" (viii).

Chase found just such a "dummy" in the eponymous hero of Melville's *Pierre*. America, Chase believed, invented adolescence, possessing neither childhood's innocence nor adulthood's wisdom. Although the postwar United States was said to be "coming of age" as a world power, national maturity ended up as perpetual adolescence, plagued by narcissistic self-satisfaction and hackneyed ideals. In such a state, American critics naturally ignored *Pierre*, "pointing out to us, as it does, the enormous difficulties to be encountered in coming of age" (*HM* 140). Foremost among those difficulties, Chase believed, was America's tendency to place "the burden of humanity wholly on the shoulders of the individual" (139). Without institutions to check depravity and supplement human frailty there can be no society "in which our Pierres can survive and be fruitful," and, still without those institutions in Chase's day, "Pierre's madness is our own as no other is" (140).

America's adolescence relied on a stubborn faith in its own innocence, maintainable only in opposition to an equally extreme evil. The disastrous consequences of this phantasmagoric opposition become clear, Chase claims, in the adversarial relationship between Billy Budd and his apparently unmotivated antagonist, Claggart. Leveling unfounded charges that result in Billy's death, Claggart represents the evil supplement to Billy's innocence. For Chase, though, the real villain in *Billy Budd* is Captain Vere, who represents an America so invested in its own faultlessness that it feeds like a vampire on the innocence of others. Knowing that his own fantasies have created Billy, Vere finds innocence threateningly ephemeral and elusive. His subsequent compulsion to "nourish" that illusory innocence allegorizes America's self-construction as "innocent," which allowed it – compelled it – to feast on the rest of the world, using a purportedly evil antagonist to deny its own imperial aggressions and turning murderous the democracy it supposedly defends.

Most dangerously, Chase argues, believing in the murderous innocence thematized in *Billy Budd* allowed Americans "to present ourselves to the world as neutrals."[14] Behind the guise of neutrality, however, lurks "the sullen and defensive sell-out to a center of power or authority" into which one enters "passively, and without heroism" (*HM* 207, 208). The result of that passive acquiescence was, for Chase, the Confidence Man's stock in trade, cynicism. Ready-made hope and cost-free progress, Melville's last published novel, *The Confidence-Man*, shows, create "a universe where everything cancels out, where moral distinctions disappear."[15] Pain and disappointment are not reasons to seek easy optimism or to succumb to cynicism; rather they should inspire *realistic* hopes founded on human fallibility. Avoiding progressive quick fixes, realistic hopes keep people resilient, working for a world where confidence comes from moral distinctions, not gullible innocence. Creating such a world requires both imagination and commitment, which join to form what Chase called "a truly remarkable visionary conversion" (64), alert to "social-historical tragedy and spiritual failure," yet capable of more "imaginative views of life" (55). Resisting the Confidence Man's cynicism, Chase claimed that "the intelligentsia has its own vision of the social revolution to come" (135).

Chase's readings of Melville condemn both 1930s liberalism and a postwar America populated by "the good and loving mediocre citizen" (*HM* 63), whose "ineradicable emotional needs" were fulfilled by a "machinelike existence" (22). According to Chase, Melville similarly "deplored many of the forms American culture was taking in his time: the decay of the spirit of freedom and humanitarianism; the whole enormous shell game of American commerce and American infantile uplift progressivism and cash-value philanthropy" (65). Like Melville, Chase saw that life had become "sterile" and "withdrawn its richness and its ecstasy" (256). America's sterility, Chase believed, came about in large part because the "commercial classes were willing to be the most abject kind of dupe if only they were given in return the comfortable sense of having mastered and destroyed every high or fierce emotion" (81). Under capitalism, the only possible "emotions and intellectual endeavors," Chase asserted, "become those which protect wealth and position with force" (135). Most Americans, he claimed, experience "the perfection of life in the image of the military machine" (22), whereas Melville's Promethean heroes live "in opposition to the high capitalist-military civilization" (32). Like his Melville, therefore, Chase could "denounce and exhort with all the dark gloom of an Old Testament prophet" (283).

Chase's Melville was not only a critic, however; he was also an idealist. Those ideals appear in characters like *Pierre*'s Charles Millthorpe, who represents "rebelliousness, idealism, and the kindness of the heart" (*HM* 121). In Chase's account, the *Pequod*'s crew members' "brotherhood with other men is open, frank, and based on the deepest ties of common humanity" (viii). Knowing as they do that "life must be understood and lived in lower worlds of ecstasy" (143), these men form "a heroic democracy" where a people "free, frank, and proud" stand "opposed to the modern Diana of ill fame, 'unanimous mediocrity'" (283).

Chase's own idealism appears not only in the content but also in the form of his Melvillean allegories. Chase's Melville was a master allegorist, and Chase's analyses of Melville similarly relied on allegory. Derived from the Greek *agora*, the space where an assembly meets for discussion, allegory signals a return from withdrawal to a public where allegory can do most good. Melville was a master particularly of *modern* allegory, which, as Cleanth Brooks wrote, "is perhaps the first attempt man makes to unite the intellect and the emotions when they begin to fall apart."[16] Chase held that the conscious intellect "feeds and ruins and wastes" what he called the "simple ordinary emotional health and equilibrium."[17] He believed that such damage must "be perpetually repaired, the wasted tissue restored," likening the dialectic of destruction and repair to "the rhythm of withdrawal and return."[18] In light of Brooks's definition, Chase's "allegoricalness" (to borrow Melville's neologism), seeking to integrate emotion and intellect, became as modern as Melville's.

Allegory unites not only affect and intellect, but critique and idealism as well. Neither Melville nor Chase saw critique and repair as mutually exclusive. Theodor Adorno insists that every utopian statement is a "determined negation," that is, a critique of the present in the act of articulating a more desirable future.[19] Critique and utopianism are therefore simultaneous and inextricable. Allegory functions in a reverse manner for Chase: by articulating his critique, he implies an ideal (an integration of conscious and unconscious, intellect and emotions) against which he finds the present lacking. In Chase's allegories, therefore, every critique is a determined idealism. Occasionally Chase's idealism becomes explicit, as when he claims that the "allegorical fire" that destroys Pierre's paternal portrait "consumes the Father" – the Law of repressive convention – in order to free what he elsewhere called the "blissful, idyllic, erotic attachment to life and to one's comrades, which is the only promise of happiness."[20] Those moments are Chase at his best, returning from critique to risk the ideals that animate his allegories and convey his affection for the author who made them possible.

Shortly after publication, Chase's book was contested from all sides. Leslie Fiedler disputed Chase's charge that the Confidence Man is a *failed* liberal, asserting, "The Confidence-Man *betrays* people into *faith*." Alfred Kazin called the book "static and even provincial," "astonishingly immature," "full of the most reckless guesses and assumptions." More broadly, Kazin condemned Chase's New Liberalism as "the intellectual wing of the party now in power," legitimizing "that master Confidence Man, F.D.R." Philip Rahv labeled Chase's study "a Talmudic elaboration of mythology pretentious to the point of stupefaction" and, contesting Chase's reading of *The Confidence-Man*, claimed that he "put a load of interpretation upon the book which it cannot carry." Newton Arvin could only sigh over his "boredom with HM and that whale and the whole overtreated subject" of liberalism.[21] Today the so-called myth and symbol critics, Chase among them, are typically viewed with suspicion, if they're read at all.

Reading Chase allegorically, as he read Melville, however, might provide insight into what today's Melville might look like, and how our changed reading practices might produce new and more contemporary perspectives on the author. Like Chase, we live in a world in transition. Chase wrote in the first years of the Cold War, while we're writing twenty-five years after the fall of the Berlin Wall and the Cold War's nominal end. Yet too often we continue, as readers, to do what Chase said Cold Warriors do: we sever, reject, fetishize alienated emotions, dismiss previous generations, "puff our inner righteousness into an image of the universe and annihilate every other image" (*HM* 301). As memories of the Cold War fade, criticism (with Melville criticism often at the forefront) has undergone a vertiginous series of "turns" – aesthetic, hemispheric, temporal, formalist, ethical, religious, and so forth – that suggest a twitchy dissatisfaction with critical suspicion and a desire to find in criticism something affirmative as well as critical, more like Chase's Melville. What R. W. B. Lewis said in 1955 of life at the start of the Cold War might be equally true after its end: "We stand in need of more stirring impulsions, of greater perspectives and more penetrating controversies," disrupting "the sheer dullness of unconscious repetition" and invigorating the "sense of possibility."[22]

A "sense of possibility" is another way of saying idealism, and it's with a hope for more critical idealism that I want to end. For Chase, Melville's finest allegories combined critique and idealism. His criticism both created and celebrated that Melville. Today, we're very good at critiques, necessarily so since, as Melville showed Chase, "we must reject, sever, and annihilate everything that denies our ultimate freedom" (*HM* 301). But after critique, what? Is a socially engaged criticism possible without a motivating ideal, without a want to follow a don't want? Are we having "stirring controversies" about such ideals? What would a straightforward critical articulation of what a *just* world, an *effective* politics, and the ethical values of identity look like? We can state those ideals in inverse form as critique. Or we can state them *as* ideals, based on possibilities of *what could be*, and perhaps, by doing so, generate "more stirring impulsions" than we have now. Developing ways to state ideals will be embarrassing, risking derision and dismissal. But that might be preferable to drowning in the whirlpool of proliferating "turns" as we struggle to find a methodological successor to New Historicism. With this collection, Melville gains a new companion. Revisiting one of the greatest allegorists of the antebellum period might be an occasion to discover a Melville for our time, and to investigate new approaches for enlivening that Melville, one of which might be to affirm, as Melville and Chase did, the imaginative idealism possible in and through literature. Apologizing to Arvin for his "too many emotional tones of praise or blame" in setting forth his readings of Melville, Chase added, "I thought it was probably the time to be vehement, if ever."[23] Maybe, decades after the Cold War's end, that time has come again.

NOTES

1 Gretchen Murphy, "Ahab as Capitalist, Ahab as Communist: Revising *Moby-Dick* for the Cold War," *Surfaces* 4 (1994), http://www.pum.umontreal.ca/revues/surfaces/vol4/murphy.html.

2 Donald E. Pease, "*Moby Dick* and the Cold War," in *The American Renaissance Reconsidered*, ed. Walter Benn Michaels and Donald E. Pease (Baltimore, MD: Johns Hopkins University Press, 1985), 115.

3 Ibid., 144.

4 Ibid., 113.

5 Richard Chase, letter to Newton Arvin, February 15, 1950, Richard V. Chase papers, Columbia University Butler Library.

6 Murphy, "Ahab as Capitalist," 20.

7 Chase, letter to Arvin, February 15, 1950.

8 Chase, letter to Newton Arvin, January 15, 1949, Richard V. Chase papers, Columbia University Butler Library.

9 John Lewis Gaddis, *The Cold War: A New History* (New York: Penguin, 2006), 32.

10 Richard Chase, *Herman Melville: A Critical Study* (1949, rpt. New York: Hafner Publishing, 1971), ix. Subsequent page references to *Herman Melville* (*HM*) are noted parenthetically in the text.

11 Richard Chase, "Melville's Confidence Man," *The Kenyon Review* 11.1 (Winter 1949): 139.

12 Chase, letter to Arvin, February 15, 1950.

13 Ibid.

14 Chase, "Melville's Confidence Man," 137.

15 Ibid., 138.

16 Quoted in F. O. Matthiessen, *American Renaissance: Art and Expression in the Age of Emerson and Whitman* (New York: Oxford University Press, 1941), 246.

17 Quoted in Clare L. Spark, *Hunting Captain Ahab: Psychological Warfare and the Melville Revival* (Kent, OH: Kent State University Press, 2001), 530, 529.

18 Quoted in ibid., 530.

19 Theodore Adorno, "Something's Missing: A Discussion between Ernst Bloch and Theodor Adorno," in Ernst Bloch, *The Utopian Function of Art and Literature: Selected Essays*, trans. Jack Zipes (Cambridge, MA: MIT Press, 1989), 10.

20 Richard Chase, *The American Novel and Its Tradition* (Baltimore, MD: Johns Hopkins University Press, 1957), 107.

21 Leslie Fiedler, letter to Richard Chase, January 30, 1949, Richard V. Chase papers, Columbia University Butler Library; Alfred Kazin, "On Melville as Scripture," *Partisan Review* 17.1 (January 1950): 67, 70; Philip Rahv, "Melville and His Critics," *Partisan Review* 17.7 (September–October, 1950): 732, 734; Newton Arvin, letter to Richard Chase, September 14, 1951, Richard V. Chase papers.

22 R. W. B. Lewis, *The American Adam: Innocence, Tragedy, and Tradition in the Nineteenth Century* (Chicago, IL: University of Chicago Press, 1955), 9, 10.

23 Richard Chase, letter to Newton Arvin, February 9, 1950, Richard V. Chase papers, Columbia University Butler Library.

SELECTED BIBLIOGRAPHY

Critical studies of Melville's works are numerous. This bibliography emphasizes book-length studies published in the last twenty years, though seminal early works and a sampling of provocative recent articles are also included.

I. Melville's Writings

The Northwestern-Newberry Edition (N-N) of *The Writings of Herman Melville* (Evanston and Chicago, IL: Northwestern University Press and The Newberry Library, 1968–), edited by Harrison Hayford, Hershel Parker, and G. Thomas Tanselle, is standard and nearly complete. For an annotated edition that has had a significant influence on Melville studies, see also the Hendricks House series *The Complete Works of Herman Melville* (New York, 1947–). Other important editions include Robert Charles Ryan, ed., *Weeds and Wildings Chiefly: With a Rose or Two* (Evanston, IL: Northwestern University Press, 1967); Douglass Robillard, ed., *The Poems of Herman Melville* (Kent, OH: Kent State University Press, 2000); and John Bryant and Haskell Springer, eds., *Moby-Dick: A Longman Critical Edition* (New York: Pearson, 2007). In the following list of the most widely used scholarly editions, the first publication date is provided parenthetically. Also noted parenthetically, where appropriate, are titles of the first British publications.

Billy Budd, Sailor (An Inside Narrative). Ed. Harrison Hayford and Merton M. Sealts, Jr. Chicago, IL: University of Chicago Press, 1962.

Clarel: A Poem and Pilgrimage in the Holy Land (1876). Ed. Harrison Hayford, Hershel Parker, and G. Thomas Tanselle. N-N, 1991.

The Confidence-Man: His Masquerade (1857). Ed. Harrison Hayford, Hershel Parker, and G. Thomas Tanselle. N-N, 1984.

Correspondence. Ed. Lynn Horth. N-N, 1993.

Israel Potter: His Fifty Years of Exile (1855). Ed. Harrison Hayford, Hershel Parker, and G. Thomas Tanselle. N-N, 1982.

Journals. Ed. Howard C. Horsford and Lynn Horth. N-N, 1989.

Mardi and a Voyage Thither (1849). Ed. Harrison Hayford, Hershel Parker, and G. Thomas Tanselle. N-N, 1970.

Melville's Marginalia. Ed. Walker Cowan. 2 volumes. New York: Garland, 1987.

Moby-Dick; or, The Whale (1851; *The Whale*). Ed. Harrison Hayford, Hershel Parker, and G. Thomas Tanselle. N-N, 1988.

Omoo: A Narrative of Adventures in the South Seas (1847). Ed. Harrison Hayford, Hershel Parker, and G. Thomas Tanselle. N-N, 1968.

The Piazza Tales and Other Prose Pieces, 1839–1860 [Includes *The Piazza Tales*, 1856]. Ed. Harrison Hayford, Alma A. MacDougall, and G. Thomas Tanselle. N-N, 1987.

Pierre; or, The Ambiguities (1852). Ed. Harrison Hayford, Hershel Parker, and G. Thomas Tanselle. N-N, 1971.

Published Poems: Battle-Pieces [1866], John Marr [1888], Timoleon [1891]. Ed. Robert C. Ryan, Harrison Hayford, Alma MacDougall Reising, and G. Thomas Tanselle. N-N, 2009.

Redburn: His First Voyage, Being the Sailor-boy Confessions and Reminiscences of the Son-of-a-Gentleman, in the Merchant Service (1849). Ed. Harrison Hayford, Hershel Parker, and G. Thomas Tanselle. N-N, 1969.

Typee: A Peep at Polynesian Life (1846; *Narrative of a Four Months' Residence among the Natives of a Valley of the Marquesas Islands*). Ed. Harrison Hayford, Hershel Parker, and G. Thomas Tanselle. N-N, 1968.

White-Jacket: or, The World in a Man-of-War (1850). Ed. Harrison Hayford, Hershel Parker, and G. Thomas Tanselle. N-N, 1970.

II. Biographical Studies and Resources

Important archival material may be found in the Melville Family Papers, Gansevoort-Lansing Collection, The New York Public Library, New York City; and at The Houghton Library of Harvard University. Other Melville repositories include The Newberry Library, The Berkshire Athenaeum, and the Clifton Waller Barrett Library at the University of Virginia. Parker's two-volume biography has the facts and more; Andrew Delbanco's relatively compact biography may be the best life for the general reader.

Delbanco, Andrew. *Melville: His World and Work*. New York: Knopf, 2005.

Dillingham, William B. *Melville and His Circle: The Last Years*. Athens: University of Georgia Press, 1997.

Garner, Stanton. *The Civil War World of Herman Melville*. Lawrence: University Press of Kansas, 1993.

Gilman, William H. *Melville's Early Life and Redburn*. New York: New York University Press, 1951.

Heflin, Wilson. *Herman Melville's Whaling Years*. Ed. Mary K. Bercaw Edwards and Thomas Farel Heffernan. Nashville, TN: Vanderbilt University Press, 2004.

Leyda, Jay, ed. *The Melville Log: A Documentary Life of Herman Melville, 1819–1891*. 1951. 2 vols. Reprint with supplement. New York: Gordian Press, 1969.

Metcalf, Eleanor. *Herman Melville: Cycle and Epicycle*. Cambridge, MA: Harvard University Press, 1953.

Miller, Edwin Haviland. *Herman Melville: A Biography*. New York: Braziller, 1975.

Parker, Hershel, *Herman Melville: A Biography*. 2 vols. Baltimore, MD: Johns Hopkins University Press, 1996 and 2002.

Robertson-Lorant, Laurie. *Melville: A Biography*. New York: Clarkson Potter, 1996.

Rogin, Michael Paul. *Subversive Genealogy: The Politics and Art of Herman Melville*. New York: Alfred A. Knopf, 1983.

Sealts, Merton M., Jr. *The Early Lives of Melville: Nineteenth-Century Biographical Sketches and Their Authors.* Madison: University of Wisconsin Press, 1974.
Sealts, Merton M.. *Melville as Lecturer.* Cambridge, MA: Harvard University Press, 1957.

III. Critical Reception and Bibliography

In addition to the following texts, useful information on critical reception and bibliography can be found in the Melville chapter in *American Literary Scholarship: An Annual* (Durham, NC: Duke University Press, 1963–), *Leviathan: A Journal of Melville Studies* (published three times a year), the annual MLA Bibliography, and the bibliographic discussions in the Northwestern-Newberry Edition.

Hayes, Kevin J., ed. *The Critical Response to Herman Melville's* Moby-Dick. Westport, CT: Greenwood Press, 1994.
Higgins, Brian. *Herman Melville: An Annotated Bibliography, 1846–1930.* Boston: G. K. Hall, 1979.
Herman Melville: A Reference Guide, 1931–1960. Boston, MA: G. K. Hall, 1987.
Higgins, Brian, and Hershel Parker, ed. *Herman Melville: The Contemporary Reviews.* Cambridge: Cambridge University Press, 1995.
Lee, A. Robert, ed. *Herman Melville: Critical Assessments.* 4 vols. Mountfield, East Sussex: Helm Information, 2001.
Yothers, Brian. *Melville's Mirrors: Literary Criticism and America's Most Elusive Author.* Rochester, New York: Camden House, 2011.

IV. Source Studies

Bercaw, Mary K. *Melville's Sources.* Evanston, IL: Northwestern University Press, 1987.
Coffler, Gail H. *Melville's Allusions to Religion: A Comprehensive Index and Glossary.* Westport, CT: Praeger, 2004.
Melville's Classical Allusions: A Comprehensive Index and Glossary. Westport, CT: Greenwood Press, 1985.
Grey, Robin, ed. *Melville and Milton: An Edition and Analysis of Melville's Annotations on Milton.* Pittsburgh, PA: Duquesne University Press, 2004.
Sealts, Merton M., Jr. *Melville's Reading. Revised and enlarged edition.* Columbia: University of South Carolina Press, 1988.
Wright, Nathalia. *Melville's Use of the Bible.* Durham, NC: Duke University Press, 1949.

V. Collections of Critical Essays

Argersinger, Jana L., and Leland S. Person, eds. *Hawthorne and Melville: Writing a Relationship.* Athens: University of Georgia Press, 2008.
Barnum, Jill, Wyn Kelley, and Christopher Sten, eds. *"Whole Oceans Away": Melville and the Pacific.* Kent, OH: Kent State University Press, 2007.

Brodhead, Richard, ed. *New Essays on* Moby-Dick. Cambridge: Cambridge University Press, 1986.

Bryant, John, ed. *A Companion to Melville Studies*. Westport, CT: Greenwood Press, 1986.

Bryant, John, Mary K. Bercaw Edwards, and Timothy Marr, eds. *Ungraspable Phantom: Essays on* Moby-Dick. Kent, OH: Kent State University Press, 2006.

Bryant, John and Robert Milder, eds. *Melville's Evermoving Dawn: Centennial Essays*. Kent, OH: Kent State University Press, 1997.

Burkholder, Robert, ed. *Critical Essays on Herman Melville's "Benito Cereno."* New York: G. K. Hall, 1992.

Frank, Jason. *A Political Companion to Herman Melville*. Lexington: University of Kentucky Press, 2013.

Gunn, Giles, ed. *A Historical Guide to Herman Melville*. New York: Oxford University Press, 2005.

Higgins, Brian, and Hershel Parker, eds. *Critical Essays on Herman Melville's* Moby-Dick. New York: G. K. Hall, 1992.

Jehlen, Myra, ed. *Herman Melville: A Collection of Critical Essays*. Englewood Cliffs, NJ: Prentice-Hall, Inc., 1994.

Kelley, Wyn, ed. *A Companion to Herman Melville*. Oxford: Blackwell, 2006.

Jędrzejko, Pawel et al., eds. *Secret Sharers: Melville, Conrad and Narratives of the Real*. Zabrze (Poland): M-Studio, 2011.

Levine, Robert S., ed. *The Cambridge Companion to Herman Melville*. Cambridge: Cambridge University Press, 1998.

Levine, Robert S., and Samuel Otter, eds. *Frederick Douglass and Herman Melville: Essays in Relation*. Chapel Hill: University of North Carolina Press, 2008.

Marovitz, Sanford E. and A. C. Christodoulou, eds. *Melville among the Nations*. Kent, OH: Kent State University Press, 2001.

Otter, Samuel, and Geoffrey Sanborn, eds. *Melville and Aesthetics*. New York: Palgrave Macmillan, 2011.

Parker, Hershel, and Harrison Hayford, eds. Moby-Dick *as Doubloon: Essays and Extracts (1851–1970)*. New York: Norton, 1970.

Schultz, Elizabeth, and Haskell Springer, eds. *Melville and Women*. Kent, OH: Kent State University Press, 2006.

Sten, Christopher, ed. *Savage Eye: Melville and the Visual Arts*. Kent, OH: Kent State University Press, 1991.

Yannella, Donald, ed. *New Essays on* Billy Budd. Cambridge: Cambridge University Press, 2002.

VI. Studies of Melville

Adler, Joyce. *War in Melville's Imagination*. New York: New York University Press, 1981.

Arsić, Branka. *Passive Constitutions or 7½ Times Bartleby*. Stanford, CA: Stanford University Press, 2007.

Baym, Nina. "Melville's Quarrel with Fiction," *PMLA* 94 (1979): 903–23.

Bellis, Peter. *No Mysteries Out of Ourselves: Identity and Textual Form in the Novels of Herman Melville*. Philadelphia: University of Pennsylvania Press, 1990.

Berthoff, Warner. *The Example of Melville*. Princeton, NJ: Princeton University Press, 1962.

Berthold, Dennis. *American Risorgimento: Herman Melville and the Cultural Politics of Italy*. Columbus: Ohio State University Press, 2009.

Brodtkorb, Paul Jr. *Ishmael's White World: A Phenomenological Reading of Moby-Dick*. New Haven, CT: Yale University Press, 1965.

Bryant, John. *Melville and Repose: The Rhetoric of Humor in the American Renaissance*. New York: Oxford University Press, 1993.

Melville Unfolding: Sexuality, Politics, and the Versions of Typee: A Fluid-text Analysis. Ann Arbor: University of Michigan Press, 2008.

Buell, Lawrence. "The Unkillable Dream of the Great American Novel: *Moby-Dick* as Test Case." *American Literary History* 20 (2008): 132–55.

Chase, Richard. *Herman Melville: A Critical Study*. New York: Macmillan, 1949.

Colatrella, Carol. *Literature and Moral Reform: Melville and the Discipline of Reading*. Gainesville: University of Florida Press, 2002.

Cook, Jonathan A. *Inscrutable Malice: Theodicy, Eschatology, and the Biblical Sources of Moby-Dick*. DeKalb: University of Illinois Press, 2012.

Cotkin, George. *Dive Deeper: Journeys with Moby-Dick*. New York: Oxford University Press, 2012.

Creech, James. *Closet Writing / Gay Reading: The Case of Melville's Pierre*. Chicago, IL: University of Chicago Press, 1993.

DeLombard, Jeannine Marie. "Salvaging Legal Personhood: Melville's 'Benito Cereno.'" *American Literature* 81 (2009): 35–64.

Dillingham, William B. *Melville's Later Novels*. Athens: University of Georgia Press, 1986.

Dimock, Wai-chee. *Empire for Liberty: Melville and the Poetics of Individualism*. Princeton, NJ: Princeton University Press, 1989.

Dowling, David. *Chasing the White Whale: The Moby-Dick Marathon; or, What Melville Means Today*. Iowa City: University of Iowa Press, 2010.

Dryden, Edgar A. *Melville's Thematics of Form: The Great Art of Telling the Truth*. Baltimore, MD: Johns Hopkins University Press, 1968.

Monumental Melville: The Formation of a Literary Career. Stanford, CA: Stanford University Press, 2004.

Duban, James. *Melville's Major Fiction: Politics, Theology, and Imagination*. DeKalb: University of Illinois Press, 1983.

Evans, K. L. *Whale!* Minneapolis: University of Minneapolis Press, 2003.

Evelev, John. *Tolerable Entertainment: Herman Melville and Professionalism in Antebellum New York*. Amherst: University of Massachusetts Press, 2006.

Fisher, Marvin. *Going Under: Melville's Short Fiction and the American 1850s*. Baton Rouge: Louisiana State University Press, 1977.

Franklin, H. Bruce. *The Wake of the Gods: Melville's Mythology*. Stanford, CA: Stanford University Press, 1963.

Freeburg, Christopher. *Melville and the Idea of Blackness: Race and Imperialism in Nineteenth-Century America*. Cambridge: Cambridge University Press, 2012.

Hayford, Harrison. *Melville's Prisoners*. Evanston, IL: Northwestern University Press, 2003.

Herbert, T. Walter. *Marquesan Encounters: Melville and the Meaning of Civilization*. Cambridge, MA: Harvard University Press, 1980.

Moby-Dick and Calvinism: A World Dismantled. New Brunswick, NJ: Rutgers University Press, 1977.

Higgins, Brian and Hershel Parker. *Reading Melville's Pierre; or, The Ambiguities*. Baton Rouge: Louisiana State University Press, 2006.

James, C. L. R. *Mariners, Renegades and Castaways: The Story of Herman Melville and the World We Live In*. 1953. Introduction, Donald E. Pease. Hanover, NH: University Press of New England, 2001.

Karcher, Carolyn. *Shadow over the Promised Land: Slavery, Race, and Violence in Melville's America*. Baton Rouge: Louisiana State University Press, 1980.

Kelley, Wyn. *Herman Melville: An Introduction*. Malden, MA: Blackwell, 2008.

Melville's City: Urban and Literary Form in Nineteenth-Century New York. Cambridge: Cambridge University Press, 1996.

Markels, Julian. *Melville and the Politics of Identity: From* King Lear *to* Moby-Dick. Urbana: University of Illinois Press, 1993.

Marrs, Cody. "A Wayward Art: *Battle-Pieces* and Melville's Poetic Turn." *American Literature* 82 (2010): 91–119.

Martin, Robert K. *Hero, Captain, and Stranger: Male Friendship, Social Critique, and Literary Form in the Sea Novels of Herman Melville*. Chapel Hill: University of North Carolina Press, 1986.

McCall, Dan. *The Silence of Bartleby*. Ithaca, NY: Cornell University Press, 1989.

Milder, Robert. *Exiled Royalties: Melville and the Life We Imagine*. New York: Oxford University Press, 2006.

Olson, Charles. *Call Me Ishmael: A Study of Melville*. San Francisco, CA: City Lights Books, 1947.

Otter, Samuel. *Melville's Anatomies*. Berkeley: University of California Press, 1999.

Pardes, Ilana. *Melville's Bibles*. Berkeley: University of California Press, 2008.

Parker, Hershel. *Reading* Billy Budd. Evanston, IL: Northwestern University Press, 1990.

Melville: The Making of the Poet. Evanston, IL: Northwestern University Press, 2008.

Melville Biography: An Inside Narrative. Evanston, IL: Northwestern University Press, 2013.

Peretz, Eyal. *Literature, Disaster, and the Enigma of Power: A Reading of* Moby-Dick. Stanford, CA: Stanford University Press, 2003.

Philbrick, Nathaniel. *Why Read* Moby-Dick? New York: Viking, 2011.

Post-Lauria, Sheila. *Correspondent Colorings: Melville in the Marketplace*. Amherst: University of Massachusetts Press, 1996.

Potter, William. *Melville's* Clarel *and the Intersympathy of Creeds*. Kent, OH: Kent State University Press, 2004.

Renker, Elizabeth. *Strike through the Mask: Herman Melville and the Scene of Writing*. Baltimore, MD: Johns Hopkins University Press, 1996.

Robillard, Douglas. *Melville and the Visual Arts: Ionian Form, Venetian Tint*. Kent, OH: Kent State University Press, 1997.

Samson, John. *White Lies: Melville's Narrative of Facts*. Ithaca, NY: Cornell University Press, 1989.

Sanborn, Geoffrey. *The Sign of the Cannibal: Melville and the Making of the Postcolonial Reader*. Durham, NC: Duke University Press, 1998.

Schultz, Elizabeth. *Unpainted to the Last: Moby-Dick and Twentieth-Century American Art*. Lawrence: University Press of Kansas, 1995.

Sealts, Merton M., Jr. *Pursuing Melville, 1940–1980*. Madison: University of Wisconsin Press, 1982.

Seelye, John. *Melville: The Ironic Diagram*. Evanston, IL: Northwestern University Press, 1971.

Short, Bryan C. *Cast by Means of Figures: Herman Melville's Rhetorical Development*. Amherst: University of Massachusetts Press, 1992.

Spanos, William V. *The Errant Art of* Moby-Dick: *The Canon, the Cold War, and the Struggle for American Studies*. Durham, NC: Duke University Press, 1995.

———. *Herman Melville and the American Calling: The Fiction after* Moby-Dick, *1851–1857*. Albany: State University Press of New York, 2008.

———. *The Exceptionalist State and the State of Exception: Herman's Melville* Billy Budd, Sailor. Baltimore, MD: Johns Hopkins University Press, 2011.

Spark, Clare L. *Hunting Captain Ahab: Psychological Warfare and the Melville Revival*. Kent, OH: Kent State University Press, 2001.

Sten, Christopher. *The Weaver-God, He Weaves: Melville and the Poetics of the Novel*. Kent, OH: Kent State University Press, 1996.

Stuckey, Sterling. *African Culture and Melville's Art: The Creative Process in* Benito Cereno *and* Moby-Dick. New York: Oxford University Press, 2009.

Szendy, Peter. *Prophecies of Leviathan: Reading Past Melville*. New York: Fordham University Press, 2010.

Tally, Robert T., Jr. *Melville, Mapping and Globalization: Literary Cartography in the American Baroque Writer*. London: Continuum, 2009.

Thompson, Lawrence R. *Melville's Quarrel with God*. Princeton, NJ: Princeton University Press, 1952.

Tolchin, Neal L. *Mourning, Gender, and Creativity in the Art of Herman Melville*. New Haven, CT: Yale University Press, 1988.

Vincent, Howard P. *The Trying Out of* Moby-Dick. Kent, OH: Kent State University Press, 1980.

Wallace, Robert K. *Melville and Turner: Spheres of Love and Fright*. Athens: University of Georgia Press, 1992.

Warren, Robert Penn. "Melville the Poet." *Kenyon Review* 8 (1946): 208–23.

Wenke, John. *Melville's Muse: Literary Creation and the Forms of Philosophical Fiction*. Kent, OH: Kent State University Press, 1995.

VII. Literary and Historical Studies with Sections on Melville

Some of the most influential work on Melville has appeared in contextual and theoretical studies that address a range of authors. The Melville texts that provide the focus of discussion, when limited to one or two, are indicated parenthetically.

Aaron, Daniel. *The Unwritten War: American Writers and the Civil War*. New York: Oxford University Press, 1973. [*Battle-Pieces*]

Agamben, Giorgio. *Potentialities: Collected Essays in Philosophy*. Stanford, CA: Stanford University Press, 2000. ["Bartleby"]

Berger, Jason. *Antebellum at Sea: Maritime Fantasies in Nineteenth-Century America*. Minneapolis: University of Minnesota Press, 2012.

Bercovitch, Sacvan. *The Rites of Assent: Transformations in the Symbolic Construction of America*. New York: Routledge, 1993. [*Pierre*]

Blum, Hester. *The View from the Masthead: Maritime Imagination and Antebellum Sea Narratives*. Chapel Hill: University of North Carolina Press, 2008.

Brodhead, Richard H. *Hawthorne, Melville, and the Novel*. Chicago, IL: University of Chicago Press, 1976.

Bromell, Nicholas K. *By the Sweat of the Brow: Literature and Labor in Antebellum America*. Chicago, IL: University of Chicago Press, 1993. [*Redburn*]

Brown, Gillian. *Domestic Individualism: Imagining Self in Nineteenth-Century America*. Berkeley: University of California Press, 1990. [*Pierre*, "Bartleby"]

Cameron, Sharon. *The Corporeal Self: Allegories of the Body in Melville and Hawthorne*. Baltimore, MD: Johns Hopkins University Press, 1981.

Impersonality: Seven Essays. Chicago, IL: University of Chicago Press, 2007. [*Billy Budd*]

Casarino, Cesare. *Modernity at Sea: Melville, Marx, Conrad in Crisis*. Minneapolis: University of Minnesota Press, 2002. [*White-Jacket, Moby-Dick*]

Cassuto, Leonard. *The Inhuman Race: The Racial Grotesque in American Literature and Culture*. New York: Columbia University Press, 1997. [*Typee*, "Benito Cereno"]

Castiglia, Christopher. *Interior States: Institutional Consciousness and the Inner Life of Democracy in the Antebellum United States*. Durham, NC: Duke University Press, 2008. [*Pierre*]

Castronovo, Russ. *Fathering the Nation: American Genealogies of Slavery and Freedom*. Berkeley: University of California Press, 1995. [*Moby-Dick, Israel Potter*]

Charvat, William. *The Profession of Authorship in America, 1800–1870: The Papers of William Charvat*. Ed. Matthew J. Bruccoli. Columbus: Ohio State University Press, 1978.

Coviello, Peter. *Intimacy in America: Dreams of Affiliation in Antebellum Literature*. Minneapolis: University of Minnesota Press, 2005. [*Moby-Dick*]

Deleuze, Gilles. *Essays Critical and Clinical*. Minneapolis: University of Minnesota Press, 1997. ["Bartleby"]

Dinius, Marcy J. *The Camera and the Press: American Visual and Print Culture in the Age of the Daguerreotype*. Philadelphia: University of Pennsylvania Press, 2012. [*Pierre*]

Douglass, Ann. *The Feminization of American Culture*. New York: Alfred A. Knopf, 1977.

Engel, William E. *Early Modern Poetics in Melville and Poe: Memory, Melancholy, and the Emblematic Tradition*. Burlington, VT: Ashgate, 2012. ["The Encantadas," *Moby-Dick*]

Franchot, Jenny. *Roads to Rome: The Antebellum Protestant Encounter with Catholicism*. Berkeley: University of California Press, 1994. ["The Two Temples," "Benito Cereno"]

Gilmore, Michael T. *American Romanticism and the Marketplace*. Chicago, IL: University of Chicago Press, 1985. [*Moby-Dick*, "Bartleby"]

The War on Words: Slavery, Race, and Free Speech in American Literature. Chicago, IL: University of Chicago Press, 2010. [*Billy Budd*]

Greeson, Jennifer Rae. *Our South: Geographic Fantasy and the Rise of National Literature*. Cambridge, MA: Harvard University Press, 2010. ["Hawthorne and His Mosses," *Pierre*]

Greiman, Jennifer. *Democracy's Spectacle: Sovereignty and Public Life in Antebellum American Writing*. New York: Fordham University Press, 2010. [*The Confidence-Man*]

Grey, Robin. *The Complicity of Imagination: The American Renaissance, Contests of Authority, and Seventeenth-Century English Culture*. Cambridge: Cambridge University Press, 1997.

Hardack, Richard. *"Not Altogether Human": Pantheism and the Dark Nature of the American Renaissance*. Amherst: University of Massachusetts Press, 2012.

Hsu, Hsuan L. *Geography and the Production of Space in Nineteenth-Century American Literature*. Cambridge: Cambridge University Press, 2010.

Huang, Yunte. *Transpacific Imaginations: History, Literature, Counterpoetics*. Cambridge, MA: Harvard University Press, 2008. [*Moby-Dick*]

Johnson, Barbara. *The Critical Difference: Essays in the Contemporary Rhetoric of Reading*. Baltimore, MD: Johns Hopkins University Press, 1980. [*Billy Budd*]

Jones, Gavin. *American Hungers: The Problem of Poverty in U.S. Literature, 1840–1945*. Princeton, NJ: Princeton University Press, 2008.

Lawrence, D. H. *Studies in Classic American Literature*. 1923. New York: Penguin Books, 1977. [*Typee, Moby-Dick*]

Lee, Maurice S. *Slavery, Philosophy, and American Literature, 1830–1860*. Cambridge: Cambridge University Press, 2005. ["Benito Cereno"]

Uncertain Chances: Science, Skepticism, and Belief in Nineteenth-Century American Literature. New York: Oxford University Press, 2012. [*Moby-Dick, Pierre*]

Leverenz, David. *Manhood and the American Renaissance*. Ithaca, NY: Cornell University Press, 1989. [*Moby-Dick*]

Levine, Robert S. *Conspiracy and Romance: Studies in Brockden Brown, Cooper, Hawthorne, and Melville*. Cambridge: Cambridge University Press, 1989. ["Benito Cereno"]

Dislocating Race and Nation: Studies in Nineteenth-Century American Literary Nationalism. Chapel Hill: University of North Carolina Press, 2008. [*Pierre*]

Luciano, Dana. *Arranging Grief: Sacred Time and the Body in Nineteenth-Century American Literature*. New York: New York University Press, 2007.

Machor, James L. *Reading Fiction in Antebellum America: Informed Response and Reception Histories, 1820–1865*. Baltimore, MD: Johns Hopkins University Press, 2011.

Marr, Timothy. *The Cultural Roots of American Islamicism*. Cambridge: Cambridge University Press, 2006.

Matthiessen, F. O. *American Renaissance: Art and Expression in the Age of Emerson and Whitman*. New York: Oxford University Press, 1941.

McWilliams, John P., Jr. *The American Epic: Transforming a Genre, 1770–1860*. Cambridge: Cambridge University Press, 1989. [*Moby-Dick*]

Michael, John. *Identity and the Failure of America: From Thomas Jefferson to the War on Terror*. Minneapolis: University of Minnesota Press, 2008. [*Moby-Dick*]

Miller, Perry. *The Raven and the Whale: The War of Words and Wits in the Era of Poe and Melville*. New York: Harcourt Brace & World, 1956.

Morrison, Toni. "Unspeakable Things Unspoken: The Afro-American Presence in American Literature." *Michigan Quarterly Review* 28 (1989): 1–34. [*Moby-Dick*]

Nabers, Deak. *Victory of Law: The Fourteenth Amendment, the Civil War, and American Literature, 1852–1867*. Baltimore, MD: Johns Hopkins University Press, 2006. [*Battle-Pieces*]

Nelson, Dana D. *The Word in Black and White: Reading "Race" in American Literature, 1638–1867*. New York: Oxford University Press, 1992. ["Benito Cereno"]

Ngai, Sianne. *Ugly Feelings*. Cambridge, MA: Harvard University Press, 2005. [*Pierre, The Confidence-Man*]

Obenzinger, Hilton. *American Palestine: Melville, Twain, and the Holy Land Mania*. Princeton, NJ: Princeton University Press, 1999. [*Clarel*]

Otter, Samuel. *Philadelphia Stories: America's Literature of Race and Freedom* (New York: Oxford University Press, 2010. ["Benito Cereno"]

Phillips, Christopher N. *Epic in American Culture: Settlement to Reconstruction*. Baltimore, MD: Johns Hopkins University Press, 2012.

Powell, Timothy B. *Ruthless Democracy: A Multicultural Interpretation of the American Renaissance*. Princeton, NJ: Princeton University Press, 2000. [*Moby-Dick*]

Ramussen, Birget Brander. *Queequeg's Coffin: Indigenous Literacies and Early American Literature*. Durham, NC: Duke University Press, 2012.

Reising, Russell T. *Loose Ends: Closure and Crisis in the American Social Text*. Durham, NC: Duke University Press, 1996. [*Israel Potter*]

Reynolds, Larry J. *European Revolutions and the American Literary Renaissance*. New Haven, CT: Yale University Press, 1988. [*Moby-Dick*]

Righteous Violence: Revolution, Slavery, and the American Renaissance. Athens: University of Georgia Press, 2011. [*Billy Budd*]

Rowe, John Carlos. *Literary Culture and U.S. Imperialism*. New York: Oxford University Press, 2000. [*Typee*]

Ruttenburg, Nancy. *Democratic Personality: Popular Voice and the Trial of American Authorship*. Stanford, CA: Stanford University Press, 1998. [*Billy Budd*]

Ryan, Susan M. *The Grammar of Good Intentions: Race and the Antebellum Culture of Benevolence*. Ithaca, NY: Cornell University Press, 2003. ["Benito Cereno," *The Confidence-Man*]

Said, Edward. *Reflections on Exile and Other Essays*. Cambridge, MA: Harvard University Press, 2000. [*Moby-Dick*]

Sanborn, Geoffrey. *Whipscars and Tattoos: The Last of the Mohicans, Moby-Dick, and the Maori*. New York: Oxford University Press, 2011.

Sedgwick, Eve Kosofsky. *Epistemology of the Closet*. Berkeley: University of California Press, 1990. [*Billy Budd*]

Spengemann, William. *Three American Poets: Walt Whitman, Emily Dickinson, and Herman Melville*. Notre Dame, IN: Notre Dame University Press, 2010.

Sundquist, Eric J. *Home as Found: Authority and Genealogy in Nineteenth-Century American Literature*. Baltimore, MD: Johns Hopkins University Press, 1979. [*Pierre*]

To Wake the Nations: Race in the Making of American Literature. Cambridge, MA: Harvard University Press, 1993. ["Benito Cereno"]

Sweet, Timothy. *Traces of War: Poetry, Photography, and the Crisis of the Union.* Baltimore, MD: Johns Hopkins University Press, 1990. [*Battle-Pieces*]

Thomas, Brook. *Cross-Examinations of Law and Literature: Cooper, Hawthorne, Stowe, and Melville.* Cambridge: Cambridge University Press, 1987.

Thompson, Graham. *Male Sexuality under Surveillance: The Office in American Literature.* Iowa City: University of Iowa Press, 2003.

Wald, Priscilla. *Constituting Americans: Cultural Anxiety and Narrative Form.* Durham, NC: Duke University Press, 1995. [*Pierre*]

Wallace, Robert K. *Douglass and Melville: Anchored Together in Neighborly Style.* New Bedford, MA: Spinner Publications, Inc., 2005.

Frank Stella's Moby-Dick: *Words and Shapes.* Ann Arbor: University of Michigan Press, 2000.

Warner, Michael. "What Like a Bullet Can Undeceive?" *Public Culture* 15 (2003): 41–54. [*Battle-Pieces*]

Weinstein, Cindy. *Family, Kinship, and Sympathy in Nineteenth-Century American Literature.* Cambridge: Cambridge University Press, 2004. [*Pierre*]

The Literature of Labor and the Labor of Literature: Allegory in Nineteenth-Century American Fiction. Cambridge: Cambridge University Press, 1995.

Weisbuch, Robert. *Atlantic Double-Cross: American Literature and British Influence in the Age of Emerson.* Chicago, IL: University of Chicago Press, 1986. ["Bartleby"]

Wilson, Ivy G. *Specters of Democracy: Blackness and the Aesthetics of Politics in the Antebellum U.S.* (New York: Oxford University Press, 2011. ["Benito Cereno"]

VIII. Digital Scholarship and Websites

The *Melville Electronic Library* is in progress and will make available a wide range of newly edited Melville texts, along with pertinent contexts; it promises to be the primary digital research archive for Melville studies. *Melville's Marginalia* offers invaluable material on Melville's reading. The Melville Society website has links to texts, archival resources, conferences, and Melville-inspired events. The URLs given below are current as of 2013.

Bryant, John and Wyn Kelley. *Melville Electronic Library.* http://mel.hofstra.edu/.

Bryant, John, ed. *Herman Melville's* Typee: *A Fluid Text Edition.* Charlottesville: University of Virginia Press, 2009. http://rotunda.upfress.virginia.edu/melville/.

The Melville Society. http://melvillesociety.org/.

Olson-Smith, Steven, Peter Norberg, and Dennis C. Marmon. *Melville's Marginalia Online.* http://melvillesmarginalia.org/front.php.

INDEX

INDEX

"Benito Cereno" (Melville) (*cont.*)
  Blum's discussion of, 4
  magazine publication of, 107–8
  racism in, 117–18
  skepticism in, 115–16
  slavery and authority in, 32–34, 51–52
Bennett, Frederick Debell, 79–80
"Berg: A Dream, The" (Melville), 18–19, 193
Bersani, Leo, 155–56, 166–67
Berthold, Dennis, 38–39
Beyond the Pleasure Principle (Freud), 224
Bible, references in *Moby-Dick* to, 26–31
Billson, James, 136
Billy Budd, Sailor (An Inside Narrative)
  (Melville), 124
  adaptations of, 217
  biographical elements in, 96
  Chase's interpretation of, 223–24, 227–31
  Crane's discussion of, 4–5, 6
  democracy in, 46–47
  digital edition of, 215–17
  judgment in, 142–53
  Northwestern University edition of,
    139–40
  picturesque in, 170–71, 180–81
  poetry in, 128
  primitivism in, 198–99
  queer literary criticism and, 160–61
  "testament of acceptance" interpretation
    of, 144
  "testament of resistance" interpretation
    of, 144–45
  Versions of Billy Budd, 216–17
"Billy in the Darbies" (Melville), 128, 142,
  215–17
Biographia Literaria (Coleridge), 88
biography, Melville's use of, 85–87
Bleak House (Dickens), 99–100, 104
blindness, Melville's fear of, 176–77
Blum, Hester, 4, 22–35
Boston Evening Traveller, 108–9
Boswell, William, 88
Breughel, Pieter, 170–71, 210
Briggs, Charles, 107–8
Britten, Benjamin, 217
Brooks, Cleanth, 229
Browne, Thomas, 78–79
Bryant, John, 8, 71–72, 175
Buell, Lawrence, 135
"Burgundy Club" (poetry), 128
Burnet, John, 172, 178, 202–17
Butler, Judith, 155–56
*Byron (Lord), 78–79

Cambridge Companion to Herman Melville
  (1998), 1–2
  new edition of, 2–9
Cameron, Sharon, 146–47
Campbell, Thomas, 148
capitalism, "Bartleby" as a critique of,
  100–1
Cardozo, Benjamin, 148–49
Cardozo Studies in Law and Literature, 143
Caruth, Cathy, 204–6
Castiglia, Christopher, 8
Cavell, Stanley, 119–20, 123–24
cetology, in *Moby-Dick*, 27–28, 30,
  68–69, 70–71
Chapman, Robert, 217
Chase, Owen, 28–30, 88
Chase, Richard, 8, 219, 222–31
China, Melville's references to, 34–35
Cicero, 120–21
circle imagery, in Melville's writing, 37–50,
  120–21
City of Dreadful Night, The (Thomson), 136
Civilization and Its Discontents, 224
civil society, Tocqueville's discussion
  of, 39–40
Civil War
  cultural discourse on, 130
  poetry about, 130–31
*Clarel: A Poem and Pilgrimage in the Holy
  Land* (Melville), 18, 85–87, 135–36,
    189–91, 192–93
  polar imagery in, 193–94
  primitivism in, 198–99
Clark, T. J., 82
class structure, in *White-Jacket*, 51–66
Claude glass technique, 183
Clough, Arthur Hugh, 135
"Cock-A-Doodle-Doo! Or, The Crowing
  of the Noble Cock Beneventano"
  (Melville), 3–4, 107
  nonhuman life in, 13, 18–19
  synopsis of, 15–16
  transitory exclamatoriness in, 16–18
"Coke and Blackstone," 148
Cold War, Melville criticism in context of,
  219–31
Coleridge, Samuel Taylor, 88
"College Colonel, The," 131–32
colonialism
  maritime literature and, 25–26
  in Melville's writing, 191–96
Colored Patriots of the American Revolution
  (Nell), 85–87

246

beast imagery in, 208–11
Chase's criticism of, 226–27
as cultural phenomena, 102
early rejection of, 101
exclamatory writing in, 13–14
Gansevoort Melville's editing of, 205
nature imagery in, 197
oceanic references in, 22–26
picturesque in, 170–71
planetary perspective in, 188
quaintness in, 108–9
queer theory interpretations of,
    157–59, 162
skepticism in, 115–16
success of, 127
tree imagery in, 18, 197–98
volcanic imagery in, 188–89
writing and publication of, 101–3, 105

"Unpardonable Sin, The" (Hawthorne),
    103–4
"Upon Appleton House" (Marvell), 128
USS *Somers* mutiny, 143
Ustinov, Peter, 217

Van Swanevelt, Herman, 179
Vedder, Elihu, 170–71, 183
Vincent, Howard, 71–72
vision theory, Melville's work and, 169–84
volcanic imagery in Melville's work, 193,
    194–95

Wallace, Robert K., 170–71, 172
Warren, Robert Penn, 136
Warren, Rosanna, 132
Waste Land, The (Eliot), 136
Weaver, Raymond, 127–28, 216

"*Weeds and Wildings Chiefly: with a Rose
    or Two* by Herman Melville" (Ryan),
    139–40
*Week on the Concord and Merrimack
    Rivers, A* (Thoreau), 120
Weems, Mason Locke, 5, 85–87
Weisberg, Richard, 143
Wensley (Quincy), 104–5
Whale, The (English edition of
    Moby-Dick), 71–72
*White-Jacket: or, The World in a
    Man-of-War* (Melville), 4–5
democracy in, 41, 46–47
endurance in, 199
identity in, 119
oceanic references in, 22–26
paganism and religion in, 192
planetary perspective in, 188,
    189–91
shark images in, 195–96
slavery in, 51–66
whiteness
images in Melville's work of, 56
in *Moby-Dick*, 204
Whitman, Walt, 122, 123, 128–29,
    136–37, 196
Wiley & Putnam, 101
Wilkes, Charles, 73
Williams, Raymond, 68–69
Wilson, Richard, 179
Women of the American Revolution, The
    (Ellet), 85–87
Wonders of Engraving, The (Duplessis),
    172, 183
Wordsworth, William, 122, 131
wound imagery, in Melville's writing,
    204–8

Cambridge Companions to...

Lucretius edited by Stuart Gillespie and Philip Hardie

Machiavelli edited by John M. Najemy

David Mamet edited by Christopher Bigsby

Thomas Mann edited by Ritchie Robertson

Christopher Marlowe edited by Patrick Cheney

Andrew Marvell edited by Derek Hirst and Steven N. Zwicker

Herman Melville (first edition) edited by Robert S. Levine

Arthur Miller edited by Christopher Bigsby (second edition)

Milton edited by Dennis Danielson (second edition)

Molière edited by David Bradby and Andrew Calder

Toni Morrison edited by Justine Tally

Nabokov edited by Julian W. Connolly

Eugene O'Neill edited by Michael Manheim

George Orwell edited by John Rodden

Ovid edited by Philip Hardie

Harold Pinter edited by Peter Raby (second edition)

Sylvia Plath edited by Jo Gill

Edgar Allan Poe edited by Kevin J. Hayes

Alexander Pope edited by Pat Rogers

Ezra Pound edited by Ira B. Nadel

Proust edited by Richard Bales

Pushkin edited by Andrew Kahn

Rabelais edited by John O'Brien

Rilke edited by Karen Leeder and Robert Vilain

Philip Roth edited by Timothy Parrish

Salman Rushdie edited by Abdulrazak Gurnah

Shakespeare edited by Margareta de Grazia and Stanley Wells (second edition)

Shakespeare on Film edited by Russell Jackson (second edition)

Shakespeare and Popular Culture edited by Robert Shaughnessy

Shakespeare on Stage edited by Stanley Wells and Sarah Stanton

Shakespearean Comedy edited by Alexander Leggatt

Shakespearean Tragedy edited by Claire McEachern

Shakespeare's History Plays edited by Michael Hattaway

Shakespeare's Last Plays edited by Catherine M. S. Alexander

Shakespeare's Poetry edited by Patrick Cheney

George Bernard Shaw edited by Christopher Innes

Shelley edited by Timothy Morton

Mary Shelley edited by Esther Schor

Sam Shepard edited by Matthew C. Roudané

Spenser edited by Andrew Hadfield

Laurence Sterne edited by Thomas Keymer

Wallace Stevens edited by John N. Serio

Tom Stoppard edited by Katherine E. Kelly

Harriet Beecher Stowe edited by Cindy Weinstein

August Strindberg edited by Michael Robinson

Jonathan Swift edited by Christopher Fox

J. M. Synge edited by P. J. Mathews

Tacitus edited by A. J. Woodman

Henry David Thoreau edited by Joel Myerson

Tolstoy edited by Donna Tussing Orwin

Anthony Trollope edited by Carolyn Dever and Lisa Niles

Mark Twain edited by Forrest G. Robinson

John Updike edited by Stacey Olster

Mario Vargas Llosa edited by Efrain Kristal and John King

Virgil edited by Charles Martindale

Voltaire edited by Nicholas Cronk

Edith Wharton edited by Millicent Bell

Walt Whitman edited by Ezra Greenspan

Oscar Wilde edited by Peter Raby

Tennessee Williams edited by Matthew C. Roudané

August Wilson edited by Christopher Bigsby

Mary Wollstonecraft edited by Claudia L. Johnson

Virginia Woolf edited by Susan Sellers (second edition)

Wordsworth edited by Stephen Gill

W. B. Yeats edited by Marjorie Howes and John Kelly

Zola edited by Brian Nelson

TOPICS

Made in the USA
Las Vegas, NV
07 June 2021